Lecture Notes in Computer Science 2874

Edited by G. Goos, J. Hartmanis, and J. van Leeuwen

Springer
Berlin
Heidelberg
New York
Hong Kong
London
Milan
Paris
Tokyo

Corrado Priami (Ed.)

Global
Computing

Programming Environments, Languages, Security, and Analysis of Systems

IST/FET International Workshop, GC 2003
Rovereto, Italy, February 9-14, 2003
Revised Papers

 Springer

Series Editors

Gerhard Goos, Karlsruhe University, Germany
Juris Hartmanis, Cornell University, NY, USA
Jan van Leeuwen, Utrecht University, The Netherlands

Volume Editor

Corrado Priami
Università di Trento, Dipartimento di Informatica e Telecomunicazioni
Via Sommarive, 14, 38050 Povo (TN), Italy
E-mail: priami@dit.unitn.it

Cataloging-in-Publication Data applied for

A catalog record for this book is available from the Library of Congress.

Bibliographic information published by Die Deutsche Bibliothek
Die Deutsche Bibliothek lists this publication in the Deutsche Nationalbibliografie;
detailed bibliographic data is available in the Internet at <http://dnb.ddb.de>.

CR Subject Classification (1998): D.2, D.3, F.3, D.4, D.1, C.2

ISSN 0302-9743
ISBN 3-540-20583-7 Springer-Verlag Berlin Heidelberg New York

Springer-Verlag is a part of Springer Science+Business Media

springeronline.com

© Springer-Verlag Berlin Heidelberg 2003
Printed in Germany

Typesetting: Camera-ready by author, data conversion by Olgun Computergrafik
Printed on acid-free paper   SPIN: 10969496   06/3142   5 4 3 2 1 0

Preface

The goal of the IST/FET proactive initiative on Global Computing is to obtain models, frameworks, methods, algorithms to build systems that are flexible, dependable, secure, robust and efficient. The dominant concerns are those of handling the co-ordination and interaction, security, reliability, robustness, failure modes, and control of risk of the entities in the system and the overall design, description and performance of the system itself. Completely different paradigms of computer science may have to be developed to tackle these issues effectively. The research should concentrate on systems having the following characteristics:

- The systems are composed of autonomous computational entities where activity is not centrally controlled, either because global control is impossible or impractical, or because the entities are controlled by different owners.
- The computational entities are mobile, due to the movement of the physical platforms or movement of the entity from one platform to another.
- The configuration varies over time. For instance, the system is open to the introduction of new computational entities and likewise their deletion. The behavior of the entities may vary over time.
- The systems operate with incomplete information about the environment. For instance, information becomes rapidly out of date and mobility requires information about the environment to be discovered.

The ultimate goal of the research action is to provide a solid scientific foundation for the design of such systems, and to lay the groundwork for achieving effective principles for building and analyzing such systems.

The workshop covered the aspects related to languages and programming environments as well as analysis of systems and resources involving nine projects (AGILE, DART, DEGAS, MIKADO, MRG, MYTHS, PEPITO, PROFUNDIS, SECURE) out of the 13 founded under the initiative. After a year from the start of the projects, the goal of the workshop was to determine the state of the art in the topics studied in the two clusters related to programming environments and the analysis of systems, and to devise strategies and new ideas to profitably continue the research effort towards the overall objective of the initiative.

Before starting the technical contribution, we gave a brief description of the nine projects involved in the meeting.

We acknowledge the Dipartimento di Informatica and Telecomunicazioni of the University of Trento, the Comune di Rovereto, the DEGAS project for partially funding the event, and the Events and Meetings Office of the University of Trento for the valuable collaboration.

Rovereto,   Corrado Priami
15 September 2003

AGILE

Full Title: **Architectures for Mobility**
Contact Person: Wirsing, Martin – Ludwig-Maximilians-Universitaet Muenchen

Architecture-based approaches have been promoted as a means of controlling the complexity of system construction and evolution, namely for providing systems with the agility required to operate in turbulent environments and adapt very quickly to changes in the enterprise world. Recent technological advances in communication and distribution have made mobility an additional factor of complexity, one for which current architectural concepts and techniques are not prepared for. AGILE will provide means for addressing this new level of complexity by developing an architectural approach in which mobility aspects can be modelled explicitly and mapped onto the distribution and communication topology made available at physical levels. The whole approach will be developed over a uniform mathematical framework based on graph-oriented techniques that will support sound methodological principles, formal analysis, and refinement.

Objectives: AGILE will develop an integrated architectural approach to the development of systems in which mobility is a key factor, including:

1. primitives for explicitly addressing mobility within architectural models;
2. algebraic models of the evolution processes that result from system reconfiguration caused by mobility of components;
3. extensions to modelling languages like the UML that make the architectural primitives available to practitioners, together with tools for supporting animation and early prototyping;
4. analysis techniques for supporting compositional verification of properties addressing evolution of computation, coordination and distribution; and
5. refinement techniques for relating logical modelling levels with the distribution and communication topology available at physical levels.

Work description: In order to meet the proposed goals, AGILE will capitalize on the experience that the members of the consortium have accumulated in the areas of formal software architectures, algebraic and logical development techniques, process calculi, concurrency, combination of formal and semiformal modelling techniques, graph-based semantics, and software development in business domains characterized by a high volatility of requirements. More precisely, AGILE will follow three main strands of research:

1. the extension of our previous work on the development of a categorical framework supporting software architectures on the basis of the separation between 'computation' and 'coordination' with an additional dimension for 'distribution' and, consequently, 'mobility', providing primitives – distribution contracts in line with the coordination contracts that we have been developing – with which the distribution topology can be explicitly modelled and refined across different levels of abstraction;

2. the definition of algebraic models for the underlying evolution processes, relating the reconfiguration of the coordination structure and the mobility of components across the distribution topology, again capitalizing on our previous work in graph transformation techniques, and laying down the basis for logical analysis of evolution properties as well as tools for animation and early prototyping; and

3. the extension of existing modelling languages and processes like the UML with the concepts and techniques that will have been developed in the other workpackages, including tools for animation and early prototyping. A fourth line of work consisting of case study development and prototyping will ensure that the project will develop a joint awareness of the problems and solutions to be developed, and that the three different technical strands will actually come together as part of a unified and effective architectural approach to mobility.

DART

Full Title: **Dynamic Assembly, Reconfiguration and Type-Checking**
Contact Person: Moggi, Eugenio – Università di Genova

The project will develop formalisms for dynamic assembly, reconfiguration and type-checking of complex distributed software systems, such as telephone and banking systems, that should be kept running as they evolve through patches or upgrades, and should be able to adapt to changes in the environment.

Such formalisms will advance the state of the art in modelling the "temporal" dimension of Global Computing (GC), where the ability to interleave meta-programming activities, like assembly and reconfiguration, with computational activities is a must.

The development of these calculi will rely on decisive progress in three areas: calculi for dynamic assembly, calculi for object evolution and adaptation, flexible and compositional type systems.

Objectives: The project aims to advance the state of the art in modelling and programming software evolution while retaining safety. More specifically:

- We will provide foundational calculi for dynamic assembly and reconfiguration which will be able to describe separate compilation, run-time code generation, dynamic linking and loading.
- We will design foundational calculi supporting objects capable of changing their behavior, e.g., by changing class, as well as calculi that are environment adaptable, e.g., able to test the existence of objects in the execution environment.
- We will develop type systems that support "compositional analysis" through the existence of "principal typings," show how to use such type systems for separate compilation and incremental type inference, and address the issue of combining dynamic type-checking with dynamic assembly and reconfiguration.

Work description: The project is organized into five workpackages (WPs). The first three WPs
1. Frameworks and Calculi for Dynamic Software Assembly,
2. Flexible and Compositional Type Systems, and
3. Calculi for Object Evolution
aim to develop the calculi and type systems identified as key project objectives.

The main goal will be to carry out the foundational work, which will take the form of frameworks for dynamic assembly and reasoning about properties of different assembly strategies, calculi for object evolution and adaptation, type systems with properties that will make them particularly suitable for use in a dynamic context. The other two WPs
4. Applications to Prevalent Languages, and
5. Flexible Dynamic Type-Checking for Dynamic Software Assembly
are downstream (their feasibility will be reassessed at the first review point at month 12 of the project); their rationale is:

– to test the portability of innovative ideas expected from WPs 1 and 3, namely facilities supporting object evolution (i.e., allowing an object to change its class or the code of its methods) and environment-adaptable programming, to a major programming language. Such a language will be chosen (at the time of the first review) from among the prevalent ones for GC. The emphasis on objects is motivated by the expectation that in any successful language for GC the object paradigm will play a major role.
– to test how the innovative ideas expected from WPs 1 and 2 (and developed fairly independently, but with portability in mind) can be merged in a unifying framework that will account for dynamic assembly, reconfiguration and type-checking.

The combination of dynamic type checking with dynamic assembly and reconfiguration is essential, since addressing these issues separately will either fail to guarantee safety and efficiency or be significantly less useful in the GC environment.

DEGAS

Full title: **Design Environments for Global Applications**
Contact person: Priami, Corrado – Università di Trento

DEGAS aims to combine structured (semiformal) graphical methods for specification by picture and animation of global applications with formal methods for their analysis and verification. We will investigate to what extent UML is already suitable to model global applications and we will propose extensions. We will propose formal models of these applications based on the operational semantics of foundational process calculi for mobility. Static and dynamic analysis concentrate on two key features of global computing: performance prediction and security. We will assess the foundational studies in a prototypical proof-of-concept environment that hides from the user as much as possible of the formal treatment. We will tune our development with case studies on wireless telecommunication applications.

Objectives: DEGAS addresses foundational aspects for the design of global applications by enhancing the state of the art in scientific as well as engineering principles. The main concerns are the specification in UML and qualitative and quantitative analysis of global applications. We plan to define the key features of global (wireless) applications that should be exposed at an abstract level of specification and analysis. We provide formal relations between the (possibly richer or incomplete) UML models and the process calculi specifications to connect the specification and the verification environment by hiding as many formal details from the designer as possible. The static and dynamic analysis with case studies should lead to the definition of new linguistic constructs and new models to analyze and reason about the performance and security of global systems.

Work description: DEGAS is organized into workpackages (WPs). Besides the management and assessment of progress and results, we have:

- WP3 (UML feasibility, modification and tool customization) customizes a tool to build the designer's interface and manipulate UML models.
- WP4 (extraction, reflection and integration) defines the interface between the specification part of the environment and the verification kernel. The extraction takes information from UML models and builds process calculi specifications; the reflection exposes to the user the results of the formal analysis in UML notation. The integration task is responsible for building a unique case tool out of the subtools developed during the project lifetime.
- WP5 (dynamic analysis) is responsible for defining new linguistic constructs and new models to carry out (quantitative and security) dynamic analysis on transition-system-based representations of global applications. The WP also exploits fine-grain models in which security and quantitative issues coexist.
- WP6 (static analysis) is responsible for specifying analysis in the flow logic and abstract interpretation approaches to determine the overall responsiveness of the system and to harden the design against denial-of-service attacks. We also investigate the usage of reachability information for controlling information leaks (to preserve confidentiality) and to ensure the correct authentication of devices.
- WP7 (case studies) is responsible for validating the development of the project as well for providing experimental guidance to the foundational studies.

The services we selected as case studies are:
(1) a pilot service for mobile entertainment, and
(2) mobile home banking.

MIKADO

Full title: **Mobile Calculi Based on Domains**
Contact person: Stefani, Jean-Bernard – INRIA

Current middleware and programming language technologies are inadequate to meet the challenges posed by a global computing environment. In particular, they tend to support only a limited range of interactions, have a limited view of components and objects, fail to properly and uniformly support properties such as mobility, predictability, security and fault-tolerance, and they are not amenable to rigorous investigation for verification, validation and test purposes. The Mikado project intends to overcome these limitations by defining and prototyping new formal models for both the specification and programming of highly distributed and mobile systems, and to develop specification and analysis techniques which can be used to build safer and more trustworthy systems, to demonstrate their conformance to specifications, and to analyze their behavior.

Objectives: The goal of the Mikado project is to construct a new formal programming model, based upon the notion of domain as a computing concept, which supports reliable, distributed, mobile computation, and provides the mathematical basis for a secure standard for distributed computing in open systems. Specifically, Mikado intends:

- to develop new formal models for both the specification and programming of large-scale, highly distributed and mobile systems;
- to develop new programming language features supporting such models, and to study their combination with functional and object-oriented programming;
- to develop specification and analysis techniques which can be used to build safer and more trustworthy systems, to demonstrate their conformance to specifications, and to analyze their behavior; and
- to prototype new virtual machine technologies which can be used to implement in a "provably correct" way such models and languages.

Work description: The project is organized around three technical work-packages (WP1–WP3) and one organizational work-package (WP4):

- WP1: Core Programming Model;
- WP2: Specification and Analysis;
- WP3: Virtual Machine Technology and Language Support;
- WP4: Project Co-ordination and Dissemination

WP1 is concerned with the definition of a core programming model for global computing, based on the notion of domain. This work-package will provide the basis for the rest of the theoretical work taking place in WP2 and for the development work taking place in WP3.

WP2 is concerned with the definition of Specification and Analysis technologies for the project's programming model. These will range from the development of type systems and static analysis techniques for expressing constraints on concurrency, mobility and resource access for the underlying execution model to providing proof technologies for assuring that mobile code, and more generally distributed systems, conform to predefined behavioral specifications. The latter will require the definition of novel co-inductive techniques for comparing the distributed behavior of systems and the elaboration of new specification logics for expressing interesting partial views of systems and programming paradigms.

WP3 is concerned with the embodiment of the Mikado programming model developed in WP1 and WP2 in concrete programming technologies. Work in WP3 will be concerned with the development of several prototypes, including:

- a virtual machine technology to support WP1's core programming model together with WP2 typing schemes; and
- language features and language extensions supporting WP1's model and WP2's type systems.

MRG

Full title: **Mobile Resource Guarantees**
Contact person: Sannella, Donald – University of Edinburgh

The use of mobile code in a global environment aggravates existing security problems and presents altogether new ones, one of which is the maintenance of bounds on quantitative resources. Without some technological foundations for providing such guarantees, global computing will be confined to applications where malfunction due to resource bound violation is accepted as normal and has little consequence. With more serious applications, resource awareness will be a crucial asset. This project aims at developing the infrastructure needed to endow mobile code with independently verifiable certificates describing resource behavior. These certificates will be condensed and formalized mathematical proofs of a resource-related property, which are by their very nature self-evident and unforgeable. Arbitrarily complex methods may be used to construct these certificates, but their verification will always be a simple computation.

Objectives:
Objective 1: Development of a framework for formal certificates of resource consumption, consisting of a cost model and a program logic for an appropriate virtual machine. In the first instance this will be a subset of the Java VM; later we will consider appropriate parameterizations allowing for mobile virtual machines.
Objective 2: Development of a notion of formalized and checkable proofs for this logic which will play the role of certificates, including the implementation of a proof checker.
Objective 3: Development of methods for machine generation of certificates for appropriate high-level code, either fully automatically or based on user-supplied annotations, e.g., in the form of invariants. Type systems will be used as the underlying formalism for this endeavor.

Objective 4: Study relaxations of proof-based certificates based on several rounds of negotiations between supplier and user of code leading to higher and higher confidence that the resource policy is satisfied.

Work description: This project aims at developing the infrastructure needed to endow mobile code with independently verifiable certificates describing resource behavior. These certificates will be condensed and formalized mathematical proofs of a resource-related property, which are by their very nature self-evident and unforgeable. Arbitrarily complex methods may be used to construct these certificates, but their verification will always be a simple computation.

The work plan consists of the following central tasks:

1. define expressive formalized resource policy (cost models);
2. define notions of independently verifiable certificates (resource- sensitive program logic with proof objects);
3. foundations for efficient generation of certificates (type systems, identification of useful programmer annotations); and
4. foundations for alternatives to generation of full certificates (proof-theoretic compression, probabilistically checkable proofs, game-theoretic approaches).

Where appropriate, each foundational task is accompanied by a prototype implementation and case studies. In addition, the project includes the following separate engineering-oriented tasks:

1. design of run-time environment including virtual machine, bytecode, implemented program logic;
2. design and implementation of a high-level programming language in which to write resource-certified code;
3. generation and integrated use of formalized certificates; and
4. parameterization by arbitrary run-time environment.

The deliverables are research papers describing our solutions to foundational problems and a working prototype which will be made available as free downloadable software.

MYTHS

Full title: **Models and Types for Security in Mobile Distributed Systems**
Contact Person: Sassone, Vladimiro – Department of Informatics, University of Sussex

Objectives: Global computing refers to computation via the sharing of an open-ended, distributed network of mobile resources by agents of all sorts. The systems range from large mainframes to mobile computers embedded in your cellphone or credit card, and agents are not tied to any specific geographical or logical network location.

The main scientific and technological challenge in this setting is that agents must operate in environments about which they possess little information, and where no a priori trustworthy agents exist. Like Pinocchio, in such conditions it is all too easy to entrust your money to the cat and the fox. The global infrastructure can only be successful if it provides adequate security guarantees. Administrative domains will want to grant access only to selected agents, and these will need to protect themselves and their data from attacks while traversing potentially hostile environments or executing remotely outside the control of their originating locations.

The overall aim of MYTHS, in short, will be to develop type-based foundational theories of security for mobile and distributed systems in order to lay the foundations for the design of robust, high-level programming paradigms for global computing.

Description of the work: MYTHS is a three-year-long project involving three partners and is articulated in the three themes below:

- *Resource access control*, i.e., the control of access to and proper use by mobile agents of computational resources distributed on the network and, possibly, not centrally owned.
- *Information flow control*, i.e., the monitoring of how information flows inside systems and whether such flows comply with the set security policies and clearance levels, such as public, restricted, and top-secret.
- *Analysis of cryptographic protocols*, i.e., the study of the correctness of protocols designed to establish secure (encrypted) communication channels.

These are central, challenging issues for global computing, with far-reaching impact on the development of high-level, reliable, network-aware programming languages. To make the network useful at all, it is imperative to ensure privacy, confidentiality, integrity and authenticity of electronic interactions, and to be able to detect or build safeguards against unwanted flows of information.

The glue that weaves themes together is provided by the pivotal notions of *models* and *types*, whence the project's title. MYTHS will develop formal models for distributed and mobile code environments based on high-level process calculi and will develop type theories to control resources and information flow, and to undertake crypto analysis.

The work is organized into workpackages (WPs). At project start, *WP1: Core Models* will analyze existing models and extend them to MYTHS's purposes. The other first-phase activities focus on modelling agents' behaviors and interactions for the analysis and enforcement of security in each theme.

- *WP2: Typed Calculi of Capabilities*. Extends the notion of capability for resource access to global computing, and devises type systems to enforce capability management policies and detect violations.
- *WP3: Types for Information Flow Control*. Identifies the flow of information determined by mobility, communication and cryptoprimitives, investigates semantic characterizations of it, and develops type systems for non-interference.

– *WP4: Types for Protocol Analysis.* Defines typed calculi and analysis techniques for cryptographic protocols (especially for e-commerce), and applies type systems for noninterference to protocol analysis.

This work leads to the central phase of the project, *WP5: Typing with Partial Knowledge*, where MYTHS extends its results to networked environments with no centralized control and in which only partial knowledge of the components of the networks may be assumed. Also, *WP6: Mutable Trust and Security Levels* investigates the management of dynamic trust levels. The project concludes with *WP7: Programming-Level Applications*, focusing on the convergence of the results achieved in the three themes and how these can collectively be applied to high-level programming languages and paradigms.

Expected results. MYTHS's results fall under the following four captions.

– TYPE SYSTEMS FOR RESOURCE ACCESS CONTROL AND MANAGEMENT OF CAPABILITIES. These will help devise alternative programming paradigms for global computing and design the corresponding programming languages and applications.
– TYPE SYSTEMS FOR INFORMATION FLOW SECURITY. These will bring advances relevant to the design and production of security middleware.
– TYPE SYSTEMS FOR PROTOCOL ANALYSIS. The results on protocol analysis will be beneficial for the design and production of cryptographic protocols, verification tools, and e-commerce and e-business applications.
– PROGRAMMING-LEVEL APPLICATIONS. This research is explicitly concerned with pointing out programming-level constructs for secure programming for global computing; its impact if successful is thus obvious.

Most of the project's outcomes will be in the form of scientific papers. We expect, however, to deliver prototype implementations of type checkers and verification tools based on them.

Project's partners: University of Sussex, UK (Coordinator); École Normale Supérieure, Paris, France; Università "Ca' Foscari," Venice, Italy.

PEPITO

Full title: **Peer-to-Peer-Implementation-and-Theory**
Contact person: Sjöland, Thomas – Swedish Institute of Computer Science

Traditional centralized system architectures are ever more inadequate. We lack a good understanding of future decentralized peer-to-peer (P2P) models for collaboration and computing, of both how to build them robustly and what can be built. The PEPITO project will investigate completely decentralized models of P2P computing.

It will:

(1) study the use-models of P2P systems, that is how they are perceived by users and what new applications are possible;

(2) develop the foundations of P2P computing, including formal foundations (calculi, proof techniques, security and resource models) and new distributed algorithms (for diffusing information and coping with multiconsistent views);

(3) provide a language-independent distribution subsystem tailored for P2P computing; and

(4) provide programming languages and platforms using this, showing that they are useful by implementing convincing demonstrator applications.

Objectives: Peer-to-peer computing (P2P) is a paradigm in which applications are connected to a shared network as peers, that is with the same capabilities and responsibilities. Current P2P applications are limited to information exchange. The objectives are to remove this limitation by:

- developing formal models to understand P2P computing;
- developing the distributed algorithms required for implementation;
- implementing a language-independent set of basic services;
- implementing languages, and devising programming techniques and convincing demonstrator applications.

Further objectives are:

- better using resources at the network's edge;
- scaling better than server-centric computing;
- allowing device mobility (independence of IP addresses);
- allowing individuals to publish information and services, and allowing individuals to collaborate while remaining anonymous.

Work description: PEPITO will assume a completely decentralized architecture in which a peer can have four simultaneous roles: it may use services, provide services, forward requests, and provide caching of information. We also assume that peer nodes connect through a virtual network that is dynamic and intermittent, and that nodes do not possess a fixed IP address. To successfully deal with the complexity of P2P systems (in which failure, reconfiguration and security are central) it is important to pursue use-model analysis, theoretical work and prototyping in a closely linked style. The complementary expertise of the PEPITO partners makes this possible: the objectives will be addressed, but enabling interaction between them is also crucial. Use-model analysis of this type of system will investigate how they are perceived by users, and what new applications are possible.

Theoretical work will study the foundational concepts of P2P systems. This includes mathematical models (calculi, proof techniques, security and resource models) and new distributed algorithms (decentralized algorithms for diffusing information, and for coping with multiconsistent computing – with simultaneous inconsistent views of entities). System design and prototyping will develop prototypes of programming languages and programming platforms (middleware) suitable for peer-to-peer computing (such platforms are lacking today; those existing are server-centric). One aspect will be a scalable and robust name/directory service based on our algorithms. Together, all these will enable the development of applications that:

– handle dynamic connectivity and device mobility;
– allow individuals to become publishers of information and services;
– permit full use of existing network resources at the edge of the network;
– and permit applications to scale better than server-centric designs.

PROFUNDIS

Full title: **Proofs of Functionality for Mobile Distributed Systems**
Contact person: Parrow, Joachim – University of Uppsala

PROFUNDIS aims at developing methods to analyze the behavior of distributed mobile systems, in order to ascertain that they function correctly. This involves modelling the systems in an abstract way and formulating rigorous correctness properties; it will be necessary to consider open and extensible systems with unknowable parts. For this purpose we shall develop operational models (based on automata), algebras, logical languages, and associated type systems. Analysis will be conducted through computer tools, both fully automatic and interactive. The novelty of the project lies in integrating several theoretical strands into one framework and one set of tools geared towards mobile distributed systems. In particular we shall consider security properties and systems used in electronic commerce.

Objectives: The objective of PROFUNDIS is to advance the state of the art of formal modelling and verification techniques to the point where key issues in mobile distributed systems, such as security protocols, authentication, access rights and resource management can be treated rigorously and with considerable automatic support. In particular we shall verify properties typical in so-called open systems, where the behavior of some parts (like intruders or adversaries) is unknowable, in extensible systems, where parts may be added or removed as the system executes, and in mobile systems, where physical and logical connectivity between parts may change. We shall implement automatic and partly automatic analysis methods for ascertaining the correct behavior of such systems. For this purpose we shall integrate and focus several strands of ongoing theoretical work.

Work description: The work builds on recent advances in key theories for process behaviors, logics and types. We shall develop automata theoretic models suitable for our applications, with a particular interest in how they can be represented efficiently and used by automatic tools, and we shall determine how they are best used in connection with advanced forms of modal logics. The logics themselves will be developed, both in terms of their expressiveness for properties related to space and structure, and in terms of their accessibility and ease of use through suitable high-level representations. We shall identify and develop analysis techniques related to these models and logics. This involves traditional behavioral equivalences and preorder checking, systematic simulation, and verification in interactive proof assistants. Here type systems will play an important role. Recent results show that types may themselves be used as crude but tractable correctness properties, and therefore type inference is highly relevant; moreover, we shall explore how advanced type information can assist the other analysis techniques. The ideas will to a large extent be implemented in a common tool set. Key issues here will be the development and adaption of algorithms for analysis, and determining the best way of using them for practical examples. We shall in particular consider examples on security properties in systems for electronic commerce.

SECURE

Full title: **Secure Environments for Collaboration Among Ubiquitous Roaming Entities**
Contact person: Cahill, Vinny – Trinity College Dublin

It is arguable whether the security mechanisms used to protect today's information systems are adequate. What is clear is that new approaches to security are needed for the infrastructure envisaged by the global computing initiative, which is characterized by decentralized control. The SECURE project will investigate a new approach to security founded on the notion of trust. The project aims to develop a model in which trust relationships are established from the record of interaction between entities, and a security mechanism expressed in terms of such trust. SECURE will also investigate how to specify access control policy based on trust. The project will formally define a computational trust model and a collaboration model capturing the dynamic aspects of the trust model; means to specify and to enforce security policies based on trust; means to evaluate security policies and implementations based on trust; and algorithms for trust management.

Objectives: The objectives of SECURE are the definition of a computational trust model allowing entities to reason about the trustworthiness of other entities for use in security-related decisions; the definition of a collaboration model capturing the issues of trust formation, trust evolution, trust propagation and trust exploitation; the definition of means to specify and to enforce security policies based on trust, including specifying the level of positive experiences required to allow a particular principal access to a specific resource; the definition of means to evaluate security policies and implementations based on trust while recognizing that there may be many different ways of establishing the required level of trust for collaboration to take place; the development of a framework encompassing algorithms for trust management, including algorithms to handle trust formation, trust evolution and trust propagation; the validation of the approach in the context of the formal model.

Work description: The application of trust leads naturally to a decentralized approach to security management that can tolerate partial information, albeit one in which there is an inherent element of risk for the trusting entity. Fundamentally, it is the ability to reason about trust that allows entities to accept risk when they are interacting with other entities, and, hence, the central problem to be addressed by SECURE is to provide entities with a basis for reasoning about trust. Thus, the heart of the SECURE workplan is the development of a computational model of trust that will provide the formal basis for reasoning about trust and for the deployment of verifiable security policies. The most important activity in the workplan is therefore the development of a formal computational trust model that captures human intuitions about trust, and must especially allow computational entities to reason about the trustworthiness of other participants for use in security-related decisions. We have planned to deliver two revisions of the model during the course of the project, primarily because we expect the development of the model to be informed by the other activities in the project.

While the development of the computational trust model is at the heart of SECURE, it alone is not sufficient to allow us to deliver a feasible security mechanism for the global computing infrastructure. In this context it is equally important that we understand how trust is formed, evolves and is exploited in a system, for instance, the trust lifecycle; how security policy can be expressed in terms of trust and how access control can be implemented to reflect policy; and how algorithms for trust management can be implemented feasibly for a range of different applications. Further activities address these issues based on an understanding of trust derived from the formal model but also contributing to the understanding of trust as a feasible basis for making security decisions to be embodied in the model.

Table of Contents

UML for Global Computing⋆

Hubert Baumeister[1], Nora Koch[1], Piotr Kosiuczenko[1],
Perdita Stevens[2], and Martin Wirsing[1]

[1] Institut für Informatik
Ludwig-Maximilians-Universität München
[2] Informatics (South)
University of Edinburgh, GB
{baumeist,kochn,kosiucze,wirsing}@informatik.uni-muenchen.de
perdita@inf.ed.ac.uk

Abstract. Global systems – systems which may operate over transient networks including mobile elements and in which computation itself may be mobile – are gaining in importance. Nevertheless, the means for their modelling are still underdeveloped. The Unified Modelling Language (UML) is well developed for convenient modelling of behavior, but is not yet so useful for modelling aspects of design relevant to global systems, such as mobility. Non-functional requirements such as performance and security also assume an increased importance in the context of global systems, and here too, UML requires enhancement.

In this paper we present an extension to UML class, sequence and activity diagrams to model mobile systems. We also describe extensions to model performance and security characteristics. We will describe how, wherever possible, we reuse existing work in these areas.

1 Introduction

The latest developments in information and communication technology impose enormous challenge of defining and exploiting dynamically configured systems of mobile entities that interact in novel ways with their environment to achieve or control their computational tasks. The emergence of the World Wide Web provides new computational paradigms in which computation is distributed over the net and highly dynamic, with the network itself changing continuously. The network topology, which was carefully hidden in LAN, starts to play a fundamental role. This situation fostered new concepts like global and mobile computing.

If dependable global systems are to be built efficiently, it is essential to be able to model their requirements and their design, since modelling is an essential part of modern software development practice. Modelling permits designers to solve many problems at an early stage of development that might otherwise be discovered much later. Models are also essential to the maintenance of systems and to their analysis.

⋆ This research has been partially sponsored by the EC 5th Framework projects: AG-ILE (IST-2001-32747) and DEGAS (IST-2001-32072).

C. Priami (Ed.): GC 2003, LNCS 2874, pp. 1–24, 2003.

The Unified Modeling Language (UML) [13] is a widely adopted standard for modelling object-oriented software systems. It consists of several diagram types providing different views of the system model. UML is a semi-formal language defined by a combination of UML class diagrams, natural language and formal constraints written in the object constraint language (OCL). An important feature of UML is that it was designed to be specialised, and mechanisms for defining specialised variants of UML are available.

In order to use UML to model global applications we have to consider both the nature of the applications themselves and the issues which will most occupy their designers. One of the key feature of global applications which distinguishes their models from models of most other applications is their use of *mobility*. In this paper we present two extensions of UML diagrams for modeling mobile systems. The first notation, the so called Sequence Diagrams for Mobility (SDM), add appropriate primitives for modelling of object topology and mobility and can be seen as a generalization of UML Sequence Diagrams [12]. The second one extends in a similar way UML Activity and Object Flow Diagrams [2]. The idea of our approach is similar to the idea of ambients or Maude in that a mobile object can migrate from one location to another, that it can be the location for other mobile objects and that it may interact with other objects. Locations can be arbitrarily nested, generalizing the limited place-agent nesting of most agent and place languages. We introduce into UML the concepts of location, mobile object, mobile location, `move` action and `clone` action. These concepts are defined by using UML stereotypes, tagged values and OCL-constraints.

There are several other issues which may occupy designers of mobile systems, but two areas seem to be of major concern. Global computing raises particular concerns for *security*, where the system includes mobile devices which cannot be trusted. Equally, in an environment where network connections may behave, fail and recover unpredictably, *performance* is harder to predict through intuition alone. Another reason why performance considerations may be important is that battery life of the mobile devices used may be a limiting factor.

In Sect. 2 we explain or choice to use the UML and discuss its extension mechanism. In Sect. 3 we present the basic concepts of mobile systems followed in Sect. 4 and Sect. 5 by the extension to UML Sequence and Activity Diagrams to model mobile systems. Security is considered in Sect. 6, performance in section 7.

2   UML Extensions

One of the basic ideas of the AGILE [1] and DEGAS [5] projects is to allow developers to design global applications using as far as possible the design notation which is familiar to them: the Unified Modelling Language. There are several reasons for this, generally consequences of the fact that UML is now the dominant modelling language for object-oriented software systems:

1. Desire to take advantage of existing expertise
2. Availability of a wide range of commercial and free tools

3. Availability of books and training, ability to recruit people already familiar with UML
4. Perception that UML has a good blend of precision and flexibility for most purposes (though there are some concerns)

However, UML, as defined by the OMG, is not in itself adequate for the modelling of global applications and for analysis of their properties including mobility, performance and security. UML does not contain features that permit the description of how parts of the system are mobile, nor that permit the expression of security or performance features. Accordingly we have decided that we need to define a variant of UML which extends the language's capabilities to express mobility, performance and security features.

The next question is how to specialise UML. We could of course define a variant of UML in any way which suited us. However, UML does provide a standard mechanism for extending UML to suit the needs of different application areas. One defines a UML *profile*, which is essentially a dialect of UML; see [13] for details. Several profiles for different application areas have themselves been standardised by the OMG, and many more have been defined by their users.

There are several advantages of using UML extenxion mechanisms, in particular:

- Not needing to define a language specialisation mechanism of our own
- Acceptability within the UML community
- Makes it straightforward to build on existing UML profiles
- Potential availability of tools supporting profiles

Sometimes, the mechanisms for defining profiles are not sufficiently expressive for defining the desired UML extensions. For example, it is difficult to define a new diagram type in a profile unless it is closely related to an existing UML diagram type. In such cases, one can choose instead to extend the UML metamodel. This gives a heavyweight extension of UML, which will not automatically be supported by tools.

At present, the main commercial tools do not support semantics of user defined profiles. However, there are signs that this is changing; for example, Artisan Software has recently released a version of their tool with support for profiles.

Therefore the approach we take to extending UML within the AGILE [1] and DEGAS [5] projects is to define a profile that meets our needs, wherever possible, both in order to save ourselves effort and in order to maximise the acceptance of our work in the wider community. DEGAS builds exclusively on profiles that already exist, whereas AGILE introduces its own notation when necessary.

3 Mobility Concepts

Mobility is one of the most important aspects of global computation. Code mobility emerged in some scripting languages for controlling network applications like Tcl and is one of the key features of the Java programming language. Agent mobility has been supported by Telescript, AgentTcl, or Odyssey (cf. e.g. [8]). In addition, hardware can be mobile too. Mobile hosts like laptops, WAPs and PDAs can move between networks. Moreover, entire networks can be mobile, like for example IBM's Personal Area Network (PAN) and networks of sensors in airplanes or trains. For example, Fig. 1 shows in an informal way a person having a PAN who boards an airplane, flies from one location to another and deplanes.

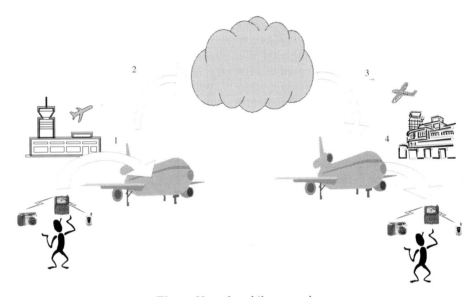

Fig. 1. Nested mobile networks.

Mobile computations can cross barriers and move between virtual and physical locations, therefore they can turn remote calls to local calls avoiding the latency limits. But there is a price to pay since the administrative barriers and multiple access pathways interact in very complex ways. This requires special means for the specification and implementation of mobile systems.

There exist already some extensions to UML for modeling mobile systems. In [16] an extension of collaboration diagrams is presented to model dynamic change of the composition relationship. It defines a form of aggregation link between objects — a component link — with the additional semantics that a component link may change over time. In addition, it proposes the use of component boundaries to emphasize the relationship between a component and its immediate components. It is an interesting approach, but it modellsm mobility in a rather indirect way and does not explain how these extensions fit into the UML metamodel.

Another extension is presented in [11]. It is similar to the early idea of Use Case Maps [3]. Stereotyped classes and packages are used to model mobility. Objects moving from one location to another are modeled by stereotyped messages.

This approach can be used when there are only two kinds of objects: mobile objects and static locations. It is not well suited for modeling objects which are both locations and mobile.

In the following we introduce the main structural concepts for modelling mobility we use in this paper: locations, mobile objects and actions moving mobile objects.

3.1   Locations

The concept of location plays an important role in the case of mobile systems. To denote classes whose instances are locations we use the stereotype «location». For example, the airport Charles de Gaulle (CDG) is an instance of the stereo-typed class Airport. Similar to the ambient calculus [4] we allow locations to be nested (cf. Fig. 2). For example, the airport Charles de Gaulle is contained in France, an instance of class Country, which is also a location. We require that any location is contained in at most one location and that a location cannot be contained in itself (directly or indirectly). We do not require that the hierarchy of locations has a single top element. Thus the hierarchy of locations forms a forest. Note that these assumptions, in particular the assumption that a location is contained in at most one location, simplifies the semantics and in consequence the analysis of mobile systems.

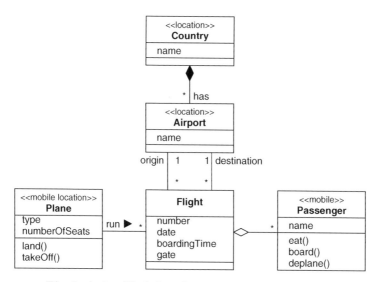

Fig. 2. A simplified class diagram modeling an airport.

3.2   Mobile Objects

A mobile object is an object that can change its location. A class representing mobile objects is indicated by the stereotype «mobile». The current location of a mobile object is indicated by the atLoc relation. As in the case of locations, a mobile object can only be contained in at most one location. In our airport example, a particular passenger is a mobile object, as he may move from one location to another, for example, from Munich to Paris (cf. Fig. 2).

Note that the atLoc relation is not explicitly presented in Fig. 2. One reason is that this would unduly complicate the diagram. For example, a passenger can be located either at a plane, an airport, or a country. The second reason is that the existence of the atLoc relation is implied by the use of the mobility stereotypes.

Locations can be mobile too. This allows us to model passengers in an airplane and flying the airplane from one airport to another. In this case the stereotype «mobile location» is used. The stereotype «mobile location» inherits from the stereotype «location» and the stereotype «mobile» for mobile objects. This was the only way to define mobile locations by stereotypes with the UML 1.3, because a model element could have only one stereotype attached to it. However, from UML 1.4 on it is possible to attach more than one stereotype to a model element. In this case we could give the class Airplane the stereotypes «mobile» and «location» to denote that it is a mobile location. However, we feel that using the stereotype «mobile location» conveys better the concept of mobile locations.

For mobile locations we require that the atLoc relation inherited from mobile objects is the same as the atLoc relation inherited from locations. To ensure this, stereotypes «mobile» and «location» inherit from a common stereotype «spatial» which denotes classes of objects that can be at a location (cf. Fig. 3).

Figure 3 shows the metamodel for the stereotypes «location», «mobile» and «mobile location».

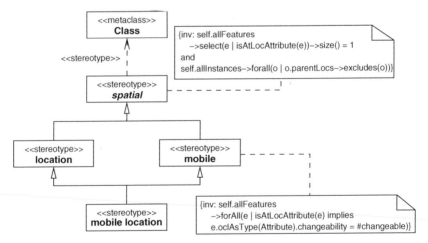

Fig. 3. Metamodel for stereotypes «location», «mobile», and «mobile location».

To model the atLoc relation, we require that each class with stereotype «location» or «mobile» provides its instances with an attribute atLoc. Since we

want to state the requirement only once, we introduce the abstract stereotype
«spatial» and state the requirement for that stereotype. Then the stereotypes
«location» and «mobile» inherit the requirement. To express this as an OCL-
constraint, we define an additional predicate isAtLocAttribute on features,
i.e. instances of metaclass Feature. In the metamodel each class is associated
with a set of features describing the methods and attributes of the class and
its instances. A feature e is an atLoc attribute, i.e. isAtLocAttribute(e), if e
is an instance attribute, has the name atLoc and its multiplicity is zero or one.
Further, the attribute can hold instances of classes having stereotype «location»:

$$\text{isAtLocAttribute}(e : \text{Feature}) =$$
$$e.\text{oclIsKindOf}(\text{Attribute}) \text{ and}$$
$$e.\text{name} = \text{'atLoc' and}$$
$$\text{let } e' = e.\text{oclAsType}(\text{Attribute}) \text{ in}$$
$$e'.\text{ownerScope} = \#\text{instance and}$$
$$e'.\text{multiplicity} = 0..1 \text{ and}$$
$$e'.\text{targetScope} = \#\text{instance and}$$
$$e'.\text{type.oclIsKindOf}(\text{Class}) \text{ and}$$
$$e'.\text{type.stereotype.name->includes}(\text{'location'})$$

Now we require that each class with stereotype «spatial» has a unique atLoc
attribute and that the atLoc relation does not contain cycles:

$$\text{self.allFeatures->select}(e \mid \text{isAtLocAttribute}(e))\text{->size}() = 1 \text{ and}$$
$$\text{self.allInstances->forAll}(o \mid o.\text{parentLocs->excludes}(o))$$

The additional operation parentLocs computes the set of all parent locations
for an instance of a class with stereotype «spatial»:

$$\text{self.parentLocs} = \text{self.atLoc->union(self.atLoc.parentLocs)}$$

For mobile objects we require in addition that they are able to change their
location, which means that their atLoc attribute can change its value. This can
be expressed by requiring that the changeability attribute of atLoc has the value
#changeable for all classes with stereotype «mobile», in addition to the exis-
tence of an atLoc attribute — which is inherited from stereotype «spatial»:

$$\text{self.allFeatures->forAll}(e \mid \text{isAtLocAttribute}(e) \text{ implies}$$
$$e.\text{oclAsType}(\text{Attribute}).\text{changeability} = \#\text{changeable})$$

The operation allFeatures is an additional operation on Classifier defined in
the UML 1.5 semantics. It collects the features of a classifier together with all
features of its parents.

4   Sequence Diagrams for Mobility

In this section we study the use of Sequence Diagrams for modelling mobile systems. We show that the standard form of UML Sequence Diagrams can be hardly used for modelling of mobile systems. We present therefore a new notation, the so called Sequence Diagrams for Mobility [12]. SDM models mobile, nested and dynamically changing structure by generalizing the concept of object lifeline of UML sequence diagrams. This idea generalizes the idea of Use Case Maps [3] and allows us to specify mobile objects with nested structure.

4.1   Modeling with Standard UML Sequence Diagrams

In this subsection we consider modelling of mobile systems with standard UML Sequence Diagrams.

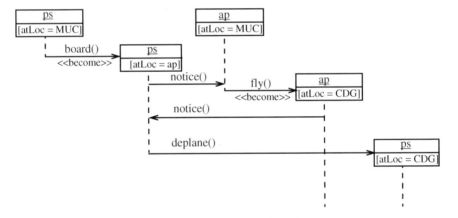

Fig. 4. Boarding, flying and deplaning.

Let us model a passenger *ps* who boards an airplane *ap* at Munich *MUC* airport, flies to Paris Charles De Gaulle *CDG* and then deplanes (cf. Fig. 4). It is not easy to model this using sequence diagrams only, since there exist no direct means for modelling change of state nor change of topology (for example the fact that a passenger is in airport and then in a airplane). The state description can be contained in the box; the fact that the person is at Paris airport is indicated by [atLoc = CDG:Airport]. This kind of modelling has the disadvantage, that when an object changes its state, we need a new box. Such boxes can be connected by a message arrow with stereotype «become». Let us observe that boarding an airplane involves an airplane and a passenger, but here boarding is modelled indirectly as the change of state of a passenger. To disallow a plane to fly without a passenger we need *notice*() message to 'inform' the plane that the passenger boarded.

As we see, UML sequence diagrams can model mobility in an indirect way and even in this simple example the diagram is rather hard to read. There are also other possibilities to model this using standard UML Sequence Diagrams but they do not yield readable specifications either. Therefore, in the following we introduce a new kind of sequence diagrams which are better suited for modelling mobility.

4.2   Sequence Diagrams for Mobility: Basic Concepts

In this subsection we present the basics of Sequence Diagrams for Mobility, an extension to UML Sequence Diagrams for modelling mobile systems. We show how to model artifacts like crossing barriers or communication. Like in Maude [6] a mobile object can migrate from one host to another , it can be also a host for other mobile objects. It may interact with other objects. Like a location, a mobile object can host other mobile objects, it can locally communicate and receive messages from other places. Objects can be arbitrarily nested, generalizing the limited place-agent nesting of most agent and place languages. In the ambient calculus [4] communication across a single barrier is synchronous; communication across multiple barriers is performed via other ambients which navigate from one location to another. In UML but also in Maude, objects can communicate in synchronous or asynchronous way. We stick to this principle. Unlike ambients, in our notation it is possible to express actions at a distance (like RMI) even if many barriers are involved, so that multiple steps can be rendered atomic. In general, we do not want to restrict the language artificially; if something is easy to specify in our notation, then we allow it without bothering whether it is easy to implement or not. But of course, if necessary one can define a dialect disallowing some expressions.

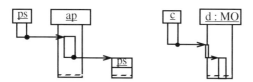

Fig. 5. Object mobility.

A mobile object can change its location performing a move action. For example, a passenger may enter an airplane and then leave it; in this case the topology changes too (cf. lhs. of Fig. 5). A virus may cross a firewall in a message (cf. rhs. of Fig. 5). To model this, the object lifeline in sequence diagrams is blown up to an action box; it models actions performed by a mobile object and indicates the boundaries of the object. Consequently, in our two dimensional representation we have two lines which denote the same thread. This implies that different arrows must be attached to different levels of an action box.

A description of a mobile object's behavior starts with a box containing optionally the object name or class. A mobile object may move into another object, or move out of an object. If an object moves into or out of another object, then the action box ends in the former location and the object is moved to another location. This **move** action is indicated by a stereotyped message arrow which starts with a black circle; we call it move arrow. We use here a notation similar to UML state machines to indicate that after the move the moving object starts its operation in a new location. A mobile object can not continue its operation outside of its new host, if it is already inside another host; consequently the arrow starts strictly at the end of the first action box to indicate that all other actions in the box must precede the move. We assume, that the mobile objects can not be bi-located or merged, therefore an object box may have at most one move arrow attached to the top and at most one arrow attached to the bottom. If a mobile object starts its operation (and was not active before anywhere else), then this is indicated by a special box like in the case of sequence diagrams. If a mobile object was already active somewhere else, then there must exist a move arrow such that its sharp end is attached to the left or right upper corner of the corresponding action box. This requirement corresponds to the fact that mobile objects can not be merged, nor appear out of nowhere. An action box of an object which already performed a move may optionally start with the objects name and/or class. We indicate the end of mobile object description by two horizontal lines, where the upper line is dashed.

Figure 5 shows what a mobile object looks like. As in the case of sequence diagrams, the object's names must be underlined. In the left hand side of the figure, a passenger *ps* enters airplane *ap*. Since there is no conflict concerning the identity of objects inside *ap*, the corresponding action box does not bear any name. Then *ps* deplanes *ap* and starts its operation outside *ap*. The name in the action box is not necessary either, since the identity of ps can be uniquely traced. No message arrow is attached to the corresponding action box except of the move. The right hand side of Fig. 5 shows a mobile object *c* entering object *d* of class *MO* by activating an operation of *d* (like a virus which sends itself in an e-mail). After the operation is finished the objects starts to operate inside *d*.

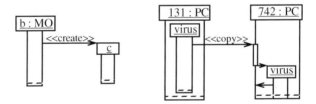

Fig. 6. Object creation and copying.

The left hand side of Fig. 6 shows the creation of a new object. The right hand side of this figure shows a proliferating virus. This virus starts a procedure on another PC to enter it. We use a message with stereotype «copy» [13], the copy is then assumed to behave as its original would do inside the new location.

Another important operation is **open** (cf. Fig. 7), this operation opens an object making its hosted objects visible. If a mobile object is opened, then it

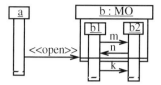

Fig. 7. Opening an object.

ends its life, but its sub-objects continue to operate. This operation is similar to operation open in the ambient calculus [4], but it may be synchronous as well as asynchronous, depending on the type of message used. The opening of an object is indicated by a horizontal line. Object a sends message open to b, then object b is opened and the hosted objects $b1$ and $b2$ continue to operate. A mobile object can be also terminated, in this case all its hosted objects are terminated too, it can be of course expressed by a series of open operations. The recursive termination is indicated by a continuous line. For the recursive termination caused by an other object we use a message with stereotype «destroy» (cf. Fig. 8) (cf. [4]). In Fig. 8, object a terminates object b. After terminating b, all its sub-objects are terminated too. The termination is indicated by a continuous line stretching across all objects.

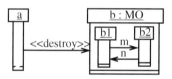

Fig. 8. Destroy.

4.3 Abstraction

In this subsection we present the zoom facility allowing one to abstract from the internal details or, vice versa, to show them. Abstraction is one of the most important concepts to manage complexity. In the case of Sequence Diagrams for Mobility we can abstract from internal object details like the behavior of hosted objects, behavior of an object during move actions and so on, or display them, depending on the desired level of detail.

The left hand side of Fig. 9 shows the virus attack (cf. Fig. 6), in the zoom-out view, as perceived by the user of the attacked PC. He/she can usually not look inside the PC hosting the virus. For an external observer who can only see the communication network, the whole situation may look like the right hand side of the figure.

It is possible to zoom into an object's move arrow to see the behavior of the participating objects. Figure 10 shows flight from Munich to Paris in a zoom-out view. The details of the flight can be seen on Fig. 10.

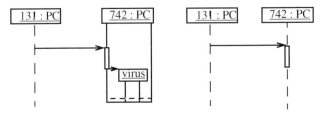

Fig. 9. Zoom-out.

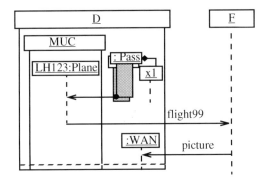

Fig. 10. Flight example.

4.4   Example

In this subsection we consider a person flying from Munich to Paris. Figure 10 shows a simple story of a passenger $x1$ who boards an airplane in Munich airport, flies to Paris and publishes a picture in a WAN. This story is described from the perspective of an observer on the German side. The person $x1$ together with other passengers enters the airport and then boards the airplane $LH123$. The airplane flies to Paris (the flight number is 99), but the only thing the observer can see is that the airplane is airborne but not what happens inside the airplane nor further details of this flight. The next event which the observer is able to notice is the appearance of a picture in the WAN. To model several passengers (i.e. objects of class `Passenger`), we use the multi-object notation [13], which allows us to present in a compact way several passengers playing the same role. Person $x1$ is distinguished using composition relationship.

This simple view shows some of the barriers person $x1$ has to cross while flying. There are political boundaries which regulate the movement of people and devices, like airplanes, computers and so on. Within those boundaries, there are other boundaries like those protecting airports and single airplanes against intruders. We specify explicitly such boundaries and the moves across them. In the view presented in Fig. 10, we have abstracted from several details. The view of passenger $x1$ is much more detailed (cf. Fig. 11).

We can see what happens inside the airplane during the flight; the move arrow contains the action box of the airplane $LH123$. Passenger $x1$ makes pictures with his digital camera; the pictures are send then to the WAN. As usual, a

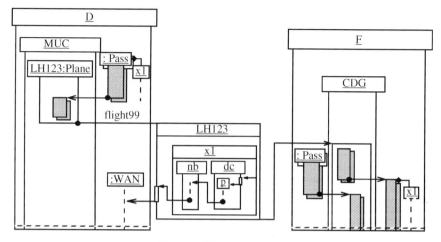

Fig. 11. Flight's details.

digital camera does not allows him to send pictures directly to the *WAN*. It is also forbidden to use mobile phones during the flight. Therefore the passenger saves the pictures to his notebook *nb*, logs into the on-board network and then transmits the pictures to *WAN* via the on-board network. We abstract here from the structure of the *WAN* network (indicated by dashed line). Let us point out that the sending of the picture by passenger $x1$ is not temporally related to crossing any border like those over *D*, *EU* and so on. The only thing we can say is that it happens between the start of the airplane and its landing. Finally, all the passengers leave the airplane and the airport. The passenger can see that the airplane is boarded by new passengers. The dashed line in the head of the last box of passenger $x1$ means that the history of this passenger started earlier and that the head of the object box is not beginning of its lifeline, but a continuation.

5   Modeling with Activity Diagrams

In this section we introduce two variants of activity diagrams for modeling mobility. These diagrams were introduced in [2]. The first variant is responsibility centered and uses swimlanes to model who is responsible for an action. The second is location centered and uses the notation of composite objects to visualize the hierarchy of locations.

Basically, there are two primitives that change the location of a mobile object. A mobile object can move from one location to another — a so called move action; or a copy of an object is moved to a new location [7] — a so called clone action. These actions act on objects and their containment relationship wrt. locations. Given a move action on an object *o* which is contained in location *l*, i.e. *o*.atLoc = *l*, to another location *l'*, then after performing the move operation object *o* is contained in location *l'*, i.e. *o*.atLoc = *l'*. Operation clone works similar; however, instead of moving the object itself, first a copy of the object is created which is then moved to the new location.

The stereotypes «move» and «clone» for action states in activity diagrams are used to denote `move` actions and `clone` actions, respectively. Actions have two additional attributes, the first one indicates who is performing the action, and the second one is the location where the action is performed.

Calculi for mobility restrict these primitives further by omitting the `clone` operation. Instead, the `clone` operation is defined as the composition of a copy operation followed by a `move` action. For notational convenience we decide to take `clone` as a primitive. Commonly, these calculi also restrict the target location of a move, for example, to move only one level in the containment hierarchy [4,14].

In the following, we present two notations for the above mentioned mobility concepts in the context of activity diagrams. The first notation is responsibility centered and focuses on *who* is performing an action and is based on the standard notation for activity diagrams. The second notation is location centered and focuses on *where* an action is performed, given by the atLoc relation between mobile objects and locations, and how activities change this relation.

5.1 Responsibility Centered View

The first notation uses object-flow states with classifier in states to model the atLoc relation. In the airport example consider a passenger Hubert who is boarding a plane at the airport of Munich. This can be modeled as a `move` action as shown in Fig. 12. The source of the `move` action is the object-flow state Hubert:Passenger [atLoc = MUC:Airport] and the target an object-flow state Hubert:Passenger [atLoc = LH123:Plane]. The passenger Hubert moves from his previous location, Munich airport (MUC), to his new location, the plane $LH123$. More precisely this means, if in an object configuration there is a passenger Hubert, an airplane $LH123$ and an airport MUC such that Hubert is contained in MUC and also $LH123$ is contained in MUC, the `move` operation changes the configuration in such a way that Hubert is no longer directly contained in the airport MUC, instead it is contained in the plane $LH123$. The containment of the plane does not change; therefore Hubert is still indirectly contained in MUC. Swimlanes can be used to show who is performing the action; in this case it is the passenger who boards the plane.

The `clone` operation is shown in Fig. 13 for a list of passengers (*lop*). One copy of the list is kept by the airport staff and another copy of the list is moved into the plane. The difference in the semantics of this diagram to the previous diagram is that given the configuration as before, the `clone` operations creates a new document list of passengers *lop'* which differs from *lop* only in the fact that it is contained in $LH123$. In addition *lop* is still contained in MUC, i.e. *lop* has not moved at all.

Note that by the UML it is possible to omit the «become» stereotype in the output of the `move` action in Fig. 12, as it is the default that the input and the output are the same objects if the type of the object flow states are the same. In the same way, the «copy» stereotype in the output of the `clone` action in Fig. 13 can be omitted because this stereotype can be deduced from the stereotype «clone» of the `clone` action.

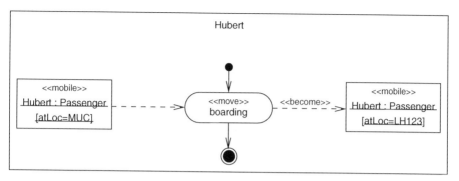

Fig. 12. The move action.

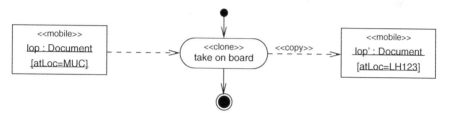

Fig. 13. The clone action.

A more complex example is given in Fig. 14. The activity diagram starts with the boarding activity of the passenger at the Munich airport. This activity changes the location of the passenger Hubert from the airport (MUC) to the particular plane $LH123$. The next activity is the take-off activity of the plane. This activity changes the location of the plane from the Munich airport (MUC) to a not specified destination, that is we are not interested in the location where the plane is when it is flying. During the flight, the plane performs the flying activity and the passenger the send mail activity. These activities happen in parallel. Note that before landing, the passenger has to stop the send mail activity because the use of electronic devices is not allowed during take-off and landing. When landing, the location of the plane is changed to the destination airport, in this case the Paris airport (CDG). Finally, the passenger deplanes and is now located at the Paris airport. This notation is responsibility centered as the swimlanes are indicating who is performing a particular activity.

5.2   Location Centered View

The second notation uses containment of the boxes for mobile objects/locations in the boxes of other locations to show the atLoc relation. For that we use the same UML notation as for composite objects. A difference is that the atLoc relation is not an aggregation. Another difference is that we also allow action states to be drawn inside composite objects of stereotype «location». This indicates that the action is performed at the corresponding location. Figure 15 shows this notation for the move operation depicted in Fig. 12.

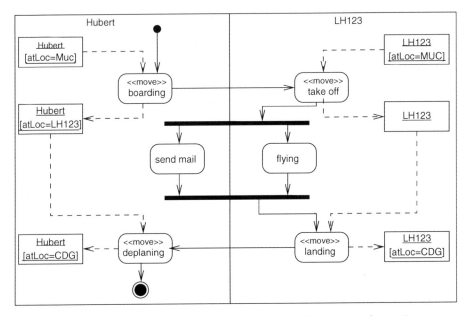

Fig. 14. The airport example using the responsibility centered notation.

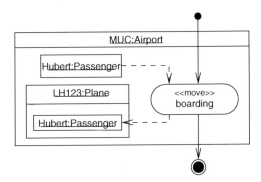

Fig. 15. The move action.

Note, that in addition to the fact that the passenger is in the plane, we can model also that the plane is parked at the airport. This is an information that cannot be represented in the responsibility centered approach as shown in Fig. 12. What Fig. 15 also shows is that activities can be drawn inside locations to indicate that the operation is performed at that location. In the example, boarding takes place at the airport. While it is still possible to use swimlanes to indicate who is performing an action, most likely, more complex diagrams will have to concentrate on either the topology of locations or on the actor performing an activity to avoid an overloaded diagram.

Note that the box containing the airport may be omitted if this is not relevant for the presentation.

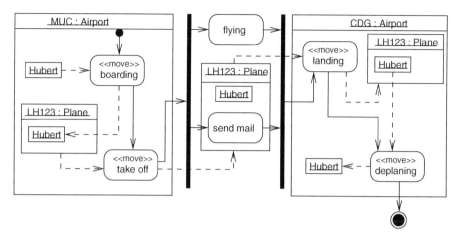

Fig. 16. The airport example using the location centered notation.

Figure 16 presents a location centered view of the activities of Fig. 14. Again, the first activity changes the location of the passenger from the airport to the plane. However, in contrast to the responsibility centered notation it is visible that the passenger is still located indirectly in the Munich airport, because the plane has not moved yet. Also one can see that the boarding activity happens at the airport. The next activity, the take-off, takes again place at the airport. In the location centered variant the notation indicates that the plane has left the airport after take-off. Again, during the flight the activities flying and send mail happen in parallel. In contrast to the information provided by the responsibility-centered notation, this notation shows that the send mail activity happens *in* the plane, while flying does not take place inside the plane. Note that for simplicity reasons, the box denoting the passenger during the flight can be omitted. Landing and deplaning are similar to the activities boarding and take-off.

6   Security

There is a very wide range of security requirements and design features which, ultimately, we would like to be able to record in our variant of UML and analyse with formal tools [5]. Much of this is outside the scope of formal techniques, for example because it pertains to information that is legal, psychological or sociological rather than mathematical. Nevertheless we do not wish to limit our UML profile to expressing only the characteristics that the tools can analyse.

Our main source for security features is a profile UMLsec developed by Jan Jürjens [10,9]. The most detailed source of information is his PhD thesis *Principles for Secure System Development* [9]. His fifth chapter, entitled *Secure Systems Development with UML*, defines the profile. (Note that the thesis also includes a formal semantics based on ASMs for a restricted fragment of UML. We do not adopt the semantics, since it is not suitable for our tool support and the fragment of UML is not appropriate to our needs. However, the profile itself does not depend on the formal semantics, so adopting the profile but not the semantics is reasonable.)

We do not reproduce UMLsec's definition here, but to give an overview of its capabilities we first quote Jürjens' list of requirements on the profile, and then give an example, also taken from [9].

6.1   Requirements on UMLsec

Security requirements. One needs to be able to formulate basic security requirements such as secrecy and integrity of data in a precise way. Formalizations of basic security requirements are provided via stereotypes, such as «secrecy» and «integrity».

Threat scenarios. It should be possible to consider various situations that give rise to different possibilities of attacks. Threat scenarios are incorporated using the formal semantics and depending on the modelled underlying physical layer via the sets of actions available to the adversary of a particular kind.

Security concepts. One should be able to employ important security concepts (for example that of tamper-resistant hardware). To incorporate security concepts such as tamper-resistant hardware, threat scenarios can be used.

Security mechanisms. One needs to be able to incorporate security mechanisms such as control access. For example, modeling the Java security architecture access control mechanisms.

Security primitives. On a more fine-grained level, one needs to model security primitives. They are either built in (such as symmetric and asymmetric encryption), or can be treated (such as security protocols).

Underlying physical security. It is necessary to take into account the level of security provided by the underlying physical layer. This can be addressed by the stereotype *secure link* in deployment diagrams.

Security management. Security management questions (such as secure workflow) need to be addressed. This can be considered by using activity diagrams.

6.2   Example of UMLsec

Figure 17 shows an example concerning communication link security which can be used in our airport case study for describing the login of a passenger into a network. The client workstation and the server are linked via a communication link; here a stereotype «internet» shows that the link is of a specific kind (the Internet). There is also a dashed-arrow dependency going from the web server to the client through the client application's interface. The component *web server* uses the services of the component *client apps*. The stereotype «secrecy» is used to indicate the precise dependency between the two.

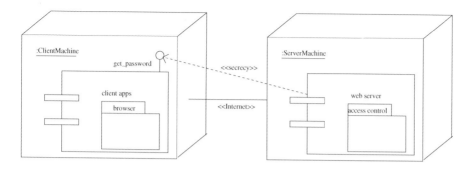

Fig. 17. Secure links usage.

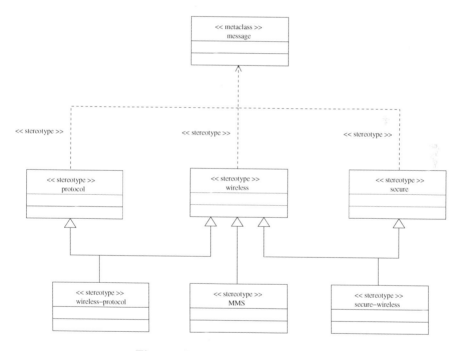

Fig. 18. Security added stereotypes.

6.3   Global Computing Requirements beyond UMLsec

Although UMLsec is a good basis for the security aspects of our profile, it does not completely meet all requirements for global computing. In particular, we have to extend UMLsec by stereotypes for messages in sequence diagrams to represent requirements on the communication medium to be used for that particular message. For example, we have to be able to represent by a stereotype «secure», that a particular message is communicated via a secure medium. Figure 18 gives an overview of our security related stereotypes.

7   Performance

Performance requires more sophisticated extensions to UML than in many other areas. The OMG's standard profile for Schedulability, Performance and Time [15] meets quite closely what performance modellers are looking for. There are some areas where changes are needed and many open questions which can only be answered by further practical experience within the project, which is ongoing at the time of writing.

7.1   Introduction to the Performance Aspects of [15]

One of the reasons why a performance profile is more complex than a security or mobility profile is that it needs to support a variety of related, but different, aims. The performance modeller does not simply record information about performance requirements that must be taken into consideration, or perhaps verified. Several different kinds of information must be recorded: requirements, measured performance, performance assumptions and performance predictions, for example. Some of this information will be output from a performance analysis or simulation tool; other parts of the information will be input to such tools, used in various ways. The profile must support the user in recording all these kinds of information and in differentiating between them.

Quoting from [15] p135:

The profile provides facilities for:

- Capturing performance requirements within the design context
- Associating performance-related QoS characteristics with selected elements of a UML model
- Specifying execution parameters which can be used by modeling tools to compute predicted performance characteristics
- Presenting performance results computed by modeling tools or found in testing

Typical tools for this kind of analysis provide two important functions. The first is to estimate the performance of a system instance, using some kind of model. The second function is assistance with determining how the system can be improved, by identifying bottlenecks or critical resources. A system designer will typically want to analyse the system under several scenarios using different parameter values for each scenario while maintaining the same overall system structure.

Providing UML extensions that allow designers to do these tasks using any one of a number of different analysis techniques is challenging. The authors of [15] have separated two tasks.

First, they have designed an extensible collection of abstract modelling *concepts* to describe the information necessary for performance (and more generally, schedulabilty and real time) analysis. Their collection is layered for manageability. The most abstract level is the *general resource model* describing the relationships between a range of basic analysis concepts, such as *resource* and various quality of service attributes. Several packages, including the performance modelling package which is our concern, extend this basic model. There is the possibility of extending the model further for global systems specific purposes, though we have not so far felt the need to do so. An analysis technique is defined in terms of the concepts, and can then apply to any notation, graphical or otherwise, from which the information embodied in the "concepts" can be derived.

Second, [15] provides a collection of UML stereotypes (i.e. specialised versions of UML model elements) and mappings from these to the concepts. This allows the relevant performance information to be expressed in a UML model. The information is then mapped to the "concepts", and so an analysis technique defined in terms of the concepts can be applied. The whole process of applying an analysis technique to a UML model can be automated.

It is not practical or useful to attempt to reproduce here all the facilities provided by [15]; instead we give examples and refer the interested reader to [15] for fuller information.

One of the fundamental concepts for the underlying performance model is a *step*. Several different kinds of UML model element (Message, Stimulus, Action State and Subactivity State) may be used to represent a step. Each of them may be labelled with the stereotype «PAstep» to indicate that a performance model should include a step corresponding to this model element. The stereotype «PAstep» has seven tags: *PAdemand, PArespTime, PAprob, PArep, PAdelay, PAextOp, PAinterval*. The three tags used in our example are:

- *PAdemand* is the total execution demand of the step on its host resource. Every scenario step in Fig. 19 has a *PAdemand* tagged value indicating its estimated mean execution time on the host processor.
- *PAextOp* is used to specify the set of operations of resources used in the execution of a step but not explicitly represented in the model. Each operation attribute identifies the operation and the number of times it is repeated.
- *PAprob* is the probability, in situations where its predecessor step has multiple successors, that this step will be executed.

Figures 19 and 20 show examples of the use of the stereotype and these tags.

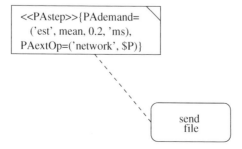

Fig. 19. External operation.

Figure 19 means that here our tagged value expression represents a demand in the scenario step with an estimated mean value of 0.2 milliseconds. It calls an external operation called 'network', 'P' times.

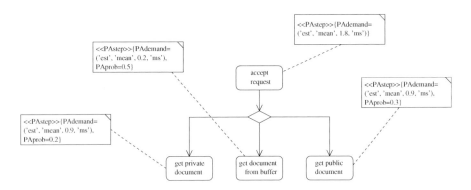

Fig. 20. Probability.

In Fig. 20 when the request is accepted, there is a probability of 0.5 that the document will be read from the buffer, 0.2 from the disk containing the private documents, 0.3 from the disk containing the public documents.

Our last example, Fig. 21, illustrates the use of nodes.

Here the *ClientWorkstation* is a host processor. The stereotype «PAhost» has seven tags: *PAschdPolicy, PArate, PAutilisation, PActxtSwT, PAprioRange, PApreemptable, PAthroughput*. The four tags used in our example are:

- *PAschdPolicy* is the access control policy for handling requests from scenario steps. The scheduling policy offers a choice of six tag types : here *PR* means Priority Inheritance.
- *PArate* is a relative speed factor for the processor expressed as a percentage of some normative processor.
- *PAutilisation* is the mean number of concurrent users of the resource.
- *PActxtSwT* is the length of time (overhead) required by the processing resource to switch from the execution of one scenario to a different one. Here the estimated mean value is 40 microseconds.

8   Conclusion and Future Work

In this paper we have presented extensions to UML sequence and activity diagrams to model the mobility aspects of global systems. We have also discussed how UML may be extended to model the performance and security aspects of global systems.

We have defined stereotyped classes to model locations and mobile objects, as well as stereotyped action states to model **move** and **clone** actions. To model

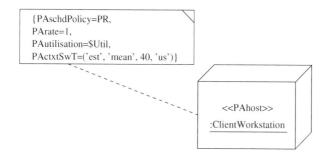

Fig. 21. Node.

complex systems it is desirable to have the concepts for expressing mobility as part of the language — as we have done in this paper — instead of modeling these defining these concepts indirectly using special encoding. The new form of Sequence and Activity Diagrams provide a powerful graphical notation for modelling mobility. They allow one to model in a clear way complex behavior. For example, a formal specification of the flying person would be rather very complicated, but a graphical representation would make it much easier to understand.

Within the two projects primarily concerned with this work, AGILE and DEGAS, work is proceeding as follows. Within AGILE, we are currently investigating the appropriateness of UML for the specification of structural and behavioral aspects of mobile systems. Our next step will be to validate the proposed notations in a bigger case study. The objective of AGILE is to develop an architectural approach in which mobility aspects can be modeled explicitly. Within DEGAS, we are connecting standard UML tools with a variety of formally based tools which are capable of performance and security analysis.

We plan to develop a formal semantics for the extended activity and sequence diagrams to provide a precise meaning of the presented concepts which is needed for formal analysis and reasoning about models. In addition, we plan to develop tools that support animation, early prototyping and analysis of mobile systems.

References

1. AGILE. Architectures for mobility. www.pst.informatik.uni-muenchen.de, 2003.
2. Hubert Baumeister, Nora Koch, Piotr Kosiuczenko, and Martin Wirsing. Extending activity diagrams to model mobile systems. In M. Aksit, M. Mezini, and R. Unland, editors, *Objects, Components, Architectures, Services, and Applications for a Networked World*, LNCS 2591, pages 278–293, Berlin-Heidelberg, October 2002. Springer-Verlag.
3. Raymond Buhr and Ronald Casselman. *Use Case Maps for Object-Oriented Systems*. Prentice-Hall, USA, 1995.
4. Luca Cardelli and Andrew Gordon. Mobile ambients. In Maurice Nivat, editor, *First Conference on Foundations of Software Science and Computation Structure*, LNCS 1378, pages 140–155. Springer Verlag, March 1998.

5. DEGAS. Design Environments for Global Applications. www.omnys.it/degas.
6. Francisco Durán, Steven Eker, Patrick Lincoln, and José Meseguer. Principles of Mobile Maude. In David Kotz and Friedemann Mattern, editors, *Agent Systems, Mobile Agents, and Applications, Second International Symposium on Agent Systems and Applications and Fourth International Symposium on Mobile Agents, ASA/MA 2000*, LNCS 1882, pages 73–85. Springer, 2000.
7. FIPA. FIPA agent management: Support for mobility specification. www.fipa.org, August 2001.
8. Jin Jing, Abdelsalam Helal, and Ahmed Elmagarmid. Client-server computing in mobile environments. *ACM Computing Surveys*, 31(2):117–157, 1999.
9. Jan Jürjens. *Principles for Secure System Development (submitted draft)*. PhD thesis, University of Oxford, UK, 2002.
10. Jan Jürjens. UMLsec: Extending UML for secure systems development. In *In proceedings of UML2002*, LNCS. Springer, 2002.
11. Cornel Klein, Andreas Rausch, Marc Sihling, and Zhaojun Wen. Extension of the Unified Modeling Language for mobile agents. In K. Siau and T. Halpin, editors, *Unified Modeling Language: Systems Analysis, Design and Development Issues*, chapter VIII. Idea Group Publishing, Hershey, PA and London, 2001.
12. Piotr Kosiuczenko. Sequence diagrams for mobility. In Stefano Spaccapietra, editor, *21 International Conference on Conceptual Modeling (ER2002)*. Springer-Verlag, October 2002. to appear.
13. OMG. Unified Modeling Language (UML), version 1.5. www.omg.org, March 2005.
14. Dirk Pattinson and Martin Wirsing. Making components move: A separation of concerns approach. In *Proc. First Internat. Symposium on Formal Methods for Components and Objects, FMCO'02, Leiden, November 2002*, LNCS, 2003. To appear.
15. Bran Selic, Alan Moore, Murray Woodside, Ben Watson, Morgan Bjorkander, Mark Gerhardt, and PDorina Petriu. Response to the OMG RFP for Schedulability, Performance, and Time, revised, June 2001. OMG document number: ad/2001-06-14.
16. Axel Wienberg, Florian Matthes, and Marko Boger. Modeling dynamic software components in UML. In Robert France and Bernhard Rumpe, editors, *UML'99 - The Unified Modeling Language. Proceedings*, LNCS 1723, pages 204–219. Springer-Verlag, 1999.

Reflecting Mobile Ambients into the π-Calculus[*]

Linda Brodo[1], Pierpaolo Degano[2], and Corrado Priami[3]

[1] ITC-IRST
via Sommarive, 18 I-38050 Povo (Trento)
brodo@itc.it
[2] Dipartimento di Informatica
Università di Pisa, via F.Buonarroti,2
I-56127 Pisa
degano@di.unipi.it
[3] Dipartimento di Informatica e Telecomunicazioni
Università di Trento
via Sommarive,14 I-38050 Povo (Trento)
priami@dit.unitn.it

Abstract. We embed the transition system of the Mobile Ambients into the transition system of a subset of the π-calculus. The basic idea, applicable to other calculi as well, is to constrain the deduction of the π-calculus transitions with the suitable conditions that reflect the nesting of ambients.

1 Introduction

Many calculi based on different primitives have been proposed to describe mobile computations: Plain Chocs [20, 21], Facile [22], π-calculus [17, 16], distributed π [19], Dπ [14], Join Calculus [10], Mobile Ambients [5], Boxed Ambients [3, 7], to mention only a few. Here, we focus on the π-like calculi and the ambient-like calculi. We want to investigate the relations between the mechanisms that the two families of calculi use in expressing mobility, relying on the calculus of Mobile Ambients (MA for short) and on the π-calculus as representatives.

The π-calculus is mainly based on the notion of communication between processes. Mobility is handled by communicating channel names. Processes that share the same channels are connected and can communicate. Thus, the links between connected processes are defined by the sets of names that each process shares with the others. The interconnection topology can then dynamically change because of name passing.

The MA relies on the notion of movement of executing environments. An environment, or ambient, denoted as $n[P]$, is identified by its name n. The execution of the basic actions of the MA, called capabilities, modify the nested structure of ambients. For example, in the process $P = n[in\,m.Q]\,|\,m[R]$ there are two ambients, n and m, and there is no nesting. After the execution of the

---

[*] Work partially supported by EU-project DEGAS (IST-2001-32072) and the Progetto MIUR Metodi Formali per la Sicurezza e il Tempo (MEFISTO).

in capability, the process P evolves into the process $P' = m[n[Q] \mid R]$, where the ambient n moved into the ambient m. Additionally, processes can communicate, but only when they reside within the same ambient.

A direct consequence of the different kind of primitives adopted by the two calculi is reflected in the definition of *neighborhood* that affects possible interactions of processes.

In the case of the π-calculus, two processes are *neighbors* if they share a no-empty set of names. Along a computation, processes may *consume* the occurrences of names or can acquire some other names. Thus, processes that were neighbors may became *distant* because they share no longer names. In the MA two ambients are neighbors if they are composed through parallel composition or one is the parent of the other. Processes exercise capabilities on neighbor ambients. Summing up, the π-calculus uses an implicit notion of mobility, based on the name sharing between processes while the MA relies on an explicit notion of mobility given by ambient constructors and their movements.

As a method of investigation, we want to encode the capabilities in terms of the more classical send and receive communication primitives. Our technique consists in separating the functional aspects, *i.e.* the usage of the ambient names on which capabilities act to describe movements, from the non functional aspects, *i.e.* the localization of ambients within the global parallel structure of the MA. To carry out our analysis we first define a translation from the syntax of the MA into the syntax of the π-calculus processes, then we introduce an abstract machine which executes the π-calculus semantic rules on the translated processes, requiring some extra conditions for an action to be executed. The extra conditions consist of localizing the processes which are the translation of the MA ambients in order to maintain the ambient nesting of the MA process before exercising a capability.

Technical Overview of the Work. The main tool we use in this paper is the enhanced operational semantics (EOS for short) [9], a non-standard way of describing the behaviour of concurrent systems. In this approach, the transitions of a system from one state to another have rich labels that encode portions of their proofs in the formal systems of axiom and rules defining the semantics. These labels can also be seen as a decoration of the syntax trees of processes, where the main operator is the parallel composition. Indeed the operational semantics is defined by inducing on the syntax of the processes. So, the labels localize within a whole process its sub-processes. For instance, in the process $T = (T_0|T_1)|T_2$ depicted in Fig. 1(a), any path from the root to a leaf of its syntax tree localizes a single sub-process: $||_1$ is the address of T_2, $||_0||_0$ is the address of T_0 and $||_0||_1$ is the address of T_1.

To translate the position of an MA ambient operator, we shall adopt a special π-calculus process which cannot perform any action: $(\nu\, a)\overline{a}\langle n \rangle$ that we abbreviate as $\mathbf{0}_n$. For instance, we shall translate $n[P_0|P_1]$ as the tree in Fig. 1(a), where $T_2 = \mathbf{0}_n$ and T_0, T_1 are the translations of P_0, P_1, respectively. Capabilities will be rendered as outputs on special channels, to be matched by auxiliary inputs. Local communications are easily managed.

The structural congruences of both calculi raise some problems because syntactical manipulations of processes obviously alter their syntax trees. For example, the syntax tree of $T = (T_0 \mid T_1) \mid \mathbf{0}_n$ becomes by associativity of parallel composition $T \equiv T' = T_0 \mid (T_1 \mid \mathbf{0}_n)$ whose syntax tree is displayed in Fig. 1(b). The neat result is that the address $\|_0\|_1$ selects T_1 in Fig. 1(a), while in T' the same sub-process T_1 is reachable through the different address $\|_1\|_0$ (see Fig. 1(b)). The exact localization of sub-processes is crucial for our development. Indeed, recall that we assumed that $T = (T_0 \mid T_1) \mid \mathbf{0}_n$ (where $T_2 = \mathbf{0}_n$) is the translation of $n[P_0 \mid P_1]$ and that we used $\mathbf{0}_n$ exactly for recording that $T_0 \mid T_1$ is "within the ambient n." Now, in T' we have $T_1 \mid \mathbf{0}_n$ that encodes a different nesting: only T_1 is "within ambient n" (actually T' would be the translation of $P_0 \mid n[P_1]$). Therefore, we cannot allow the address of T_1 to change freely. In other words, we shall control the applications of congruences in both the MA and the π-calculus processes.

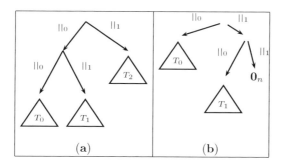

Fig. 1. Syntax trees of π-calculus processes.

The correctness of our translation is given by establishing a one-to-one correspondence between the transition system of the MA and the transition system of the π-calculus when is generated by the translation of the MA terms. An obvious consequence is that the MA transition system is strictly contained into the one of the π-calculus.

Overview of the Presentation. In Sect. 2 we shall overview the MA and in Sect. 3 we shall introduce the π_{MA}, the fragment of the higher order π-calculus that we use hereafter. In Sect. 4 we define the translation from the processes of the MA to those of the π_{MA}, which is endowed with an auxiliary transition system in Sect. 5. Section 6 shows how to deal with congruences and proves that the transition system of the MA is isomorphic to the one of the π_{MA} and included in the transition system of the π-calculus. The paper ends with an example worked in detail, and with some concluding remarks. All the proofs are in the Appendix.

2   The Mobile Ambient Calculus

In this section we briefly recall the syntax and the semantics of the MA [5].

Definition 1. *Given a set* Names *of names ranged over by* $n, m, \ldots$, *a set of variables ranged over by* x, y, z, *the syntax of the MA is described by the following BNF-like specification.*

	Capabilities		Processes
$M :=$ x	*variable*	$P, Q, R :=$ $\mathbf{0}$	*inactivity*
$\mid n$	*name*	$\mid (\nu n)P$	*restriction*
$\mid in\ M$	*can enter into* M	$\mid P\mid Q$	*composition*
$\mid out\ M$	*can exit out of* M	$\mid\ !P$	*replication*
$\mid open\ M$	*can open* M	$\mid M[P]$	*ambient*
$\mid \epsilon$	*null*	$\mid M.P$	*capability action*
$\mid M.M'$	*path*	$\mid (x).P$	*input action*
		$\mid \langle M \rangle$	*async output action*

We recall the intuitive semantics of the calculus. The $\mathbf{0}$ process cannot perform any action. The parallel operator defines the parallel composition of processes. In $P_0 \mid P_1$, P_0 and P_1 act independently and may interact. The replication $!P$ generates an unbounded number of parallel compositions of P. In $(\nu x)P$ the restriction operator creates a new name whose scope is P. The constructor $n[P]$ defines an ambient whose name is n, with the process P running inside. The processes $(x).P$ and $\langle M \rangle$ are the input/output actions, respectively. The input prefix binds the variable x in the process P, the variable will be replaced by the name that will be received along an anonymous channel. The output prefix is asynchronous and sends on an anonymous channel a name or a capability. The process $M.P$ executes the capability M and then acts as P. The capabilities, characterizing the MA, are $in\,n$, $out\,n$ and $open\,n$ which define the ambient movements. The $in\,n$ capability is performed by an ambient which enters the ambient n. An ambient laying in the ambient n executes the capability $out\,n$ if it exits n. The $open\,n$ capability is executed to drop the boundaries of the ambient n. Finally, the null capability ϵ and the path $M.M'$ have intuitive meanings. For simplifying the use of the brackets we assume the sequentialization operator to be right associative, *i.e.* $M_1.M_2.P$ is read as $M_1.(M_2.P)$.

The structural congruence $\equiv$ of the MA is defined as the minimal congruence induced by the α-conversion and by the rules in Tab. 1. The rules form two groups. Those in the upper part of the table involve the $\mid$ operator and replication; as they alter the syntax trees of processes, we shall control their application. The rules in the lower part of the table, together with the α-conversion, will be applied to put processes in a standard form that is introduced below.

Definition 2. P *is in* ν-*form if* $\exists\ \{x_1, \ldots x_n\} \subseteq$ Names *s.t.* $P = (\nu\ x_1) \ldots (\nu\ x_n)P'$, *and* P' *contains neither restrictions outside the scope of a* $!$ *operator nor* ϵ *capabilities.*
Hereafter we write $(\nu\ I)P$ *for* $(\nu\ x_1) \ldots (\nu\ x_n)P$ *if* $I = \{x_1, \ldots x_n\}$.

Table 1. Structural congruence for Mobile Ambients.

$P \mid \mathbf{0} \equiv P$	Struct Zero Par	$!P \equiv P \mid !P$	Struct Repl
$P \mid (Q \mid R) \equiv (P \mid Q) \mid R$	Struct Par Ass	$P \mid Q \equiv Q \mid P$	Struct Par Comm

$!\mathbf{0} \equiv \mathbf{0}$ Struct Zero Repl $\epsilon.P \equiv P$ Struct ϵ $(\nu n)\mathbf{0} \equiv \mathbf{0}$ Struct Zero Res

$$(\nu n)(\nu n')P \equiv (\nu n')(\nu n)P \qquad \text{Struct Res Res}$$

$$(\nu n)(P \mid Q) \equiv ((\nu n)P) \mid Q, \text{ if } n \notin fn(Q) \quad \text{Struct Res Par}$$

$$m[(\nu n)P] \equiv (\nu n)m[P], \text{ if } n \neq m \quad \text{Struct Res Amb}$$

Table 2. Reduction rules for Mobile Ambients.

Red In : $n[in\ m.P \mid Q] \mid m[R] \Rightarrow m[n[P \mid Q] \mid R]$
Red Open : $open\ n.P \mid n[Q] \Rightarrow P \mid Q$
Red Out : $m[n[out\ m.P \mid Q] \mid R] \Rightarrow n[P \mid Q] \mid m[R]$
Red Comm : $\langle M \rangle \mid (x).P \Rightarrow P\{x \leftarrow M\}$

$$\text{Red Par} : \frac{P \Rightarrow P'}{P \mid Q \Rightarrow P' \mid Q} \qquad \text{Red Amb} : \frac{P \Rightarrow P'}{n[P] \Rightarrow n[P']}$$

$$\text{Red Res} : \frac{P \Rightarrow P'}{(\nu n)P \Rightarrow (\nu n)P'}$$

$$\text{Red} \equiv : \frac{P \equiv P', P' \Rightarrow Q', Q' \equiv Q}{P \to_{MA} Q}$$

Without loss of generality, we may assume that from now onward processes are kept in ν-form. Indeed, we shall push all the restrictions to the top level of each process at the very beginning and whenever new restrictions are introduced by the application of the rule *Struct Repl* or by the execution of an action (α-conversion may be required); similarly for ϵ capabilities that could be in the initial process or introduced by a communication, see the example at the end of Section 4. As a matter of fact, our treatment can be carried out on processes not in ν-form. However, this standard form simplifies some parts, mainly the proofs.

We use a slight variant of the MA operational semantics given in [5]. Unlike the standard semantics that allows to interleave rules for transitions with congruence rules, we force all the congruence rules in the bottom of Tab. 1 to be applied as the last step of a deduction. In a sense, here we choose a sort of representative for all the equivalent derivations of the same transition, *i.e.*

all the derivations with the same root. To do so, we first define the transition relation $P \Rightarrow Q$ by the inference rules given in the upper part of Tab. 2. The processes P and Q are subject to no congruence rules, not even α-conversion, except for those in the lower part of Tab. 1. Thus, these transitions transform processes in a *rigid* manner, because no re-arrangement of sub-processes is allowed as far as the *parallel* structure of processes is concerned. For this reason sometimes we shall refer to $\Rightarrow$ as the *rigid* transition system. We then deal with structural congruence, including α-conversion if needed, in the single rule (Red $\equiv$) that defines the actual transition relation $\rightarrow_{MA}$ in the lower part of Tab. 2. The relation $\rightarrow_{MA}$ is the minimal relation defined by the congruence rules in Tab. 1, the α-conversion and the transition rules in Tab. 2. It is easy to prove by structural induction that our semantics and the original one coincide.

Property 1. The operational semantics in Tab. 2 coincides with the operational semantics in [5].

An example suffices to show the differences, if any, in deriving a transition with the original semantics and with ours. Consider the following MA process

$$P = P_0 \,|\, n[in\ m.P_1] \,|\, m[R_1] \,|\, R_0$$

where the parallel composition is left associative. In the original semantics, one derivation of its transition, moving n into m, is

$$\cfrac{\cfrac{\cfrac{\mathbf{B_1}, n[in\ m.P_1|\mathbf{0}] \,|\, m[R_1] \rightarrow m[n[P_1|\mathbf{0}] \,|\, R_1], \mathbf{B_2}}{n[in\ m.P_1|\mathbf{0}] \,|\, m[R_1] \rightarrow m[n[P_1] \,|\, R_1]}}{n[in\ m.P_1|\mathbf{0}] \,|\, m[R_1] \,|\, P_0 \rightarrow m[n[P_1] \,|\, R_1] \,|\, P_0}}{\mathbf{A_1},\ \ \mathbf{A_2},\ \ \mathbf{A_3},\ \ \mathbf{A_4}\ \ ,\ \ n[in\ m.P_1|\mathbf{0}] \,|\, m[R_1] \,|\, P_0 \,|\, R_0 \rightarrow m[n[P_1] \,|\, R_1] \,|\, P_0 \,|\, R_0}}{P_0 \,|\, n[in\ m.P_1] \,|\, m[R_1] \,|\, R_0 \rightarrow m[n[P_1] \,|\, R_1] \,|\, P_0 \,|\, R_0}$$

In the derivation we make use of the following rules for structural congruence (applied to the underlined sub-processes and then closed under the relevant context):

$\mathbf{A_1} : ((P_0 \,|\, \underline{n[in\ m.P_1]}) \,|\, m[R_1]) \,|\, R_0 \equiv ((\underline{n[in\ m.P_1]} \,|\, P_0) \,|\, m[R_1]) \,|\, R_0$

$\mathbf{A_2} : ((\underline{n[in\ m.P_1] \,|\, P_0}) \,|\, m[R_1]) \,|\, R_0 \equiv (n[in\ m.P_1] \,|\, \underline{(P_0 \,|\, m[R_1])}) \,|\, R_0$

$\mathbf{A_3} : (n[in\ m.P_1] \,|\, \underline{(P_0 \,|\, m[R_1])}) \,|\, R_0 \equiv (n[in\ m.P_1] \,|\, \underline{(m[R_1] \,|\, P_0)}) \,|\, R_0$

$\mathbf{A_4} : (n[in\ m.P_1] \,|\, \underline{(P_0 \,|\, m[R_1])}) \,|\, R_0 \equiv ((n[in\ m.P_1] \,|\, m[R_1]) \,|\, P_0) \,|\, R_0$

$\mathbf{B_1} : \underline{n[in\ m.P_1]} \,|\, m[R_1] \equiv n[in\ m.P_1|\mathbf{0}] \,|\, m[R_1]$

$\mathbf{B_2} : m[n[\underline{P_1|\mathbf{0}}] \,|\, R_1] \equiv m[n[P_1] \,|\, R_1]$

Another derivation follows, in which all the congruence rules needed are applied in a single bunch in the premise of the root of the derivation tree as suggested by our choice of representative derivations.

$$\cfrac{\cfrac{\cfrac{n[in\ m.P_1|\mathbf{0}] \,|\, m[R_1] \Rightarrow m[n[P_1|\mathbf{0}] \,|\, R_1]}{n[in\ m.P_1|\mathbf{0}] \,|\, m[R_1] \,|\, P_0 \Rightarrow m[n[P_1|\mathbf{0}] \,|\, R_1] \,|\, P_0}}{\mathbf{A_1},\ \mathbf{A_2},\ \mathbf{A_3},\ \mathbf{A_4},\ \mathbf{C_1}, \cfrac{}{n[in\ m.P_1|\mathbf{0}] \,|\, m[R_1] \,|\, P_0 \,|\, R_0 \Rightarrow m[n[P_1|\mathbf{0}] \,|\, R_1] \,|\, P_0 \,|\, R_0}},\mathbf{C_2}}{P_0 \,|\, n[in\ m.P_1] \,|\, m[R_1] \,|\, R_0 \rightarrow_{MA} m[n[P_1] \,|\, R_1] \,|\, P_0 \,|\, R_0}$$

The two new instances of congruence rules are:

$\mathbf{C_1} : n[\underline{in\ m.P_1}] \mid m[R_1] \equiv n[\underline{in\ m.P_1|\mathbf{0}}] \mid m[R_1]|P_0|R_0$
$\mathbf{C_2} : m[n[\underline{P_1|\mathbf{0}}] \mid R_1] \equiv m[n[P_1] \mid R_1]|P_0|R_0$

It is immediate to see that this is a derivation in the standard semantics as well: just substitute $\rightarrow$ for both $\Rightarrow$ and $\rightarrow_{MA}$.

3   A Fragment of the π-Calculus

In this section we overview the π-calculus [17, 16], a model of concurrent communicating processes based on the notion of *naming*. Actually we introduce a subset of the syntax of the higher order π-calculus [18], as we will not use the matching operator, the $+$ operator and the silent action τ. More importantly, we only use a very limited form of higher order, because we allow processes to be communicated that are made of sequences of prefixes, only. We will refer to this subset as π_{MA}. Its syntax is defined below.

Definition 3. *Let $\mathcal{N}$ be a countable infinite set of names ranged over by $a, b, \ldots$, $x, y, \ldots$. Let $\mathcal{V}$ be a set of process variables ranged over by $X, Y, \ldots$. Let K stand for sequences of prefixes or for a name, and let U stand for a variable or for a name. Processes (denoted by $T, T_0, \cdots \in \mathcal{P}$) are built from names according to the syntax*

$$\pi_s ::= \epsilon \mid \pi.\pi_s \qquad T ::= \mathbf{0} \mid \pi_s.T \mid T|T \mid (\nu x)T \mid !T \mid Y$$

The prefix π is $x(U)$ for input and $\overline{x}\langle K \rangle$ for output We call K and U objects and x the subject of the prefix. The empty string of prefixes is denoted by ϵ.

We assume that the operators have decreasing binding power, in the following order: $(\nu\,a), \pi., !T, |$. The sequentialization operator associates on the right, *e.g.* $\pi_1.\pi_2.T$ is the same as $\pi_1.(\pi_2.T)$, and the parallel composition on the left, *e.g.* $T_0 \mid T_1 \mid T_2$ is the same as $(T_0 \mid T_1) \mid T_2$. Functions *fn* and *bn* collect all the free and the bound names of π-calculus processes, respectively, and are defined in the standard way.

The process $\pi.T$ performs the action π and then behaves as T. The input prefix $x(U)$ binds the occurrences of the variable U in the prefixed process T. A name or a sequence of prefixes will be received on the channel x and it will substitute the free occurrences of the placeholder U in T. The output prefix $\overline{x}\langle K \rangle$ sends the name or the sequences of prefixes K along the channel x. The processes $\mathbf{0}, !T, T_1 \mid T_2$ and $(\nu\,x)T$ have the same meaning as in the MA. Note that here communications need not to be local as the parallel operator allows two input/output prefixes to interact whenever they share the same channel name, independently from their actual position.

We will consider the enhanced operational semantics [9] of the π_{MA} which differs from the standard one in [16, 18] as the labels of the transitions encode portions of their proofs. Actually we slight simplify the presentation in [9].

Table 3. Structural congruence for π_{MA}.

$T|\mathbf{0} \equiv T$ P-Zero Par $\epsilon.T \equiv T$ P-ϵ $!T \equiv T|!T$ P-Repl

$(T_0|T_1)|T_2 \equiv T_0|(T_1|T_2)$ P-Par Ass $T_0|T_1 \equiv T_1|T_0$ P-Par Comm

---

$!\mathbf{0} \equiv \mathbf{0}$ P-Zero Repl $\epsilon.T \equiv T$ P-ϵ $(\nu\,x)\mathbf{0} \equiv \mathbf{0}$ P-Zero Res

$(\nu\,x)(\nu\,x')T \equiv (\nu\,x')(\nu\,x)T$ P-Res Res

$(\nu x)(T_0|T_1) \equiv ((\nu\,x)T_0)|T_1$, if $x \notin fn(T_1)$ P-Res Par

---

Definition 4 (proof terms). *Let $\vartheta \in \{||_0\}^*$. Then the set Θ of proof terms (with metavariable θ) is defined by the following syntax*

$$\theta ::= \vartheta\mu \mid \vartheta\langle||_0\vartheta_0\overline{x}\langle K\rangle, ||_1\vartheta_1x(U)\rangle$$

where $x \in \{in, out, open, ch\}$.

The tags $||_i$, $i \in \{0,1\}$ will be used to record an action that may occur on the left ($||_0$) or on the right side ($||_1$) of a $|$ operator.

The enhanced operational semantics for the π_{MA} is given by the structural congruence $\equiv$ on processes, defined as the least congruence satisfying the α-conversion and the rules in Tab. 3, and by the semantic rules in Tab. 4. We have split the rules in Tab. 3 in two groups, as we did for the MA congruence in Tab. 1. The rules in the upper part of the table will be applied in a strictly controlled manner, by the auxiliary semantics in Sect. 5, in deriving a π_{MA} transition. As already done for the MA processes, it is convenient to impose a special form (again called ν-form) also to the π_{MA} processes, obtained by applying the congruence rules in the lower part of Tab. 3.

Definition 5. *A process T is in ν-form if $\exists\, I \subset \mathcal{N}$ such that $T = (\nu\,I)T'$, and T' contains neither restrictions outside the scope of a $!$ operator nor the empty sequence of prefixes ϵ.*

As it was the case for the MA, also here α-conversions may be in order to recover the ν-form of a process after the application of a P-Repl rule (see Tab. 3) or introduced by a communication, see the example at the end of Section 4.

Note that the inference rules in Tab. 4 are a strict sub-set of those for the π-calculus. There are no rules for the nondeterministic choice, as we discarded it from the syntax. Then we eliminate the *Open* and the *Close* rules, because the ν-form we introduced makes them useless. We do not need a symmetric rule for the $\ell\pi_{Par}$, because we shall permit a sub-process to execute an action only if it lies on the left-side of a parallel operator. We do not even include the symmetric rule of the $\ell\pi_{Com}$ as we shall allow the execution of a communication only if the output prefix lies on the left hand-side of the parallel operator. The last two

Table 4. Proved transition system for π_{MA}.

$$\ell\pi_{Act} : \pi.T \xrightarrow{\pi}_p T$$

$$\ell\pi_{Par} : \frac{T \xrightarrow{\theta}_p T'}{T|Q \xrightarrow{\|_0\theta}_p T'|Q}, bn(\theta) \cap fn(Q) = \emptyset$$

$$\ell\pi_{Res} : \frac{T \xrightarrow{\theta}_p T'}{(\nu J)T \xrightarrow{\theta}_p (\nu\ J)T'}, J \cap n(\theta) = \emptyset$$

$$\ell\pi_{Com} : \frac{T \xrightarrow{\vartheta_0\overline{x}\langle K\rangle}_p T', Q \xrightarrow{\vartheta_1 x(U)}_p Q'}{T|Q \xrightarrow{\langle\|_0\vartheta_0\overline{x}\langle K\rangle,\|_1\vartheta_1 x(U)\rangle}_p T'|Q'\{K/U\}}$$

omissions directly derive from the format of the inference rules of the MA given in Tab. 2 and from our definition of the translation function, see Def. 6.

Here we show how the proof terms are built while deducing a transition. Consider the process $\overline{x}\langle z\rangle | x(y).T_0 | T_1$ and its possible transition in the standard π-calculus semantics $\overline{x}\langle z\rangle | x(y).T_0 | T_1 \xrightarrow{\tau}_M T_0\{z/y\} | T_1$ (recall that | is left-associative). The derivation of the same transition using the enhanced operational semantics provides more expressive labels which record the occurrences of the parallel operators.

$$\frac{\overline{x}\langle z\rangle \xrightarrow{\overline{x}\langle z\rangle}_p \mathbf{0} \ , \ x(z) \xrightarrow{x(y)}_p T_0\{z/y\}}{\dfrac{\overline{x}\langle z\rangle | x(y).T_0 \xrightarrow{\langle\|_0\overline{x}\langle z\rangle,\|_1 x(y)\rangle}_p \mathbf{0} | T_0\{z/y\}}{\overline{x}\langle z\rangle | x(y).T_0 | T_1 \xrightarrow{\|_0\langle\|_0\overline{x}\langle z\rangle,\|_1 x(y)\rangle}_p \mathbf{0} | T_0\{z/y\} | T_1}}$$

Note that the sub-process responsible for the action can be selected using the parallel tags (e.g., the outermost $\|_0$ says that the acting sub-agent is $R = \overline{x}\langle z\rangle | x(y).T_0$). The labels for the communication record the input/output actions performed by the two interacting partners (e.g. $\|_0$ says that the sending sub-process is on the left of the parallel operators of R). Actually, the enriched labeling represents (portions of) the syntactic structure of the processes as the semantics is defined inducing on the syntax. In fact, the labeled syntax tree of process $\overline{x}\langle z\rangle | x(y).T_0 | T_1$ is:

4   The Translation

We define below a function, invertible on its image, that translates the MA processes into π_{MA} processes; essentially, it transforms capabilities in outputs on special channels and encodes ambient nesting through a special deadlocked process.

To simplify the next definition and the translation function in given in Sect. 5, it is convenient to extend the MA syntax with a set of distinguished auxiliary symbols $\emptyset_n$, one for every name n. These symbols will be used in the definition below to simplify the translation function as well as in Sect. 5.

Definition 6. *Let $\mathbf{0}_m$ be a shorthand for the π_{MA} process $(\nu\ a)\bar{a}\langle m\rangle.\mathbf{0}$; and assume to have a bijection from the variables of the MA to those of the π-calculus (we shall write X for the image of x). Then, the auxiliary function $\mathcal{T}: Processes \to \mathcal{P}$ is defined by structural induction on the syntax of the MA as follows*

Capabilities:		*Processes:*	

$$\mathcal{T}(0) = \mathbf{0}$$

$$\mathcal{T}(y) = Y \qquad\qquad \mathcal{T}((\nu\ n)P) = (\nu\ n)(\mathcal{T}(P))$$

$$\mathcal{T}(n) = n \qquad\qquad \mathcal{T}(P \mid Q) = \mathcal{T}(P) \mid \mathcal{T}(Q)$$

$$\mathcal{T}(in\ M) = \overline{in}\langle\mathcal{T}(M)\rangle \qquad\qquad \mathcal{T}(!P) =!\mathcal{T}(P)$$

$$\mathcal{T}(out\ M) = \overline{out}\langle\mathcal{T}(M)\rangle \qquad\qquad \mathcal{T}(M[P]) = (\mathcal{T}(P)|\mathcal{T}(\emptyset_{\mathcal{T}(M)}))$$

$$\mathcal{T}(open\ M) = \overline{open}\langle\mathcal{T}(M)\rangle \qquad\qquad \mathcal{T}(M.P) = \mathcal{T}(M).\mathcal{T}(P)$$

$$\mathcal{T}(\epsilon) = \epsilon \qquad\qquad \mathcal{T}((x)P) = ch(\mathcal{T}(x)).\mathcal{T}(P)$$

$$\mathcal{T}(M.M') = \mathcal{T}(M).\mathcal{T}(M') \qquad\qquad \mathcal{T}(\langle M\rangle) = \overline{ch}\langle\mathcal{T}(M)\rangle.\mathbf{0}$$

Additionally: $\mathcal{T}(\emptyset_m) = \mathbf{0}_m$

The translation function is:

$$\widehat{\mathcal{T}}(P) = (\nu I)(T|\widehat{T})$$

$$\text{with } \mathcal{T}(P) = (\nu\ I)T \text{ and } \widehat{T} =!in(Y)|!out(Y)|!open(Y),$$

assuming that the set I contains all the names restricted in P not occurring within the scope of a ! operator.

A capability for entering an ambient n $(in\ n)$ is rendered as an output of n on the special channel in; similarly for the others capabilities. These outputs will be matched by corresponding inputs in the replicated, additional process $\widehat{T}$. For simplicity, we shall always write $\widehat{T}$ assuming that we implicitly apply the congruence rule P-Repl for making available one of the three input actions (*i.e.* $(in(Y)\mid!in(Y))\mid!out(Y)\mid!open(Y)$) and the P-Zero rule to eliminate the $\mathbf{0}$ occurring because of a communication over the in, out or $open$ channels (*e.g.* $((\mathbf{0}\mid!in(Y))\mid!out(Y)\mid!open(Y)) \equiv \widehat{T}$). Note that in this case the application of congruence rules is not harmful, as we are manipulating a sub-process *not* derived from any MA process.

The reason why we introduced the class of processes $\mathbf{0}_m$ is to record the nesting of the ambients and their names, during the translation. We want to remark that $\mathbf{0}_m$ cannot perform any action: it is semantically equivalent to $\mathbf{0}$.

The processes in the image of $\widehat{\mathcal{T}}$ use a well characterized set of names. There are names used only as channels (in, out, $open$, ch); names never used in transitions (the subjects occurring in $\mathbf{0}_m$); names only occurring as objects (those corresponding to ambient names).

As an example consider the process $P = P_0 \,|\, n[in\, m.P_1] \,|\, m[R_1] \,|\, R_0$ of Sect. 2, the translation of which is:

$$(\mathcal{T}(P_0)|(\overline{in}\langle m\rangle.\mathcal{T}(P_1)|\mathbf{0}_n)|(\mathcal{T}(R_1)|\mathbf{0}_m)|\mathcal{T}(R_0))\,|\,\widehat{T}$$

Now we clarify why we need to introduce the ϵ prefix in the π_{MA}: given the MA process $P' = (x).x.P'' \,|\, \langle \epsilon \rangle$ its translation is

$$\widehat{T}(P') = (ch(X).X\,.\mathcal{T}(P'')|\,\overline{ch}\langle\epsilon\rangle)\,|\,\widehat{T}.$$

After firing the communication over ch we get $\epsilon.\mathcal{T}(P'')\,|\,\widehat{T}$ and P-ϵ congruence rule eliminates the ϵ prefix.

5   The Rigid Transition Relation for the π_{MA} Calculus

The standard semantics of the π-calculus allows to freely apply congruences in any point of the derivation of a transition, similarly to what happens for the MA. Analogously to what we did for the MA in Section 2, we shall here introduce a rigid transition system for the π_{MA}. We shall disallow the congruence rules in the upper part of the Tab. 3, and we only keep those in the lower part to put processes in ν-form. (Recall that the auxiliary process $\widehat{T}$, which does not correspond to any MA process, is instead subject also to the monoidal rules for the parallel operator.) The actual transitions will be introduced in the next section, and proved to be in bijection with those of the MA.

However, the transition system defined by the rules in Tab. 4 contains much more transitions than needed, because the MA processes involved in basic movements must satisfy certain neighborhood relationships; typically one ambient has to be parent, *i.e.* it contains the other one. We will check this nesting of ambients on the π_{MA} processes resulting from a translation, by resorting to side conditions to the inference rules and exploiting our special processes $\mathbf{0}_n$.

It is convenient to first introduce two additional operators for both the MA and the π_{MA}, that have quite the same structure; so, we feel free to designate both of them by the same symbol @. These operators select a sub-process within a whole process following the path $\vartheta \in \mathcal{L} = \{\|_0, \|_1\}^*$. The selector for the MA also uses the auxiliary symbols $\emptyset_n$, introduced at the beginning of Sect. 4. Indeed, as mentioned in the Introduction (see also Fig. 1), an ambient $n[P]$ is represented by a syntax tree whose left branch (at $\|_0$) is the tree originated by P and whose right branch (at $\|_1$) is the special process $\mathbf{0}_n = (\nu\, a)\overline{a}\langle n\rangle)$ to which $\emptyset_n$ will be mapped.

Definition 7. *The partial function* $\_@\_ : Processes \times \mathcal{L} \to Processes$ *is defined by structural induction on the MA processes as follows:*

$$P@\epsilon = P, \quad (\nu n)P@\vartheta = P@\vartheta, \quad (P_0|P_1)@||_i\vartheta = P_i@\vartheta, \ i \in \{0,1\}$$
$$m[P]@||_0\vartheta = P@\vartheta, \quad m[P]@||_1 = \emptyset_m$$

The definition of the selection operator for the π_{MA} processes follows.

Definition 8. *The partial function* $\_@\_ : \mathcal{P} \times \mathcal{L} \to \mathcal{P}$ *is defined by structural induction on the* π_{MA} *processes as follows:*

$$T@\epsilon = T, \quad (\nu x)T@\vartheta = T@\vartheta, \quad (T_0|T_1)@||_i\vartheta = T_i@\vartheta, \ i \in \{0,1\}$$

The following lemma shows that the translation function $\mathcal{T}(\_)$ is an $\mathcal{L}$ homomorphism for the action of the monoid $\mathcal{L}$ over the syntax trees of the MA processes.

Lemma 1 (@ lemma). *Given an MA process* P, $\forall \vartheta \in \mathcal{L}$

$$\mathcal{T}(P@\vartheta) = \mathcal{T}(P)@\vartheta$$

The definition of the rigid transition system for the π_{MA} is simplified by the notion of "localized" replacement $T\{\vartheta \mapsto T'\}$: the process T' replaces the sub-process $T@\vartheta$ in T and leaves all the other sub-processes as they are. For example, $((T_1|T_2)|T_3)\{||_0||_1 \mapsto T_4\} = (T_1|T_4)|T_3$.

Definition 9. *Given* T, T', T'' *and* $\vartheta \in \mathcal{L}$, *the operator* $\_\{\_ \mapsto \_\} : \mathcal{P} \times \mathcal{L} \times \mathcal{P} \to \mathcal{P}$ *is defined as:*

$$T\{\epsilon \mapsto T'\} = T'$$

$$(\nu x)T\{||_i\vartheta \mapsto T'\} = (\nu x)(T\{||_i\vartheta \mapsto T'\})$$

$$(T|T'')\{||_0\vartheta \mapsto T'\} = T\{\vartheta \mapsto T'\}|T''$$

$$(T|T'')\{||_1\vartheta \mapsto T'\} = T|(T''\{\vartheta \mapsto T'\})$$

We eventually define in Tab. 5 the transition relation $\Rightarrow_\pi$ which is the counterpart of the transition relation $\Rightarrow$ defined in Tab. 2; we shall sometimes call $\Rightarrow_\pi$ the *rigid* transition system of the π_{MA}. Below, we briefly comment on how the nesting of ambients is checked on the source of a transitions, also resorting to a graphical representation of the transitions.

The rule $M\pi_{in}$ corresponds to the MA input capability. The upper part of Fig. 2 displays the effects of the transition deduced, when it is applied at address $||_0 \vartheta$, as it should. The syntax tree of the source process on the left is on the form required by the rule through its side conditions, as explained below, the tree on the right shows the target of the transition. In order to be applicable, the rule requires that the sub-process performing an output at $||_0\vartheta||_0||_0||_0$ (corresponding to the capability *in m*) has $\mathbf{0}_n$ as its uncle at $||_0\vartheta||_0||_1$. If so $U = T@||_0\vartheta||_0$ is indeed the translation of a process $n[P]$, *i.e.* the condition $T@ ||_0 \vartheta ||_0||_1 = \mathbf{0}_n$ holds. Also, it should be the case that there is an ambient m into which n can enter: the condition $T@||_0\vartheta||_1||_1 = \mathbf{0}_m$ tells us this. There is a further structural condition: the capability *in m* should not be included in

Table 5. The rigid transition system of π_{MA}.

$$M\pi_{in} : \dfrac{T' \xrightarrow{\langle||_0\vartheta||_0||_0||_0 \overline{in}\langle m\rangle, ||_1||_0 in(Y)\rangle}_p T'}{(\nu\ I)T \Rightarrow_\pi (\nu\ I)T'\{||_0\vartheta \mapsto (V|W)|Z\}}, \text{ if } \begin{array}{c} T@||_0\vartheta||_1||_1 = \mathbf{0}_m \\ \wedge \\ T@||_0\vartheta||_0||_1 = \mathbf{0}_n \\ \wedge \\ T@||_0\vartheta||_0||_0||_1 \neq \mathbf{0}_k \end{array}$$

$$V = T'@||_0\vartheta||_0,\ W = T'@||_0\vartheta||_1||_0,\ Z = T'@||_0\vartheta||_1||_1$$

$$M\pi_{out} : \dfrac{T' \xrightarrow{\langle||_0\vartheta||_0||_0||_0||_0\overline{out}\langle m\rangle, ||_1||_0 out(Y)\rangle}_p T'}{(\nu\ I)T \Rightarrow_\pi (\nu\ I)T'\{||_0\vartheta \mapsto V|(W|Z)\}}, \text{ if } \begin{array}{c} T@||_0\vartheta||_1 = \mathbf{0}_m \\ \wedge \\ T@||_0\vartheta||_0||_0||_1 = \mathbf{0}_n \\ \wedge \\ T@||_0\vartheta||_0||_1 \neq \mathbf{0}_h \\ \wedge \\ T@||_0\vartheta||_0||_0||_0||_1 \neq \mathbf{0}_k \end{array}$$

$$V = T'@||_0\vartheta||_0||_0,\ W = T'@||_0\vartheta||_0||_1,\ Z = T'@||_0\vartheta||_1$$

$$M\pi_{open} : \dfrac{T' \xrightarrow{\langle||_0\vartheta||_0\overline{open}\langle m\rangle, ||_1||_0 open(Y)\rangle}_p T'}{(\nu\ I)T \Rightarrow_\pi (\nu\ I)T'\{||_0\vartheta||_1 \mapsto W\}}, \text{ if } T@||_0\vartheta||_1||_1 = \mathbf{0}_m$$

$$W = T'@||_0\vartheta||_1||_0$$

$$M\pi_{com} : \dfrac{T' \xrightarrow{||_0\vartheta\langle||_0\overline{ch}\langle K\rangle, ||_1 ch(Y)\rangle}_p T'}{(\nu\ I)T \Rightarrow_\pi (\nu\ I)T'\{||_0\vartheta \mapsto T'@||_0\vartheta||_0\}}$$

an ambient h, son of n. The condition $T@||_0\vartheta||_0||_0||_1 \neq \mathbf{0}_k$ makes it sure that this is the case. (The reader may check that if there is such an h, then this condition does not hold, e.g. in $P = h[n[in\ m.R]]|m[Q].$) Finally, note that in the conclusions of $M\pi_{in}$ the substitution $(\nu\ I)T'\{||_0\vartheta \mapsto (V|W)|Z\}$ is equivalent to the application of the congruence rule P-Par Ass of Tab. 3. In fact, $(\nu\ I)T'\langle\equiv\rangle_{(P-ParAss,||_0\vartheta)}(\nu\ I)T'\{||_0\vartheta \mapsto (V|W)|Z\}$ (for the definition of the notation $\langle\equiv\rangle_{(R,\vartheta)}$ see the beginning of paragraph 6.1).

The central part of Fig. 2 shows the rule $M\pi_{out}$, that is the counterpart of the rule Red Out. It requires that the sub-process which is going to perform the out capability at $||_0\ \vartheta\ ||_0||_0||_0||_0$ has $\mathbf{0}_n$ as uncle at $||_0\ \vartheta\ ||_0||_1$. As before, this condition says that $U = T@\ ||_0\ \vartheta\ ||_0||_0$ is indeed the translation of a process $n[P]$. Then $T@\ ||_0\ \vartheta\ ||_1$ must be $\mathbf{0}_m$ to ensure that U is lying within an ambient m, i.e. $n[P]$ is inside m. The other conditions ($T@||_0\vartheta||_0||_1 \neq \mathbf{0}_h$ and $T@||_0\vartheta||_0||_0||_0||_1 \neq \mathbf{0}_k$) ensure that the ambient n is actually son of m and of no other ambient h and that $out\ n$ is on the top-level of ambient n.

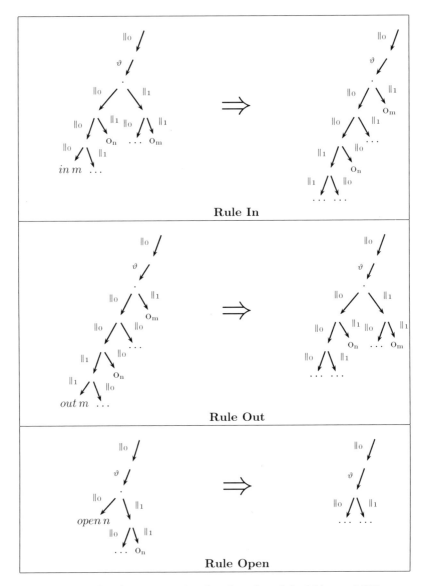

Fig. 2. Graphical representation for the rules of the MA capabilities.

Note that in the target process of the transition deduced, the substitution $(\nu\ I)T'\{\|_0\vartheta \mapsto V|(W|Z)\}$ corresponds to applying the congruence rule P-Par Ass of Tab. 3, *i.e.* $(\nu\ I)T'\langle\equiv\rangle_{(P-ParAss,\|_0\vartheta)}(\nu\ I)T'\{\|_0\vartheta \mapsto V|(W|Z)\}$.

For the rule $M\pi_{open}$, shown in the lower part of Fig. 2, we only need to know that the sub-process performing the (translation of the) open capability $U = T@\|_0\vartheta\|_0$ lies immediately outside the ambient m, *i.e.* $T@\ \|_0\ \vartheta\ \|_1\|_1 = \mathbf{0}_n$. Here, the substitution $(\nu\ I)T'\{\|_0\vartheta\|_1 \mapsto W\}$ makes it clear that $(\nu a)\overline{a}\langle m\rangle$ cannot perform any move and it is therefore equivalent to $\mathbf{0}$. Then, to obtain the target of the transition deduced, one has to apply the congruence rule P-Zero Par of Tab. 3: $(\nu\ I)T\langle\equiv\rangle_{(P-ParNew,||_0\vartheta||_1||_1)}T'\langle\equiv\rangle_{(P-ZeroPar,||_0\vartheta||_1)}(\nu\ I)T'\{||_0\vartheta||_1 \mapsto W\}$.

For the $M\pi_{com}$ rule, which corresponds to the Red Comm rule, there are no side conditions because the parallel tags in the labels of the premises are enough to ensure that the two sub-processes performing the input and the output action lay on opposite sides of the *same* parallel operator.

We end this section with the following lemma, that shows that the rigid transition systems of the MA and of the π_{MA} coincide.

Lemma 2 ($\Rightarrow$ and $\Rightarrow_\pi$ coincide). *For all $P \in Processes$*

$$P \Rightarrow Q \quad iff \quad \widehat{\mathcal{T}}(P) \Rightarrow_\pi \widehat{\mathcal{T}}(Q).$$

In the proof of the above lemma we shall use the following property, the proof of which is immediate. The property states that the deduction of rigid transitions, for both MA and π_{MA} processes, is never affected by restrictions. This fact makes it clear that name extrusion will never occur for a process $\widehat{\mathcal{T}}(P)$, as in the MA the restriction operator is only used to create new names and it never acts as a binder for a channel name.

Property 2. For all $P \in Processes$, $I \subseteq Names$

- $P \Rightarrow Q$ iff $(\nu\ I)P \Rightarrow (\nu\ I)Q$
- if P is in ν-form, then $\widehat{\mathcal{T}}(P) \Rightarrow_\pi \widehat{\mathcal{T}}(Q)$ iff $(\nu\ I)\widehat{\mathcal{T}}(P) \Rightarrow_\pi (\nu\ I)\widehat{\mathcal{T}}(Q)$

6   The Operational Semantics of the π_{MA}

The last step of our work is the definition of the transition relation $\rightarrow_\pi$ that corresponds to the transition relation $\rightarrow_{MA}$ of the MA.

So far, we only have rigid transitions $T \Rightarrow_\pi T'$ for the π_{MA}. In order to establish the wanted bijection between the transitions of an MA process P and of its translation $\widehat{\mathcal{T}}(P)$, we first record each congruence rule that have been applied to P in rule Red $\equiv$, and the sub-processes $P@\vartheta$ affected. Then we shall apply the *same* congruence rules to the sub-processes of $\widehat{\mathcal{T}}(P@\vartheta)$, so mimicking in π_{MA} each transformation in the structure of processes made on MA. This will be the purpose of the next sub-section. The proof of the correctness of our proposal will then follow easily.

6.1   Handling Congruences

As said already, the application of any MA semantic rule in the upper part of Tab. 1, alters the syntactic structure of processes. For example, the right component of $R = m[P] \mid Q$ is Q, that instead is the left one in the congruent process $Q \mid m[P]$. These changes will prevent us from recognizing that a π_{MA}

is the translation of a specific MA process. So we introduce below a simple mechanism to handle the manipulations of processes due to congruence. We shall record the sequence of congruence rules applied to a process and those sub-processes to which they are applied. As a consequence, we always know the address to which a selected sub-process moved.

We write $P \equiv_{(r,\vartheta)} Q$ to say that the MA processes Q is obtained from P by applying once the congruence rule r (defined in the upper part of the Tab. 1) at the sub-process $P@\vartheta$. For example, $(P_1 \mid (P_2 \mid \mathbf{0})) \mid P_3 \equiv_{(StructZero\ Par,\|_0\|_1)} (P_1 \mid P_2) \mid P_3$. Quite in the same manner, we write $T_1 \langle\equiv\rangle_{(R,\vartheta)} T_2$, to say that the π_{MA} process T_2 is obtained from T_1 by applying once the rule R (defined in the upper part of Tab. 3) at the sub-process $T_1@\vartheta$.

Clearly, the congruence rules for the MA in the upper part of Tab. 1 are in correspondence with those in the upper part of Tab. 3, that we slightly constrain below.

Definition 10. *Let r be any of the rules in the upper part of Tab. 1; let R be any of the rules in the upper part of Tab. 3, where $T_0, T_1, T_2 \neq \mathbf{0}_n$.*

Then we write $r \diamond R$ whenever r is on the form Struct rule and R is on the form P-rule, with rule $\in \{Zero\ Par,\ Zero\ Res,\ Par\ Comm,\ Par\ Ass,\ Repl\}$.

We also extend the relation $\diamond$ to sequences of pairs $\phi = \langle(r_0, \vartheta_0), \ldots, (r_n, \vartheta_n)\rangle$, and $\Phi = \langle(R_0, \vartheta_0) \ldots, (R_n, \vartheta_n)\rangle$, and we write $\phi \diamond \Phi$ when $\forall i.\ r_i \diamond R_i,\ i \in \{0, \ldots, n\}$.

Sometimes we shall write $P \equiv_\phi Q$ and $T_0 \langle\equiv\rangle_\Phi T_1$ with the obvious meaning.

Below, we shall prove that our translation $\widehat{T}$ commutes with the application of the congruences rules. Some attention has to be paid to the rule *Struct Repl*, in connection with our wish to have processes always in ν-form. If a restriction occurs within a replication, it may be necessary to move it at the top-level of the whole process, and this may require some α-conversions. For example, consider the following congruent processes

$$R = (!(\nu\ n)n[P]) \mid n[Q] \equiv_{(StructRepl,\|_0)}$$
$$R' = ((\nu\ n)n[P] \mid (!(\nu)\ n[P])) \mid n[Q] \equiv$$
$$R'' = (\nu\ p)((p[P\{n \leftarrow p\}] \mid (!(\nu\ n)n[P])) \mid n[Q]).$$

Now consider the congruent processes obtained by translation:

$$\widehat{T}(R) \langle\equiv\rangle_{(P-Repl,\|_0)} \widehat{T}(R').$$

In order to put $\widehat{T}(R')$ in ν-form, it is crucial to α-rename n as p at position $\|_0$, as done when passing from R' to R''. To do that, it suffices to label each renaming of a name m to q (or of a variable x to y) by a pair $(m \leftarrow q, \vartheta)$ (or by $(x \leftarrow y, \vartheta)$), where ϑ is the address of the affected sub-process (in our example the pair is $(n \leftarrow p, \|_0)$). In other words, α-conversions are to be dealt with as the congruence rules in the upper parts of the Tables 1 and 3. We prefer to leave this step implicit, assuming that to each α-conversion in a MA process there is a corresponding α-conversion in its translation, with the same choice of new names or new variables.

Lemma 3 (on the congruence). *For all sequences of pairs* ϕ, Φ *such that* $\phi \diamond \Phi$, *and* $\forall\, P, Q \in Processes$

$$P \equiv_\phi Q \quad iff \quad T(P) \langle \equiv \rangle_\Phi T(Q).$$

6.2   The Transition Relation $\rightarrow_\pi$

We are now ready to define the transition relation $\rightarrow_\pi$ for π_{MA}, that corresponds to the standard transition relation $\rightarrow_{MA}$ of the MA. It will be defined as the composition of transition relation $\Rightarrow_\pi$ with the relation $\langle \equiv \rangle_{(R, \vartheta)}$. This step can be seen as the counterpart of the rule Red$\equiv$ in Tab. 2.

Definition 11. *We define* $T \rightarrow_\pi T'$ *iff* $\exists \Phi_0, \Phi_1$ *and* T_0, T_1 *such that* $T \langle \equiv \rangle_{\Phi_0} T_0 \Rightarrow_\pi T_1 \langle \equiv \rangle_{\Phi_1} T'$.

The transition system of the MA is isomorphic to that of π_{MA}, when considering only processes in the image of the function $\widehat{T}$.

Theorem 1. *Let* $\widehat{T}(Processes) = \{\widehat{T}(P)|\ P \in Processes\}$, *then*

$$\langle Processes, \rightarrow_{MA} \rangle \text{ is isomorphic to } \langle \widehat{T}(Processes), \rightarrow_\pi \rangle.$$

As a consequence, a computation of P in MA has one and only one corresponding computation of the π_{MA} process $\widehat{T}(P)$. With the next corollary we end the proof of the operational correctness of our proposal.

Corollary 1. *For all* $P, Q \in Processes$

$$P \rightarrow^*_{MA} Q \quad iff \quad \widehat{T}(P) \rightarrow^*_\pi \widehat{T}(Q)$$

The following theorem proves that transition system defined by the rules in Tab. 5, is a fragment of the standard transition system of the higher order π-calculus. Actually, we shall consider a slight variant of the standard structural congruence $\equiv_M$, which identifies with the process that cannot perform any action the process $(\nu a)\overline{a}\langle m \rangle.\mathbf{0}$.

Theorem 2. *Let* $\equiv_M$ *be the minimal congruence induced by the standard congruence of the higher order π-calculus, and by the rule* $(\nu a)\overline{a}\langle m \rangle.\mathbf{0} \equiv_M \mathbf{0}$. *Then, for all* $T_0, T_0 \in \mathcal{P}$ *we have that* $T_0 \rightarrow_\pi T_1$ *implies* $T_0 \xrightarrow{\tau}_M T \equiv_M T_1$.

A specialization of the above theorem enforces the idea that the we are simulating the behaviour of the MA processes within a subset of the π-calculus.

Corollary 2. *For all* $P_0, P_1 \in Processes$ *let* $T_0 = \widehat{T}(P_0), T_1 = \widehat{T}(P_1)$ *then*

$$T_0 \rightarrow_\pi T_1 \text{ implies } T_0 \xrightarrow{\tau}_M T_1.$$

7   A Mobile Ambients Example: Mobile Agent Authentication

To show how our proposal works we take the following process that specifies an authentication protocol from [5], Sect. 8:

$$SYS = home[(\nu\ n)(open\ n|agent[out\ home.in\ home.n[out\ agent.open\ agent.P]])].$$

Figure 3 displays a complete computation of SYS, and splits each transition in the application of congruence rules and in the rigid transition. The changes in the abstract syntax trees of SYS and of its derivatives due to the applications of congruence rules are in Fig. 5.

The translation of SYS according to the function $\widehat{\mathcal{T}}$ is:

$$SYS_\pi = \widehat{\mathcal{T}}(SYS) = (\nu\ n)\ (\quad (\overline{open}\langle n\rangle|(\overline{out}\langle home\rangle.\overline{in}\langle home\rangle.$$
$$(\overline{out}\langle agent\rangle.\overline{open}\langle agent\rangle.P|\mathbf{0}_n)$$
$$|\mathbf{0}_{agent})$$
$$|\mathbf{0}_{home})$$
$$|\widehat{T})$$

Fig. 4 displays how the computation of SYS_π proceeds and the correspondence of its steps with those of SYS in Fig. 3. Also here we separate the application of the rigid transitions from that of the congruence rules, and we show in Fig. 6 the changes made by these on the syntax tree of $\widehat{\mathcal{T}}(SYS)$.

8   Conclusion

We presented a technique to reflect the behaviour of the MA processes into a subset of the transition system of a fragment of HOπ, called π_{MA}. We rely on the enhanced operational semantics of HOπ, that heavily exploits the structure of processes [9]. This is expressed through the abstract syntax trees of processes, built considering the parallel composition as unique operator. An MA process P is translated into an π_{MA} process $T = \widehat{\mathcal{T}}(P)$ and each ambient n is given an address exploiting the position of n within the syntax trees of P and of T. These addresses are sequences of tags $\|_0$ and $\|_1$, recording the left and the right sides of a $|$, respectively. As expected the translation respect addresses (and the nesting of ambients).

Since syntax trees are rigid, in that their structure cannot be altered, it is natural to define a rigid transition system for MA ($\Rightarrow$) and one for π_{MA} processes ($\Rightarrow_\pi$), *i.e.* for processes that do not obey any congruence laws. This is easy for MA. We took advantage from the localization of ambients by their addresses to check if the π_{MA} process $T = \widehat{\mathcal{T}}(P)$ respects the ambient nesting required to perform a specific capability; the same mechanism allows us to correctly compute the new ambient nesting caused in T by firing that capability. We proved that the two rigid transition systems coincide.

The standard transition system for MA is then obtained by collapsing all the applications of congruence rules as the last, further step of a deduction of

$$SYS_1 \equiv_{(\text{StructParComm},||_0)} SYS_2 \equiv_{(\text{StructParZero},||_0||_0||_0)} SYS_3$$

$$\Downarrow$$

$$SYS_4 = (\nu\,n)(agent[in\,home.n[out\,agent.open\,agent.P]|\mathbf{0}]|home[open\,n])$$

$$\Downarrow$$

$$SYS_5 = (\nu\,n)home[agent[n[out\,agent.open\,agent.P]|\mathbf{0}]|open\,n]$$

$$\equiv_{(\text{StructParZero},||_0||_0||_0||_0||_0)} SYS_6$$

$$\Downarrow$$

$$SYS_7 = (\nu\,n)home[(n[open\,agent.P|\mathbf{0}]|agent[\mathbf{0}])|open\,n]$$

$$\equiv_{(\text{StructParComm},||_0)} SYS_8 \equiv_{(\text{StructParAss},||_0,)} SYS_9$$

$$\Downarrow$$

$$SYS_{10} = (\nu\,n)home[(\mathbf{0}|(open\,agent.P|\mathbf{0}))|agent[\mathbf{0}]]$$

$$\equiv_{(\text{StructParZero},||_0||_0||_1)} SYS_{11} \equiv_{(\text{StructParComm},||_0||_0)}$$
$$SYS_{12} \equiv_{(\text{StructParZero},||_0||_0)} SYS_{13}$$

$$\Downarrow$$

$$SYS_{14} = (\nu\,n)home[P|\mathbf{0}]$$

$SYS_1 = (\nu\,n)home[open\,n|agent[out\,home.in\,home.n[out\,agent.open\,agent.P]]]$
$SYS_2 = (\nu\,n)home[agent[out\,home.in\,home.n[out\,agent.open\,agent.P]]|open\,n]$
$SYS_3 = (\nu\,n)home[agent[out\,home.in\,home.n[out\,agent.open\,agent.P]|\mathbf{0}]|open\,n]$
$SYS_6 = (\nu\,n)home[agent[n[out\,agent.open\,agent.P|\mathbf{0}]|\mathbf{0}]|open\,n]$
$SYS_8 = (\nu\,n)home[open\,n|(n[open\,agent.P|\mathbf{0}]|agent[\mathbf{0}])]$
$SYS_9 = (\nu\,n)home[(open\,n|n[open\,agent.P|\mathbf{0}])|agent[\mathbf{0}]]$
$SYS_{11} = (\nu\,n)home[(\mathbf{0}|open\,agent.P)|agent[\mathbf{0}]]$
$SYS_{12} = (\nu\,n)home[(open\,agent.P|\mathbf{0})|agent[\mathbf{0}]]$
$SYS_{13} = (\nu\,n)home[open\,agent.P|agent[\mathbf{0}]]$

Fig. 3. A complete computation of the MA process SYS.

the transition $P \Rightarrow P'$. The same congruence rules, applied to the sub-processes of $T = \widehat{\mathcal{T}}(P)$ at the same addresses are applied for deducing the corresponding transition of T. It is straightforward then showing that the two transition systems are in bijection. As a matter of fact, the transition system of the fragment of HOπ we use is strictly contained in the transition system of the full HOπ.

The one-to-one correspondence between the transitions of the MA and of the HOπ suggests a way of studying the behaviour of the MA process P using the available tools developed for HOπ. Given an MA process P, one carries out the analysis on its translation $\widehat{\mathcal{T}}(P)$, and then reflects its results back to the MA word. Typically, one can use the Mobility Workbench [23] to check behavioural properties. Also, one can study causality based properties of the MA processes, relying on the causality notions defined in the enhanced operational approach

$$SYS_{\pi 1}\langle\equiv\rangle_{(P-ParComm,||_0||_0)}SYS_{\pi 2}\langle\equiv\rangle_{(P-ZeroPar,||_0||_0||_0||_0)}SYS_{\pi 3}$$

$$\Downarrow_\pi \quad {}^{\langle ||_0||_0||_0||_0||_0\overline{out}\langle home\rangle,||_1||_0 out(Y)\rangle}$$

$$SYS_{\pi 4} = (\nu\ n)$$
$$((((\overline{in}\langle home\rangle.(\overline{out}\langle agent\rangle.\overline{open}\langle agent\rangle.P|\mathbf{0}_n)|\mathbf{0})|\mathbf{0}_{agent})|(\overline{open}\langle n\rangle|\mathbf{0}_{home}))|\widehat{T})$$

$$\Downarrow_\pi \quad {}^{\langle ||_0||_0||_0||_0||_0\overline{in}\langle home\rangle,||_1||_0 in(Y)\rangle}$$

$$SYS_{\pi 5} = (\nu\ n)((((((\overline{out}\langle agent\rangle.\overline{open}\langle agent\rangle.P|\mathbf{0}_n)|\mathbf{0})|\mathbf{0}_{agent})|\overline{open}\langle n\rangle)|\mathbf{0}_{home})|\widehat{T})$$

$$\langle\equiv\rangle_{(P-ZeroPar,||_0||_0||_0||_0||_0||_0)}SYS_{\pi 6}$$

$$\Downarrow_\pi \quad {}^{\langle ||_0||_0||_0||_0||_0||_0\overline{out}\langle agent\rangle,||_1||_0 out(Y)\rangle}$$

$$SYS_{\pi 7} = (\nu\ n)((((((\overline{open}\langle agent\rangle.P|\mathbf{0})|\mathbf{0}_n)|(\mathbf{0}|\mathbf{0}_{agent})|\overline{open}\langle n\rangle)|\mathbf{0}_{home})|\widehat{T})$$

$$\langle\equiv\rangle_{(P-ParComm,||_0||_0)}SYS_{\pi 8}\langle\equiv\rangle_{(P-ParAss,||_0||_0)}SYS_{\pi 9}$$

$$\Downarrow_\pi \quad {}^{\langle ||_0||_0||_0||_0\overline{open}\langle n\rangle,||_1||_0 open(Y)\rangle}$$

$$SYS_{\pi 10} = (\nu\ n)((((\mathbf{0}|(\overline{open}\langle agent\rangle.P|\mathbf{0}))|(\mathbf{0}|\mathbf{0}_{agent}))|\mathbf{0}_{home})|\widehat{T})$$

$$\langle\equiv\rangle_{(P-ZeroPar,||_0||_0||_0||_1)}SYS_{\pi 11}$$
$$\langle\equiv\rangle_{(P-ParComm,||_0||_0||_0)}SYS_{\pi 12}\langle\equiv\rangle_{(P-ZeroPar,||_0||_0||_0)}SYS_{\pi 13}$$

$$\Downarrow_\pi \quad {}^{\langle ||_0||_0||_0\overline{open}\langle agent\rangle,||_1||_0 open(Y)\rangle}$$

$$SYS_{\pi 14} = (\nu\ n)(((P|\mathbf{0})|\mathbf{0}_{agent})|\mathbf{0}_{home})|\widehat{T})$$

$$SYS_{\pi 2} = (\nu\ n)((((\overline{out}\langle home\rangle.\overline{in}\langle home\rangle.(\overline{out}\langle agent\rangle.\overline{open}\langle agent\rangle.P|\mathbf{0}_n)|\mathbf{0}_{agent})|$$
$$\overline{open}\langle n\rangle)|\mathbf{0}_{home})|\widehat{T})$$
$$SYS_{\pi 3} = (\nu\ n)(((((\overline{out}\langle home\rangle.\overline{in}\langle home\rangle.(\overline{out}\langle agent\rangle.\overline{open}\langle agent\rangle.P|\mathbf{0}_n)|\mathbf{0})|$$
$$\mathbf{0}_{agent})|\overline{open}\langle n\rangle)|\mathbf{0}_{home})|\widehat{T})$$
$$SYS_{\pi 6} = (\nu\ n)(((((((\overline{out}\langle agent\rangle.\overline{open}\langle agent\rangle.P|\mathbf{0})|$$
$$\mathbf{0}_n)|\mathbf{0})|\mathbf{0}_{agent})|\overline{open}\langle n\rangle)|\mathbf{0}_{home})|\widehat{T})$$
$$SYS_{\pi 8} = (\nu\ n)(((\overline{open}\langle n\rangle|(((\overline{open}\langle agent\rangle.P|\mathbf{0})|\mathbf{0}_n)|(\mathbf{0}|\mathbf{0}_{agent})))|\mathbf{0}_{home})|\widehat{T})$$
$$SYS_{\pi 9} = (\nu\ n)((((\overline{open}\langle n\rangle|((\overline{open}\langle agent\rangle.P|\mathbf{0})|\mathbf{0}_n)|(\mathbf{0}|\mathbf{0}_{agent})))|\mathbf{0}_{home})|\widehat{T})$$
$$SYS_{\pi 11} = (\nu\ n)((((\mathbf{0}|\overline{open}\langle agent\rangle.P)|(\mathbf{0}|\mathbf{0}_{agent})))|\mathbf{0}_{home})|\widehat{T})$$
$$SYS_{\pi 12} = (\nu\ n)((((\overline{open}\langle agent\rangle.P|\mathbf{0})|(\mathbf{0}|\mathbf{0}_{agent})))|\mathbf{0}_{home})|\widehat{T})$$
$$SYS_{\pi 13} = (\nu\ n)(((\overline{open}\langle agent\rangle.P|(\mathbf{0}|\mathbf{0}_{agent})))|\mathbf{0}_{home})|\widehat{T})$$

Fig. 4. A complete computation of $\widehat{T}(SYS)$.

for the π-calculus [8]. Furthermore, it is possible to re-use the tools for the analysis of quantitative aspects defined for the π-calculus [1, 2], *e.g.* performance or probabilistic behaviour of the MA processes.

We conclude our paper with a short list of related papers. The literature reports several ways to compare the MA and the π-calculus that often rely on an encoding of (a fragment of) one calculus into (a fragment of) the other, up

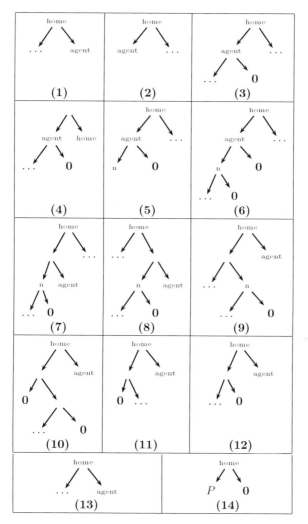

Fig. 5. The structure of the ambients along the MA computation. (The ith picture refers to the process SYS_i).

to suitable behavioural equivalences. We remark that our approach is different, instead: we proposed an injective mapping from the transition systems of the MA into that of the HOπ-calculus, using no observational equivalences.

The first work relating the two calculi is in [5, 4], that gives an encoding of the asynchronous π-calculus into the MA. This encoding has two main disadvantages: it is not compositionally, and each π-calculus channel needs a centralized ambient to handle all the input/output requests involving the channel itself. In [15] an encoding of asynchronous π-calculus into the Safe Ambients (a variant of MA) is proposed. Their authors improve on the technique of [5] by presenting

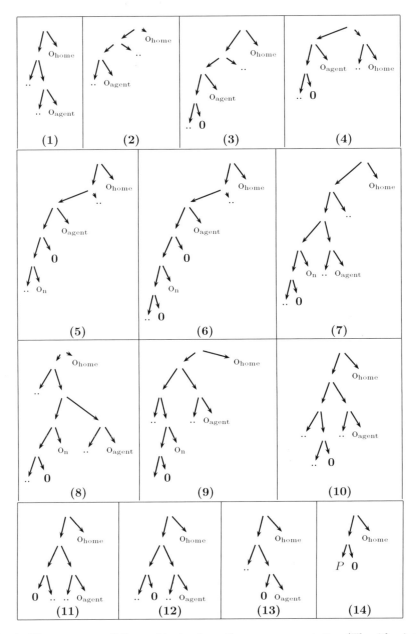

Fig. 6. The structure of the ambients along the π_{MA} computation.(The ith picture refers to the process $SYS_{\pi i}$).

a compositional and a simpler encoding because it requires no centralised ambients. In [12] a translation of the MA into the distributed Join Calculus [11] is presented. The atomic steps of the MA are decomposed into several elementary steps, each involving only local synchronizations. A distributed implementation of ambient written in Jocaml [6] is given. The translation is proved to be corrected up to the notion of a hybrid barbed bisimulation in such a way that the translation preserves and reflects a variety of global observations. The expressiveness of the Pure Mobile Ambients, *i.e.* MA where only capability actions are admitted with no local communications, is studied in [24] by encoding the synchronous π-calculus into the Pure Safe Ambients, relying on π_{esc}, an extension of the π-calculus with explicit substitutions and channels. This encoding is proved to preserve an operational correspondence. An encoding of the π_{esc} into the typed RObust AMbients (ROAM), a variant of the Safe Ambients, is presented in [13]. The goal of this work is to prove a stronger operational correspondence than the one in [24] for the encoding of the synchronous π-calculus into the Pure Safe Ambients.

References

1. L. Brodo, P. Degano, and C. Priami. A tool for quantitative analysis of π-calculus processes. In R. Gorrieri, editor, *Proceedings of Process Algebra and Performance Modelling (PAPM'00)*, Geneva, 2000. Carleton Scientific.
2. L. Brodo and C. Priami. Performance considerations on the wap secure transpor layer. In D. Nowak, editor, *Proceedings of Automated Verification of Critical Systems (AVoCS'01)*, Oxford, UK, 2001.
3. M. Bugliesi, G. Castagna, and S. Crafa. Access control for mobile agents: The calculus of boxed ambients. *ACM Transactions on Programming Languages and Systems.* to appear.
4. L. Cardelli, G. Ghelli, and A. D. Gordon. Mobility types for mobile ambients. In J. Wiedermann, P. van Emde Boas, and M. Nielsen, editors, *Proceedings of International Colloquium on Automata, Languages and Programming (ICALP'99)*, volume 1644 of *LNCS*, pages 230–239, Prague, Czech Republic, 1999. Springer-Verlag.
5. L. Cardelli and A. Gordon. Mobile Ambients. *Theoretical Computer Science*, 240/1:177–213, 2000.
6. S. Conchon and F. Le Fessant. Jocaml: Mobile agents for objective-caml. In *Proceedings of Agent Systems and Applications and International Symposium on Mobile Agents (ASA/MA '99)*, pages 22–29, Palm Springs, California, USA, 1999. IEEE Computer Society.
7. S. Crafa, M.Bugliesi, and G. Castagna. Information Flow Security in Boxed Ambients. In *Proceedings of Foundations of Wide Area Network Computing (F-WAN'02)*, number 3 in ENTCS, Malaga, Spain, 2002. Elsevier.
8. P. Degano and C. Priami. Non-interleaving semantics for mobile processes. *Theoretical Computer Science*, 216(1–2):237–270, 1999.
9. P. Degano and C. Priami. Enhanced operational semantics: a tool for describing and analyzing concurrent systems. *ACM Computing Surveys*, 33(2):135–176, 2001.
10. C. Fournet and G. Gonthier. The reflexive chemical abstract machine and the join-calculus. In *Proceedings of Principles of Programming Languages (POPL '96)*, pages 372–385, St. Petersburg Beach, Florida, USA, 1996. ACM Press.
11. C. Fournet and G. Gonthier. The Join Calculus: A language for distributed mobile programming. In G. Barthe, P. Dybjer, L. Pinto, and J. Saraiva, editors, *Proceedings of Applied Semantics (APPSEM'00)*, volume 2395 of *LNCS*, pages 268–332, Caminha, Portugal, 2002. Springer-Verlag.

12. C. Fournet, J.J. Levy, and A. Schmitt. An asynchronous, distributed implementation of mobile ambients. In J. van Leeuwen, O. Watanabe, M. Hagiya, P. D. Mosses, and T. Ito, editors, *Proceedings of the IFIP Theoretical Computer Science (IFIP TCS'00)*, volume 1872 of *LNCS*, pages 348–364, Sendai, Japan, 2000.
13. X. Guan and J. You. Encoding channels in typed ambients. unpublished manuscript.
14. M. Hennessy and J. Riely. Resource access control in systems of mobile agents. *Information and Computation*, 173(1):82–120, 2002.
15. F. Levi and D. Sangiorgi. Controlling interference in ambients. In *Proceedings of Principles of Programming Languages (POPL '00)*, pages 352–364, Boston, Massachusetts, USA, 2000. ACM Press.
16. R. Milner. *Communicating and Mobile Systems: The π Calculus*. Cambridge University Press, 1999.
17. R. Milner, J. Parrow, and D. Walker. A calculus of mobile processes. *Information and Computation*, 100(1):1–77, 1992.
18. D. Sangiorgi. *Expressing Mobility in Process Algebra*. PhD thesis, University of Edinburgh, Edinburgh, U. K., 1993.
19. P. Sewell. Global/local subtyping and capability inference for a distributed π-calculus. In *Proceedings of International Colloquium on Automata, Languages, and Programming (ICALP '98)*, volume 1443 of *LNCS*, Aalborg, Denmark, 1998.
20. B. Thomsen. A calculus of higher order communicating systems. In *Proceedings of Principles of Programming Languages (POPL'89)*, pages 143–154, Austin, Texas, USA, 1989. ACM Press.
21. B. Thomsen. Plain CHOCS: A second generation calculus for higher order processes. *Acta Informatica*, 30(1):1–59, 1993.
22. B. Thomsen, L. Leth, and T.-M. Kuo. A facile tutorial. In U. Montanari and V. Sassone, editors, *Proceedings of Concurrency Theory (CONCUR'96)*, volume 1119, pages 278–298. Springer-Verlag, 1996.
23. B. Victor and F. Moller. The Mobility Workbench — A tool for the π-calculus. In D. Dill, editor, *Proceedings of Computer Aided Verification (CAV'94)*, volume 818 of *LNCS*, pages 428–440, Stanford, California, USA, 1994. Springer-Verlag.
24. P. Zimmer. On the Expressiveness of Pure Mobile Ambients. *Mathematical Structures of Computer Science*, 13, 2003.

A   Proofs

Property 1
The operational semantics in Tab. 2 coincides with the operational semantics in [5].

Proof. The congruence rules in Tab. 1 coincide with the ones in [5]. The semantic rules in Tab. 2, with the replacement of $\rightarrow_{MA}$ with $\Rightarrow$ in the conclusions of the rule Red$\equiv$, are the same as the ones in [5] as well. By using $\Rightarrow$ as an auxiliary relation for $\rightarrow_{MA}$ in Tab. 2 we only impose a fixed structure to the derivation of transitions: the rules of structural congruence are applied all together in the last step of the derivation, instead of interleaving them with transition rules as it may happen with the semantics of [5].

Lemma 1 Given a MA process P, $\forall \vartheta \in \mathcal{L}$

$$\mathcal{T}(P@\vartheta) = \mathcal{T}(P)@\vartheta$$

Proof. The proof is by induction on the structure of P.

$\Rightarrow)$

base

$P = \mathbf{0}$ or $P = \langle M \rangle$ or $P = M.P'$ or $P = (x).P'$ or $P = !P'$.
$P@\vartheta = Q$ is defined only if $\vartheta = \epsilon$ implies
(if $P@\epsilon = Q$ then $\mathcal{T}(P)@\epsilon = \mathcal{T}(Q)$);

inductive step

$P = P_0|P_1$ $P@\vartheta$ is defined only if $\vartheta = \epsilon$ or $\vartheta = ||_0\vartheta'$ or $\vartheta = ||_1\vartheta'$:

$\quad\quad \vartheta = \epsilon$ trivial

$\quad\quad \vartheta = ||_0\vartheta'$ $P@||_0\vartheta' = (P_0|P_1)@||_0\vartheta' = P_0@\vartheta' = Q$.

$\quad\quad\quad$ Now, $\mathcal{T}(P)@||_0\vartheta' = \mathcal{T}(P_0|P_1)@||_0\vartheta' =$

$\quad\quad\quad (\mathcal{T}(P_0)|\mathcal{T}(P_1))@||_0\vartheta' = \mathcal{T}(P_0)@\vartheta'$,

$\quad\quad\quad$ and the inductive hypothesis suffices.

$\quad\quad \vartheta = ||_1\vartheta'$ it is the symmetric case

$P = n[P']$ $P@\vartheta$ is defined only if $\vartheta = \epsilon$ or $\vartheta = ||_0\vartheta'$ or $\vartheta = ||_1$:

$\quad\quad \vartheta = \epsilon$ trivial

$\quad\quad \vartheta = ||_0\vartheta'$ $P@||_0\vartheta' = n[P']@||_0\vartheta' = P'@\vartheta' = Q$.

$\quad\quad\quad$ Now, $\mathcal{T}(P)@||_0\vartheta' = \mathcal{T}(n[P'])@||_0\vartheta' =$

$\quad\quad\quad (\mathcal{T}(P')|\mathcal{T}(\emptyset_{\mathcal{T}(n)}))@||_0\vartheta' = \mathcal{T}(P')@\vartheta'$,

$\quad\quad\quad$ and the inductive hypothesis suffices.

$\quad\quad \vartheta = ||_1$ $P@||_1 = n[P']@||_1 = \emptyset_n$,

$\quad\quad\quad \mathcal{T}(P)@||_1 = \mathcal{T}(n[P'])@||_1 =$

$\quad\quad\quad (\mathcal{T}(P')|\mathcal{T}(\emptyset_{\mathcal{T}(n)}))@||_1 = \mathcal{T}(\emptyset_{\mathcal{T}(n)}) = \mathcal{T}(\mathbf{0}_n)$,

$\quad\quad\quad$ the thesis holds.

$P = (\nu\ x)P'$ $P@\vartheta = P'@\vartheta$. Now

$\quad\quad\quad \mathcal{T}(P)@\vartheta = \mathcal{T}((\nu\ x)P')@\vartheta = \mathcal{T}(P')@\vartheta$,

$\quad\quad\quad$ and the inductive hypothesis suffices.

$\Leftarrow)$

base

$P = \mathbf{0}$ or $P = \langle M \rangle$ or $P = M.P'$ or $P = (x).P'$ or $P = !P'$.
$\mathcal{T}(P)@\vartheta = \mathcal{T}(Q)$ is defined only if $\vartheta = \epsilon$ implies
(if $\mathcal{T}(P)@\epsilon = \mathcal{T}(Q)$ then $P@\epsilon = Q$)

inductive step

$P = P_0|P_1$ $\mathcal{T}(P)@\vartheta$ is defined only if $\vartheta = \epsilon$ or $\vartheta = |_0\vartheta'$ or $\vartheta = ||_1\vartheta'$

$\quad\quad \vartheta = \epsilon$ trivial

$\quad\quad \vartheta = ||_0\vartheta'$ $\mathcal{T}(P)@||_0\vartheta' = (\mathcal{T}(P_0)|\mathcal{T}(P_1))@||_0\vartheta' = \mathcal{T}(P_0)@\vartheta'$,

$\quad\quad\quad$ on the other hand $P@||_0\vartheta' = P_0|P_1@||_0\vartheta' = P_0@\vartheta'$.

$\quad\quad\quad$ The inductive hypothesis suffices.

$\quad\quad \vartheta = ||_1\vartheta'$ symmetric case

$P = n[P']$ $\mathcal{T}(P)@\vartheta$ is defined only if $\vartheta = \epsilon$ or $\vartheta = ||_0\vartheta'$ or $\vartheta = ||_1$

$\vartheta = \epsilon$ trivial

$\vartheta = ||_0\vartheta'$ $\mathcal{T}(P)@||_0\vartheta' = \mathcal{T}(n[P'])@||_0\vartheta' =$
$(\mathcal{T}(P')|\mathcal{T}(\emptyset_{\mathcal{T}(n)}))@||_0\vartheta' = \mathcal{T}(P')@\vartheta'.$
On the other hand $P@||_0\vartheta' = n[P']@||_0\vartheta' = P'@\vartheta'.$
The inductive hypothesis,
$\mathcal{T}(P')@\vartheta' = \mathcal{T}(Q)$ implies $P'@\vartheta' = Q$, suffices.

$\vartheta = ||_1$ $\mathcal{T}(P)@||_1 = \mathcal{T}(n[P'])@||_1 =$
$(\mathcal{T}(P')|\mathcal{T}(\emptyset_{\mathcal{T}(n)}))@||_1 = \mathcal{T}(\emptyset_{\mathcal{T}(n)}) = \mathbf{0}_n.$
On the other hand $P@||_1 = n[P']@||_1 = \emptyset_n$
and the thesis holds.

$P = (\nu\ x)P'$ $\mathcal{T}(P)@\vartheta = (\nu\ x)\mathcal{T}(P')@\vartheta = \mathcal{T}(P')@\vartheta.$
On the other hand $P@\vartheta = (\nu\ x)P'@\vartheta = P'@\vartheta$ and
the inductive hypothesis suffices.

Lemma 3 [on the congruences] For all sequences of pairs ϕ, Φ such that $\phi \diamond \Phi$, and $\forall\ P, Q \in$ Processes

$$P \equiv_\phi Q \ \text{ iff } \ \mathcal{T}(P)\langle\equiv\rangle_\Phi\mathcal{T}(Q).$$

Proof. The proof is by straightforward induction on the number of the congruence rules in ϕ (and Φ), once proved the base case.
Se we prove that $\forall\ \vartheta \in \mathcal{L}$ and $\forall\ P, Q \in$ Processes such that $r \diamond R$ then

$$P \equiv_{(r,\vartheta)} Q \ \text{ iff } \ \mathcal{T}(P)\langle\equiv\rangle_{(R,\vartheta)}\mathcal{T}(Q).$$

We proceed by cases on *rule* s.t. Struct *rule* $\diamond$ P-*rule*. We consider below the case when the congruence rule is applied to transform P into Q and $\mathcal{T}(P)$ into $\mathcal{T}(Q)$; the proof in the other direction is symmetric.

(Zero Par) by Lemma 1 $(P@\vartheta = P_1\ |\ \mathbf{0}$ iff $\mathcal{T}(P)@\vartheta = \mathcal{T}(P_1)|\mathcal{T}(\mathbf{0}))$
and $(Q@\vartheta = P_1$ iff $\mathcal{T}(Q)@\vartheta = \mathcal{T}(P_1)).$
Then, by definition $(\mathcal{T}(P)\langle\equiv\rangle_{(\text{Struct }rule,\vartheta)}\mathcal{T}(Q)$ iff $P \equiv_{(\text{P}-rule,\vartheta)} Q).$

(Par Comm) by Lemma 1
$(\mathcal{T}(P)@\vartheta = \mathcal{T}(P_0|P_1) = \mathcal{T}(P_0)|\mathcal{T}(P_1)$ iff $P@\vartheta = P_0\ |\ P_1)$
and $(\widehat{\mathcal{T}}(Q)@||_0\vartheta = \mathcal{T}(P_1\ |\ P_0) = \mathcal{T}(P_1)|\mathcal{T}(P_0)$ iff
$Q@\vartheta = P_1\ |\ P_0).$
Then, by definition $(\mathcal{T}(P)\langle\equiv\rangle_{(\text{Struct }rule,\vartheta)}\mathcal{T}(Q)$ iff $P \equiv_{(\text{P}-rule,\vartheta)} Q).$

(Par Assoc) by Lemma 1
$(\mathcal{T}(P)@\vartheta = \mathcal{T}(P_0|(P_1|P_2)) = \mathcal{T}(P_0)|(\mathcal{T}(P_1)|\mathcal{T}(\mathbf{0}))$ iff
$P@\vartheta = P_0\ |\ (P_1\ |\ P_2))$ and
$(Q@\vartheta = (P_0\ |\ P_1)\ |\ P_2$ iff $\mathcal{T}(Q)@\vartheta = (\mathcal{T}(P_0)|\mathcal{T}(P_1))|\mathcal{T}(P_2)).$
Then by definition $(\mathcal{T}(P)\langle\equiv\rangle_{(\text{Struct }rule,\vartheta)}\mathcal{T}(Q)$ iff $P \equiv_{(\text{P}-rule,\vartheta)} Q).$

(Repl) By Lemma 1 $(\mathcal{T}(P)@\vartheta =!\mathcal{T}(P')$ iff $P@\vartheta =!P')$ and
$(\mathcal{T}(Q)@\vartheta = (\mathcal{T}(P')|!\mathcal{T}(P'))$ iff $Q@\vartheta = (P'\ |\ !P')).$
Then by definition $(\mathcal{T}(P)\langle\equiv\rangle_{(\text{Struct }rule,\vartheta)}\mathcal{T}(Q)$ iff $P \equiv_{(\text{P}-rule,\vartheta)} Q).$

Lemma 2 [on the rigid transitions]

$$\forall P\ .\ P \Rightarrow Q \ \text{ iff } \ \widehat{\mathcal{T}}(P) \Rightarrow_\pi \widehat{\mathcal{T}}(Q)$$

Proof. We divide the proof into two step. At first we prove the following lemma.

Lemma (on contexts) Let $\vartheta \in \{||_0\}^*$, then

$$\mathcal{T}(P)@\vartheta = \mathcal{T}(Q) \quad \text{iff} \quad \mathcal{T}(P) = \mathcal{C}_\vartheta[\mathcal{T}(Q)]$$

where $\mathcal{C}_\vartheta[\_] = (\ldots(\mathcal{T}(\_)|\mathcal{T}(P_1))|\ldots|\mathcal{T}(P_n))$, for some $P_1, \ldots, P_n$, $n \geq 0$, and $\vartheta = ||_0 \ldots ||_0$, n times.

Proof. The proof is by induction on ϑ.
base: $\vartheta = \epsilon$
By definition of $-@-$ operator $\mathcal{T}(P)@\epsilon = \mathcal{T}(Q) = \mathcal{T}(P)$,
thus $\mathcal{C}_\epsilon[Q] = \mathcal{T}(Q) = \mathcal{T}(P)$.
inductive step: $\vartheta = ||_0\vartheta'$, with $\vartheta' = ||_0^{n-1}$
$\mathcal{T}(P)@||_0\vartheta'$ is defined only if $\mathcal{T}(P) = \mathcal{T}(P')|\mathcal{T}(P'')$,
thus $(\mathcal{T}(P')|\mathcal{T}(P''))@||_0\vartheta' = \mathcal{T}(P'')@\vartheta'$.
By inductive hypothesis $\mathcal{T}(P')@\vartheta' = \mathcal{T}(Q)$ implies
$\mathcal{T}(P') = \mathcal{C}_{\vartheta'}[\mathcal{T}(Q)] = (\ldots(_{n-1}\mathcal{T}(Q)|\mathcal{T}(P_1))\ldots|\mathcal{T}(P_{n-1}))_{n-1}$,
for some $P_1, \ldots, P_{n-1}$.
Now it is easy to verify that $\mathcal{T}(P')|\mathcal{T}(P'') = \mathcal{C}_{\vartheta'}[\mathcal{T}(Q)]|\mathcal{T}(P'') = \mathcal{C}_\vartheta[\mathcal{T}(Q)]$.

Now we start the proof of the main Lemma. Accordingly to Property 2, in the rest of the proof we do not mention any restriction at the top level for the MA processes and for their translations: $P = (\nu\ I)P'$, $Q = (\nu\ J)Q'$, $\widehat{\mathcal{T}}(P) = (\nu\ I)\widehat{\mathcal{T}}(P')$ and $\widehat{\mathcal{T}}(Q) = (\nu\ J)\widehat{\mathcal{T}}(Q')$.
Thus we feel free to omit below any reference to possible (and needed, due to replication) applications of congruence rules for restrictions and α-conversion.
$\Rightarrow)$
The proof is by induction on the length of the derivation.
base:
We proceed by case analysis on the rule applied: Red In, Red Out, Red Open, Red Comm.

Red In: $P = n[in\ m.P_1|P_2]|m[Q'] \Rightarrow Q = m[n[P_1|P_2]|Q']$.
By definition $\widehat{\mathcal{T}}(P) = (((\overline{in}\langle m\rangle.\mathcal{T}(P_1)|\mathcal{T}(P_2))|\mathbf{0}_n)|(\mathcal{T}(Q')|\mathbf{0}_m))|\widehat{\mathcal{T}}$.
By rule $\ell\pi_{Com}$, we derive

$$\widehat{\mathcal{T}}(P) \xrightarrow{\langle||_0||_0||_0||_0\ \overline{in}\langle m\rangle,\ ||_1||_0 in(Y)\rangle}_p T'$$
$$= (((\mathcal{T}(P_1)|\mathcal{T}(P_2))|\mathbf{0}_n)|(\mathcal{T}(Q')|\mathbf{0}_m))|\widehat{\mathcal{T}}. \tag{1}$$

All the side conditions of $M\pi_{in}$ are also satisfied: $\widehat{\mathcal{T}}(P)@||_0||_1||_1 = \mathbf{0}_m$, $\widehat{\mathcal{T}}(P)@||_0||_0||_1 = \mathbf{0}_n$ and $\widehat{\mathcal{T}}(P)@||_0||_0||_0||_1 \neq \mathbf{0}_k$. Thus, by rule $M\pi_{in}$, with premise (1), we derive: $(\mathcal{T}(P)|\widehat{\mathcal{T}}) \Rightarrow_\pi T''$, with $T'' = T'\{||_0 \mapsto ((T'@||_0||_0|T'@||_0||_1||_0)|T'@||_0||_1||_1)\}$.

Red Out: $P = m[n[out\ m.P_1|P_2]|Q'] \Rightarrow Q = n[P_1|P_2]|m[Q']$.
By definition $\widehat{\mathcal{T}}(P) = (((\overline{out}\langle m\rangle.\mathcal{T}(P_1)|\mathcal{T}(P_2))|\mathbf{0}_n)|\mathcal{T}(Q')|\mathbf{0}_m)|\widehat{T}$.
By rule $\ell\pi_{Com}$ we derive

$$\widehat{\mathcal{T}}(P) \xrightarrow{\langle||_0||_0||_0||_0||_0\ \overline{out}\langle m\rangle,||_1||_0\ out(Y)\rangle}_p T'$$
$$= (((\mathcal{T}(P_1)|\mathcal{T}(P_2))|\mathbf{0}_n)|\mathcal{T}(Q')|\mathbf{0}_m)|\widehat{T}. \tag{2}$$

All the side conditions of $M\pi_{out}$ are also satisfied: $\widehat{\mathcal{T}}(P)@||_0||_1 = \mathbf{0}_m$, $\widehat{\mathcal{T}}(P)@||_0||_0||_0||_1 = \mathbf{0}_n$, $\widehat{\mathcal{T}}(P)@||_0||_0||_0||_0||_1 \neq \mathbf{0}_k$ and $\widehat{\mathcal{T}}(P)@||_0||_0||_1 \neq \mathbf{0}_h$. Thus by rule $M\pi_{out}$, with premise (2), we derive $\widehat{\mathcal{T}}(P) \Rightarrow_\pi T''$,
with $T'' = T'\{||_0 \mapsto (T'@||_0||_0||_0|(T'@||_0||_0||_1|T'@||_0||_1))\}$.

Red Open: $P = open\ m.P'|m[Q'] \Rightarrow Q = P'|Q'$.
By definition $\widehat{\mathcal{T}}(P) = (\overline{open}\langle m\rangle.\mathcal{T}(P')|(\mathcal{T}(Q')|\mathbf{0}_m))|\widehat{T}$. By rule $\ell\pi_{Com}$ we derive

$$\widehat{\mathcal{T}}(P) \xrightarrow{\langle||_0\ \overline{open}\langle m\rangle,||_1||_0 open(Y)\rangle}_p T' = (\mathcal{T}(P')|(\mathcal{T}(Q')|\mathbf{0}_m))|\widehat{T}. \tag{3}$$

The side condition of $M\pi_{open}$ is also satisfied: $\widehat{\mathcal{T}}(P)@||_0||_1||_1 = \mathbf{0}_m$. Thus by rule $M\pi_{open}$, with premise (3), we derive: $\widehat{\mathcal{T}}(P) \Rightarrow_\pi T''$, with $T'' = T'\{||_0||_1 \mapsto T'@||_0||_1||_0\}$.

Red Comm: $P = \langle M\rangle\,|\,(x).P' \Rightarrow Q = P'\{x \leftarrow M\}$.
By definition $\widehat{\mathcal{T}}(P) = (\overline{ch}\langle\mathcal{T}(M)\rangle\,|\,ch(X).\mathcal{T}(P'))|\widehat{T}$. By rule $\ell\pi_{Com}$ we derive

$$\widehat{\mathcal{T}}(P) \xrightarrow{||_0\langle||_0\overline{ch}\langle\mathcal{T}(M)\rangle,||_1 ch(X)\rangle}_p T' = \mathcal{T}(P')\{\mathcal{T}(M)/X\}|\widehat{T}. \tag{4}$$

This is the premise to deduce, by rule $M\pi_{com}$, $\widehat{\mathcal{T}}(P) \Rightarrow_\pi T''$, with $T'' = T'\{||_0 \mapsto T'@||_0||_0\}$.

In all the above cases it is immediate to verify that $T'' = \widehat{\mathcal{T}}(Q)$.
inductive step:

We proceed by cases on the last rule to derive $P \to Q$ that could be either Red Amb or Red Par.

Red Amb: $P = n[P'] \Rightarrow Q = n[Q']$. The inductive hypothesis is $\widehat{\mathcal{T}}(P') \Rightarrow_\pi \widehat{\mathcal{T}}(Q')$, *i.e.*

$$\mathcal{T}(P')|\widehat{T} \xrightarrow{\theta}_p T|\widehat{T}, \text{ with } \mathcal{T}(Q') = (T|\widehat{T})\{||_0\vartheta \mapsto T_s\} \tag{5}$$

where T_s depends on the applied rule. We have to prove that

$$\widehat{\mathcal{T}}(P) = \mathcal{T}(P)|\widehat{T} = (\mathcal{T}(P')|\mathbf{0}_n)|\widehat{T} \Rightarrow_\pi (\mathcal{T}(Q')|\mathbf{0}_n)|\widehat{T} = \widehat{\mathcal{T}}(Q) \tag{6}$$

Recall that the rules $M\pi_s$, with $s \in \{in, out, open, com\}$ correspond, respectively, to the MA rules Red In, Red Out, Red Open, Red Comm.

By inductive hypothesis, (5) is deduced by either rule $M\pi_s$. In particular $\widehat{T}$ can be involved or not.

If $\widehat{T}$ is involved, the premise for deducing (5) has the form $\mathcal{T}(P')|\widehat{T} \xrightarrow{\langle||_0\vartheta\overline{x}\langle K\rangle,||_1||_0 x(Y)\rangle}_p T|\widehat{T}$, where ϑ and x depend on the rule applied. Its left premise is $\mathcal{T}(P') \xrightarrow{\vartheta\overline{x}\langle K\rangle}_p T$ that fulfills the premise of $\ell\pi_{Par}$ and permits to deduce $\mathcal{T}(P')|\mathbf{0}_n \xrightarrow{||_0\vartheta\overline{x}\langle K\rangle}_p T|\mathbf{0}_n$. This is the premise, together with $\widehat{T} \xrightarrow{||_0 x(Y)}_p \widehat{T}$, for rule $\ell\pi_{Com}$. So we can deduce $(\mathcal{T}(P')|\mathbf{0}_n)|\widehat{T} \xrightarrow{\langle||_0||_0\vartheta\overline{x}\langle K\rangle,||_1||_0 x(Y)\rangle}_p (T|\mathbf{0}_n)|\widehat{T}$. By inductive hypothesis all the side conditions of $M\pi_s$ still hold and we can deduce the desired (6), in fact by inductive hypothesis $\mathcal{T}(Q) = ((T|\mathbf{0}_n)|\widehat{T})\{||_0||_0\vartheta \mapsto T_s\}$. If (5) is deduced by rule $M\pi_{com}$, its premise is $\mathcal{T}(P')|\widehat{T} \xrightarrow{||_0\vartheta\langle||_0\overline{ch}\langle K\rangle,||_1 ch(Y)\rangle}_p T|\widehat{T}$, whose premise is $\mathcal{T}(P') \xrightarrow{\vartheta\langle||_0\overline{ch}\langle K\rangle,||_1 ch(Y)\rangle}_p T$. With rule $\ell\pi_{Par}$ we deduce $\mathcal{T}(P')|\mathbf{0}_n \xrightarrow{||_0\vartheta\langle||_0\overline{ch}\langle K\rangle,||_1 ch(Y)\rangle}_p T|\mathbf{0}_n$ and then $(\mathcal{T}(P')|\mathbf{0}_n)|\widehat{T} \xrightarrow{||_0||_0\vartheta\langle||_0\overline{ch}\langle K\rangle,||_1 ch(Y)\rangle}_p (T|\mathbf{0}_n)|\widehat{T}$ from which we easily deduce (6). In fact by inductive hypothesis $\widehat{T}(Q) = ((T|\mathbf{0}_n)|\widehat{T})\{||_0||_0\vartheta \mapsto T@||_0\vartheta||_0\}$.

Red Par: $P = P'|R \Rightarrow Q = Q'|R$. The inductive hypothesis is $\widehat{T}(P') \Rightarrow_\pi \widehat{T}(Q')$, i.e.

$$\mathcal{T}(P')|\widehat{T} \xrightarrow{\theta}_p T|\widehat{T}, \text{ with } \mathcal{T}(Q') = (T|\widehat{T})\{||_0\vartheta \mapsto T_s\} \qquad (7)$$

where T_s depends on the applied rule. We have to prove that

$$\widehat{T}(P) = \mathcal{T}(P)|\widehat{T} = (\mathcal{T}(P')|R)|\widehat{T} \Rightarrow_\pi (\mathcal{T}(Q')|R)|\widehat{T} = \mathcal{T}(Q) \quad (8)$$

The proof can be obtained by the one of the previous item by substituting $\mathbf{0}_n$ with R.

$\Leftarrow)$

An MA ambient constructor $m[\_]$ is translated by a π-like calculus parallel operator, $\_|\mathbf{0}_m$. Thus, any ϑ in a translated process is originated either by an ambient or a parallel composition of the MA processes.

The proof is by cases on the rules.

In each of the following case it holds that $\vartheta \in \{||_0\}^*$, because, by using $\ell\pi_{Par}$ (i.e. $\ell\pi_{Par_0}$ of Tab. 4), we can only derive actions on the left side of a parallel operator.

$M\pi_{in}$ $\widehat{T}(P) \Rightarrow_\pi \widehat{T}(Q)$, i.e. $\mathcal{T}(P)|\widehat{T} \Rightarrow_\pi \mathcal{T}(Q)|\widehat{T}$. Its premise
$$\mathcal{T}(P)|\widehat{T} \xrightarrow{\langle||_0\vartheta||_0||_0||_0 in\langle m\rangle,||_1||_0 in(Y)\rangle}_p T|\widehat{T}, \text{ must be derived by } \ell\pi_{Com}$$

and the side conditions $\widehat{\mathcal{T}}(P)@||_0\vartheta||_1||_1 = \mathbf{0}_m$, $\widehat{\mathcal{T}}(P)@||_0\vartheta||_0||_1 = \mathbf{0}_n$, $\widehat{\mathcal{T}}(P)@||_0\vartheta||_0||_0||_1 \neq \mathbf{0}_k$.
Therefore we know that, for some P', Q', R :
$\widehat{\mathcal{T}}(P)@||_0\vartheta||_0||_0||_0 = \mathcal{T}(P)@\vartheta||_0||_0||_0 = \overline{in}\langle m\rangle.\mathcal{T}(P')$,
$\widehat{\mathcal{T}}(P)@||_0\vartheta||_1||_1 = \mathcal{T}(P)@\vartheta||_1||_1 = \mathbf{0}_m$,
$\widehat{\mathcal{T}}(P)@||_0\vartheta||_0||_1 = \mathcal{T}(P)\vartheta||_0||_1 = \mathbf{0}_n$; thus
$\widehat{\mathcal{T}}(P)@||_0\vartheta = \mathcal{T}(P)@\vartheta = (\overline{in}\langle m\rangle.\mathcal{T}(P')|\mathcal{T}(Q'))|\mathbf{0}_n)|(\mathcal{T}(R)|\mathbf{0}_m)$,
and
$\widehat{\mathcal{T}}(Q)@||_0\vartheta = \mathcal{T}(Q)@\vartheta = (((\mathcal{T}(P')|\mathcal{T}(Q'))|\mathbf{0}_n)|\mathcal{T}(R))|\mathbf{0}_m$,(see
also the definition of V, W, Z in $M\pi_{in}$). Using the lemma on contexts,
$\mathcal{T}(P) = \mathcal{C}_\vartheta[((\overline{in}\langle m\rangle.\mathcal{T}(P')|\mathcal{T}(Q'))|\mathbf{0}_n)|(\mathcal{T}(R)|\mathbf{0}_m)]$
and
$\mathcal{T}(Q) = \mathcal{C}_\vartheta[(((\mathcal{T}(P')|\mathcal{T}(Q'))|\mathbf{0}_n)|\mathcal{T}(R))|\mathbf{0}_m]$.

As $\widehat{\mathcal{T}}$ is invertible on its image, $P@\vartheta = n[in\ m.P'|Q']|m[R]$ and $Q@\vartheta = m[n[P'|Q']|R]$. By rules Red In, Red Amb and Red Par, we derive $P \Rightarrow Q$.

$M\pi_{out}$ $\widehat{\mathcal{T}}(P) \Rightarrow_\pi \widehat{\mathcal{T}}(Q)$, i.e. $\mathcal{T}(P)|\widehat{T} \Rightarrow_\pi \mathcal{T}(Q)|\widehat{T}$. Its premise is
$\mathcal{T}(P)|\widehat{T} \xrightarrow{\langle ||_0\vartheta||_0||_0||_0||_0\overline{out}\langle m\rangle,||_1||_0 out(Y)\rangle}_p T|\widehat{T}$ must be derived by $\ell\pi_{Com}$
and the side conditions $\widehat{\mathcal{T}}(P)@||_0\vartheta||_1 = \mathbf{0}_m$, $\widehat{\mathcal{T}}(P)@||_0\vartheta||_0||_0||_1 = \mathbf{0}_n$,
$\widehat{\mathcal{T}}(P)@||_0\vartheta||_0||_0||_0||_1 \neq \mathbf{0}_k$, $\widehat{\mathcal{T}}(P)@||_0\vartheta||_0||_1 \neq \mathbf{0}_h$.
Therefore we know that, for some P', Q', R:
$\widehat{\mathcal{T}}(P)@||_0\vartheta||_0||_0||_0||_0 = \mathcal{T}(P)@\vartheta||_0||_0||_0||_0 = \overline{out}\langle m\rangle.\mathcal{T}(P')$,

$\widehat{\mathcal{T}}(P)@||_0\vartheta||_1 = \mathcal{T}(P)@\vartheta||_1 = \mathbf{0}_m$,
$\widehat{\mathcal{T}}(P)@||_0\vartheta||_0||_0||_1 = \mathcal{T}(P)@\vartheta||_0||_0||_1 = \mathbf{0}_n$,
thus
$\widehat{\mathcal{T}}(P)@||_0\vartheta = \mathcal{T}(P)@\vartheta = ((((\overline{out}\langle m\rangle.\mathcal{T}(P')|\mathcal{T}(Q'))|\mathbf{0}_n)|\mathcal{T}(R))|\mathbf{0}_m)$,
and
$\widehat{\mathcal{T}}(Q)@||_0\vartheta = \mathcal{T}(Q)@\vartheta = ((\mathcal{T}(P')|\mathcal{T}(Q'))|\mathbf{0}_n)|(\mathcal{T}(R)|\mathbf{0}_m)$,
(see also the definition of V, W, Z in $M\pi_{out}$). Using the lemma on
contexts ,
$\mathcal{T}(P) = \mathcal{C}_\vartheta[((((\overline{out}\langle m\rangle.\mathcal{T}(P')|\mathcal{T}(Q'))|\mathbf{0}_n)|\mathcal{T}(R))|\mathbf{0}_m)]$
and
$\mathcal{T}(Q) = \mathcal{C}_\vartheta[((\mathcal{T}(P')|\mathcal{T}(Q'))|\mathbf{0}_n)|(\mathcal{T}(R)|\mathbf{0}_m)]$.

As $\widehat{\mathcal{T}}$ is invertible on its image, $P@\vartheta = m[n[out\ m.P'|Q']|R]$ and $Q@\vartheta = n[P'|Q']|m[R]$. By rules Red Out, Red Amb and Red Par, we derive $P \Rightarrow Q$.

$M\pi_{open}$ $\widehat{\mathcal{T}}(P) \Rightarrow_\pi \widehat{\mathcal{T}}(Q)$, i.e. $\mathcal{T}(P)|\widehat{T} \Rightarrow_\pi \mathcal{T}(Q)|\widehat{T}$. Its premise
$\mathcal{T}(P)|\widehat{T} \xrightarrow{\langle ||_0\vartheta||_0\overline{open}\langle m\rangle,||_1||_0 open(Y)\rangle}_p T|\widehat{T}$ must be derived by $\ell\pi_{Com}$
and the side condition $\widehat{\mathcal{T}}(P)@||_0\vartheta||_1||_1 = \mathbf{0}_m$.

Therefore we know that, for some P', R:

$\widehat{T}(P)@||_0\vartheta||_0 = T(P)@\vartheta = \overline{open}\langle m \rangle.T(P'),$

$\widehat{T}(P)@||_0\vartheta||_1||_1 = T(P)@\vartheta||_1||_1 = \mathbf{0}_m$, thus,

$\widehat{T}(P)@||_0\vartheta = T(P)@\vartheta = \overline{open}\langle m \rangle.T(P')|(T(R)|\mathbf{0}_m),$

and

$\widehat{T}(Q)@||_0\vartheta = T(P')|T(R)$, (see also the definition of W in $M\pi_{open}$).

Using the lemma on contexts,

$T(P) = C_\vartheta[\overline{open}\langle m \rangle.T(P')|(T(R)|\mathbf{0}_m)]$ and $T(Q) = C_\vartheta[T(P')|T(Q')]$.

As $\widehat{T}$ is invertible on its image, $P@\vartheta = open\ m.P'|m[R]$ and $Q@\vartheta = P'|R$. By rules Red Open, Red Amb and Red Par, we derive $P \Rightarrow Q$.

$M\pi_{com}$ $\widehat{T}(P) \Rightarrow_\pi \widehat{T}(Q)$, i.e. $T(P)|\widehat{T} \Rightarrow_\pi T(Q)|\widehat{T}$. Its premise

$T(P)|\widehat{T} \xrightarrow{||_0\vartheta\langle||_0\overline{ch}\langle K \rangle,||_1 ch(Y)\rangle}_p T|\widehat{T}$ must be derived by $\ell\pi_{Com}$.

By the label of the above premise, we know that, for some P', M:

$\widehat{T}(P)@||_0\vartheta = T(P)@\vartheta = \overline{ch}\langle K \rangle | ch(Y).T(P')$, and $\widehat{T}(Q)@||_0\vartheta = T(Q)@\vartheta = T(P')\{K/Y\}$, see the conclusion of rule $M\pi_{comm}$. Using the lemma on contexts,

$T(P) = C_\vartheta[\overline{ch}\langle K \rangle | ch(Y).T(P')]$ and $T(Q) = C_\vartheta[T(P')]$.

As $\widehat{T}$ is invertible on its image, $P@\vartheta = \langle M \rangle | ch(y).P'$ and $Q@\vartheta = P'\{y \leftarrow M\}, with T(M) = K$. By rules Red Comm, Red Amb and Red Par, we derive $P \Rightarrow Q$.

Theorem 1 Let $\mathcal{A} = \{P \in Processes \mid P$ is in ν-form$\}$, and

$$\widehat{T}(\mathcal{A}) = \{\widehat{T}(P)| P \in \mathcal{A}\},$$

then

$$\langle \mathcal{A}, \rightarrow_{MA} \rangle \text{ is isomorphic to } \langle \widehat{T}(\mathcal{A}), \rightarrow_\pi \rangle.$$

Proof. $(\nu\ I)P \Rightarrow (\nu\ I)Q$ iff $\widehat{T}((\nu\ I)P) \Rightarrow_\pi \widehat{T}((\nu\ I)Q)$ by Lemma 2. $\forall \phi, \Phi$, with $\phi \diamond \Phi$, $P \equiv_\phi Q$ iff $\widehat{T}(P)\langle \equiv \rangle_\Phi T(Q)$, by Corollary 3, and α-conversion does not affect isomorphism.

Theorem 2 Let $\equiv_M$ be the minimal congruence induced by the standard congruence of the higher order π-calculus, and by the rule $(\nu a)\overline{a}\langle m \rangle.\mathbf{0} \equiv_M \mathbf{0}$. Then

$$T_0 \rightarrow_\pi T_1 \text{ implies } T_0 \xrightarrow{\tau}_M T \equiv_M T_1.$$

Proof. For the sake of readability we shall call P-Par New the congruence rule $(\nu\ a)\overline{a}\langle m \rangle \equiv_M \mathbf{0}$ By definition, $T_0 \rightarrow_\pi T_1$ iff $\exists T_0', T_1', \Phi_1, \Phi_2$ s.t. $T_0\langle \equiv \rangle_{\Phi_1} T_0' \Rightarrow_\pi T_1'\langle \equiv \rangle_{\Phi_2} T_1$. As $\rightarrow_M$ is defined up to structural congruence, and $\langle \equiv \rangle_\Phi \subseteq \equiv_M$, we only need to prove that if $T_0' \Rightarrow_\pi T_1'$ then $T_0' \xrightarrow{\tau}_M T_1'$.

The semantic rules for $\rightarrow_p$ in Tab. 4 are a proper subset of those for the higher order π-calculus $\rightarrow_M$ after relabeling transitions with ℓ function, in Def. 4. Furthermore, the $\rightarrow_p$ transitions do not allow congruence rules and α-conversion to be applied, except for the $\widehat{T}$ process.

The transition $T_0' \Rightarrow_\pi T_1'$ is derived by either rule: $M\pi_{in}, M\pi_{out}, M\pi_{open}, M\pi_{com}$.

$M\pi_{in}$ its premise is $T_0' \xrightarrow{\langle\|_0\vartheta\|_0\|_0\|_0\overline{in}\langle m\rangle, \|_1\|_0 in(Y)\rangle}_p T$, for such a T that

$T@\|_0\vartheta = ((T_2|T_3)|\mathbf{0}_n)|(T_4|\mathbf{0}_m)$, for some T_2, T_3, T_4.

Now, $T_1' = T\{\|_0\vartheta \mapsto (V|W)|Z\}\langle\equiv\rangle_{(P-ParAss,\|_0\vartheta)}T\{\|_0\vartheta \mapsto V|(W|Z)\} = T$,

(for V, W, Z as in the definition of the rule $M\pi_{in}$). Thus,

$T_1' = T\{\|_0\vartheta \mapsto (T@\|_0\vartheta\|_0|T@\|_0\vartheta\|_1\|_0)|T\|_0@\|_1\|_1\}\langle\equiv\rangle_{(P-ParAss,\|_0\vartheta)}$

$T\{\|_0\vartheta \mapsto T@\|_0\vartheta\|_0|(T@\|_0\vartheta\|_1\|_0|T\|_0@\|_1\|_1)\} = T$.

$M\pi_{out}$ its premise is $T_0' \xrightarrow{\langle\|_0\vartheta\|_0\|_0\|_0\|_0\overline{out}\langle m\rangle, \|_1\|_0 out(Y)\rangle}_p T$, for such a T that

$T@\|_0\vartheta = (((T_2|T_3)|\mathbf{0}_n)|T_4)|\mathbf{0}_m$, for some T_2, T_3, T_4.

Now, $T_1' = T\{\|_0\vartheta \mapsto V|(W|Z)\}\langle\equiv\rangle_{(P-ParAss,\|_0\vartheta)}T\{\|_0\vartheta \mapsto (V|W)|Z\} = T$,

(for V, W, Z as in the definition of the rule $M\pi_{out}$. Thus,

$T_1' = T\{\|_0\vartheta \mapsto T_1@\|_0\vartheta\|_0|_0|(T_1@\|_0\vartheta\|_0\|_1|T_1@\|_0\vartheta\|_1)\}\langle\equiv\rangle_{(P-ParAss,\|_0\vartheta)}$

$T\{\|_0\vartheta \mapsto (T_1@\|_0\vartheta\|_0|_0|T_1@\|_0\vartheta\|_0\|_1)|T_1@\|_0\vartheta\|_1\}$.

$M\pi_{open}$ its premise is $T_0' \xrightarrow{\langle\|_0\vartheta\|_0\overline{open}\langle m\rangle, \|_1\|_0 open(Y)\rangle}_p T$, for such a T that

$T@\|_0\vartheta = T_2|(T_3|\mathbf{0}_m)$, for some T_2, T_3. Now,

$T_1' = T\{\|_0\vartheta \mapsto T_2|T_3\}\langle\equiv\rangle_{(P-ZeroPar,\|_0\vartheta\|_1)}T\{\|_0\vartheta \mapsto T_2|(T_3|\mathbf{0})\}$

$\langle\equiv\rangle_{(P-ParNew,\|_0\vartheta\|_1\|_1)}T\{\|_0\vartheta \mapsto T_2|(T_3|\mathbf{0}_m)\} = T$. Thus, $T_1' =$

$T\{\|_0\vartheta\|_1 \mapsto T@\|_0\vartheta\|_1\|_0\}\langle\equiv\rangle_{(P-ZeroPar,\|_0\vartheta\|_1)}T@\{\|_0\vartheta\|_1 \mapsto T@\|_0\vartheta\|_1\|_0|\mathbf{0}\}$

$\langle\equiv\rangle_{(P-ParNew,\|_0\vartheta\|_1)}T@\{\|_0\vartheta\|_1 \mapsto T@\|_0\vartheta\|_1\|_0|\mathbf{0}_m\} = T$.

$M\pi_{com}$ its premise is $T_0' \xrightarrow{\|_0\vartheta\langle\|_0\overline{ch}\langle K\rangle, \|_1 ch(Y)\rangle}_p T$, for such a T that $T@\|_0\vartheta = T_2|\mathbf{0}$,

for some T_2.

Now, $T_1' = T\{\|_0\vartheta \mapsto T_2\}\langle\equiv\rangle_{(P-ZeroPar,\|_0\vartheta)}T\{\|_0\vartheta \mapsto T_2|\mathbf{0}\} = T$. Thus,

$T_1' = T\{\|_0\vartheta \mapsto T@\|_0\vartheta\|_0\}\langle\equiv\rangle_{(P-ZeroPar,\|_0\vartheta)}T\{\|_0\vartheta \mapsto T@\|_0\vartheta\} = T$.

In all the above cases $T_0' \xrightarrow{\tau}_M T \equiv T_1$ holds because $\ell(\vartheta\langle\vartheta_0\pi_0, \vartheta_1\pi_1\rangle) = \tau$ and because the $\to_M$ transitions have no side-conditions on the parallel structure.

Extensible Objects: A Tutorial[*]

Viviana Bono

Università di Torino, Dipartimento di Informatica
corso Svizzera 185, 10149 Torino, Italy
bono@di.unito.it

Abstract. In the object-oriented realm, class-based languages dominate the world of production languages, but object-based languages have been extensively studied to provide the foundations of the object-oriented paradigm. Moreover, object-based languages are undergoing a Renaissance thanks to the growing popularity of scripting languanges, which are essentially object-based.

We focus on *extensible* object-based calculi, which feature method addition, together with classical method override and method invocation. Extensible objects can be seen as a way to bridge the gap between the class-based setting and the pure object-based setting.

Our aim is to provide a brief but rigorous view on extensible objects, following a thread suggested by the concept of "self" (which is the reference to the executing object) and its related typing problems.

This tutorial may be seen as a complementary contribution to the literature which has explored and compared extensively pure object-based and class-based foundations (for example, as in the books by Abadi and Cardelli, and Bruce, respectively), but which generally neglected extensible objects.

Keywords: object-oriented calculi, object-based calculi, extensible objects, types

1   Introduction

Object-oriented programming languages enjoy an ever growing popularity, as they are a tool for designing maintainable and expandable code, and are also suited for developing web applications and mobile code. It is possible to distinguish among class-based languages and object-based languages. Class-based ones relies on class hierarchies and objects are the class instances, while object-based ones offer objects as the only computational entities, on which also inheritance is defined. Production languages, such as Java [AG96], are usually class-based. They are considered suited to design software *in-the-large*, because they are well-coupled with software engineering principles, thanks to the abstraction mechanism offered by the class hierarchies. In object-based languages (such as Self

---

[*] This work has been partially supported by EU FET - Global Computing initiative, project DART IST-2001-33477, and by MIUR project NAPOLI. The funding bodies are not responsible for any use that might be made of the results presented here.

[US87], Obliq [Car95], or Cecil [CG]), new objects may be constructed from already existing objects, inheriting properties from the latter, so inheritance plays its rôle directly at the object level. Most object-based languages and calculi offer an *override* operation (to modify the components of the parent object), while few of them feature also an *addition* operation (to add new components to the parent object), giving rise to *extensible objects* and to a more complete form of inheritance which resembles class-based inheritance. Object-based languages have not been popular thus far as production languages, but have been the basis of more than fifteen years of study on the theoretical foundations of object-oriented languages. Object-oriented languages have introduced a number of ideas, concepts and techniques, which have proved to be useful and effective in programming, but which needed (and some of them still need) to be fully formalized, in order to understand, exploit and ameliorate them. Many techniques to prove program soundness have been developed in the object-based setting, because the concept of "object" is seen as more primitive from a formal-mathematical point of view than the concept of "class".

However, object-based languages, and in particular the ones featuring extensible objects, nowadays are becoming interesting also for practical purposes, thanks to the new challenges that come from the Internet. The growing use of a network as a primary environment for developing, distributing and running programs requires new supporting infrastructures. In particular, there is the need of a greater flexibility, allowing software to execute in different environments essentially without changes, and the requirement to develop working prototypical applications in a relatively short time. That is why scripting languages, like JavaScript [Fla99], that offer a set of easy-to-use primitives to program web applications, are becoming increasingly popular. There is a number of ongoing researches on foundations for scripting languages [BDG02,DG03], as well as for prototyping *delegation*-based languages [AD02b,ABDD03] (whose objects' main feature is to keep a link to the objects they were created from, which gives them the ability to *delegate* the execution of a method to another object). Research in these fields is especially oriented towards the design of type systems, balancing the need of a certain degree of safety during the program execution (in the style of "a well-typed program cannot go wrong") and the requirement of flexibility (not to restrain reusability and not to slow down the design of prototypes).

Extensible objects are the right tool to formalize both scripting and fast-prototyping calculi, as well as hybrid object-based/class-based languages (which try to exploit the best of both approaches as in, for instance, [AD02a]), and to experiment with appropriate type systems: therefore, extensible objects are back in use. With this tutorial we would like to give an essential survey on the basics of the topic, which is lacking in the object-oriented literature, that generally focused on pure object-based calculi (a reference on this topic is the book by Abadi and Cardelli [AC96a]), and on class-based languages (a reference on this other topic is the book by Bruce [Bru02]).

In this tutorial we present a functional object-based calculus with *fields* (otherwise called *instance variables*) and methods, equipped with method and field invocation, method and field addition and method and field override, and we analyze it in a classical way, that is, from the point of view of its type system. Prerequisites for this tutorial are a general knowledge of the object-oriented terminology and of functional calculi and their type systems. A book that may provide the appropriate background is the one by Pierce [Pie02]. Another reference that is useful to grasp the basics of the object-based language approach (also from an implementation point of view) is Chapter 4 of [AC96a].

The tutorial is structured as follows. Section 2 discusses extensible objects from the point of view of their typing, and presents some informal examples motivating the introduction of *MyType* inheritance. Section 3 introduces the calculus $\mathtt{Obj}^+$, through its syntax and operational semantics, then in Section 4 $\mathtt{Obj}^+$'s type system is illustrated. Section 5 gives an overview on a semantics by encoding of $\mathtt{Obj}^+$, casting some light on the formal meaning of extensible objects. Section 6 present a way of modelling classes following the "Classes = Extensible Objects + Encapsulation" model of [Fis96]. Finally, in Sections 7 we discuss some related work.

This paper is partly based on the material for the lectures given by the author at the "Mini-Ecole Chambéry-Turin d'Informatique Théorique" (29 January – 1 February 2003).

2   An Overview of *MyType*

A type discipline is important for object-oriented languages to ensure safety (i.e., absence of *message-not-understood* run-time errors), and the design of safe type systems depends on the knowledge of the semantics of the object-oriented language in question. In fact, safety is proved via a *Subject Reduction* theorem based on a (usually intuitive) operational semantics that mimic program execution. Subject Reduction states that if a program is well-typed (with type τ), then the result of its computation is well-typed (with type τ). From this theorem, it is possible to prove a formal safety property ensuring that "well-typed programs cannot go wrong".

Typing object-oriented programs is an hard task, because one must take in account many features which may be in conflict with each other. We will hint at the well-known conflict between inheritance and subtyping in Section 4.2, and instead discuss in this section some other important issues about the typing of object-oriented calculi. In particular, we will concentrate on the concept of *self* (sometimes called *this*, e.g., in Java, and here denoted with SELF), which is of paramount importance in object-oriented languages. SELF is a special variable that allows reference to the object executing the current method, and therefore permits the invocation of the sibling methods and the access to the object's fields.

We now overview briefly some concepts that will lead us to understand how to treat SELF in a functional object-based calculus with extensible objects.

Objects. Records are an intuitive way to model objects since both are collections of name/value pairs. The records-as-objects approach was in fact developed in the pioneering work on object-oriented calculi [CW85], in which inheritance was modeled by record subtyping. Unlike records, however, object methods should be able to modify fields and invoke sibling methods [Coo89]. To be capable of updating the object's internal state, methods must be functions of the host object (SELF). Therefore, objects must be *recursive* records. Moreover, SELF must be appropriately updated when a method is inherited, since new methods and fields may have been added and/or old ones redefined in the new host object.

Object Updates. If all object updates are imperative, SELF can be bound to the host object when the object is instantiated from the class. We refer to this approach as *early* SELF binding. SELF then always refers to the same record, which is modified imperatively in place by the object's methods. The main advantage of early binding is that the fixed-point operator (which gives to methods the possibility to reference the host object, i.e., SELF) has to be applied only once, at the time of object instantiation. If functional updates must be supported — which is, obviously, the case for purely functional object calculi — early binding does not work (see, for example, [AC96a], where early binding is called *recursive semantics*). With functional updates, each change in the object's state creates a new object. If SELF in methods is bound just once, at the time of object instantiation, it will refer to the old, incorrect object and not to the new, updated one. Therefore, SELF must be bound each time a method is invoked. We refer to this approach as *late* SELF binding.

Object Extension. Object extension in an object-based calculus is typically modelled by an operation that extends objects by adding new methods and fields to them. There are two constraints on such an operation: (*i*) the type system must prevent addition of a component to an object which already contains a component with the same name, and (*ii*) since an object may be extended again after addition, the actual host object may be larger than the object to which a method was originally added. Thus, method bodies must behave correctly in any extension of the original host object. Therefore, they must have a polymorphic type with respect to SELF. The fulfillment of the two constraints can be achieved, for instance, via polymorphic types built on row schemes [BF98] that use kinds to keep track of methods' presence. Even more complicated is the case when object extension must be supported in a functional calculus. In the functional case, all methods modifying an object have the type of SELF as their return type. Whenever an object is extended or has its components redefined (overriden), the type given to SELF in all inherited methods must be updated to take into account new and/or redefined components. Therefore, the type system should include the notion of the "type of SELF", called *MyType* (a.k.a. *SelfType*), so that the inherited methods can be specialized properly. Support for *MyType* generally leads to more complicated type systems, in which forms of recursive types are required. *MyType* can be supported by using row variables combined with recursive types [FHM94,FM95,Fis96], by means of special forms of second-order quantifiers such as the *Self* quantifier of [AC96a], or with match-bound type variables as in [BB99,BBC02] and in the calculus presented in this tutorial.

Our calculus $\mathtt{Obj}^+$, which will be introduced in Section 3, is chosen to give a complete example of a calculus with extensible objects and a functional semantics of method addition. This is, in our opinion, the most difficult semantics to grasp, and should serve the purpose of giving the reader enough tools to tackle other calculi.

We now introduce two examples to show the gain of introducing an appropriate type *MyType* for the host object SELF. The examples are expressed in a syntactic-sugared functional object-based pseudo-language (which offers the same features of the formal calculus we will introduce in Section 3) where:

1. we distinguish among fields and methods — in particular, each method uses SELF (i.e., it is a implicit function of SELF);
2. a dot '.' represents component selection;
3. the symbol ':=' stands for (functional) field override, and the keyword **extends** represents component addition;
4. ';' indicates concatenation of statements. This is codifiable in any functional language[1].

The first example we present is a simple and standard one.

let $Point \equiv \langle\; x = 0, \;\; move(d) = (\text{SELF}.x := (\text{SELF}.x + d); \textbf{return } \text{SELF})\; \rangle$
     in let $(ColorPoint \textbf{ extends } Point) \equiv \langle\; color = blue,$
                              $setcolor(c) = (\text{SELF}.color := c; \textbf{return } \text{SELF}),$
                                $\ldots\; \rangle$
         in $/ * \mathbf{main} * / \; ColorPoint.move.setcolor$

The object *ColorPoint* inherits the methods from *Point*; in particular, it inherits the method *move* which returns a modified SELF (i.e., a new object is created from the host object by modifying the field x through an update of the field x itself with a value computed from its current value plus a displacement d). The main program executes without errors, but within traditional type systems it is not typable, since *ColorPoint.move* would either be of type of *Point*, and *Point* does not have a *setcolor* method, or of the most general type possible (e.g., in Java it would be `Object`), again making impossible calling the specific methods of *ColorPoint*. The solution adopted in traditional programming languages to make this program type check is to use *typecasts*, which are explicit declarations made by the programmer on the expected actual type of the method result according to the type of the object the method is invoked upon. Typecasts are unsafe — the programmer must be "sure" about the actual type of the returned object, since little or even no static checking is performed on typecasts, as happens, respectively, in Java or in C++. Moreover typecasts certainly do not improve readability of code, which has a negative impact on the debugging phase. An alternative to typecasts is the introduction of *selftype* (otherwise known as *MyType*), with the meaning "the type of the current object", i.e., "the type of self". If we annotate **move** with the *MyType* as its return type, then *ColorPoint.move* and *ColorPoint* will have the *same* type and the main

---

[1] Of course in call-by-value calculi codification of statement concatenation is easier.

program will typecheck and work without typecasts, because *MyType specialize* along the *Point/ColorPoint* hierarchy (that is why the use of *MyType* is also known as *MyType specialization*).

The second example defines a linked/double-linked list, and it is largely inspired to a class-based example that can be found in Bruce's book [Bru02] on page 41.

```
let Node ≡ ⟨ val = 0,  next = null,
              getVal = (return SELF.val),
              setVal(nv) = (SELF.val := nv; return SELF),
              getNext = (return SELF.next),
              setNext(nn) = (SELF.next := nn; return SELF),
              attachRight(nn) = (return SELF.setNext(nn); ⟩
  in let (DbleNode extends Node) ≡ ⟨ prev = null,  getPrev = (return SELF.prev),
                                     setPrev(np) = (SELF.prev := np; return SELF),
                                     attachRight(nn) =
                                         (return nn.setPrev(SELF.setNext(nn))) ⟩
    in /* main */
```

We type this example by giving *MyType* as the type for the fields *next* and *prev*[2], as the return type of *setVal, getNext, setNext, attachRight, getPrev, setPrev*, and also as the type of the parameters *nn* of *setNext* and *attachRight*, and *np* of *setPrev*. Therefore, *setNext* has type $MyType \to MyType$, with *MyType* "changing of meaning" according to the object the method is invoked upon: *Node.getNext* has type $Nodetype \to Nodetype$, and *DbleNode.getNext* has type $DbleNodetype \to DbleNodetype$. The same "changing of meaning" is reproduced for *attachRight*.

Note that in an imperative setting, where the update of the fields can be done by side-effects, there is no need to return SELF, and, as a consequence, the return types of *setVal, setNext, attachRight, setPrev* can be a "void" type without losing expressive power. However, it would be impossible to give a sensible type to parameters such as *nn*, since *setNext*'s parameter must have the *same* type as the object on which *setNext* is invoked upon (i.e., it must have a *Node* type if it is invoked on a *Node*, or a *DbleNode* type if it is invoked on a *DbleNode*). Methods such as *setNext* are called *binary* methods [BCC+95]. Being able to type binary methods is a special feature of functional calculi supporting *MyType*.

3   The Calculus

Our specimen calculus is called Obj$^+$, and is a fully fledged object-based calculus that supports message passing and constructs for object update and extension. Obj$^+$ is a variant of the *Lambda Calculus of Objects* of [FHM94], the first calculus that provided a formal type system for extensible objects. The differences from the original proposal of [FHM94] are as follows: (*i*) method bodies are ς-abstractions over a SELF variable rather than λ-abstractions, and (*ii*) methods are distinguished from fields, both syntactically and semantically. The use of

---

[2] We assume to have a term constant *null* whose type is *MyType*.

ς-binders eases the comparisons between our calculus and related calculi in the literature (with ς-binders, the syntax of Obj^+ is a proper extension of the untyped ς-calculus [AC96a]). As for the distinction between methods and fields, a part from being a common practice in object-oriented languages and calculi, it arises as a result of a retrospective analysis of the interpretation of objects and object types. In fact, as proven in [BBC02], the qualitative nature of the target theory used in the interpretation changes significantly depending on the kind of overrides (otherwise called *updates* in the literature) supported by the source calculus. Specifically, recursive types suffice for the interpretation of *external* and *self-inflicted* field updates, and *external* method updates[3]. On the other hand, *self-inflicted* method updates require a non-trivial extension of the target theory, one in which recursion and least fixed points are available not only for types, but also for type operators.

Obj^+ is an untyped version of the calculus Ob^+ presented in [BBC02]. Ob^+ served the purpose of being the source calculus of a type preserving and computationally adequate interpretation into a functional calculus. Ob^+ was explicitly typed for a technical reason: to ensure that well-typed objects had unique types, a property that was missing in [FHM94] and necessary to have a fully formal encoding. We will give an overview of such encoding results in Section 5, but, since we are not going into technical details in the present tutorial, we preferred to use as a tutorial example an untyped calculus, which is easier to describe and work with.

The syntax of Obj^+ terms is defined by the following productions:

$$a, b, c ::= \textit{Terms}$$

x		*variable*
$\langle v_i = c_i{}^{i \in I}, m_j = \varsigma(x)b_j\{x\}^{j \in J} \rangle$		*object*
		(v_i's and m_j's distinct)
$a.v$		*field selection*
$a.v \leftarrow b$		*field update*
$a.v \leftarrow\!\!+\, b$		*field addition*
$a \circ m$		*method invocation*
$a \circ m \leftarrow \varsigma(x)b\{x\}$		*method update*
$a \circ m \leftarrow\!\!+\, \varsigma(x)b\{x\}$		*method addition*

Terms of the form $\langle v_i = c_i{}^{i \in I}, m_j = \varsigma(x)b_j\{x\}^{j \in J} \rangle$ denote objects, i.e., collections of named fields and methods that can be selected, updated, or added. As in [AC96a], each method is an abstraction of the host object SELF, represented by the ς-bound variable x. The notation $b\{x\}$ emphasizes that the variable x may occur free in b. Given $b\{x\}$, we write $b\{a\}$ (or, equivalently $b\{x := a\}$) to denote the term that results from substituting the term a for every free occurrence of x in b.

---

[3] The adjective *external* refers to invocation/override operations performed on objects, while the adjective *self-inflicted* refers to invocation/override operations performed on SELF, inside a method body.

Each of the primitive operations on objects come in two versions, for fields and methods. $a \circ m$ invokes the method associated with the label m in a, while $a \bullet v$ selects the field v; $a \circ m \leftarrow \varsigma(x)b\{x\}$ replaces the current body of m in a with $\varsigma(x)b\{x\}$, while $a \bullet v \leftarrow b$ performs the corresponding operation on the field v; finally, $a \circ m \leftarrow\!\!+ \varsigma(x)b\{x\}$ extends a by adding a new method m with associated body $\varsigma(x)b\{x\}$, and $a \bullet v \leftarrow\!\!+ b$ does the same with the field v.

Terms that differ only for renaming of bound variables, or for the relative order of method and field labels are considered equal, i.e., syntactically identical: we write $a \equiv b$ to state that a and b are equal. To ease the notation, we use ℓ to denote method or field labels whenever the distinction between methods and fields may be disregarded soundly, and write $a \cdot \ell$ to denote $a \circ \ell$ or $a \bullet \ell$.

The evaluation of $\mathtt{Obj}^+$ expressions is defined by a big-step operational semantics that rewrites closed terms into results[4]. A *result* r is defined to be a term in object form. We write $a \Downarrow_o r$ to denote that evaluating a closed term a returns the result r, and say that a converges – written $a \Downarrow_o$ – if there exists a result r such that $a \Downarrow_o r$. The operational semantics is defined below, rule by rule, and it is an extension of the corresponding semantics in [AC96a] that handles field and method addition. The following notation is used in the operational semantics rules:

$$\langle \ell_i = \mathbf{b}_i\{x\}^{i \in I \cup J} \rangle \triangleq \langle v_i = c_i{}^{i \in I}, m_j = \varsigma(x)b_j\{x\}^{j \in J} \rangle$$
$$a \cdot \ell \triangleq a \circ \ell \text{ or } a \bullet \ell$$
$$a \cdot \ell \leftarrow \mathbf{b}\{x\} \triangleq a \circ \ell \leftarrow \varsigma(x)b\{x\} \text{ or } a \bullet \ell \leftarrow b$$
$$a \cdot \ell \leftarrow\!\!+ \mathbf{b}\{x\} \triangleq a \circ \ell \leftarrow\!\!+ \varsigma(x)b\{x\} \text{ or } a \bullet \ell \leftarrow\!\!+ b$$

The rules are rather intuitive, and for the ones dealing with updates and additions we do not need to distinguish among fields and methods.

Results : $r = \langle v_i = c_i{}^{i \in I}, m_j = \varsigma(x)b_j\{x\}^{j \in J} \rangle$

(Select$_\mathrm{v}$) $\dfrac{a \Downarrow_o \langle \ldots, v_j = c_j, \ldots \rangle \quad c_j \Downarrow_o r}{a \bullet v_j \Downarrow_o r}$

(Select$_\mathrm{m}$) $\dfrac{a \Downarrow_o \widehat{a} \quad b_j\{\widehat{a}\} \Downarrow_o r \quad (\widehat{a} \equiv \langle \ldots, m_j = \varsigma(x)b_j\{x\}, \ldots \rangle)}{a \circ m_j \Downarrow_o r}$

(Update) $\dfrac{a \Downarrow_o \langle \ell_i = \mathbf{b}_i\{x\}^{i \in I \cup J} \rangle \quad k \in I \cup J}{a \cdot \ell_k \leftarrow \mathbf{b}\{x\} \Downarrow_o \langle \ell_i = \mathbf{b}_i\{x\}^{i \in I \cup J - \{k\}}, \ell_k = \mathbf{b}\{x\} \rangle}$

(Extend) $\dfrac{a \Downarrow_o \langle \ell_i = \mathbf{b}_i\{x\}^{i \in I \cup J} \rangle \quad \ell \notin \{\ell_i\}^{i \in I \cup J}}{a \cdot \ell \leftarrow\!\!+ \mathbf{b}\{x\} \Downarrow_o \langle \ell = \mathbf{b}\{x\}, \ell_i = \mathbf{b}_i\{x\}^{i \in I \cup J} \rangle}$

Field selection and method invocation (rules (Select$_\mathrm{v}$) and (Select$_\mathrm{m}$)) are computed by evaluating the recipient of the selection/invocation to a result (that

---

[4] The definition of a small-step operational semantics can be found in Appendix A.3.

is, to an object), then by selecting and evaluating the sought component body. The only difference is that a retrieved method body must have the host object substituted for the SELF variable (represented formally in the calculus by x) before being evaluated, to accomplish with the intended semantics of objects, so to make it possible to invoke sibling methods and access object fields. Updating (rule (Update)) must ensure that the component we want to update exists in the object which the recipient of the updating operation evaluates to, before updating the component. Vice-versa, for the extension (rule (Extend)) we must ensure that the component is not present yet before adding it.

3.1 Formalized Examples

In this section, we present some examples illustrating the behavior of the calculus Obj^+. We start from an expression representing an infinite computation:

$$\Omega \equiv \langle m = \varsigma(x)x \circ m \rangle \circ m$$

This expression reduces to itself forever, therefore never to a result r (i.e., it does not converge), as the following derivation in the big-step semantics shows.

$$
(\text{Select}_m) \ \frac{\begin{array}{c} \langle m = \varsigma(x)x \circ m \rangle \Downarrow_o \langle m = \varsigma(x)x \circ m \rangle \\ (x \circ m)\{\langle m = \varsigma(x)x \circ m \rangle\} \equiv \Omega \\ (x \circ m)\{\langle m = \varsigma(x)x \circ m \rangle\} \Downarrow_o ?? \end{array}}{\Omega \Downarrow_o ??}
$$

It is possible to show formally that Obj^+ is Turing-complete (that is, it can codify all partial recursive functions). In [FHM94], an encoding in the Lambda Calculus of Objects of Object numerals, Zero test, Predecessor and fixed-point operator (using the Ω expression shown above, written in their syntax) is presented. We prefer to take the Abadi-Cardelli's approach (presented on pages 66–67 of [AC96a]), that is, encoding the untyped lambda calculus in Obj^+ (we recall that the symbol ':=' denotes a substitution):

$[\![x]\!] \equiv x$ (variable);
$[\![a\ b]\!] \equiv [\![a]\!] \bullet [\![b]\!]$ (application), where $p \bullet q \equiv (p.arg \leftarrow q) \circ val$;
$[\![\lambda x.a\{x\}]\!] \equiv \langle\, arg = y, val = \varsigma(x) [\![a\{x\}]\!] \{x := x.arg\} \,\rangle$
(lambda abstraction),
with y a fresh variable.

The reader may want to check that this encoding preserves β-reduction.

Since Obj^+ is Turing-complete, we can add integers as shortcuts for numerals to Obj^+ terms, in order to ease the task of writing examples. An example that we could not left out is the Point/ColorPoint one, expressed in the Obj^+ syntax:

$\text{Point} \equiv \langle\, pos = 0, move = \varsigma(x)(x.pos \leftarrow ((x.pos) + 1)) \,\rangle$
$\text{ColorPoint} \equiv \text{Point}.c \leftarrow\!\!+\ = blue$

It is possible to note that a *move* is performed by a self-inflicted field selection $(x.pos)$, that returns the value of *pos* which is then incremented by 1, and through an updating of *pos* with the new value via a self-inflicted override $(x.pos \leftarrow (\ldots))$. Let us consider now some computations:

ColorPoint reduces in few operational big-steps to the object:
$\langle\, pos = 0, move = \varsigma(x)(x.pos \leftarrow ((x.pos) + 1)), c = blue \,\rangle$;

ColorPoint $\circ$ *move* reduces in few operational big-steps to the object:
$\langle\, pos = 1, move = \varsigma(x)(x.pos \leftarrow ((x.pos) + 1)), c = blue \,\rangle$.

We advise the reader to perform both of the above reductions in detail. The second one, in particular, shows how the host-object SELF-substitution works.

4   Types and Typing Rules

In this section we describe the type system of the calculus $\mathtt{Obj}^+$. The syntax of types is as follows.

$$A, B, C ::= \quad Types$$
$$X, U \qquad\qquad\qquad\qquad variable$$
$$\mathtt{pro}(X)\langle\!\langle v_i : C_i{}^{i \in I}, m_j : B_j\{X\}^{j \in J} \rangle\!\rangle \ object\ type\ (v_i\text{'s and }m_j\text{'s distinct})$$

An object type $A \equiv \mathtt{pro}(X)\langle\!\langle v_i : C_i{}^{i \in I}, m_j : B_j\{X\}^{j \in J} \rangle\!\rangle$ is the type of all the objects with fields v_i ($i \in I$), and methods m_j ($j \in J$). The keyword $\mathtt{pro}$ [5] binds all free occurrences of X in the $B_j\{X\}^{j \in J}$. When invoked, each field v_i returns a value of type C_i, and each method m_j returns a value of type $B_j\{A\}$, that is the type B_j with every free occurrence of the variable X substituted by the type A itself. This type substitution reflects the *self-substitution* semantics of method invocation. As in the syntax of terms, we use the notation $\mathtt{pro}(X)\langle\!\langle \ell_i : B_i\{X\}^{i \in I} \rangle\!\rangle$ for $\mathtt{pro}$-types, whenever there is no reason to distinguish methods from fields. Object types that differ in the order of the component labels, or for the names of bound variables are considered equal: we write $A \equiv B$ to state that the types A and B are equal.

As hinted in Section 2, functional method addition needs a form of *MyType* inheritance, in order to specialize the method types as methods are inherited. The typing rules for $\mathtt{Obj}^+$ rely on the form of match-bounded polymorphism that was studied in [BB99] for the *Lambda Calculus of Objects* [FHM94]. Polymorphic types arise in the typing of methods as a result of (*i*) method bodies being dependent on SELF, and (*ii*) the possibility for a method to be invoked on extensions of the object where it was first installed. To ensure sound typing of method invocation, method bodies are typed in a context that assumes the so-called *MyType* for the SELF variable x. In this context, *MyType* is a *match-bounded type variable* representing the types of the objects resulting from *all the possible extensions* of the host object with new methods and fields. The *matching* relation ($<\!\#$) was introduced in [Bru94]. A full study about matching and its various application other than *MyType* inheritance can be found in [Bru02].

---

[5] The notation $\mathtt{pro}$ was introduced in [FHM94] and it is maintained here for historical reasons.

The most significant rule for matching in our context is the following:

(Match pro)

$$\frac{\Gamma \vdash \mathtt{pro}(X)\langle\!\langle \ell_i : B_i\{X\}^{i \in 1..n+k}\rangle\!\rangle}{\Gamma \vdash \mathtt{pro}(X)\langle\!\langle \ell_i : B_i\{X\}^{i \in 1..n+k}\rangle\!\rangle \mathrel{\#\!\!\#} \mathtt{pro}(X)\langle\!\langle \ell_i : B_i\{X\}^{i \in 1..n}\rangle\!\rangle}$$

This rule superficially looks like the *subtyping-in-width rule*, but the use of matching in place of the more standard relation of subtyping is central to the type system, because matching, unlike subtyping, does not support subsumption: since objects are extensible, absence of subsumption on pro-types is crucial for type soundness (see Section 4.2 for a quick overview on the problem, and [BB99] for a deeper discussion).

All of the typing rules for $\mathtt{Obj}^+$ are collected in Appendix A.4. The most interesting rules are given and commented below.

(Val Object: $A \equiv \mathtt{pro}(X)\langle\!\langle v_i : C_i{}^{i \in I}, m_j : B_j\{X\}^{j \in J}\rangle\!\rangle$)

$$\frac{\Gamma \vdash c_i : C_i \qquad \Gamma, U \mathrel{\#\!\!\#} A, x : U \vdash b_j\{x\} : B_j\{U\} \qquad \forall\, i \in I, j \in J}{\Gamma \vdash \langle v_i = c_i{}^{i \in I}, m_j = \varsigma(x)b_j\{x\}^{j \in J}\rangle : A}$$

(VAL OBJECT) is the rule for object formation. *MyType* is the type variable U match-bounded in the context of the typing judgements of method bodies, and it is given to the SELF variable x as its type $(x{:}U)$. Note that the return type of each method depends polymorphically on *MyType*: this allows the (return) type of methods to be soundly specialized upon method addition. The rule also emphasizes the distinction between methods and fields: since the latter do not depend on SELF, their type need not depend on *MyType*.

(Val Select)

$$\frac{\Gamma \vdash a : A \qquad \Gamma \vdash A \mathrel{\#\!\!\#} \mathtt{pro}(X)\langle\!\langle \ell : B\{X\}\rangle\!\rangle}{\Gamma \vdash a \cdot \ell : B\{A\}}$$

(VAL SELECT) is the rule for field and method invocation. An invocation for (the field or) method ℓ on an object a requires a to have a pro-type containing the label ℓ. The result of the call has the type B listed in the pro-type of a, with A substituted for X (if ℓ is a field, this substitution is vacuous). Note that A may either be a pro-type matching $\mathtt{pro}(X)\langle\!\langle \ell : B\{X\}\rangle\!\rangle$, or else an unknown type (i.e., a type variable) occurring (match-bounded) in the context Γ. Rules like the one above are sometimes referred to as *structural rules* [AC96a], and their use is critical for an adequate rendering of *MyType* polymorphism: it is the ability to refer to possibly unknown types that allows methods to act parametrically over any $U \mathrel{\#\!\!\#} A$, where U is the type of SELF, and A is a given pro-type.

(Val Field Addition: $A^+ \equiv \mathtt{pro}(X)\langle\!\langle \ell : B\{X\}, \ell_i : B_i\{X\}^{i \in I}\rangle\!\rangle$)

$$\frac{\Gamma \vdash a : \mathtt{pro}(X)\langle\!\langle \ell_i : B_i\{X\}^{i \in I}\rangle\!\rangle \quad \Gamma \vdash c : B \quad (\ell \neq \ell_i \; \forall i \in I)}{\Gamma \vdash a.\ell \leftarrow\!\!+ c : A^+}$$

(Val Method Addition: $A^+ \equiv \mathtt{pro}(X)\langle\!\langle \ell : B\{X\}, \ell_i : B_i\{X\}^{i \in I}\rangle\!\rangle$)

$$\frac{\Gamma \vdash a : \mathtt{pro}(X)\langle\!\langle \ell_i : B_i\{X\}^{i \in I}\rangle\!\rangle \quad \Gamma, U \not\!\!\#\, A^+, x : U \vdash b\{x\} : B\{U\}}{(\ell \neq \ell_i \; \forall i \in I)}$$
$$\Gamma \vdash a \circ \ell \leftarrow\!\!+ \varsigma(x)b\{x\} : A^+$$

(VAL FIELD ADDITION) and (VAL METHOD ADDITION) are the typing rules for field and method additions. The label ℓ is assumed to be different from all of the ℓ_i's, $i \in I$, and the type of the object a being extended to be a pro-type: since no subtyping is available on pro-types, this implies that an object extension is typed with *exact* knowledge of the type of a. Note that in rule (Val Method Addition) the return type of the added method depends polymorphically on *MyType*, while in the rule (Val Field Addition) the field type is not required to depend on *MyType*.

(Val Field Update)

$$\frac{\Gamma \vdash a : A \quad \Gamma \vdash A \not\!\!\#\, \mathtt{pro}(X)\langle\!\langle v : C\rangle\!\rangle \quad \Gamma \vdash c : C}{\Gamma \vdash a.v \leftarrow c : A}$$

(VAL FIELD UPDATE) is a structural rule: as in (Val Select), the type A of the object a being updated may either be a type variable, or a pro-type. When it is a pro-type, the update is *external*; when it is a type variable, the update is *self-inflicted*. The judgement $\Gamma \vdash A \not\!\!\#\, \mathtt{pro}(X)\langle\!\langle v : C\rangle\!\rangle$ requires A (hence $a : A$) to have a field v with type C, and the remaining judgement ensures that the update preserves the type of the object.

(Val Method Update (external only)): $(A \equiv \mathtt{pro}(X)\langle\!\langle v_i : C_i^{\,i \in I}, m_j : B_j\{X\}^{j \in J}\rangle\!\rangle)$

$$\frac{\Gamma \vdash a : A \quad \Gamma, U \not\!\!\#\, A, x : U \vdash b\{x\} : B_k\{U\} \quad k \in J}{\Gamma \vdash a \circ m_k \leftarrow \varsigma(x)b\{x\} : A}$$

(VAL METHOD UPDATE) handles the case of updates for methods: unlike the corresponding rule for fields, (Val Method Update) is non-structural, as the type A of the object being updated is required to be a pro-type. As a consequence, method updates may *not* be self-inflicted; instead, it is available as an *external* operation which can only be performed from outside the object. This restriction could safely be lifted, without consequences on the operational behavior of the source calculus or on the operational soundness of the type system. The rule accounting both for external and self-inflicted method updates would have the following form:

(Val Method Update' (external and self-inflicted))

$$\frac{\Gamma \vdash a : A \quad \Gamma \vdash A \mathbin{\#} \mathtt{pro}(X)\langle\!\langle m_k : B_k\{X\} \rangle\!\rangle \quad \Gamma, U \mathbin{\#} A, x : U \vdash b\{x\} : B_k\{U\}}{\Gamma \vdash a \circ m_k \leftarrow \varsigma(x)b\{x\} : A}$$

On the one hand, type soundness in the presence of both external and self-inflicted method updates can be proved as in the calculus described in [BB99]. On the other hand, as we mentioned, self-inflicted method updates do have significant impact on the semantic interpretation, so, since we want to account for the semantics by encoding (in Section 5), is worth to present the two rules separately.

We conclude the presentation of the source calculus stating the main properties of the type system. Proofs for the results below are essentially the same as those given in full detail in [BB99].

Theorem 1 (Subject Reduction). *If $\Gamma \vdash a : A$ in* $\mathtt{Obj}^+$, *and $a \Downarrow_o r$, then also $\Gamma \vdash r : A$.*

Theorem 2 (Soundness). *Let c be a closed expression such that $\varnothing \vdash c : A$ for some type A. Then:*

1. *if c is one of: $a \circ \ell \leftarrow \varsigma(x)b\{x\}$, $a.\ell \leftarrow b$, $a \cdot \ell$, and $a \Downarrow_o r$, then r is an object containing a label ℓ.*
2. *if c is one of: $a \circ \ell \leftarrow\!\!+ \varsigma(x)b\{x\}$, $a.\ell \leftarrow\!\!+ b$, and $a \Downarrow_o r$, then r is an object that does not contain a label ℓ.*

The soundness theorem states that if an expression is well-typed, no *message-not-understood* error will arise at run-time.

4.1   Some Examples of Typing

As we added integers to the $\mathtt{Obj}^+$ terms, we now consider also their type int to type the Point/ColorPoint example:

$$\mathtt{Point} \equiv \langle\, pos = 0, move = \varsigma(x)(x.pos \leftarrow_X ((x.pos) + 1)) \,\rangle \;:$$
$$\mathtt{pro}(X)\langle\!\langle pos\text{:}int, move\text{:}X \rangle\!\rangle;$$

$$\mathtt{ColorPoint} \equiv \mathtt{Point}.c \leftarrow\!\!+ = \mathtt{blue} \;:\; \mathtt{pro}(X)\langle\!\langle pos\text{:}int, move\text{:}X, c\text{:}color \rangle\!\rangle$$

The type derivation is left to the reader as an exercise. We will show, instead, the type derivation for $\langle\, m = \varsigma(x)x \circ m \,\rangle : \mathtt{pro}(X)\langle\!\langle m\text{:}X \rangle\!\rangle$ ($\langle\, m = \varsigma(x)x \circ m \,\rangle$ is part of Ω, presented in Section 3.1). We need basically[6] a (Val Object) application and a (Val Select) application (from bottom to top).

$$\frac{\dfrac{x : U \vdash x : U \quad U \mathbin{\#} \mathtt{pro}(X)\langle\!\langle m\text{:}X \rangle\!\rangle \vdash U \mathbin{\#} \mathtt{pro}(X)\langle\!\langle m\text{:}X \rangle\!\rangle}{U \mathbin{\#} \mathtt{pro}(X)\langle\!\langle m\text{:}X \rangle\!\rangle, x : U \vdash x \circ m : X\{U\} \equiv U}}{\Gamma \vdash \langle\, m = \varsigma(x)x \circ m \,\rangle : \mathtt{pro}(X)\langle\!\langle m\text{:}X \rangle\!\rangle}$$

---

[6] We omit checking well-formedness for $x : U$ and $U \mathbin{\#} \mathtt{pro}(X)\langle\!\langle m\text{:}X \rangle\!\rangle$ in the derivation.

4.2   Subtyping

A concept of paramount importance in the object-oriented realm is *subtyping*: A is a subtype of B, written $A <: B$, iff a value of type A can be used in any context expecting a value of type B. Connected to the notion of subtyping is the *subsumption* rule: if P:A and $A <: B$, then P:B. If $A <: B$, a value of type A can be: (*i*) used for a parameter of type B; and (*ii*) assigned to a variable of type B, so that the value of an expression can correspond to a subtype of its static type. We discuss briefly subtyping for the most common structures used in the object-oriented setting, and then some anomalies by showing three examples.

Subtype for Records (co-variant). If $r : \{l_i : B_i\}^{i \in 1..k}$ then $r.l_i : B_i$. When is $\{l_j : A_j\}^{j \in 1..n} <: \{l_i : B_i\}^{i \in 1..k}$? Assume $r' : \{l_j : A_j\}^{j \in 1..n}$. We still need $r'.l_i : B_i$, $i \in 1..k$. Therefore, $\{l_j : A_j\}^{j \in 1..n} <: \{l_i : B_i\}^{i \in 1..k}$ if $k \leq n$ (*subtyping-in-width*) and $\forall\, i \in 1..k, A_i <: B_i$ (*subtyping-in-depth*).

Subtype for Functions (co/contra-variant). If $F : A \to B$ and $a : A$ then $F(a) : B$. When is $A' \to B' <: A \to B$? If $F' : A' \to B'$, we still need $F'(a) : B$. Therefore, $A' \to B' <: A \to B$ if $A <: A'$ and $B' <: B$, i.e., subtyping behaves contra-variant for parameters and co-variant for results. This rather counter-intuitive behavior is source of "troubles" when subtyping on function types, obviously applied to methods, meets inheritance.

Example 1: Inheritance Is Not Subtyping [CHC90]. Can inherited methods break when called on "subobjects"? Unfortunately, yes. Let us consider this fragment of pseudo-code that we assume inserted in a program `let`-defining two *Node*'s called $nd1, nd2$ and a *DbleNode* called dnd (*Node* and *DbleNode* where introduced in Section 2).

```
...in
    let Break ≡ ⟨ breakit(n1, n2) = n1.attachRight(n2) ⟩
        in /* main */ Break.breakit(nd1, nd2); Break.breakit(dnd, nd1)
```

The first call $Break.breakit(nd1, nd2)$ is safe, but a problem arises from the second call $Break.breakit(dnd, nd1)$ because it triggers $dnd.attachRight(nd1)$, which in turn tries to set the non-existing *prev* of $nd1$, making the program crash (since the invoked *attachRight* is the one of *DbleNode*). This happens being *DbleNode* not a subtype of *Node*, because of *MyType* appearing in a contra-variant position in *attachRight* (i.e., as the type of its parameter)[7].

We can conclude that $\mathtt{pro}(X)\langle\!\langle m_j : A_j\{X\}^{j \in 1..n}\rangle\!\rangle <: \mathtt{pro}(X)\langle\!\langle m_i : B_i\{X\}^{i \in 1..k}\rangle\!\rangle$ if and only if $k \leq n$ and for all $i \in 1..k$, $A_i\{X\} <: B_i\{X\}$, *but* no $B_i\{X\}$ has a contra-variant occurrence of X, that is, no parameters in the methods of the supertype can have the same type *MyType* of SELF.

Therefore, if two object types are subtypes, then they match, but not vice-versa. For example (using the usual informal notation), *DbleNodetype* $\#$ *Nodetype* but not *DbleNodetype* $<:$ *Nodetype*. For a careful study of the conflict between inheritance and subtyping, see the work of Castagna et al. (for

---

[7] These problems are well-known in the recursive type setting, and *MyType* is nothing else than a form of recursive type.

instance, in [Cas96]), where, among other things, another approach for object-oriented languages is presented, alternative to the "objects-as-records" one: the "methods-as-overloaded-functions" model.

Example 2: Subtyping-in-Width versus Method/Field Addition. In an object with two components ℓ_1 and ℓ_2 of types A_1 and A_2, the component ℓ_1 may require ℓ_2 to be of type A_2. "Forgetting" ℓ_2 by subtyping may result in a possible re-addition of ℓ_2 with another, incompatible, type A_3, making the invocation of ℓ_1 fail (even though the whole expression is well-typed).

Example 3: Subtyping-in-Depth versus Method/Field Override. Consider the following object:

$$\texttt{UseLog} \equiv \langle\, n = 10, m = \varsigma(x)Log(x.n)\,\rangle : \texttt{pro}(X)\langle\!\langle n : posint, m : int \rangle\!\rangle$$

The method m selects the value of the field n and calculates its base-10 logarithm. Now, by subtyping, $posint <: int$, so we may have $\texttt{UseLog} : \texttt{pro}(X)\langle\!\langle n : int, m : int \rangle\!\rangle$, which would allow to update n with a negative value. This clearly would make the invocation of m fail (even though the whole expression is well-typed).

In the literature, there are two main ways to make subtyping and operations on objects living together harmlessly.

– Limiting subtyping, for instance by collecting the mutual dependencies among methods and allowing subtyping applications only if they involve methods that are not used by other methods [BL95,Rém98].
– Defining two states in which an object can be. In *state 1*, objects can be extended/overridden (i.e., in this state, objects play a rôle similar to the one of classes), while in *state 2*, objects can be subtyped.

The solution of [FM95] belongs to the second "family", and it is formalized by the following rule:

(Sub $\texttt{probj}$FM95)

$$\frac{\Gamma, Y, X <: Y \vdash B_i'\{X\} <: B_i\{Y\} \qquad (i = 1..n)}{\Gamma \vdash \texttt{probj}(X)\langle\!\langle \ell_i : B_i'\{X\}^{i\in 1..n+k} \rangle\!\rangle <: \texttt{obj}(Y)\langle\!\langle \ell_i : B_i\{Y\}^{i\in 1..n} \rangle\!\rangle}$$

When an object is in its $\texttt{pro}$-totypical state, it can be modified by override and addition, but subtyping does not apply. When an object changes state, becoming a "true" $\texttt{obj}$-ect, it is as "sealed" and cannot be modified anymore, but then subtyping (both in-width and in-depth, as the above rule shows) applies. The drawback of this approach is that, since the passage from the $\texttt{pro}$-state to the $\texttt{obj}$-state is done by using the same subtyping rule, when an object contains a binary method it cannot be "promoted" from $\texttt{pro}$- to $\texttt{obj}$-, otherwise we run into the problem described in the Example 1 above.

5   Semantics by Encoding

Interpretations of object-oriented programming are typically defined in terms of reductions to procedural or functional programming, and help provide sound and formal foundations to object-oriented languages and their specific constructs and techniques. The reduction is not straightforward: difficulties arise principally at the level of types, when trying to validate the subtyping properties of the source languages. A number of object encodings for the so-called *object-based* calculi have subsequently been proposed by [PT94,AC96a,ACV96,BCP97], and recently by [Cra99]. These interpretations apply to a rich variety of object calculi with constructs for object formation, message send and (functional) method update: they succeed in validating the operational semantics of these calculi as well as the expected subtyping relationships over object types; finally they extend smoothly to the case of *Self Types* and other object-oriented constructs. None of these proposals, however, appears to scale to calculi of extensible objects, where there are two major difficulties in dealing with their interpretations. The first is the presence of the *MyType*. The second difficulty arises from the co-existence of subtyping and object extension, two mechanisms that we have seen being essentially incompatible in Section 4.2, and hence difficult to combine in sound and flexible type systems. Summarizing, the fact that inheritance and client-use of the objects components happen both at the same level, that is, on the same entities (i.e., the objects), complicates the semantics a great deal.

In this section, we summarize the paper [BBC02], where an interpretation of extensible objects is presented that addresses both these problems. In particular, subtyping is accounted for by distinguishing between extensible and nonextensible objects, as proposed by [FM95] (their main rule is (Sub probjFM95), presented in Section 4.2). The interpretation is an encoding: the target calculus is a polymorphic λ-calculus with records, recursive types and (higher-order) subtyping. Within this calculus, an extensible object is interpreted as a pair of two components: the object *generator*, which is made available to contexts where the structure of the object is extended with new methods or fields, and the *interface*, a recursive record that provides direct access for the object's clients to the methods and fields of the object itself. Technically, the two components are collectively grouped into a single recursive record by a technique which is inspired by, and generalizes, the *split-method* interpretation of [ACV96]. The resulting interpretation is faithful to the source calculus in that (*i*) it preserves the validity of typing judgements, and (*ii*) it validates the operational semantics, i.e., the encoding is computationally adequate. Besides providing a fully formal interpretation of extensible objects, the encoding of [BBC02] also clarifies the relationship between calculi of extensible and nonextensible objects presented in the recent literature. In fact, the encoding specializes smoothly to the case of nonextensible objects and object types, validating the expected subtyping relationships. Although the focus is one particular calculus – specifically, on one approach to combining object extension with subtyping – the translation is sufficiently general to capture other notions of subtyping over object types (a notable example are the rules for covariant subtyping of [AC96a]).

5.1   The Target Calculus $F_{\omega<:\mu}$

The target calculus of the translation is a variant of the polymorphic typed λ-calculus $F^{\omega}_{\leq:}$. We briefly review the syntax, introducing notation and terminology on type operators and recursive types.

	K ::=	*Kinds*	
		T	type
		K $\Rightarrow$ K	type operator

	A, B ::=	*Constructors*	
		X	constructor variable
		Top	greatest constructor of kind T
		A$\rightarrow$B	function type
		$[m_1 : \text{B}, \ldots, m_k : \text{B}]$	record type
		$\forall (X <: \text{A} :: \text{K})\text{A}$	bounded universal type
		$\mu(X)\text{A}$	recursive type
		$\lambda(X :: \text{K})\text{B}$	operator
		B(A)	operator application

	M, N ::=	*Expressions*	
		x	variable
		$\lambda(x : A)M$	abstraction
		$M\,N$	application
		$\Lambda(X <: \text{A} :: \text{K})e$	type-abstraction
		$M\,\text{A}$	type-application
		$[m_1 = M_1, \ldots, m_k = M_k]$	record
		$M.m$	record selection
		$\texttt{fold}(\text{A}, M)$	recursive fold
		$\texttt{unfold}(M)$	recursive unfold
		$\texttt{let } x = M \texttt{ in } N$	local definition
		$\texttt{letrec } f(x : A) : \text{B} = M \texttt{ in } N$	recursive local definition

A type operator is a function from types to types. Types and type operators are collectively called *constructors*. The notation A :: K indicates that the constructor A has kind K. The typing rules, found in the paper [BBC02], are standard (see also Chapter 20 of [AC96a]). Type equality is defined by judgements of the form $\Gamma \vdash \text{A} \leftrightarrow \text{B}$, modulo renaming of bound variables. The following notation is used throughout: $Op \equiv \text{T} \Rightarrow \text{T}$ is the kind of type operators, $\text{A} \leq \text{B}$ denotes subtyping over type operators, whereas $\text{A} <: \text{B}$ denotes subtyping over the kind T of types. We also use the following shorthands from [AC95] to emphasize the relationships between type operators and their fixed points. Given the type operator A :: Op, $\text{A}^{*} \equiv \mu(X)\text{A}(X)$ is the (least) fixed point of A; dually, given the recursive type A :: T $\equiv \mu(X)\text{B}(X)$, $\text{A}^{\text{OP}} \equiv \lambda(X)\text{B}(X)$ :: Op is the type operator whose (least) fixed point is A. As in [AC95], A^{OP} is defined in terms of the syntactic form $\mu(X)\text{B}(X)$ of A: the notation A^{OP} is well-defined because we rely on a weak notion of type equality whereby a recursive type is isomorphic, rather than equal, to its unfoldings. Results, or values, are lambda abstractions, records, and recursive folds. We write $M \Downarrow_f r$ to denote that M (a closed term) evaluates to a result r, and say that M converges – written $M \Downarrow_f$ – if there exists a result r such that $M \Downarrow_f r$. A standard call-by-name operational semantics for this target calculus can be found in [BBC02].

5.2   Encoding of Extensible Objects and Types: An Overview

To understand the encoding and its subtleties, it is useful to proceed by steps, and first discuss solutions that are intuitively simple but do not give a correct encoding. We keep the discussion informal, and look at a simplified case in which objects have no fields, and for which the only available operators are method addition and invocation. Then we extend the analysis to objects with fields, and show how to account for field selection, addition and update. Finally we look at method updates, distinguishing *external* from *self-inflicted* updates: we show that the former can be encoded in $F_{\omega<:\mu}$ with no additional machinery, and discuss the extensions to $F_{\omega<:\mu}$ required to handle the latter. The paper [BBC02] presents the fully-formal encoding.

Failures of Self-application. We first consider objects without fields. Looking at the reduction rules, it would be tempting to interpret these objects as in the *self-application* semantics of [Kam88]. In this semantics, methods are functions of the SELF parameter, objects are records of such functions, and method invocation is field selection plus self-application. This semantics was originally proposed as an interpretation of nonextensible objects, and its properties are well-known [AC96a]: it works well in the untyped case, but fails in the typed case because it does not validate the expected subtyping relationships over object types.

A similar problem arises for our extensible objects, even though pro-types can *not* be subtyped. Following the self-application semantics, one would interpret the type $\mathtt{pro}(X)\langle\!\langle m{:}B\rangle\!\rangle$ as the recursive record type $A \equiv \mu(X)[m : X \to B]$ which solves the type equation $A = [m : A{\to}B]$. Now, given (the interpretation of) an object $a : A$, consider extending a with (the interpretation of) a new method $m' = \lambda(s)b$. The extension is interpreted as the formation of the new record $[m = a.m, m' = \lambda(s)b]$, whose type is $A^+ \equiv \mu(X)[m : X{\to}B, m' : X \to B']$. Typing the new record requires the type of $a.m$ to be subsumed to $A^+ \to B$, but the subtype relationship $A{\to}B <: A^+{\to}B$ fails due to the contravariant occurrence of the types A and A^+.

To circumvent the use of subsumption, a seemingly correct solution would be to refine the self-application semantics by using polymorphic methods and interpreting pro-types as recursive types of the form $\mu(X)[m : \forall(U \mathbin{\#\!\!<} X)U{\to}B\{U\}]$. Unfortunately this attempt fails when trying to reduce matching to subtyping in $F_{\omega<:\mu}$, as in [AC95]: the reason is essentially the same as before, as the universal quantifier is again contravariant in its bound.

In both the previous attempts, the actual source of the problem is the poor interaction between the subtyping rules for recursive types and the contravariant

occurrence of the recursion variable in the types of methods: we need to break
that problematic dependency.

Methods and Split Labels. Looking at the typing rules of $\texttt{Obj}^+$ (cf. Section 4), one may identify two distinguished views of methods. The rule (Val
Object) shows this distinction clearly: in the premises, methods are viewed and
typed as concrete values – abstractions of SELF – whereas in the conclusion they
are seen as "abstract services" that can be invoked by messages. This observation
suggests an interpretation that splits methods into two parts, in ways similar to,
but different from, the translation of [ACV96] (see [BBC02]). In the untyped
case, the object[8] $\langle m_i = \varsigma(x)b_i{}^{i\in 1..n}\rangle$ can be interpreted as the recursive record
that satisfies the following equation:

$$M = [m_i^{gen} = \lambda(x)[\![b_i]\!]^{i\in 1..n}, \; m_i^{sel} = M.m_i^{gen}(M)^{\;i\in 1..n}]$$

Each method m_i is represented by two components: the *generator* m_i^{gen}, associated with a function representing the actual body of m_i, and the *selector* m_i^{sel},
which results from self-applying m_i^{gen} to the host object and can be directly invoked by selection, without self-application at selection time. Thus, *clients* of the
object can access the object's methods by means of the selectors, while *derived
objects*, obtained by the addition of new methods, inherit the generators and
re-install the corresponding selectors to rebind SELF to the extended structure
of the host object. In other words, the set of selectors can be thought of as the
abstract interface that the object provides for its clients, while the generators
are available in contexts where the structure of the object needs to be extended
with new methods.

This idea works well also in the typed case. The interface associated with
an $\texttt{Ob}^+$ type $A \equiv \texttt{pro}(X)\langle\!\langle m_i : B_i\{X\}^{i\in 1..n}\rangle\!\rangle$ is represented by the type operator
A^{IN} defined by $\mathsf{A}^{\text{IN}}(X) \equiv [m_i^{sel} : \mathsf{B}_i\{X\}^{i\in 1..n}]$, that includes the method selectors
(here, and below, B_i is the translation of B_i). The type A, in turn, is interpreted
as the recursive record type that collects the components representing generators
and selectors for each of the m_i:

$$\mathsf{A} \equiv \mu(X)[m_i^{gen} : \forall(U \leq \mathsf{A}^{\text{IN}})U^* {\to} \mathsf{B}_i\{U^*\}^{\;i\in 1..n}, m_i^{sel} : \mathsf{B}_i\{X\}^{\;i\in 1..n}].$$

The generators have polymorphic types corresponding to the match-bounded
types used in the typing rules of the source calculus: following [AC95], matching
is interpreted as higher-order subtyping.

The typed translation of terms derives immediately from the untyped translation and the translation of types. The object $\varsigma(X{=}A)\langle m_i = \varsigma(x:X)b_i\{X\}^{i\in 1..n}\rangle$
is interpreted as the following recursive record, where A^{OP} is the type operator
corresponding to A:

$$M = [m_i^{gen} = \Lambda(U \leq \mathsf{A}^{\text{IN}})\lambda(x:U^*)[\![b_i\{U\}]\!]^{i\in 1..n}, m_i^{sel} = M.m_i^{gen}(\mathsf{A}^{\text{OP}})(M)^{i\in 1..n}]$$

---

[8] The form $\langle m_i = \varsigma(x)b_i{}^{i\in 1..n}\rangle$ is a shortcut notation for the object expression
$\langle m_i = \varsigma(x)b_i\{x\}^{i\in 1..n}\rangle$.

Exposing the interface A^{IN} in the (higher-order) subtype constraint $U \leq A^{IN}$ of the generators insures that each method may legally invoke its sibling methods via SELF. The use of the interface A^{IN} in the bounded quantifier is critical for well-typedness: besides exposing the selectors for use within each method body, it validates the subtyping relationships

$$\forall (U \leq A^{IN})U^* \to B_i\{U^*\} \leq \forall (U \leq (A^+)^{IN})U^* \to B_i\{U^*\}$$

needed to inherit the generators upon object extension, as well as the relationship $A^{OP} \leq A^{IN}$ needed to type the self-application $M.m_i^{gen}(A^{OP})$. Note also that the interface hides the generators to reflect that objects cannot be self-extended.

Fields and Field Update. Fields are handled easily in the interpretation: they need no generator components *gen*, as they do not depend on SELF, and their evaluation is independent of the structure of the object and of its extensions. On the other hand, field updates require a different treatment (and interpretation) of the recursive nature of SELF. The problem is well-known [AC96a]: defining objects by *direct* recursion, as we did above, does not quite reflect their computational behavior. Specifically, field updates do not work if the recursion freezes SELF to be the object at the time of creation or extension: subsequent updates on a field are not reflected in the invocation of a method that depended on that field through SELF. The solution, as in [ACV96,AC96a], is to give a recursive definition not of the object itself, but rather of the dependency of the object on its methods. In the untyped case, this correspond to the following interpretation of $\langle m_i = \varsigma(x)b_i^{i \in 1..n} \rangle$.

$$
\begin{aligned}
&\texttt{letrec } mkobj(f_1, \ldots, f_n) = \\
&\quad [m_i^{gen} = f_i^{i \in 1..n}, \ m_i^{sel} = f_i(mkobj(f_1, \ldots, f_n))^{i \in 1..n}] \\
&\texttt{in } mkobj(\lambda(x)[\![b_1]\!], \ldots, \lambda(x)[\![b_n]\!])
\end{aligned}
$$

Now it is the definition of *mkobj*, i.e., of the function that creates the object, that is recursive, not the object itself. This enables a correct interpretation of field updates that uses the *updaters* of [ACV96]. The interpretation of a, now complete, object of the form $\langle v_i = c_i^{i \in 1..n}, m_j = \varsigma(x)b_j^{j \in 1..m} \rangle$ can be defined as follows:

$$
\begin{aligned}
&\texttt{letrec } mkobj(w_i^{i \in 1..n}, f_j^{j \in 1..m}) = \\
&\quad [v_i^{sel} = w_i^{i \in 1..n}, \\
&\quad v_i^{upd} = \lambda(z)mkobj(w_1, \ldots, w_{i-1}, z, w_{i+1}, \ldots, w_n, f_j^{j \in 1..m})^{i \in 1..n}, \\
&\quad m_j^{gen} = f_j^{j \in 1..m}, \\
&\quad m_j^{sel} = f_j(mkobj(w_i^{i \in 1..n}, f_j^{j \in 1..m}))^{j \in 1..m}] \\
&\texttt{in } mkobj([\![c_i]\!]^{i \in 1..n}, \lambda(x)[\![b_j]\!]^{j \in 1..m})
\end{aligned}
$$

Fields are also split into two components: the selector v^{sel} provides access to the contents of the field, the updater v^{upd} takes the new value and returns a new object with the value installed in place of the original. A field update may then be translated by a simple call to the updater associated with that field.

The translation extends smoothly to the typed case: to allow field selection and update, the interface and the type of the object are extended with new components corresponding to the selectors and updaters associated with the object's fields. If $A \equiv \mathtt{pro}(X)\langle\!\langle v : C, \ldots \rangle\!\rangle$, the type of the selector v^{sel} is C, and the type of the updater v^{upd} is $C \to A$, that is the type of a function that, given an argument with the same type as the value to be updated, returns an object which has the same type as the object prior to the update.

Method Update. In the untyped case, method updates can be dealt with in exactly the same way as field updates, by introducing an updater m_i^{upd} for each method, and interpreting a method update as a call to the corresponding updater. Unfortunately, the typing of method updaters poses a non-trivial problem.

Self-inflicted Updates. Take $A \equiv \mathtt{pro}(X)\langle\!\langle m : B\{X\} \rangle\!\rangle$ and $a : A$, and consider updating the method m of a. Using method updaters, the translation of A would be the recursive type:

$$A = \mu(X)[\, m^{gen} : \forall(U \leq \mathsf{A^{IN}})U^* \to B\{U^*\},$$
$$m^{upd} : (\forall(U \leq \mathsf{A^{IN}})U^* \to B\{U^*\}) \to X,$$
$$m^{sel} : B\{X\}]$$

As in the case of fields, the updater m^{upd} expects an argument of the same type as the actual method body — the type of m^{gen} — and returns a modified copy of the object, preserving the original type. The problem is that to allow self-inflicted method updates the updaters must be exposed in the interface $\mathsf{A^{IN}}$. This leads to a new definition of the interface associated to the type A, as the type operator that satisfies the following equation:

$$\mathsf{A^{IN}}(X) = [m_i^{upd} : (\forall(U \leq \mathsf{A^{IN}})U^* \to B_i\{U^*\}) \to X, \ m_i^{sel} : B_i\{X\}]$$

The problem with this equation is that it involves type operators rather than types: solving equations of this kind requires a significant extension to the target theory $F_{\omega<:\mu}$, one that allows fixed points to be taken not only at types, but also at type operators. To our knowledge, this extended theory has not been studied in the literature, and its soundness is still an open problem. For this reason, in the formal treatment [BBC02], we disregard method updaters, and focus attention on the simpler case in which method update is an operation that may only be performed from outside the object. External updates, which are legal in the source calculus, can still be accounted for in $F_{\omega<:\mu}$, as we discuss below.

External Updates. The translation of external method updates relies on the same technique discussed for method addition. Given the object $a \equiv \langle m_i = \varsigma(x)b_i{}^{i \in 1..n} \rangle$, the interpretation of $a \circ m_j \leftarrow \varsigma(x)b$ is the call

$$mkobj(\, [\![\, a\,]\!]\, .m_1^{gen}, \dots, [\![\, a\,]\!]\, .m_{j-1}^{gen}, \lambda(x)\, [\![\, b\,]\!]\, , [\![\, a\,]\!]\, .m_{j+1}^{gen}, \dots, [\![\, a\,]\!]\, .m_n^{gen})$$

which forms a new object containing new body for m_j and the methods inherited from a. Note that this interpretation of method updates does *not* work for the self-inflicted case. As we already pointed out, the generators m_i^{gen} cannot be invoked from within a method body, as they are not exposed by the interface of the object: on the other hand, exposing the generators in the interface (i.e. using A^{OP} in place of A^{IN}) would break the subtyping required to type an object extension (for $(A^+)^{OP} \leq A^{OP}$ fails due to the contravariant occurrence of the universal quantifier in the type of the generators).

6   From Extensible Objects to Classes

The main insight of the object-based model is that class-based notions need not to be assumed, but instead they can be emulated by more primitive notions. Moreover, these more primitive notions can be combined in more flexible way than in a strict class discipline. Therefore, one way to evaluate object-based calculi is with respect to how well they support class-based programming. The main contribution of the paper [BF98] is the formal study of a calculus of encapsulated extensible objects (that uses bounded existential quantifier), which are used to model class hierarchies. This calculus is imperative, and simplifies the type system for the calculus described in Fisher's dissertation [Fis96] (which is functional and supporting *MyType*). The paper [BF98] presents an (imperative) operational semantics, and gives a sound and complete typing algorithm. We summarize the paper in this tutorial and, to motivate the study, we report a comparison between this approach to modeling classes and the well-known *record-of-premethods* approach. This comparison, which is an overview of [FM98], reveals why extensible calculi are relevant to class-based programming.

6.1   Premethod Model

In the context of object calculi, it seems natural to define inheritance using *premethods*, functions that are written with the intent of becoming object methods, but which are not yet installed in any object. Premethods are functions that explicitly depend on the "object itself," typically assumed to be the first parameter to the function. Following this idea, Abadi and Cardelli encoded classes in a pure object system using records of premethods [AC96a]; these ideas are also used by Reppy and Riecke [RR96]. In this approach, a class is an object that contains a record of premethods and a constructor function used to package these premethods into objects.

The primary advantage of the record-of-premethods encoding is that it does not require a complicated form of object. All that is needed is a way of forming an object from a list of component definitions. However, this approach has some serious drawbacks. We discuss these drawbacks using a list of criteria [FM98] that characterizes the rôle of classes in class-based languages.

Does the Class Construct Provide a Coherent, Extensible Collection?
The combination of a record of premethods and a constructor function may be
thought of as a coherent, extensible collection. Because premethods are simply
fields in a record, nothing requires that they be coherent until a constructor
function is supplied. Since the constructor function installs the premethods into
an object, however, the fact that a given constructor is typable implies that the
premethods it uses are coherent. Notice, however, that nothing requires a given
constructor to mention all of the premethods in a given premethod record.

Does the Class Construct Guarantee Initialization? In more elaborate
record-of-premethod models, the code to initialize private instance variables is
guaranteed to run if any of the associated premethods is installed into an object.
However, constructor functions cannot be reused usefully in derived classes. A
consequence is that if a class designer puts initialization code into a class constructor, that code will not be executed for derived classes. There are several
program-development scenarios where this weakness would be a serious problem.
For example, class designers may wish to perform some kind of bookkeeping
whenever objects are instantiated from a class or its descendants. To achieve
it, programmers need a place to put code that will execute whenever an object
is instantiated. With the record-of-premethods approach, however, there is no
appropriate place: no base class constructor function will be called for derived
classes, and a premethod function may be called without creating an object.

Does the Class Construct Provide an Explicit Type Hierarchy? In
many existing class-based languages, it is possible to restrict the subtypes of an
"implementation" object type (i.e., a class) to classes that inherit all or part
of the object's implementation. This restriction may be useful for optimizing
operations on objects, allowing access to argument objects in binary methods,
and guaranteeing semantic consistency beyond type considerations [KLM94]. A
special case of this capability is the ability to define *final* classes, as recognized
in work on Rapide [KLM94] and incorporated (presumably independently) as
a language feature in Java. This ability is lacking in the record-of-premethods
approach since any object whose type is a structural subtype of another type τ
can be used as an object of type τ.

**Does the Class Mechanism Automatically Propagate Base Class
Changes?** Because derived class constructors must explicitly name the methods
that they wish to inherit, the record-of-premethods approach does not automatically propagate base class method changes. In particular, if a derived class D is
defined from a base class B in Java or related languages, then adding a method to
B will result in an additional method of D, and similarly for every other class derived from B (and there may be many). With the record-of-premethods approach,
derived class constructors must be explicitly rewritten each time base classes
change. Since object-oriented programs are typically quite large and maintenance may be distributed across many people, the person who maintains a base
class may fail to inform those maintaining its derived classes of its change, caus-

ing unpredictable errors. There is no mechanism in this approach to detect such errors automatically.

6.2   Extensible Object Model

While we readily admit that its simplicity is a virtue, the above discussion reveals that several important and desirable features of class-based programming are lost in the record-of-premethods model. Extensible objects provide a rich alternative. A principled way to think about class-based object-oriented languages is as the combination of two orthogonal components [Fis96,FM98]: (i), an object system that supports inheritance and message sending and (ii), an encapsulation mechanism that provides hiding. We call this model of classes the "Classes = Extensible Objects + Encapsulation" approach. Referring to the class-evaluation checklist we used to evaluate the pre-methods model, we can see that this approach successfully addresses each of the points listed there: it provides an extensible coherent collection, guarantees initialization, supports an explicit type hierarchy, and automatically propagates base class changes.

Extensible, Coherent Collection. Extensible objects obviate the need for premethods, since collections of methods that are already installed in objects may be extended. Because of this fact, we may impose static constraints on the ways in which one method may be combined with others. For example, if an object contains two mutually recursive methods, then we cannot replace one with another of a different type. In contrast, in the record-of-premethods approach, it is possible to form a record of premethods without a "covering" constructor that checks to be sure that all of the premethods are coherent.

Guaranteed Initialization. A second advantage of extensible objects is that class constructors and initialization code can be inherited, i.e., reused in derived classes. For example, to create `ColorPoint` objects, we may invoke a `Point` class constructor and add color methods to the resulting extensible object. This process guarantees that the `Point` class has the opportunity to initialize any inherited components properly. It also guarantees that the designers of the `Point` class have the opportunity to update any bookkeeping information they may be keeping about instantiations of `Point` objects.

Explicit Type Hierarchy. A further advantage is the rich subtyping structure of this approach. In particular, it provides "implementation" types that subtype along the inheritance hierarchy, "interface" types that subtype via structural subtyping rules, and a hybrid subtyping relation that allows implementation types to be subtypes of interface types. With this subtyping structure, programmers can use implementation types where the extra information is useful and interface types where more generality is required.

Automatic Propagation of Changes. Another advantage arises with private (or protected) methods. In the extensible-object formulation, methods always remain within an object, even when it is extended. These hidden methods exist in all future extensions, but they can only be accessed by methods that were defined before the method became hidden. Furthermore, these private methods need not be manipulated explicitly by derived class constructors to insure that they are treated properly.

These advantages may be seen in the encoding of the traditional Point and ColorPoint hierarchy, studied in the paper [BF98]. In this tutorial we present it in its pseudo-type-theory version only, to develop intuitions for the formal model.

6.3 Pseudo-Type-Theoretic Point, ColorPoint Hierarchy

In the "Classes = Extensible Objects + Encapsulation" model of classes [Fis96,FM98], extensible objects support the inheritance aspects of classes, while an encapsulation mechanism provides the hiding. We illustrate the ideas behind this model by encoding the familiar Point, ColorPoint hierarchy in pseudo-type theory. The code, which appears in Figure 1, contains two class declarations followed by "*Client Code.*"

Class Declarations

    Class Point **implements** *"Point_public_interface"*, *"Point_protected_interface"*

    exports newP : *int* → *"extensible obj. type from* Point *class"*

    is

        { *"Point_private_interface"*; *"code to implement* newP *"* }

    end;

    Class ColorPoint **implements** *"CP_public_interface"*, *"CP_protected_interface"*

    exports newCP : *color* → *int* → *"non-extensible obj. type from* ColorPoint *class"*

    is

        { *"CP_private_interface"*; *"code to implement* newCP *"* }

    end;

in

    "If desired, restrict return types of non-final constructors;"

    "Client Code"

end

Fig. 1. Point, ColorPoint hierarchy.

To explain the model, we focus on the **Class** encapsulation construct, which provides the outer wrapping for each of the class declarations. In it, the **Class** clause names the abstraction-as-class, Point in the first case, ColorPoint in the second. The **implements** clause gives the public and protected interfaces supported by the class, *"Point_public_interface"* and *"Point_protected_interface,"* respectively, in the Point case. A public interface lists the methods available from instances of its class. Such a list for a simple Point class might be of the form ⟨getX : *int*, setX : *int* → *unit*⟩, revealing that objects of the class contain getX and setX methods of the indicated types. At the discretion of the class designer, a class's public interface may explicitly name its parent class, if one exists. For example, the ColorPoint public interface might be of the form ⟨Point | getC : *color*, setC : *color* → *unit*⟩. The Point portion of this interface indicates that objects created from the ColorPoint class were formed via inheritance from the Point class; hence, they have the Point class methods. In addition, by thus indicating the parent class, the ColorPoint class designer declares that the "implementation type" associated with the ColorPoint class is a subtype of the Point class's "implementation type." Through this declaration mechanism, the model supports an explicit type hierarchy. The second half of the ColorPoint public interface indicates that the ColorPoint class added getC and setC methods.

The protected interface augments the public one with information for deriving classes. In this model, this information consists of method and field names that may not be used in derived classes without introducing name clashes.

The **exports** clause of the encapsulation mechanism reveals the names and types of the non-dynamically dispatched operations defined by the class. In general, this clause lists constructor and "friend" functions. In the example, the Point class designer chose to export a single constructor function, newP of type *int* → "*extensible object type from* Point *class*." By making the return type an extensible object type, the class designer enabled inheritance from this class: a derived class calls newP to get the implementation of the Point class and then adds and redefines components as necessary. Since the ColorPoint class designer made newCP return a non-extensible object, the ColorPoint class is "final," in the sense that no other class can be formed by extending its implementation. The Point class designer opted to make the return type of newP flag its defining class (via the "*from* Point *class*" annotation). Because this information is present in the constructor type, the ColorPoint class designer can export its parent's identity. Without it, the derived class could reuse its parent's implementation but could not reveal this fact nor make the ColorPoint implementation type a subtype of the Point implementation type.

The **is** clause of the encapsulation mechanism has two pieces. The first part, the private interface, lists all the methods defined within the class. For a simple Point class, this interface might be of the form ⟨x : *int*, getX : *int*, setX : *int* → *unit*⟩, where x is a private field.

The second piece of a class implementation is the code to implement the constructor and friend functions listed in the **exports** clause. In the Point class case, this code simply defines an extensible object with field x and methods getX and setX. For the ColorPoint class, the constructor implementation first calls newP to inherit the Point class behavior and then adds color-related fields and methods. If the ColorPoint class advertises the fact that it inherits from Point in its public interface, then the type system insures that the ColorPoint constructor function calls newP and returns an extension of the resulting object. Thus the type system guarantees that the Point class has a chance to initialize its private variables and set up its desired invariants for any object instantiated from it, either directly or via a derived class.

Because the **Class** construct is an encapsulation mechanism, only the aspects of the **is** code specifically mentioned in the **implements** and **exports** clauses can be used in the rest of the program. Hence in the encoding, this mechanism ensures the privacy of private methods and fields.

After we process all the class declarations in the pseudo-code, we are almost ready to execute the *"Client Code."* Without any further adjustment, however, non-final classes have constructor functions that return extensible objects, which enable run-time inheritance. If we wish to disable this feature, we may restrict the return types of these constructor functions to return "non-extensible" objects instead. This type restriction does not involve changing the values in any way; it simply adjusts the types. The restriction is safe because every extensible object type in the system is a subtype of the corresponding non-extensible version.

7 Related Work

In the Lambda Calculus of Objects [FHM94], *MyType* inheritance is rendered via *row variables* (instead of being modelled by match-bound quantification as it is for Obj^+). The type of SELF is a partially non-defined row-type, where the non-defined part is a row-variable representing all possible extensions that the host object may be subjected to. Rows are validated by using *kinds*. Also the calculus of [BF98] we presented informally in Section 6 is based on row-variables.

The work [Liq98] presents a detailed comparison among four type systems for the Lambda Calculus of Objects: the original one [FHM94], the Fisher's thesis one [Fis96], an earlier version of Obj^+ [BB99], and a system based on bounded polymorphism.

In the literature, there are proposals that integrate extensible objects in broader contexts. We mention three of them:

- Baby Modula 3 [Aba94] is a toy language that provides extensible objects. In order to ensure safety with respect to subtyping, all of the object extensions must be done before applying any form of subsumption. This language also accounts for a notion of "incomplete objects", for which completions are fixed ahead of time, prior to any addition. A calculus that offers a more complex form of incomplete objects is presented in [BBDCL99].
- The calculus presented in [Rém98] is a version of the Abadi and Cardelli calculus [AC96b] equipped with extensible objects, as it is our Obj^+, but its type system is richer. The underlying idea is to trace subtyping, in such a way method addition and subtyping-in-width can co-exists. This extra-information allows also to model a form of *virtual* methods (i.e., it models a form of incomplete objects). Moreover, when sufficient type information is available, objects play a rôle similar to the one of classes; such information can be then hidden progressively, objects regaining their proper rôle.
- The paper [DHL98] extends the Lambda Calculus of Objects with a form of *self-inflicted* method addition. Relationships between this calculus and foundations for dynamic re-classification of objects [DDDCG02] are under study.

References

[Aba94]   M. Abadi. Baby Modula–3 and a Theory of Objects. *Journal of Functional Programming*, 4(2):249–283, 1994.

[ABDD03]   C. Anderson, F. Barbanera, M. Dezani-Ciancaglini, and S. Drossopoulou. Can addresses be types? (a case study: objects with delegation). In *WOOD'03*, volume 82.8 of *ENTCS*. Elsevier, 2003.

[AC95]   M. Abadi and L. Cardelli. On Subtyping and Matching. In *Proceedings of ECOOP'95: European Conference on Object-Oriented Programming*, volume 952 of *LNCS*, pages 145–167. Springer–Verlag, 1995.

[AC96a]   M. Abadi and L. Cardelli. *A Theory of Objects*. Monographs in Computer Science. Springer, 1996.

[AC96b]   M. Abadi and L. Cardelli. A Theory of Primitive Objects: Untyped and First-Order System. *Information and Computation*, 125(2):78–102, March 1996.

[ACV96]   M. Abadi, L. Cardelli, and R. Viswanathan. An Interpretation of Objects and Object Types. In *Proc. of POPL'96*, pages 396–409, 1996.

[AD02a]   C. Anderson and S. Drossopoulou. Babyj - from object based to class based programming via types. In *Proc. of WOOD'03*, volume 82.8 of *ENTCS*, 2002. Workshop of ETAPS'03.

[AD02b]   C. Anderson and S. Drossopoulou. δ - an imperative object based calculus. Presented at the workshop USE in 2002, Malaga, 2002.

[AG96]   K. Arnold and J. Gosling. *The Java Programming Language*. Addison-Wesley, 1996.

[BB99]   V. Bono and M. Bugliesi. Matching for the Lambda Calculus of Objects. *Theoretical Computer Science*, 212(1/2):101–140, 1999.

[BBC02]   V. Bono, M. Bugliesi, and S. Crafa. Typed interpretations of extensible objects. *ACM Transactions on Computational Logic*, 2002.

[BBDCL99]   V. Bono, M. Bugliesi, M. Dezani-Ciancaglini, and L. Liquori. A Subtyping for Extensible, Incomplete Objects. *Fundamenta Informaticae*, 38(4):325–364, 1999.

[BCC⁺95]   K.B. Bruce, L. Cardelli, G. Castagna, The Hopkins Object Group, G. Leavens, and B. Pierce. On Binary Methods. *Theory and Practice of Software Systems*, 1(3):217–238, 1995.

[BCP97]   K.B. Bruce, L. Cardelli, and B. Pierce. Comparing Object Encodings. In *Proc. of TACS'97*, volume 1281 of *LNCS*, pages 415–438. Springer-Verlag, 1997.

[BDG02]   V. Bono, F. Damiani, and P. Giannini. A calculus for "environment-aware" computation. In *F-WAN'02*, volume 66.3 of *ENTCS*. Elsevier, 2002.

[BF98]   V. Bono and K. Fisher. An Imperative, First-Order Calculus with Object Extension. In *Proc. of ECOOP'98*, volume 1445 of *LNCS*, pages 462–497, 1998. A preliminary version already appeared in Proc. of 5th Annual FOOL Workshop.

[BL95]   V. Bono and L. Liquori. A Subtyping for the Fisher-Honsell-Mitchell Lambda Calculus of Objects. In *Proc. of CSL'94*, volume 933 of *LNCS*, pages 16–30. Springer-Verlag, 1995.

[Bru94]   K.B. Bruce. A Paradigmatic Object-Oriented Programming Language: Design, Static Typing and Semantics. *Journal of Functional Programming*, 4(2):127–206, 1994.

[Bru02]   K.B. Bruce. *Foundations of Object-Oriented Languages – Types and Se-mantics.* The MIT Press, 2002.

[Car95]   L. Cardelli. A Language with Distribuite Scope. *Computing Systems*, 8(1):27–59, 1995.

[Cas96]   G. Castagna.   *Object-Oriented Programming: a Unified Foundation.* Birkauser, 1996.

[CG]   UW Cecil Group. UW Cecil Group : Home. Cecil's language home page.

[CHC90]   W. Cook, W. Hill, and P. Canning. Inheritance is not Subtyping. In *Proc. of ACM Symp. POPL'90*, pages 125–135. ACM Press, 1990.

[Coo89]   W.R. Cook. *A Denotational Semantics of Inheritance.* PhD thesis, Brown University, 1989.

[Cra99]   K. Crary. Simple, efficient object encoding using intersection types. Tech. rep., CMU-CS-99-100, Cornell University, 1999.

[CW85]   L. Cardelli and P. Wegner. On Understanding Types, Data Abstraction and Polymorphism. *Computing Surveys*, 17(4):471–522, 1985.

[DDDCG02]   S. Drossopoulou, F. Damiani, M. Dezani-Ciancaglini, and P. Giannini. More dynamic object re-classification: Fickle$_{II}$. *ACM Transactions On Programming Languages and Systems*, 24(2):153–191, 2002.

[DG03]   F. Damiani and P. Giannini. Alias types for "environment-aware" com-putations. In *WOOD'03*, volume 82.8 of *ENTCS*. Elsevier, 2003.

[DHL98]   P. Di Gianantonio, F. Honsell, and L. Liquori. A Lambda Calculus of Objects with Self-inflicted Extension. In *Proc. of ACM-SIGPLAN OOP-SLA, International Symposium on Object Oriented, Programming, Sys-tem, Languages and Applications*, pages 166–178. The ACM Press, 1998.

[FHM94]   K. Fisher, F. Honsell, and J. C. Mitchell. A Lambda Calculus of Objects and Method Specialization. *Nordic Journal of Computing*, 1(1):3–37, 1994. A preliminary version appeared in *Proc. of IEEE Symp. LICS'93*.

[Fis96]   K. Fisher. *Type Systems for Object-Oriented Programming Languages.* PhD thesis, Stanford University, 1996. Available as Stanford Computer Science Technical Report number STAN-CS-TR-98-1602.

[Fla99]   D. Flannanghan. *JavaScript: The definitive guide.* O'Reilly, 1999.

[FM95]   K. Fisher and J. C. Mitchell. A Delegation-based Object Calculus with Subtyping. In *Proc. of FCT*, volume 965 of *LNCS*, pages 42–61. Springer-Verlag, 1995.

[FM98]   K. Fisher and J.C. Mitchell. On the relationship between classes, objects, and data abstraction. *Theory and Practice of Object Systems*, 4(3), 1998. Special Issue on Third Workshop on Foundations of Object-Oriented Lan-guages (FOOL 3). Preliminary version appeared in Marktoberdorf '97 proceedings.

[Kam88]   S. Kamin. Inheritance in Smalltalk-80: a denotational definition. In *Proc. of POPL'88*, pages 80–87. ACM Press, 1988.

[KLM94]   D. Katiyar, D. Luckham, and J.C. Mitchell. A type system for proto-typing languages. In *Proc. 21st of Symp. on Principles of Programming Languages.* ACM, 1994.

[Liq98]   L. Liquori. On Object Extension. In *Proc. of ECOOP, European Con-ference on Object Oriented Programming*, volume 1445 of *Lecture Notes in Computer Sciences*, pages 498–552. Springer Verlag, 1998.

[Pie02]   B.C. Pierce. *Types and Programming Languages.* The MIT Press, 2002.

[PT94]   B. Pierce and D. Turner. Simple type-theoretic foundations for object-oriented programming. *Journal of Functional Programming*, 4(2):207–248, 1994.

[Rém98]   D. Rémy. From classes to objects via subtyping. In *Proceedings of ESOP'98*, volume 1381 of *Lecture Notes in Computer Science*. Springer-Verlag, 1998.

[RR96]   J.H. Reppy and J.G. Riecke. Classes in Object ML via modules. In *Proc. of FOOL3 Workshop*, 1996.

[US87]   D. Ungar and R. B. Smith. Self: the Power of Simplicity. In *Proc. of OOPSLA'87*, pages 227–241. ACM Press, 1987.

A   Obj$^+$

A.1   Notation

$$\langle \ell_i = \mathbf{b}_i\{x\}^{i\in I\cup J}\rangle \triangleq \langle v_i = c_i{}^{i\in I}, m_j = \varsigma(x)b_j\{x\}^{j\in J}\rangle$$

$$a \cdot \ell \triangleq a \circ \ell \text{ or } a.\ell$$

$$a \cdot \ell \leftarrow \mathbf{b}\{x\} \triangleq a \circ \ell \leftarrow \varsigma(x)b\{x\} \text{ or } a.\ell \leftarrow b$$

$$a \cdot \ell \leftarrow\!\!\!+ \mathbf{b}\{x\} \triangleq a \circ \ell \leftarrow\!\!\!+ \varsigma(x)b\{x\} \text{ or } a.\ell \leftarrow\!\!\!+ b$$

A.2 $\Downarrow_o$: Big-Step Operational Semantics

Results : $r = \langle v_i = c_i{}^{i\in I}, m_j = \varsigma(x)b_j\{x\}^{j\in J}\rangle$

(Select$_v$) $$\dfrac{a \Downarrow_o \langle\ldots, v_j=c_j,\ldots\rangle \quad c_j \Downarrow_o r}{a.v_j \Downarrow_o r}$$

(Select$_m$) $$\dfrac{a\Downarrow_o \widehat{a} \quad b_j\{\widehat{a}\} \Downarrow_o r \quad (\widehat{a} \equiv \langle\ldots, m_j = \varsigma(x)b_j\{x\},\ldots\rangle)}{a \circ m_j \Downarrow_o r}$$

(Update) $$\dfrac{a \Downarrow_o \langle \ell_i = \mathbf{b}_i\{x\}^{i\in I\cup J}\rangle \quad k \in I\cup J}{a \cdot \ell_k \leftarrow \mathbf{b}\{x\} \Downarrow_o \langle \ell_i = \mathbf{b}_i\{x\}^{i\in I\cup J-\{k\}}, \ell_k = \mathbf{b}\{x\}\rangle}$$

(Extend) $$\dfrac{a \Downarrow_o \langle \ell_i = \mathbf{b}_i\{x\}^{i\in I\cup J}\rangle \quad \ell \notin \{\ell_i\}^{i\in I\cup J}}{a \cdot \ell \leftarrow\!\!\!+ \mathbf{b}\{x\} \Downarrow_o \langle \ell = \mathbf{b}\{x\}, \ell_i = \mathbf{b}_i\{x\}^{i\in I\cup J}\rangle}$$

A.3 $\succ_o$: Small-Step Operational Semantics

$a \equiv \langle v_i = c_i{}^{i\in I}, m_j = \varsigma(x)b_j\{x\}^{j\in J}\rangle$

(*Select$_v$*) $a.v_i \succ_o c_i$ $i \in I$

(*Select$_m$*) $a \circ m_j \succ_o b_j\{a\}$ $j \in J$

$a \equiv \langle \ell_i = \mathbf{b}_i\{x\}^{i\in I\cup J}\rangle$

(*Extend*) $\ell \notin \{\ell_i\}^{i\in I\cup J}$
$\quad\quad a \cdot \ell \leftarrow\!\!\!+ \mathbf{b}\{x\} \succ_o \langle \ell = \mathbf{b}\{x\}, \ell_i = \mathbf{b}_i\{x\}^{i\in I\cup J}\rangle$

(*Update*) $k \in I\cup J$
$\quad\quad a \cdot \ell_k \leftarrow \mathbf{b}\{x\} \succ_o \langle \ell_i = \mathbf{b}_i\{x\}^{i\in I\cup J-\{k\}}, \ell_k = \mathbf{b}\{x\}\rangle$

A.4   Typing Rules

Context Formation

(Ctx $\varnothing$)   (Ctx X)   (Ctx Match)

$$\frac{}{\varnothing \vdash *} \qquad \frac{\Gamma \vdash * \quad X \notin Dom(\Gamma)}{\Gamma, X \vdash *} \qquad \frac{\Gamma \vdash \mathtt{pro}(X)\langle \ell_i : B_i\{X\}^{i\in I}\rangle \quad U \notin Dom(\Gamma)}{\Gamma, U \lessgtr\!\!\# \, \mathtt{pro}(X)\langle \ell_i : B_i\{X\}^{i\in I}\rangle \vdash *}$$

Type formation

(Type X)   (Type Match U)   (Type $\mathtt{pro}$)

$$\frac{\Gamma', X, \Gamma'' \vdash *}{\Gamma', X, \Gamma'' \vdash X} \quad \frac{\Gamma', U \lessgtr\!\!\# A, \Gamma'' \vdash *}{\Gamma', U \lessgtr\!\!\# A, \Gamma'' \vdash U} \quad \frac{\Gamma, X \vdash B_i\{X\}}{\Gamma \vdash \mathtt{pro}(X)\langle \ell_i : B_i\{X\}^{i\in I}\rangle}$$

Term Formation

(Val x)   (Val Select)

$$\frac{\Gamma', x : A, \Gamma'' \vdash *}{\Gamma', x : A, \Gamma'' \vdash x : A} \quad \frac{\Gamma \vdash a : A \quad \Gamma \vdash A \lessgtr\!\!\# \, \mathtt{pro}(X)\langle \ell : B\{X\}\rangle}{\Gamma \vdash a \cdot \ell : B\{A\}}$$

(Val Object: $A \equiv \mathtt{pro}(X)\langle v_i : C_i^{\,i\in I}, m_j : B_j\{X\}^{j\in J}\rangle$)

$$\frac{\Gamma \vdash c_i : C_i \qquad \Gamma, U \lessgtr\!\!\# A, x : U \vdash b_j\{x\} : B_j\{U\} \qquad \forall\, i \in I, j \in J}{\Gamma \vdash \langle v_i = c_i^{\,i\in I}, m_j = \varsigma(x)b_j\{x\}^{j\in J}\rangle : A}$$

(Val Field Addition: $A^+ \equiv \mathtt{pro}(X)\langle \ell : B\{X\}, \ell_i : B_i\{X\}^{i\in I}\rangle$)

$$\frac{\Gamma \vdash a : \mathtt{pro}(X)\langle \ell_i : B_i\{X\}^{i\in I}\rangle \quad \Gamma \vdash c : B \quad (\ell \neq \ell_i \; \forall i \in I)}{\Gamma \vdash a.\ell \hookleftarrow c : A^+}$$

(Val Method Addition: $A^+ \equiv \mathtt{pro}(X)\langle \ell : B\{X\}, \ell_i : B_i\{X\}^{i\in I}\rangle$)

$$\frac{\Gamma \vdash a : \mathtt{pro}(X)\langle \ell_i : B_i\{X\}^{i\in I}\rangle \quad \Gamma, U \lessgtr\!\!\# A^+, x : U \vdash b\{x\} : B\{U\} \quad (\ell \neq \ell_i \; \forall i \in I)}{\Gamma \vdash a \circ \ell \hookleftarrow \varsigma(x)b\{x\} : A^+}$$

(Val Field Update)

$$\frac{\Gamma \vdash a : A \quad \Gamma \vdash A \lessgtr\!\!\# \, \mathtt{pro}(X)\langle v : C\rangle \quad \Gamma \vdash c : C}{\Gamma \vdash a.v \leftarrow c : A}$$

(Val Method Update: $A \equiv \mathtt{pro}(X)\langle v_i : C_i^{\,i\in I}, m_j : B_j\{X\}^{j\in J}\rangle$)

$$\frac{\Gamma \vdash a : A \quad \Gamma, U \lessgtr\!\!\# A, x : U \vdash b\{x\} : B_k\{U\} \quad k \in J}{\Gamma \vdash a \circ m_k \leftarrow \varsigma(x)b\{x\} : A}$$

Matching

(Match U)   (Match Refl)   (Match Trans)

$$\frac{\Gamma', U \lessgtr\!\!\# A, \Gamma'' \vdash *}{\Gamma', U \lessgtr\!\!\# A, \Gamma'' \vdash U \lessgtr\!\!\# A} \quad \frac{\Gamma', U \lessgtr\!\!\# A, \Gamma'' \vdash U}{\Gamma', U \lessgtr\!\!\# A, \Gamma'' \vdash U \lessgtr\!\!\# U} \quad \frac{\Gamma \vdash U \lessgtr\!\!\# B \quad \Gamma \vdash B \lessgtr\!\!\# A}{\Gamma \vdash U \lessgtr\!\!\# A}$$

(Match $\mathtt{pro}$)

$$\frac{\Gamma \vdash \mathtt{pro}(X)\langle \ell_i : B_i\{X\}^{i\in 1..n+k}\rangle}{\Gamma \vdash \mathtt{pro}(X)\langle \ell_i : B_i\{X\}^{i\in 1..n+k}\rangle \lessgtr\!\!\# \, \mathtt{pro}(X)\langle \ell_i : B_i\{X\}^{i\in 1..n}\rangle}$$

The Klaim Project: Theory and Practice*

Lorenzo Bettini[1], Viviana Bono[2], Rocco De Nicola[1], Gianluigi Ferrari[3],
Daniele Gorla[1], Michele Loreti[1], Eugenio Moggi[4], Rosario Pugliese[1],
Emilio Tuosto[3], and Betti Venneri[1]

[1] Dip. Sistemi e Informatica, Univ. di Firenze
v. Lombroso 6/17, 50134 Firenze, Italy
[2] Dip. Informatica, Univ. di Torino
Corso Svizzera 185, 10149 Torino, Italy
[3] Dip. Informatica, Univ. di Pisa
v. Buonarroti 2, 56100 Pisa, Italy
[4] Dip. Informatica e Scienze dell'Informazione
Univ. di Genova
v. Dodecaneso 35, 16146 Genova, Italy

Abstract. KLAIM (*Kernel Language for Agents Interaction and Mobility*) is an experimental language specifically designed to program distributed systems consisting of several mobile components that interact through multiple distributed tuple spaces. KLAIM primitives allow programmers to distribute and retrieve data and processes to and from the nodes of a net. Moreover, localities are first-class citizens that can be dynamically created and communicated over the network. Components, both stationary and mobile, can explicitly refer and control the spatial structures of the network.

This paper reports the experiences in the design and development of KLAIM. Its main purpose is to outline the theoretical foundations of the main features of KLAIM and its programming model. We also present a modal logic that permits reasoning about behavioural properties of systems and various type systems that help in controlling agents movements and actions. Extensions of the language in the direction of object oriented programming are also discussed together with the description of the implementation efforts which have lead to the current prototypes.

Keywords: Process Calculi, Mobile Code, Distributed Applications, Network Awareness, Tuple Spaces, Type Systems, Temporal Logics, Java.

1 Introduction

The distributed software architecture (model) which underpins most of the wide area network (WAN) applications typically consists of a large number of heterogeneous computational entities (sometimes referred to as nodes or sites of the

* This work has been partially supported by EU FET - Global Computing initiative, project AGILE IST-2001-32747, project DART IST-2001-33477, project MIKADO IST-2001-32222, project PROFUNDIS IST-2001-33100, and by MIUR project NAPOLI. The funding bodies are not responsible for any use that might be made of the results presented here.

C. Priami (Ed.): GC 2003, LNCS 2874, pp. 88–150, 2003.

network) where components of applications are executed. Network sites are generally managed by different authorities with different administrative policies and security requirements. Differently from traditional middlewares for distributed programming, the structure of the underlying network is made manifest to components of WAN applications. Indeed, a key design principle of WAN computing is *network awareness*. This is because often applications need to be aware of the administrative domains where they are currently located, and need to know how to cross administrative boundaries and move to other locations. Components of WAN applications are characterized by a highly dynamic behavior and have to deal with the unpredictable changes over time of the network environment (due to the unavailability of connectivity, lack of services, node failures, reconfiguration, and so on). Moreover, nomadic or mobile components must be designed to support heterogeneity and interoperability because they may disconnect from a node and reconnect later to a different node. Therefore, a distinguished feature of WANs and WAN applications is that their overall structure can change dynamically and unpredictably. We refer the interested reader to [Car99] for a comprehensive analysis of the issues related to the design and development of WAN applications.

The problems associated with the development of WAN applications have prompted the study of *new* paradigms and programming languages with mechanisms for handling code and agent mobility, for managing security, and for coordinating and monitoring the use of resources. Mobility provides a suitable abstraction to design and implement WAN applications. The usefulness of mobility emerges when developing both applications for nomadic devices with intermittent access to the network (*physical mobility*), and network services with different access policies (*logical mobility*). Mobility has produced new interaction paradigm [FPV98], that significantly differ from the traditional client-server pattern, and permit exchange of active units of behavior and not just of raw data:

- *Remote Evaluation*: processes send for execution to remote hosts;
- *Code On-Demand*: processes download code from remote hosts to execute it locally;
- *Mobile Agents*: processes can suspend and migrate to new hosts, where they can resume execution.

Among these design paradigms, Code On-Demand is probably the most widely used (e.g. Java Applets). The one based on mobile agents is, instead, the most challenging because it has a number of distinguishing features and poses a number of demands:

- an agent needs an *execution environment*: a server is needed that supplies resources for execution;
- an agent is *autonomous*: it executes independently of the user who created it (*goal driven*);
- an agent is able to detect changes in its operational environment and to act accordingly (*reactivity* and *adaptivity*).

Another interesting feature of mobile agents is the possibility of executing *disconnected operations* [PR98]: a software component may be remotely executed even if the user (its owner) is not connected; if this is the case, the agent may decide to "sleep" and to periodically try to reestablish the connection with its owner. Conversely, the user, when reconnected, may try to *retract* the component back home. In addition to this scenario, *ad hoc networks* [CMC99] allow connection of nomadic devices without a fixed network structure and *peer-to-peer architectures* (e.g. Napster and Gnutella) introduce a new pattern for Internet interaction by sharing information, that changes dynamically, among distributed components.

There are a few programming languages and systems that provide basic facilities for mobility. A well-known example is the Java programming language. Another interesting example is provided by Oracle [Ora99], which supports access to a database from a mobile device by exploiting mobile agents. However, current technologies provide only limited solutions to the general treatment of mobility.

At a foundational level, several process calculi have been developed to gain a more precise understanding of network awareness and mobility. We mention the Distributed Join-calculus [FGL+96], the Distributed π-calculus [HR02], the Ambient calculus [CG00], the Seal calculus [CV99], and Nomadic Pict [WS99]. Other foundational models adopt a logical style toward the analysis of mobility. *MobileUnity* [MR98] and *MobAdtl* [FMSS02] are program logics specifically designed to specify and reason about mobile systems exploiting a Unity-like proof system. The aforementioned approaches have improved the formal understanding of the complex mechanisms underlying network awareness.

Some of the above mentioned calculi deal also with the key issue of security, namely *privacy* and *integrity* of data, hosts and agents. It is important to prevent malicious agents from accessing private information or modifying private data. Tools are thus needed that enable sites receiving mobile agents for execution to set demands and limitations to ensure that the agents will not violate privacy or jeopardize the integrity of the information. Similarly, mobile agents need tools to ensure that their execution at other sites will not disrupt them or compromise their security. The problem of modelling resource access control of highly distributed and autonomous components has been faced by exploiting suitable notions of type [HR02,BCC01,CGZ01].

1.1   The Klaim Approach

KLAIM (*Kernel Language for Agents Interaction and Mobility*, [DFP98]) is an experimental language specifically designed to program distributed systems made up of several mobile components interacting through multiple distributed tuple spaces. KLAIM components, both stationary and mobile, can explicitly refer and control the spatial structures of the network at any point of their evolution. KLAIM primitives allow programmers to distribute and retrieve data and processes to and from the nodes of a net. Moreover, localities are first-class citizens, they can be dynamically created and communicated over the network and are handled via sophisticated scoping rules.

KLAIM communication model builds over, and extends, Linda's notion of *generative communication* through a single shared tuple space [Gel85]. A tuple space is a multiset of tuples that are sequences of information items. Tuples are *anonymous* and are picked up from tuple spaces by means of a *pattern-matching* mechanism (*associative selection*). Interprocess communication is *asynchronous*: producer (i.e. sender) and consumer (i.e. receiver) of a tuple do not need to synchronize. The Linda model, was originally proposed for parallel programming on isolated machines. Multiple, possibly distributed, tuple spaces have been advocated later [Gel89] to improve modularity, scalability and performance. The obtained communication model has a number of properties that make it appealing for WAN computing (see, e.g., [DWFB97,CCR96,Deu01]). The model permits *time uncoupling* (data life time is independent of the producer process life time), *destination uncoupling* (the producer of a datum does not need to know the future use or the destination of that datum) and *space uncoupling* (communicating processes need to know a single interface, i.e. the operations over the tuple space). The success of the tuple space paradigm is witnessed by the many tuple space based run-time systems, both from industries (e.g. SUN JavaSpaces [Sun99,AFH99] and IBM T Spaces [WMLF98]) and from universities (e.g. PageSpace [CTV+98], WCL [Row98], Lime [PMR99] and TuCSoN [OZ99]).

KLAIM programming paradigm emphasizes a clear separation between the computational level and the net coordinator/administrator level. Intuitively, programmers design computational units (processes and mobile agents), while coordinators design nets. Hence, coordinators manage the initial distribution of processes and set the security policies for controlling access to resources and mobility of processes. Coordinators have complete control over changes of configuration of the network that may be due to addition/deletion of software components and sites, or to transmission of programs and of sites references.

Thus, differently from other programming notations with explicit mechanisms for distribution and mobility, in KLAIM the network infrastructure is clearly distinguishable from user processes and explicitly modelled. We argue that this feature permits a more accurate handling of WAN applications. Indeed, structuring applications in terms of processes and coordinators provides a clean and a powerful abstraction device for WAN programming. In particular, it is instrumental to define security policies and their enforcement mechanisms.

KLAIM has been implemented [BDP02] by exploiting Java and has proved to be suitable for programming a wide range of distributed applications with agents and code mobility [DFP98,DFP00,BDL03,FMP03].

1.2   This Paper

This paper reports our experience in the design and development of KLAIM. Its purpose is to outline the theoretical foundations of the main features of KLAIM and of its programming model together with the description of the implementation efforts which have lead to the current prototype.

The rest of the paper is organized as follows. Section 2 introduces, step by step, the foundations of KLAIM as a process calculus. We start by presenting cKLAIM (*Core* KLAIM), that can be seen as a variant of the π-calculus with process distribution, process mobility, and asynchronous communication of names through shared located repositories. We then continue by introducing μKLAIM (*Micro* KLAIM), that exploits the full power of Linda coordination primitives (tuples and pattern-matching), and move to introducing KLAIM, that is also equipped with higher-order communication and with a naming service facility. The section ends with the presentation of OPENKLAIM, a KLAIM dialect equipped with constructs for explicitly modelling connectivity between network nodes and for handling changes of the network topology. Section 3 defines a temporal logics for μKLAIM that permits specification and verification of dynamic properties of networks (e.g., resource allocation, access to resources and information disclosure). Section 4 introduces two type systems for controlling processes activities, namely access to resources and mobility, in μKLAIM networks. Section 5 introduces HOTKLAIM (*Higher-Order Typed* KLAIM), an enrichment of KLAIM with the powerful abstraction mechanisms and types of system F. This permits to conveniently deal with highly parameterized mobile components and to dynamically enforce host security policies. Section 6 presents O'KLAIM, a linguistic integration of object-oriented features with KLAIM, which is used as the coordination language for exchanging mobile object-oriented code among processes in a network. Section 7 presents X-KLAIM (*eXtended* KLAIM), an experimental programming language obtained by extending KLAIM with a high level syntax (including variable declarations, assignments, conditionals, sequential and iterative process composition). The pragmatics of the language is illustrated by means of simple programming examples which demonstrate how well established programming paradigms for mobile applications can be naturally programmed in KLAIM. Finally, in the last section we draw a few conclusions on our work on KLAIM.

2   Klaim as a Process Calculus

In this section, we present the foundations of KLAIM as a process calculus. We shall introduce the main features of KLAIM step by step, by defining appropriate process calculi of increasing complexity. The main advantage of the approach is that it provides a scalable context where the semantics of each construct is self-contained and simple. We start by presenting cKLAIM (*Core* KLAIM) a variant of the π-calculus [MPW92] with process distribution, process mobility, and asynchronous communication of names through shared located repositories instead of channel-based communication primitives. Then, we introduce μKLAIM (*Micro* KLAIM) which is obtained by enriching cKLAIM with the full power of Linda coordination primitives: tuples and pattern-matching. KLAIM is then obtained by extending μKLAIM with higher-order communication and with a naming service facility. Finally, we present OPENKLAIM, a KLAIM dialect with constructs for explicitly modeling connectivity between network nodes and for handling changes in the network topology.

Table 1. cKlaim syntax.

$N ::=$		Nets	$a ::=$		Actions
	$l :: P$	single node		$\mathbf{out}(\ell')@\ell$	output
	$l :: \langle l' \rangle$	located datum		$\mathbf{in}(T)@\ell$	input
	$N_1 \parallel N_2$	net composition		$\mathbf{eval}(P)@\ell$	migration
				$\mathbf{newloc}(u)$	creation
$P ::=$		Processes			
	$\mathbf{nil}$	null process	$T ::=$		Templates
	$a.P$	action prefixing		ℓ	name
	$P_1 \mid P_2$	parallel composition		$! u$	formal
	A	process invocation			

2.1   cKlaim

The syntax of cKlaim [GP03a] is reported in Table 1. We assume existence of
two disjoint sets: the set $\mathcal{L}$, of *localities*, ranged over by $l, l', l_1, \ldots$, and the set $\mathcal{U}$,
of *locality variables*, ranged over by $u, u', u_1, \ldots$. Localities are the addresses (i.e.
network references) of nodes and are the syntactic ingredient used to express the
idea of administrative domain: computations at a given locality are under the
control of a specific authority. Moreover, localities provide the abstract counterpart of *resources* and are the cKlaim communicable objects. The set of *names*
$\mathcal{N}$, ranged over by $\ell, \ell', \ldots$, will denote the union of sets $\mathcal{L}$ and $\mathcal{U}$. Finally, we
assume a set $\mathcal{A}$, of *process identifiers*, ranged over by $A, B, \ldots$.

Nets are finite collections of nodes where processes and data can be allocated.
Nodes are pairs, the first component is a locality (l is the address of the node)
and the second component is either a process or a datum.

Processes are the cKlaim active computational units. They may be executed
concurrently either at the same locality or at different localities and can perform
four different basic operations, called *actions*. Two actions manage data repositories: adding/withdrawing a datum to/from a repository. One action activates
a new thread of execution, viz. a process. The last action permits creation of
new network nodes. The latter action is not indexed with an address because
it always acts locally; all other actions indicate explicitly the (possibly remote)
locality where they will take place. Action **in** exploits *templates* as patterns to
select data in shared repositories.

Processes are built up from the special process **nil**, that does not perform
any action, and from the basic operations by means of action prefixing, parallel composition and process definition. Recursive behaviours are modelled via
process definitions. It is assumed that each process identifier A has a *single*
defining equation $A \stackrel{\triangle}{=} P$. Hereafter, we do not explicitly represent equations for
process definitions (and their migration to make migrating processes complete),
and assume that they are available at any locality of a net.

Table 2. Structural congruence.

(COM) $N_1 \parallel N_2 \equiv N_2 \parallel N_1$	(ASSOC) $(N_1 \parallel N_2) \parallel N_3 \equiv N_1 \parallel (N_2 \parallel N_3)$
(ABS) $l::P \equiv l::(P\vert\mathbf{nil})$	(PRINV) $l::A \equiv l::P$ if $A \stackrel{\triangle}{=} P$
(CLONE) $l::(P_1\vert P_2) \equiv l::P_1 \parallel l::P_2$	

Names occurring in cKLAIM processes and nets can be *bound*. More precisely, action prefixes $\mathbf{in}(!\,u)@\ell.P$ and $\mathbf{newloc}(u).P$ bind u in P (namely, P is the scope of the bindings made by the action). A name that is not bound is called *free*. The sets $fn(\cdot)$ and $bn(\cdot)$ (respectively, of free and bound names of a process/net term) are defined accordingly. The set $n(\cdot)$ of names of a term is the union of its sets of free and bound names. As usual, we say that two terms are *α-equivalent*, written $\equiv_\alpha$, if one can be obtained from the other by renaming bound names. Hereafter, we shall work with terms whose bound names are all distinct and different from the free ones. Moreover, we will use σ to range over *substitutions*, i.e. functions with finite domain from locality variables to localities, and write $\circ$ to denote substitutions composition and ϵ to denote the 'empty' substitution.

The operational semantics of cKLAIM is given in terms of a structural congruence and of a reduction relation over nets. The *structural congruence*, $\equiv$, identifies nets which intuitively represent the same net. It is defined as the smallest congruence relation over nets that satisfies the laws in Table 2. The structural laws express that $\parallel$ is commutative and associative, that the null process can always be safely removed/added, that a process identifier can be replaced with the body of its definition, and that it is always possible to transform a parallel of co-located processes into a parallel over nodes. Notice that commutativity and associativity of '$\vert$' is somehow derived from rules (COM), (ASSOC) and (CLONE).

The *reduction relation*, $\rightarrowtail$, is the least relation induced by the rules in Table 3. Net reductions are defined over configurations of the form $L \vdash N$, where L is a finite set of names such that $fn(N) \subseteq L \subset \mathcal{N}$. Set L keeps track of the names occurring free in N and is needed to ensure global freshness of new network localities. Whenever a reduction does not generate any fresh addresses we write $N \rightarrowtail N'$ instead of $L \vdash N \rightarrowtail L \vdash N'$.

We now comment on the rules in Table 3. All rules for (possibly remote) process actions require existence of the target node. The assumption that all the equations for process definitions are available everywhere greatly simplifies rule (EVAL) because it permits avoiding mechanisms for code inspection to find the process definitions needed by Q. Rule (IN) requires existence of the chosen datum in the target node. Moreover, the rule says that action $\mathbf{in}(!\,u)@l'$ looks for any name l'' at l' that is then used to replace the free occurrences of u in the continuation of the process performing the input, while action $\mathbf{in}(l'')@l'$ looks exactly for the name l'' at l'; in both cases, the matched datum is consumed. With abuse of notation, we use $\mathbf{nil}$ to replace data that have been consumed to avoid disappearance of the hosting node (whenever, in the initial configuration,

Table 3. CKLAIM operational semantics.

(OUT)	$l :: \mathbf{out}(l'')@l'.P \parallel l' :: P' \succ\!\!\longrightarrow l :: P \parallel l' :: P' \parallel l' :: \langle l'' \rangle$
(EVAL)	$l :: \mathbf{eval}(Q)@l'.P \parallel l' :: P' \succ\!\!\longrightarrow l :: P \parallel l' :: P' \vert Q$
(IN)	$l :: \mathbf{in}(T)@l'.P \parallel l' :: \langle l'' \rangle \succ\!\!\longrightarrow l :: P\sigma \parallel l' :: \mathbf{nil}$ where $\sigma = \begin{cases} [l''/u] & \text{if } T = !\,u \\ \epsilon & \text{if } T = l'' \end{cases}$
(NEW)	$L \vdash l :: \mathbf{newloc}(u).P \succ\!\!\longrightarrow L \cup \{l'\} \vdash l :: P[l'/u] \parallel l' :: \mathbf{nil} \qquad \text{if } l' \notin L$
(PAR)	$\dfrac{L \vdash N_1 \succ\!\!\longrightarrow L' \vdash N_1'}{L \vdash N_1 \parallel N_2 \succ\!\!\longrightarrow L' \vdash N_1' \parallel N_2}$
(STRUCT)	$\dfrac{N \equiv N_1 \quad L \vdash N_1 \succ\!\!\longrightarrow L' \vdash N_2 \quad N_2 \equiv N'}{L \vdash N \succ\!\!\longrightarrow L' \vdash N'}$

it only contains tuples) due to data consumption. In rule (NEW), the premise exploits the set L to choose a fresh address l' for naming the new node. Notice that the address of the new node is not known to any other node in the net. Hence, it can be used by the creating process as a *private* name. Rule (PAR) says that if part of a net makes a reduction step, the whole net reduces accordingly. Finally, rule (STRUCT), that relates structural congruence and reduction, says that all structural congruent nets can make the same reduction steps.

Process interaction in CKLAIM is asynchronous: no synchronization takes place between sender and receiver processes (only existence of target nodes is checked). Moreover, communication is anonymous and associative because data have no names and are accessed via matching. Intuitively, data could be understood as *services* and matching provides a basic *service discovery* mechanism.

2.2 μKlaim

We now enrich CKLAIM with tuples and pattern-matching (and with a primitive for accessing tuples without consuming them) thus getting μKLAIM [GP03c]. Table 4 illustrates the syntactical categories for μKLAIM that differ from the corresponding ones in the syntax of CKLAIM. We shall use $x, y, z, \ldots$ as generic value variables, and still use ℓ to denote a locality l or a locality variable u.

In μKLAIM, communicable objects (the arguments of **out**) are *tuples*: sequences of actual fields. These contain expressions, localities or locality variables. The *tuple space* (TS, for short) of a node consists of the tuples located there. The precise syntax of *expressions* e is deliberately not specified. We assume that expressions contain, at least, basic values V and variables x. *Templates* are sequences of actual and formal fields, and are used as patterns to select tuples in a tuple space. Formal fields are written $!\,x$ or $!\,u$ and are used to bind variables to values. Notice that, syntactically, templates include tuples.

Processes can also read tuples without removing them from the tuple space by executing action **read**$(T)@\ell$. Only evaluated tuples can be added to a TS

Table 4. μKLAIM syntax.

$N ::=$		NETS	$T ::= F \mid F,T$			TEMPLATES
	$l::P$	*single node*	$F ::= f \mid !x \mid !u$			TEMPLATE FIELDS
	$\mid l::\langle et \rangle$	*located tuple*	$t ::= f \mid f,t$			TUPLES
	$\mid N_1 \parallel N_2$	*net composition*	$f ::= e \mid \ell \mid u$			TUPLE FIELDS
			$et ::= ef \mid ef,et$			EVALUATED TUPLES
$a ::=$		ACTIONS	$ef ::= V \mid l$			EVALUATED TUPLE
	$\mathbf{out}(t)@\ell$	*output*				FIELDS
	$\mid \mathbf{in}(T)@\ell$	*input*	$e ::= V \mid x \mid \ \dots$			EXPRESSIONS
	$\mid \mathbf{read}(T)@\ell$	*read*				
	$\mid \mathbf{eval}(P)@\ell$	*migration*				
	$\mid \mathbf{newloc}(u)$	*creation*				

Table 5. Matching rules.

$$(\text{M}_1) \quad match(V,V) = \epsilon \qquad\qquad (\text{M}_2) \quad match(!x,V) = [V/x]$$

$$(\text{M}_3) \quad match(l,l) = \epsilon \qquad\qquad (\text{M}_4) \quad match(!u,l) = [l/u]$$

$$(\text{M}_5) \quad \frac{match(eF,ef) = \sigma_1 \qquad match(eT,et) = \sigma_2}{match(\ (eF,eT)\ ,\ (ef,et)\ ) = \sigma_1 \circ \sigma_2}$$

and templates must be evaluated before they can be used for retrieving tuples. Template evaluation consists in computing the value of the expressions occurring in the template. Localities and formal fields are left unchanged by evaluation. Templates with variables in actual fields cannot be evaluated. We shall write $[\![\,T\,]\!]$ to denote the template resulting from evaluation of T when evaluation succeeds.

To define the operational semantics, we first formalize the pattern-matching mechanism which is used to select (evaluated) tuples from TSs according to (evaluated) templates. The *pattern-matching* function *match* is defined in Table 5. The meaning of the rules is straightforward: an evaluated template matches against an evaluated tuple if both have the same number of fields and corresponding fields do match; two values (localities) match only if they are identical, while formal fields match any value of the same type. A successful matching returns a substitution function associating the variables contained in the formal fields of the template with the values contained in the corresponding actual fields of the accessed tuple (of course, in μKLAIM, substitutions can also encompass values and value variables).

While the structural congruence is left unchanged, the reduction relation, $\rightarrowtail$ refines that given in Table 3 for CKLAIM. In the rest of this section, we comment on the different reduction rules. Rule (OUT) becomes

Table 6. KLAIM syntax.

$N ::=$	NETS	$P \mathrel{+=} X$	*process variable*
$l::_\rho P$	*single node*	$F \mathrel{+=} \,!\,X$	
$\mid\ l::\langle et \rangle$	*located tuple*	$f \mathrel{+=} P$	
$\mid\ N_1 \parallel N_2$	*net composition*	$ef \mathrel{+=} P$	

$$(\textsc{Out}) \quad \frac{[\![\,t\,]\!] = et}{l::\mathbf{out}(t)@l'.P \parallel l'::P' \;\longmapsto\; l::P \parallel l'::P' \parallel l'::\langle et \rangle}$$

and expresses that the tuple resulting from the evaluation of the argument t of
out is added to the TS at l' (therefore, the **out** can be performed only when t
is evaluable). Rule (IN) becomes

$$(\textsc{In}) \quad \frac{match([\![\,T\,]\!], et) = \sigma}{l::\mathbf{in}(T)@l'.P \parallel l'::\langle et \rangle \;\longmapsto\; l::P\sigma \parallel l'::\mathbf{nil}}$$

The rule expresses that the process performing the operation can proceed only
if the argument T of **in** is evaluable and pattern-matching succeeds. In this case,
the tuple is removed from the TS and the returned substitution is applied to the
continuation of the process performing the operation. A similar rule is introduced
to model the semantics of action **read**, namely

$$(\textsc{Read}) \quad \frac{match([\![\,T\,]\!], et) = \sigma}{l::\mathbf{read}(T)@l'.P \parallel l'::\langle et \rangle \;\longmapsto\; l::P\sigma \parallel l'::\langle et \rangle}$$

that differs from (IN) just because the accessed tuple is still left in the TS.

2.3   Klaim

We are now able to introduce all features of KLAIM. Table 6 illustrates the syntax
of the calculus that differs from the corresponding part of the syntax of μKLAIM;
in particular, the productions for nets replace those in Table 1 and the productions for tuple fields replace those in Table 4. As a matter of notation, given a
grammar such as $e::= p_1 \mid \ \ldots \ \mid p_m$, we write $e\mathrel{+=} p_{m+1} \mid \ \ldots \ \mid p_{m+n}$ as a
shorthand for $e::= p_1 \mid \ \ldots \ \mid p_{m+n}$.

A *network node* becomes a term of the form $l::_\rho P$, where ρ is an *allocation
environment* that binds the locality variables occurring free in P. Allocation environments provide a name resolution mechanism by mapping locality variables
u into localities l. The distinguished locality variable $\mathtt{self}$ is used by processes
to refer to the address of their current hosting node.

Remark 1. This is different from previous presentations of KLAIM where, besides
(physical) localities and locality variables, we also used the syntactical category
of *logical localities* and defined allocation environments as maps from logical

localities to (physical) localities. To simplify the resulting calculus, in this paper we preferred to incorporate the syntactical category of logical localities into that of locality variables.   □

One significant design choice underlying KLAIM is abstraction of the exact physical allocation of processes and resources over the net. Indeed, in the initial configuration, localities cannot occur in templates/tuples argument of process actions because they cannot occur as actual fields anymore. Therefore, processes have no direct access to nodes and can get knowledge of a locality either through their (local) naming facilities, viz. allocation environment, or by communicating with other processes (which, again, exploit other allocation environments). To this aim, the operational semantics will use localities alike locality variables (i.e. it will be defined over nets generated from an extended syntax that allows localities to occur wherever we can have locality variables).

We say that a net is *well-formed* if for each node $l::_\rho P$ we have that $\rho(\texttt{self}) = l$, and if for any pair of nodes $l::_\rho P$ and $l'::_{\rho'} P'$, $l = l'$ implies $\rho = \rho'$. Hereafter, we will only consider well-formed nets.

The second important extension with respect to μKLAIM is higher-order communication. This feature enables processes to exchange pieces of code through the communication actions. We will explain later how this form of code migration differs from the one provided by **eval**.

As far as the operational semantics is concerned, the structural congruence is modified in the obvious way (thus, it is not shown): the most significant law is $l::_\rho (P_1|P_2) \equiv l::_\rho P_1 \parallel l::_\rho P_2$. Allocation environments affects the evaluation of templates when evaluating locality variables. To this purpose, the template evaluation function takes as parameter the allocation environment of the node where evaluation takes place. The function has the form $[\![\cdot]\!]_\rho$ and the main clauses of its definition are given below:

$$[\![u]\!]_\rho = \begin{cases} \rho(u) & \text{if } u \in dom(\rho) \\ undef & \text{otherwise} \end{cases} \qquad\qquad [\![P]\!]_\rho = P\{\rho\}$$

where $P\{\rho\}$ denotes the process term obtained from P by replacing any free occurrence of a locality variable $u \in dom(\rho)$ that is not within the argument of an **eval** with $\rho(u)$. Process $[\![P]\!]_\rho$ is deemed to be well-defined only if $P\{\rho\}$ does not contain free locality variables outside the arguments of **eval**. Two examples of process evaluation are $[\![out(P)@\ell.Q]\!]_\rho = out([\![P]\!]_\rho)@\rho(\ell).Q\{\rho\}$ and $[\![eval(P)@\ell.Q]\!]_\rho = eval(P)@\rho(\ell).Q\{\rho\}$. We shall write $[\![t]\!]_\rho = et$ to denote that evaluation of tuple t using ρ succeeds and returns the evaluated tuple et.

The most significant rules of the reduction relation are reported in Table 7, where we write $\rho(\ell) = l$ to denote that either $\ell = l$ or ℓ is a locality variable that ρ maps to l. In rule (OUT), the local allocation environment is used both to determine the name of the node where the tuple must be placed and to evaluate the argument tuple. This implies that if the argument tuple contains a field with a process, the corresponding field of the evaluated tuple contains the process resulting from the evaluation of its locality variables. Hence, processes in a tuple are transmitted after the interpretation of their free locality variables

Table 7. KLAIM operational semantics.

(OUT)	$$\frac{\rho(\ell) = l' \qquad [\![\, t \,]\!]_\rho = et}{l::_\rho \mathbf{out}(t)@\ell.P \parallel l'::_{\rho'} P' \succ\!\!\longrightarrow l::_\rho P \parallel l'::_{\rho'} P' \parallel l'::\langle et \rangle}$$
(EVAL)	$$\frac{\rho(\ell) = l'}{l::_\rho \mathbf{eval}(Q)@\ell.P \parallel l'::_{\rho'} P' \succ\!\!\longrightarrow l::_\rho P \parallel l'::_{\rho'} P'|Q}$$
(IN)	$$\frac{\rho(\ell) = l' \qquad match([\![\, T \,]\!]_\rho, et) = \sigma}{l::_\rho \mathbf{in}(T)@\ell.P \parallel l'::\langle et \rangle \succ\!\!\longrightarrow l::_\rho P\sigma \parallel l'::\mathbf{nil}}$$
(READ)	$$\frac{\rho(\ell) = l' \qquad match([\![\, T \,]\!]_\rho, et) = \sigma}{l::_\rho \mathbf{read}(T)@\ell.P \parallel l'::\langle et \rangle \succ\!\!\longrightarrow l::_\rho P\sigma \parallel l'::\langle et \rangle}$$
(NEW)	$$\frac{l' \notin L}{L \vdash l::_\rho \mathbf{newloc}(u).P \succ\!\!\longrightarrow L \cup \{l'\} \vdash l::_\rho P[l'/u] \parallel l'::_{\rho[l'/\texttt{self}]} \mathbf{nil}}$$

through the local allocation environment. This corresponds to having a *static scoping* discipline for the (possibly remote) generation of tuples. A *dynamic linking* strategy is adopted for the **eval** operation, rule (EVAL). In this case the locality variables of the spawned process are not interpreted using the local allocation environment: the linking of locality variables is done at the remote node. Finally, in rule (NEW), the environment of a new node is derived from that of the creating one with the obvious update for the **self** variable. Therefore, the new node inherits all the bindings of the creating node.

We end this section with a simple example that should throw light on the differences between the two forms of mobility supplied by KLAIM. One form is mobility with static scoping: a process moves along the nodes of a net with a fixed binding of resources. The other form is mobility with dynamic linking: process movements break the links to local resources. For instance, consider a net consisting of two localities l_1 and l_2. A client process C is allocated at locality l_1 and a server process S is allocated at locality l_2. The server can accept processes for execution. The client sends process Q to the server. The code of processes is:

$$C \overset{\triangle}{=} \mathbf{out}(Q)@u.\mathbf{nil}$$
$$Q \overset{\triangle}{=} \mathbf{in}(\text{"foo"}, !x)@\texttt{self}.\mathbf{out}(\text{"foo"}, x+1)@\texttt{self}.\mathbf{nil}$$
$$S \overset{\triangle}{=} \mathbf{in}(!X)@\texttt{self}.X$$

The behaviour of the processes above depends on the meaning of u and **self**. It is the allocation environment that establishes the links between locality variables and localities. Here, we assume that the allocation environment of locality l_1, ρ_1, maps **self** into l_1 and u into l_2, while the allocation environment of locality l_2, ρ_2, maps **self** into l_2. Finally, we assume that the tuple spaces located at l_1 and l_2 both contain the tuple $\langle \text{"foo"}, 1 \rangle$. The following KLAIM program represents the net described above:

$$l_1::_{\rho_1} C|\langle''\!foo'', 1\rangle \;\; \| \;\; l_2::_{\rho_2} S|\langle''\!foo'', 1\rangle.$$

After the execution of **out**$(Q)@u$, the tuple space at locality l_2 contains a tuple where the code of process Q is stored. Indeed, it is the process Q' that is stored in the tuple:

$$Q' \triangleq \mathbf{in}(''\!foo'', !x)@l_1.\mathbf{out}(''\!foo'', x+1)@l_1.\mathbf{nil}.$$

The locality variables occurring in Q are evaluated using the environment at locality l_1 where the action **out** has been executed. Hence, when executed at the server's locality the mobile process Q increases tuple $''\!foo''$ at the client's locality.

In order to move process Q for execution at l_2 without keeping the original linkage to resources, the client code should be **eval**$(Q)@u.\mathbf{nil}$. When **eval**$(Q)@u$ is executed, Q is spawned at the remote node *without* evaluating its locality variables according to the allocation environment ρ_1. Thus, the execution of Q will depend only on the allocation environment ρ_2 and Q will increase tuple $''\!foo''$ at the server's locality.

2.4   OpenKlaim

In this section, we present an extension of KLAIM, called here OPENKLAIM, that has been first presented in [BLP02] and was specifically designed for enabling users to give more realistic accounts of *open systems*. Indeed, open systems are dynamically evolving structures: new nodes can get connected or existing nodes can disconnect. Connections and disconnections can be temporary and unexpected. Thus, the assumption that the underlying communication network will always be available is too strong. Moreover, since network routes may be affected by restrictions (such as temporary failures or firewall policies), *naming* may not suffice to establish connections or to perform remote operations. Therefore, to make KLAIM suitable for dealing with open systems, the need arises to extend the language with constructs for explicitly modeling connectivity between network nodes and for handling changes in the network topology.

OPENKLAIM is obtained by equipping KLAIM with mechanisms to dynamically update allocation environments and to handle node connectivity, and with a new category of processes, called *nodecoordinators*, that, in addition to standard KLAIM operations, can execute privileged operations that permit establishing new connections, accepting connection requests and removing connections. The new privileged operations can also be interpreted as movement operations: entering a new administrative domain, accepting incoming nodes and exiting from an administrative domain. The KLAIM extensions that lead to OPENKLAIM are reported in Table 8.

OPENKLAIM processes can be thought of as user programs and differs from KLAIM processes in the following three respects.

Table 8. OPENKLAIM syntax.

$a ::=$		ACTIONS	$f +=$		TUPLE FIELDS
	$\mathbf{out}(t)@\ell$	output		$*l$	Dereferentiation
$\mid$	$\mathbf{in}(T)@\ell$	input			
$\mid$	$\mathbf{read}(T)@\ell$	read	$\mathbb{C} ::=$		NODECOORDINATORS
$\mid$	$\mathbf{eval}(P)@\ell$	migration		P	(standard) process
$\mid$	$\mathbf{bind}(u,l)$	bind	$\mid$	$pa.\mathbb{C}$	action prefixing
			$\mid$	$\mathbb{C}_1 \mid \mathbb{C}_2$	parallel composition
$pa ::=$		PRIVILEGED ACTIONS	$\mid$	$\mathbb{A}$	node coordinator invocation
	a	(standard) action			
$\mid$	$\mathbf{newloc}(u,\mathbb{C})$	creation	$N ::=$		NETS
$\mid$	$\mathbf{login}(\ell)$	login		$\mathbf{0}$	empty net
$\mid$	$\mathbf{logout}(\ell)$	logout	$\mid$	$l ::_\rho^S \mathbb{C}$	single node
$\mid$	$\mathbf{accept}(u)$	accept	$\mid$	$l :: \langle et \rangle$	located tuple
			$\mid$	$N_1 \parallel N_2$	net composition

- When tuples are evaluated, locality names resolution does not take place automatically anymore. Instead, it has to be explicitly required by putting the operator $*$ in front of the locality that has to be evaluated. For instance, $(3,l)$ and $(s,\mathbf{out}(s_1)@s_2.\mathbf{nil})$ are fully-evaluated while $(3,*l)$ and $(*l,\mathbf{out}(l)@\mathtt{self}.\mathbf{nil})$ are not.
- Operation **newloc** cannot be performed by user processes anymore. It is now part of the syntax of node coordinator processes because, when a new node is created, it is necessary to install one such process at it and, for security reasons, user processes cannot be allowed to do this.
- Operation **bind** has been added to enable user processes to enhance local allocation environments with name bindings. For instance, $\mathbf{bind}(u,l)$ enhances the local allocation environment with the pair (u,l).

NodeCoordinators can be thought of as processes written by node managers, a sort of superusers. Thus, in addition to the standard KLAIM operations, such processes can execute coordination operations to establish new connections (viz. $\mathbf{login}(\ell)$), to accept connection requests (viz. $\mathbf{accept}(u)$), and to remove connections (viz. $\mathbf{logout}(\ell)$). These operations are not indexed with a locality, since they always act locally at the node where they are executed. Node coordinators are stationary processes and cannot be used as tuple fields. They are installed at a node either when the node is initially configured or when the node is dynamically created, e.g. when a node coordinator performs $\mathbf{newloc}(u,\mathbb{C})$ (where $\mathbb{C}$ is a node coordinator).

A network node is now either a located tuple $l :: \langle et \rangle$ or a 4-tuple of the form $l ::_\rho^S \mathbb{C}$, where S gives the set of nodes connected to l and $\mathbb{C}$ is the parallel composition of user and node coordinator processes. A net can be an empty net $\mathbf{0}$, a single node or the parallel composition of two nets N_1 and N_2 with disjoint sets of node addresses (in this setting, we do not use structural congruence, thus we don't have an analogous of rule (CLONE) of Table 2).

Table 9. Process semantics (sample rules).

$$l::\langle et \rangle \xrightarrow[l]{\langle et \rangle @l} \mathbf{0} \quad (\text{Tuple}) \qquad\qquad l::^S_\rho \mathbb{C} \xrightarrow[l]{l::^S_\rho \mathbb{C}} \mathbf{0} \quad (\text{Node})$$

$$\frac{N_1 \xrightarrow[l_1]{\lambda} N_1' \quad N_2 \xrightarrow[l_2]{l_2::^{\{l_1\} \cup S}_\rho \mathbb{C}} N_2'}{N_1 \parallel N_2 \xrightarrow[l_2]{\lambda\{\rho\}} N_1' \parallel N_2' \parallel l_2::^{\{l_1\} \cup S}_\rho \mathbb{C}} \quad (\text{Env})$$

$$l::^S_\rho \mathbf{bind}(u, l_1).\mathbb{C} \xrightarrow[l]{\mathbf{b}(l, u, l_1)} l::^S_{\rho[l_1/u]} \mathbb{C} \quad \textit{if } \rho(u) \textit{ is undefined} \quad (\text{Bind})$$

$$l::^S_\rho \mathbf{out}(t)@\ell.\mathbb{C} \xrightarrow[l]{\mathbf{o}(l, [\![t]\!]_\rho, \rho(\ell))} l::^S_\rho \mathbb{C} \quad (\text{Out})$$

$$l::^S_\rho \mathbf{in}(T)@\ell.\mathbb{C} \xrightarrow[l]{\mathbf{i}(l, [\![T]\!]_\rho, \rho(\ell))} l::^S_\rho \mathbb{C} \quad (\text{In})$$

If $l::^S_\rho \mathbb{C}$ is a node in the net, then we will say that the nodes in S are *logged in* l and that l is a *gateway* for those nodes. A node can have more than one gateway. Moreover, if l_1 is logged in l_2 and l_2 is logged in l_3 then l_3 is a gateway for l_1 too.

Remark 2. Our approach aims at a clean separation between the coordinator level (made up by node coordinator processes) and the user level (made up by standard processes). This separation has a considerable impact. From an abstract point of view, the coordinator level may represent the network operating system running on a specific computer and the user level may represent the processes running on that computer. The new privileged operations are then system calls supplied by the network operating system. From a more implementative point of view, the coordinator level may represent the part of a distributed application that takes care of the connections to a remote server (if the application is a client) or that manages the connected clients (if the application is a server). The user level then represents the remaining parts of the application that can interact with the coordinator by means of specific protocols.   □

To save space, here we do not show the full operational semantics of OPEN-KLAIM (we refer the interested reader to [BLP02]), rather we show the most significant rules. The semantics of nets, given by the reduction relation $\rightarrowtail$ (partially) defined in Table 11, exploits two labelled transitions: $\xrightarrow[l]{\lambda}$, (partially) defined in Table 9, accounts for the execution of standard actions and for the availability of net resources (tuples and nodes); $\xrightarrow{\lambda}$, (partially) defined in Table 10, accounts for the execution of privileged actions. Within the transition labels, l indicates the gateway that makes an action possible, while λ represents

Table 10. *Node coordinator* semantics (sample rules).

$$\frac{l_2 \notin L}{L \vdash l_1::_\rho^S \textbf{newloc}(u, \mathbb{C}).\mathbb{C}' \xrightarrow{\ \textbf{n}(l_1,\mathbb{C},l_2)\ } L \cup \{l_2\} \vdash l_1::_\rho^S \mathbb{C}'[l_2/u]} \quad (\text{NEWLOC})$$

$$l_1::_\rho^S \textbf{login}(l_2).\mathbb{C} \xrightarrow{\ \textbf{lin}(l_1,-,l_2)\ } l_1::_\rho^S \mathbb{C} \quad (\text{LOGIN})$$

$$l_1::_\rho^S \textbf{logout}(l_2).\mathbb{C} \xrightarrow{\ \textbf{lout}(l_1,-,l_2)\ } l_1::_\rho^S \mathbb{C} \quad (\text{LOGOUT})$$

$$l_1::_\rho^S \textbf{accept}(u).\mathbb{C} \xrightarrow{\ \textbf{acc}(l_1,-,l_2)\ } l_1::_\rho^{S\cup\{l_2\}} \mathbb{C}[l_2/u] \quad (\text{ACCEPT})$$

Table 11. OPENKLAIM operational semantics (sample rules).

$$\frac{N_1 \xrightarrow[l]{\ \textbf{b}(l_2,u,l_1)\ } N_2}{N_1 \longmapsto N_2} \quad (\text{NETBIND})$$

$$\frac{N_1 \xrightarrow[l]{\ \textbf{o}(l_1,et,l_2)\ } N_1' \quad N_1' \xrightarrow[l]{\ l_2::_\rho^S P\ } N_2}{N_1 \longmapsto N_2 \parallel l_2::_\rho^S \langle et\rangle | P} \quad (\text{NETOUT})$$

$$\frac{N_1 \xrightarrow[l]{\ \langle et\rangle @ l_2\ } N_1' \quad N_1' \xrightarrow[l]{\ \textbf{i}(l_1,[\![\,T\,]\!]_\rho,l_2)\ } N_2 \quad match([\![\,T\,]\!]_\rho, et) = \sigma}{N_1 \longmapsto N_2\sigma} \quad (\text{NETIN})$$

$$\frac{N_1 \xrightarrow{\ \textbf{n}(l_1,\mathbb{C},l_2)\ } N_2}{N_1 \longmapsto N_2 \parallel l_2::_{[l_2/\texttt{self}]}^\emptyset \mathbb{C}} \quad (\text{NETNEW})$$

$$\frac{N_1 \xrightarrow{\ \textbf{lin}(l_1,-,l_2)\ } N_1' \quad N_1' \xrightarrow{\ \textbf{acc}(l_2,-,l_1)\ } N_2}{N_1 \longmapsto N_2} \quad (\text{NETLOGIN})$$

$$\frac{N_1 \xrightarrow{\ \textbf{lout}(l_1,-,l_2)\ } N_1' \quad N_1' \xrightarrow[l_2]{\ l_2:_{l_2}^{\{l_1\}\cup S}\mathbb{C}\ } N_2 \quad \rho' = \rho \setminus l_1}{N_1 \longmapsto N_2 \parallel l_2::_{\rho'}^S \mathbb{C}} \quad (\text{NETLOGOUT})$$

the intended operation and has the form $\textbf{x}(l_1, arg, l_2)$, where $\textbf{x}$ is the operation, l_1 is the node performing the operation, l_2 is the target node, and arg is the argument of $\textbf{x}$. For instance, $\textbf{i}(l_1, [\![\,T\,]\!]_\rho, l_2)$ represents operation $\textbf{in}(T)@l_2$ performed at l_1.

Rule (TUPLE) signals the presence of the tuple $\langle et\rangle$ in the tuple space of l and, similarly, rule (NODE) signals the presence of node $l::_\rho^S \mathbb{C}$ in the net. These information are used to enable execution of standard actions different from **bind**. Rule (ENV) permits changing the gateway used by an action. This is important for remote interaction because two nodes can interact only if there exists a node that acts as gateway for both. Moreover, rule (ENV) implements a *name resolution* mechanism (akin those of DNS servers): node l_1, that uses l_2 as a gateway, can exploit l_2's allocation environment for resolving localities that it is not able to resolve by itself (this is not shown in detail here but this is what notation $\lambda\{\rho\}$ means). Rules (BIND) and (NETBIND) enhance the local allocation environment with the new alias u for l_1. Rules (OUT) and (NETOUT) model tuple output. To this aim, it is checked existence of the target node (by using rule (NODE)) and existence of a gateway shared between the source and the target nodes (by using rule (ENV)). Similarly, rules (IN) and (NETIN) model communication; in this case, it is checked existence of a matching tuple at the target node (by using rule (TUPLE)) and, again, existence of a shared gateway.

Rules (NEWLOC) and (NETNEW) say that $\mathbf{newloc}(u, \mathbb{C})$ creates a new node in the net, binds its address to u in the local allocation environment and installs the node coordinator $\mathbb{C}$ at the new node. Differently from KLAIM, the new node does not inherit the binders of the creating node (inheritance could be programmed by appropriately using **bind** in $\mathbb{C}$). We have also that a **newloc** does not automatically log the new node in the generating one. This can be done by installing in the new node a node coordinator that performs a **login**. Rule (LOGIN) says that $\mathbf{login}(l_2)$ logs the executing node l_1 in l_2. Rules (ACCEPT) and (NETLOGIN) say that, for a $\mathbf{login}(l_2)$ executed at l_1 to succeed, there must be at l_2 a node coordinator process of the form $\mathbf{accept}(l_1).\mathbb{C}'$. As a consequence of this synchronization, l_1 is added to the set S of nodes logged in l_2. Rules (LOGOUT) and (NETLOGOUT) say that $\mathbf{logout}(l_2)$ disconnects the executing node l_1 from l_2; as a consequence, l_1 is removed from the set S of nodes logged in l_2 and any *alias* for l_1 is removed from the allocation environment ρ of l_2 (notation $\rho \setminus l_1$). The second premise of rule (NETLOGOUT) checks existence of a node of the form $l_2::_\rho^{\{l_1\}\cup S} \mathbb{C}$ in N_1' and returns the net N_2 obtained by removing that node from N_1'.

Remark 3. OPENKLAIM can be viewed as a core calculus to describe net infrastructures. The calculus can be easily extended with powerful constructs definable atop the basic primitives. For example, a few such constructs have been introduced in [BLP02]. In X-KLAIM such derived operations are provided as primitives for efficiency reasons (see Section 7.1). $\qquad\square$

The design principles underlying OPENKLAIM have been exploited in [DFM+03] to define KAOS, a calculus that can be considered as an extension of μKLAIM with OPENKLAIM node coordinators. The main peculiarity of KAOS is that connections among nodes are labelled by *costs*, namely special values that abstract connection features. Costs are the formal tool for programming *Quality of Service* (QoS) attributes at the level of WAN applications. Indeed, KAOS costs measure *non-functional* properties (e.g., *timely response* and *security*) that programmers can specify and that depend on the application. The underlying algebraic structure of costs is a *constraint semi-ring* [BMR97] and this permits performing operations over costs, such as addition and comparison.

Hence, it is possible to take into account costs when paths between nodes must be determined.

3   A Modal Logic for μKlaim

For agent-based calculi, as well as for other formalisms, it is crucial to have tools for establishing deadlock freeness, liveness and correctness with respect to given specifications. However for programs involving different actors and authorities it is also important to establish other properties such as resources allocation, access to resources and information disclosure. In [DL02,Lor02] a temporal logics has been proposed for specifying and verifying dynamic properties of mobile agents specified in KLAIM. The inspiration for the proposal was Hennessy-Milner Logics [HM85] but it needed significant adaptations due to the richer operating context. In this section, we re-work on the logics of [DL02] and propose a simplified variant of the logic for μKLAIM.

In order to do this, we need to reconsider the operational semantics of μKLAIM that was given as a set of rewriting rules in Section 2. We need here a labelled operational semantics that makes evident the involved localities and the information transmitted over the net. Our labels carry information about the action performed, the localities involved in the action and the transmitted information. Transition labels have the following structure:

$$\mathbf{x}(l_1, arg, l_2),$$

where $\mathbf{x}$ denotes the action performed. The set *Lab* of transition labels a is defined by the following grammar:

$$a ::= \mathbf{o}(l_1, et, l_2) \mid \mathbf{i}(l_1, et, l_2) \mid \mathbf{r}(l_1, et, l_2) \mid \mathbf{e}(l_1, P, l_2) \mid \mathbf{n}(l_1, -, l_2)$$

Locality l_1 denotes the node where the action is executed, while l_2 is the node where the action takes effect. Finally, arg is the argument of the action and can be either a tuple or a process. For instance, if a process running at l_1 inserts $[\![t]\!]$ in the tuple space located at l_2, by executing $\mathbf{out}(t)@l_2$, then the net evolves with a transition whose label is $\mathbf{o}(l_1, [\![t]\!], l_2)$. The rules of the labelled operational semantics are presented in Table 12. Notice that, the proposed semantics is completely in accordance with the one presented in Table 3. In fact, the rules are the same apart for the labels.

Temporal properties of nets are expressed by means of the *diamond* operator ($\langle \mathcal{A} \rangle \phi$) indexed with a predicate over transition labels. A net N satisfies a formula $\langle \mathcal{A} \rangle \phi$ if there exists a label a and a net N' such that we have: $N \succ\!\!\xrightarrow{a} N'$, a satisfies $\mathcal{A}$ and N' satisfies ϕ.

Specific process predicates are introduced to describe *static* properties of processes that are spawned to be evaluated remotely. These predicates permit specifying accesses to resources (data and nodes) by processes and the causal dependencies of their actions.

The logic provides also state formulae for specifying the distribution of resources (i.e. data stored in nodes) in the system.

Table 12. μKLAIM labelled operational semantics.

(OUT)	$$\dfrac{[\![\,t\,]\!] = et}{l::\mathbf{out}(t)@l'.P \parallel l::P' \xrightarrow{\;\mathrm{o}(l,et,l')\;} l::P \parallel l::P' \parallel l'::\langle et\rangle}$$
(EVAL)	$$l::\mathbf{eval}(Q)@l'.P \parallel l'::P' \xrightarrow{\;\mathrm{e}(l,Q,l')\;} l::P \parallel l'::P'|Q$$
(IN)	$$\dfrac{match([\![\,T\,]\!],et) = \sigma}{l::\mathbf{in}(T)@l'.P \parallel l'::\langle et\rangle \xrightarrow{\;\mathrm{i}(l,et,l')\;} l::P\sigma \parallel l'::\mathbf{nil}}$$
(READ)	$$\dfrac{match([\![\,T\,]\!],et) = \sigma}{l::\mathbf{read}(T)@l'.P \parallel l'::\langle et\rangle \xrightarrow{\;\mathrm{r}(l,et,l')\;} l::P\sigma \parallel l'::\langle et\rangle}$$
(NEW)	$$\dfrac{l' \notin L}{L \vdash l::\mathbf{newloc}(u).P \xrightarrow{\;\mathrm{n}(l,-,l')\;} L \cup \{l'\} \vdash l::P[l'/u] \parallel l'::\mathbf{nil}}$$
(PAR)	$$\dfrac{L \vdash N_1 \xrightarrow{\;a\;} L' \vdash N_1'}{L \vdash N_1 \parallel N_2 \xrightarrow{\;a\;} L' \vdash N_1' \parallel N_2}$$
(STRUCT)	$$\dfrac{N \equiv N_1 \quad L \vdash N_1 \xrightarrow{\;a\;} L' \vdash N_2 \quad N_2 \equiv N'}{L \vdash N \xrightarrow{\;a\;} L' \vdash N'}$$

Table 13. The logic for μKLAIM.

$$\Phi ::= \mathtt{true} \mid \langle t\rangle@\ell \mid \langle \mathcal{A}\rangle\phi \mid \kappa \mid \nu\kappa.\phi \mid \phi \vee \phi \mid \neg\phi$$

$$\mathcal{A} ::= \circ \mid \alpha \mid \mathcal{A}_1 \sqcap \mathcal{A}_2 \mid \mathcal{A}_1 \cup \mathcal{A}_2 \mid \mathcal{A}_1 - \mathcal{A}_2 \mid \forall u. \mathcal{A}$$

$$\alpha ::= \mathtt{O}(\ell_1,\ell,\ell_2) \mid \mathtt{I}(\ell_1,\ell,\ell_2) \mid \mathtt{R}(\ell_1,\ell,\ell_2) \mid \mathtt{E}(\ell_1,\mathtt{pp},\ell_2) \mid \mathtt{N}(\ell_1,-,\ell_2)$$

$$\mathtt{pp} ::= \mathtt{1_P} \mid \mathtt{ap} \to \mathtt{pp} \mid \mathtt{pp} \wedge \mathtt{pp}$$

$$\mathtt{ap} ::= \mathtt{o}(\ell)@\mathtt{lp} \mid \mathtt{i}(T)@\mathtt{lp} \mid \mathtt{r}(T)@\mathtt{lp} \mid \mathtt{e}(\mathtt{pp})@\mathtt{lp} \mid \mathtt{n}(u)$$

Below, we introduce syntax and semantics of the logic. We let Φ be the set of logic formulae defined by the grammar of Table 13, where:

- ϕ is used to denote logical formulae that characterize properties of μKLAIM systems;
- κ belongs to the set of logical variables $VLog$;
- $\mathcal{A}$ denotes a *label predicate*, i.e. a predicate that finitely specifies an infinite set of transition labels;
- pp denotes a *process predicate* that express *static* properties of processes.

In the rest of this section, we explain first syntax and semantics of formulae, then introduce label predicates and their interpretation. We conclude the section with the definition of process predicates.

3.1   Logical Formulae

A formula ϕ can be either true, that is satisfied by any net, or a composed formula; a net N satisfies $\phi_1 \vee \phi_2$ if N satisfies either ϕ_1 or ϕ_2, while N satisfies $\neg\phi$ if N does not satisfies ϕ. Specific state formulae ($\langle t \rangle @\ell$) are introduced for specifying properties related to the data placement over the nodes. N satisfies $\langle t \rangle @\ell$ if and only if N contains node ℓ and tuple $\langle [\![t]\!] \rangle$ is stored in the tuple space located at ℓ. Dynamic properties of μKLAIM systems are specified using the operator $diamond$ ($\langle \mathcal{A} \rangle \phi$) that is indexed with predicates specifying properties of transition labels. We will rely on the interpretation function $\mathbb{A}[\![\cdot]\!]$ that will be formally defined later. It interprets each label predicate $\mathcal{A}$ as a set of pairs $\langle a, \sigma \rangle$ where a is a transition label and σ is a substitution.

The intuitive interpretation of $\langle \mathcal{A} \rangle \phi$ will be:

– a net N satisfies $\langle \mathcal{A} \rangle \phi$ if there exist $\langle a, \sigma \rangle \in \mathbb{A}[\![\mathcal{A}]\!]$ and N' such that $N \succ\!\!\xrightarrow{a} N'$ and N' satisfies $\phi\sigma$;

Recursive formulae $\nu\kappa.\phi$ are used to specify $infinite$ properties of systems. To guarantee well that the interpretation function of formulae be well-defined, we shall assume that no variable κ occurs negatively (i.e. under the scope of an odd number of $\neg$ operators) in ϕ.

Other formulae like $[\mathcal{A}]\phi$, $\phi_1 \wedge \phi_2$ or $\mu\kappa.\phi$ can be expressed in ϕ. Indeed $[\mathcal{A}]\phi = \neg\langle \mathcal{A} \rangle\neg\phi$, $\phi_1 \wedge \phi_2 = \neg(\phi_1 \vee \phi_2)$ and $\mu\kappa.\phi = \neg\nu\kappa.\neg\phi[\neg\kappa/\kappa]$. We shall use these derivable formulae as $macros$ in ϕ.

The interpretation function of formulae makes use of $logical\ environments$. A logical environment is a function that, given a logical variable and a substitution, yields a set of nets.

Definition 1. *Let $VLog$ be the set of logical variables, $Subst$ be the set of substitutions and Net be the set of μ*KLAIM *nets, we define the* logical environment Env *as*

$$Env \subseteq [VLog \rightarrow Subst \rightarrow 2^{Net}]$$

We will use ε, sometime with indexes, to denote elements of Env.

The interpretation function $\mathbb{M}[\![\cdot]\!]: \Phi \rightarrow Env \rightarrow Subst \rightarrow 2^{Net}$ that, using a substitution environment and a logical environment, for each $\phi \in \Phi$, yields the set of nets that satisfy ϕ or, equivalently, the set of nets that are $models$ for ϕ with respect to given substitution and logical environment. Function $\mathbb{M}[\![\cdot]\!]$ is formally defined in Table 14.

3.2   Label Predicates

A label predicate $\mathcal{A}$ is built from $abstract\ actions$ and $\circ$, that denotes the set of all transition labels, by using disjunction ($\cdot \cup \cdot$), conjunction ($\cdot \cap \cdot$) and difference ($\cdot - \cdot$).

$Abstract\ actions$ denote set of labels by singling out the kind of action performed (**out**, **in**, ...), the localities involved in the transition and the information

Table 14. Interpretation function of formulae.

$$\mathrm{M}[\![\mathbf{true}]\!]\varepsilon\sigma = Net$$
$$\mathrm{M}[\![\kappa]\!]\varepsilon\sigma = \varepsilon(\kappa)\sigma$$
$$\mathrm{M}[\![\langle t\rangle@l]\!]\varepsilon\sigma = \{N|N \equiv N_1 \parallel l::\langle\,[\![\,t\sigma\,]\!]\,\rangle\}$$
$$\mathrm{M}[\![\langle\mathcal{A}\rangle\phi]\!]\varepsilon\sigma = \{N|\exists a, \sigma', N'. \ N \overset{a}{\succ\!\!\longrightarrow} N', (a, \sigma') \in \mathrm{A}[\![\mathcal{A}\{\sigma\}]\!], N' \in \mathrm{M}[\![\phi]\!]\varepsilon\sigma' \cdot \sigma\}$$
$$\mathrm{M}[\![\phi_1 \vee \phi_2]\!]\varepsilon\sigma = \mathrm{M}[\![\phi_1]\!]\varepsilon\sigma \cup \mathrm{M}[\![\phi_2]\!]\varepsilon\sigma$$
$$\mathrm{M}[\![\neg\phi]\!]\varepsilon\sigma = Net - \mathrm{M}[\![\phi]\!]\varepsilon\sigma$$
$$\mathrm{M}[\![\nu\kappa.\phi]\!]\varepsilon\sigma = \bigcup\{g|g \subseteq f^{\phi}_{\kappa,\varepsilon}(g)\} \text{ where } f^{\phi}_{\kappa,\varepsilon}(g) = \mathrm{M}[\![\phi]\!]\varepsilon \cdot [\kappa \mapsto g]$$

Table 15. Label predicates interpretation.

$$\mathrm{A}[\![\circ]\!] = Lab$$
$$\mathrm{A}[\![\mathsf{O}(\ell_1, t, \ell_2)]\!] = \{(\mathbf{o}(l_1, t, l_2); \emptyset)\}$$
$$\mathrm{A}[\![\mathsf{I}(\ell_1, T, \ell_2)]\!] = \{(\mathbf{i}(l_1, T, l_2); \emptyset)\}$$
$$\mathrm{A}[\![\mathsf{R}(\ell_1, T, \ell_2)]\!] = \{(\mathbf{i}(l_1, T, l_2); \emptyset)\}$$
$$\mathrm{A}[\![\mathsf{E}(\ell_1, \mathsf{pp}, \ell_2)]\!] = \{(\mathbf{e}(l_1, P, l_2); \emptyset)|P \in \mathbb{P}[\![\mathsf{pp}]\!]\}$$
$$\mathrm{A}[\![\mathsf{N}(\ell_1, -, \ell_2)]\!] = \{(\mathbf{n}(l_1, -, l_2); \emptyset)\}$$
$$\mathrm{A}[\![\mathcal{A}_1 \cup \mathcal{A}_1]\!] = \mathrm{A}[\![\mathcal{A}_1]\!] \cup \mathrm{A}[\![\mathcal{A}_2]\!]$$
$$\mathrm{A}[\![\mathcal{A}_1 \cap \mathcal{A}_1]\!] = \{(a; \sigma_1 \cdot \sigma_2)|(a; \sigma_1) \in \mathrm{A}[\![\mathcal{A}_1]\!], (a; \sigma_2)\mathrm{A}[\![\mathcal{A}_2]\!]\}$$
$$\mathrm{A}[\![\mathcal{A}_1 - \mathcal{A}_2]\!] = \{(a; \sigma)|(a; \sigma) \in \mathrm{A}[\![\mathcal{A}_1]\!], \forall\sigma' \ (a; \sigma') \notin \mathrm{A}[\![\mathcal{A}_2]\!]\}$$
$$\mathrm{A}[\![\forall u.\mathcal{A}]\!] = \bigcup_{l\in\mathcal{L}}\{(a; \sigma \cdot [u/l])|(a; \sigma) \in \mathrm{A}[\![\mathcal{A}[l/u]]\!]\}$$

transmitted. Abstract actions have the same structure of transition labels; but have *process predicates* instead of processes.

Finally, predicates $\forall u.\mathcal{A}$ is used to quantify over localities, where $\langle a, \sigma \cdot [l/u]\rangle$ belongs to $\mathrm{A}[\![\forall u.\mathcal{A}]\!]$ if and only if $\langle a, \sigma\rangle$ belongs to $\mathrm{A}[\![\mathcal{A}[l/u]]\!]$.

Formal interpretation of labels predicates is defined by means of interpretation function $\mathrm{A}[\![\cdot]\!]$. This function takes a label predicate $\mathcal{A}$ and yields a set of pairs *<transition label-substitution>*. Intuitively, $(a, \sigma) \in \mathrm{A}[\![\mathcal{A}]\!]$ if transition label a *satisfies* $\mathcal{A}$ with respect to the substitution σ. Function $\mathrm{A}[\![\cdot]\!]$ is defined in Table 15.

Notice that, $\forall u$ plays the role of *existential quantification* if it is used inside a $\langle\cdot\rangle$, while it works like an *universal quantification* when used inside $[\cdot]$. Moreover, in $\langle\mathcal{A}\rangle\phi$, $\mathcal{A}$ acts as binder for quantified variables in $\mathcal{A}$ that appear in ϕ.

Process predicates are used for characterizing properties processes involved in the transition. For instance:

- $\mathcal{A}_1 = \mathtt{I}(l_1, l, l_2)$ is satisfied by a transition label if a process, located at l_1, retrieves locality l from the tuple space at l_2;
- $\mathcal{A}_2 = \forall u_1 \mathtt{I}(u_1, l, l_2)$ is satisfied by a transition label if a process, located at a generic locality, retrieves locality l from the tuple space at l_2;
- $\mathcal{A}_2 - \mathcal{A}_1$ is satisfied by a transition label if a process, that is not located at l_1, retrieves locality l from the tuple space at l_2.

3.3   Process Predicates

Process predicates shall be used to specify the kind of accesses to the resources of the net (data and nodes) that a process might perform in a computation. These accesses are composed for specifying their causal dependencies. The causal properties we intend to express for processes are of the form *"first read something and then use the acquired information in some way"*.

We use 1_P for a generic process and $\mathsf{pp}_1 \wedge \mathsf{pp}_2$ for the set of processes that *satisfy* pp_1 and pp_2. A process satisfies $\mathsf{ap} \to \mathsf{pp}$ if it may perform an access (i.e. an action) that satisfies ap and use the acquired information as specified by pp. The satisfaction relation between actions ($\mathtt{act}$) and access predicates ($\mathtt{ap}$) is quite intuitive and can be defined inductively as follows:

$$\mathbf{out}(t)@\ell_2 \text{ satisfies } \mathsf{o}(t)@\ell_2$$
$$\mathbf{in}(T)@\ell \text{ satisfies } \mathsf{i}(T)@\ell$$
$$\mathbf{read}(T)@\ell \text{ satisfies } \mathsf{r}(T)@\ell$$
$$\mathbf{eval}(P)@\ell \text{ satisfies } \mathsf{e}(\mathsf{pp})@\ell \Leftrightarrow P \text{ satisfies } \mathsf{pp}$$
$$\mathbf{newloc}(u) \text{ satisfies } \mathsf{n}(u)$$

Process predicates can be thought of as types that reflect the possible accesses a process might perform along its computation; they also carry information about the possible use of the acquired resources.

To formally define functions $\mathbb{P}[\![\cdot]\!]$ that yields the set of process satisfying a given process predicates, we need to introduce a transition relation for describing possible computations of processes. The operational semantics proposed in Table 12, is not adequate, because it describes the actual computation of nets and processes. The relation we need, instead, has to describe, using a sort of *abstract interpretation*, the structured sequences of actions a process might perform during its computation.

Let $\mathcal{V}$ be a set of variables, we will write $\mathcal{V} \vdash P \xrightarrow{act} Q$ whenever:

- the process P, at some point of its computation, might perform the action act;
- all the actions that syntactically precede act in P, that are execute before act, do not bind variables in $\mathcal{V}$.

Let $P \to_\mathcal{V} Q$ be the relation defined in Table 16, $\mathcal{V} \vdash P \xrightarrow{act} Q$ is inductively defined as follows:

- for every $\mathcal{V}$,

$$\mathcal{V} \vdash act.P \xrightarrow{act} P$$

Table 16. Abstract interpretation of processes.

$$
\begin{array}{ll}
act.P \to_\mathcal{V} P \ (1) & A \to_\mathcal{V} P \ (2) \\
P|Q \to_\mathcal{V} P & P|Q \to_\mathcal{V} Q \\
P + Q \to_\mathcal{V} P & P + Q \to_\mathcal{V} Q
\end{array}
$$

(1) act does not bind variables in $\mathcal{V}$
(2) $A \overset{def}{=} P$

Table 17. Process predicates interpretation functions.

$$\mathbb{P}[\![1_\mathsf{P}]\!] = Proc$$

$$\mathbb{P}[\![\mathsf{ap} \to \mathsf{pp}]\!] = \{P | \exists act, Q_1, Q_2 :$$
$$P \equiv_\alpha Q_1, \mathtt{fv}(\mathsf{ap} \to \mathsf{pp}) \vdash Q_1 \overset{act}{\Longrightarrow} Q_2, act \in \mathbb{AC}[\![\mathsf{ap}]\!], Q_2 \in \mathbb{P}[\![\mathsf{pp}]\!]\}$$

$$\mathbb{P}[\![\mathsf{pp}_1 \wedge \mathsf{pp}_2]\!] = \mathbb{P}[\![\mathsf{pp}_1]\!] \cap \mathbb{P}[\![\mathsf{pp}_2]\!]$$

$$\mathbb{AC}[\![\mathsf{o}(t)@\ell]\!] = \{\mathbf{out}(t)@\ell\} \qquad\qquad \mathbb{AC}[\![\mathsf{i}(T)@\ell]\!] = \{\mathbf{in}(T)@\ell\}$$

$$\mathbb{AC}[\![\mathsf{r}(T)@\ell]\!] = \{\mathbf{read}(T)@\ell\}$$
$$\mathbb{AC}[\![\mathsf{e}(\mathsf{pp})@\ell]\!] = \{\mathbf{eval}(Q)@\ell | Q \in \mathbb{P}[\![\mathsf{pp}]\!]\sigma\}$$

$$\mathbb{AC}[\![\mathsf{n}(u)]\!] = \{\mathbf{newloc}(u')\}$$

– if $P \to_\mathcal{V} P'$ and $\mathcal{V} \vdash P' \overset{act}{\Longrightarrow} Q$ then

$$\mathcal{V} \vdash P \overset{act}{\Longrightarrow} Q$$

The process predicates interpretation function $\mathbb{P}[\![\cdot]\!]$ is inductively defined in Table 17. We will write $P \colon \mathsf{pp}$ to denote that $P \in \mathbb{P}[\![\mathsf{pp}]\!]$. Conversely, we will write $\neg(P \colon \mathsf{pp})$ whenever $P \notin \mathbb{P}[\![\mathsf{pp}]\!]$. Furthermore, we assume that process predicates are equal up to contraction (i.e. $\mathsf{pp} \wedge \mathsf{pp} = \mathsf{pp}$), commutative and associative properties; for instance $\mathsf{pp}_1 \wedge (\mathsf{pp}_2 \wedge \mathsf{pp}_1) = \mathsf{pp}_1 \wedge \mathsf{pp}_2$.

We would like to remark that process predicates represent *set* of *causal dependent* sequences of *accesses* that a single process *might* perform and not actual computational sequences.

That follows is a typical properties that one can prove using the logic. Let us consider the set of processes that, after reading the name of a locality from l_1, spawn a process to the read locality:

$$\mathsf{i}(!u)@l_1 \to \mathsf{e}(1_\mathsf{P})@u \to 1_\mathsf{P}$$

This predicate is by

$$\mathbf{in}(!u_1)@l_1.\mathbf{in}(!x)@u_1.\mathbf{eval}(P)@u_1.Q$$

but it is not satisfied by

$$\mathbf{in}(!u_2)@l_1.\mathbf{read}(!u_2)@l_2.\mathbf{eval}(P)@u_2.\mathbf{nil}$$

since no process is evaluated at the locality retrieved from l_1. Indeed a locality from l_1 is retrieved, but the one used to evaluate P is the locality read from l_2.

The process predicate above could be used for specifying a security policies. For instance, one could ask that *never a process that, after reading the name of a locality from l_1, spawns a process to the read locality, is evaluated at site l_2.* This property can be formalized using the following formula:

$$\nu\kappa.[\forall u.\mathtt{E}(u,\mathtt{i}(!u)@l_1 \to \mathtt{e}(1_\mathtt{P})@u \to 1_\mathtt{P},l_2)]\mathtt{false} \wedge [\circ]\kappa$$

3.4   An Automatic Tool for Supporting Analysis

To simplify the analysis of μKLAIM programs, we use the framework KLAIML [Lor02] that permits simulating an μKLAIM program and generating its reachability graph. Moreover, using KLAIML, it is possible to verify whether a program satisfies a formula.

The core of the system, which is implemented in OCaml [LRVD99], consists of two components: `klaimlgraph` and `klaimlprover`. The first one permits analyzing the execution of μKLAIM programs and generating their reachability graphs. The second one, after loading a net N and a formula ϕ, tests the satisfaction of ϕ by N. If the analyzed program has a finite reachability graph, `klaimlprover` exhibits the actual tree structure of the proof either for ϕ or for $\neg\phi$.

The results produced by `klaimlgraph` and `klaimlprover` are stored in XML format. These files can be visualized using the *front-end* components of the system: `jgraphviewer` and `jproofviewer`.

4   Types for Access and Mobility Control in μKlaim

In the design of programming languages for mobile agents, the integration of security mechanisms is a major challenge; indeed, a great effort has been recently devoted to embed security issues within standard programming features. Several sensible language-based security techniques have been proposed in literature, including type systems, control and data flow analysis, in-lined reference monitoring and proof-carrying code; some of these techniques are analyzed and compared in [SMH00].

An important topic deeply investigated for KLAIM is the use of type systems for security [DFP97,DFP99,DFPV00,DFP00,GP03c,GP03b], namely for controlling accesses to tuple spaces and mobility of processes. To better clarify the problems we were faced with, let us consider a simple scenario. Imagine that a publisher P has an on-line repository (implemented by a node whose address is l_R) containing all its available papers. It is then reasonable to want enforcing some minimal security requirements, like, e.g., that only authorized users can read P papers (*secrecy* of P's data) and no user other than P can put/remove papers in l_R (*integrity* of P's data). The only (unsatisfactory) mechanism available in KLAIM for protecting P publications is to make l_R a reserved address; in this way, P can communicate it only to trusted entities. However, the behaviour of this "trusted" entities is out of P's control: they could (maliciously or incidentally) make l_R public and, from then onwards, no security property on P's data can be ensured.

The idea of statically controlling the execution of a program via types dates back in time. The traditional property enforced by types, i.e. *type safety*, implies that every data will be used consistently with its declaration during the computation (e.g., an integer variable will always be assigned integer values). However, to better deal with global computing problems, we generalized traditional types to *behavioural types*. Intuitively, behavioural types are abstractions of process behaviours and provide information about the *capabilities of processes*, namely the operations processes can perform at a specific locality (downloading/consuming a tuple, producing a tuple, activating a process, and creating a new node). By using behavioural types, each KLAIM node comes equipped with a security policy, specified by a net coordinator in terms of execution privileges: the policy of node l describes the actions processes located at l are allowed to execute. Type checking will guarantee that only processes whose intentions match the rights granted by coordinators are allowed to proceed.

In this section we shall summarize the type theory developed for KLAIM and illustrate how to use type systems to enforce the policies mentioned above. For the sake of presentation, we concentrate on μKLAIM and leave aside the treatment of equations for process definitions (we refer the interested reader to the original papers for a full account of the theories presented).

4.1   A Capability-Based Type System

In this section, we illustrate the basic ideas underlying various type systems, increasingly more powerful, developed for μKLAIM. The development of μKLAIM applications proceed in two phases. In the first phase, node administrators assign policies to the nodes of the net, and processes are programmed while ignoring the access rights of the hosting nodes. In the second phase, processes are allocated over the nodes of the net, while type checking their intentions against the policy of the hosting node. Finally, through a mix of both static and dynamic typing, μKLAIM type system guarantees that only processes with intentions that match the access rights as granted by the net coordinators are allowed to proceed.

We start by presenting a basic framework for our type theory; further developments are given is Sections 4.2 and 4.3. As we already said, μKLAIM types provide information about the legality of process actions: downloading/consuming tuples, producing tuples, activating processes and creating new nodes. We use r, i, o, e and n to indicate *capabilities*, where each symbol stands for the operation whose name begins with it; e.g., r denotes the capability of executing a **read** action. We let π to range over subsets of $\{r, i, o, e, n\}$. *Types*, ranged over by δ, are functions mapping localities (and locality variables) into subsets of capabilities. For the sake of readability, types will be written according to the following notation $[\ell_1 \mapsto \pi_1, \ldots, \ell_n \mapsto \pi_n]$. By taking advantage of the fact that types are functions, we express *subtyping* in terms of the standard pointwise inclusion of functions. Hence, we write $\delta_1 \preceq \delta_2$ if $\delta_1(\ell) \subseteq \delta_2(\ell)$ for every $\ell \in \mathcal{L} \cup \mathcal{U}$.

Each node can be decorated with a type, set by the node administrator, that determines the access policy of the node in terms of access rights on the other nodes of the net. For example, the capability e is used to control process mobility; thus, the privilege $[l' \mapsto \{e\}]$ in the type of locality l will enable processes running at l to perform **eval** actions over l'. From this perspective, subtyping formalizes degrees of restrictions, i.e. if $\delta_1 \preceq \delta_2$, then δ_1 expresses a less permissive policy than δ_2. Hence, the syntax of μKLAIM nets becomes

$$N ::= \quad l::^{\delta} P \quad | \quad l::\langle et \rangle \quad | \quad N_1 \parallel N_2$$

Nodes of the form $l::\langle et \rangle$ represent located resources. We assume that the located resources in the initial configuration have been produced by the net coordinator and, then, are reliable (i.e. no checks are needed).

A static type checker verifies whether the processes in the net do comply with the security policies of the nodes where they are allocated. To this aim, two syntactic constructs are now explicitly typed. Firstly, the **newloc** construct becomes **newloc**$(u{:}\delta)$, where δ specifies the security policy of the new node. Moreover, template formal parameters are now of the shape $!\,u{:}\pi$, where π specifies the access rights corresponding to the operations that the receiving process wants to perform at u. In both cases, the type information is not strictly necessary: it increases the flexibility of the **newloc** action (otherwise, some kind of 'default policy' should be assigned to the newly created node) and enables a simpler static type checking.

Thus, for each node of a net, say $l::^{\delta} P$, the static type checker procedure can determine if the actions that P intends to perform when running at l are enabled by the access policy δ or not. Moreover, the type checker verifies that in $a._{-}$ the continuation process behaves consistently with the declarations made for locality variables bound by a. This fact is expressed by the type judgment $\delta \vdash_{\overline{l}} P$. A net is deemed *well-typed* if for each node $l::^{\delta} P$ it holds that $\delta \vdash_{\overline{l}} P$.

To give the flavour of our typing inference system, we show and comment on three significant typing rules concerning **eval**, **in** and **newloc** actions. The rules are

$$\frac{e \in \delta(\ell) \qquad \delta \vdash_{\overline{l}} P}{\delta \vdash_{\overline{l}} \textbf{eval}(Q)@\ell.P} \qquad \frac{i \in \delta(\ell) \qquad \delta[\widetilde{u \mapsto \pi}]_{!u:\pi \in T} \vdash_{\overline{l}} P}{\delta \vdash_{\overline{l}} \textbf{in}(T)@\ell.P}$$

$$\frac{n \in \delta(l) \qquad \delta' \preceq \delta[u \mapsto \delta(l)] \qquad \delta[u \mapsto \delta(l)] \vdash_{\overline{l}} P}{\delta \vdash_{\overline{l}} \textbf{newloc}(u{:}\delta').P}$$

In $\delta \vdash_{\overline{l}} P$, the δ is called *typing environment*; it records the privileges granted to P and provides information about P's free variables. In all rules, the static checker must verify the existence of the privilege for executing the checked action in the current typing environment. When typing **eval**$(Q)@\ell.P$, notice that in general nothing can be statically said about the legacy of Q at ℓ. Indeed, ℓ can be a locality variable and, thus, the locality name replacing it (and hence its associated policy) will be known only at run-time. When typing $\mathbf{in}(T)@\ell.P$, the continuation process P can intend to perform actions on the locality variables bound by T. Thus, P must be typed in the environment obtained from δ by adding information about such variables, as stated by T; this is written $\delta[\widetilde{u \mapsto \pi}]_{!u:\pi \in T}$, where $\delta_1[\delta_2]$ denotes the pointwise union of functions δ_1 and δ_2. Thus, the static checking of P in this extended environment will verify that the declarations contained in T for its bound variables will be respected by P. When typing $\mathbf{newloc}(u:\delta').P$, we assume that the creating node owns over the created one all the privileges it owns on itself (thus, the continuation process P will be typed in the environment δ extended with the association $[u \mapsto \delta(l)]$). Moreover, the check $\delta' \preceq \delta[u \mapsto \delta(l)]$ verifies that the access policy δ' for the new node is in agreement with the policy δ of the node executing the operation[1].

Type information contained in processes play a crucial role in the operational semantics, thus enabling/disabling process migrations and data communications. This fact is expressed by modifying the new operational rules for actions $\mathbf{eval}$ and $\mathbf{in/read}$ as follows. The new reduction rule for $\mathbf{eval}$ is

$$\frac{\delta' \vdash_{\overline{l'}} Q}{l::^{\delta}\mathbf{eval}(Q)@l'.P \parallel l'::^{\delta'} P' \longrightarrow l::^{\delta} P \parallel l'::^{\delta'} P'|Q}$$

Notice that the process Q must be dynamically typechecked against the policy of node l', now that the target of the migration (and hence its security policy) is known. The reduction rule for creation of new nodes is

$$\frac{l' \notin L}{L \vdash l::^{\delta}\mathbf{newloc}(u:\delta').P \longrightarrow L \cup \{l'\} \vdash l::^{\delta[l' \mapsto \delta(l)]} P[l'/u] \parallel l'::^{\delta'[l'/u]} \mathbf{nil}}$$

Notice that in this case all checks have been made statically, but the point here is that a new node with its policy is added and that the policy of the creating of node change accordingly. The reduction rule for action $\mathbf{in}$ (the corresponding rule for $\mathbf{read}$ is omitted) becomes:

$$\frac{match_{\delta}(\llbracket T \rrbracket, et) = \sigma}{l::^{\delta}\mathbf{in}(T)@l'.P \parallel l'::\langle et \rangle \longrightarrow l::^{\delta} P\sigma \parallel l'::\mathbf{nil}}$$

The new pattern matching function $match_{\delta}$ is defined like $match$ but it also verifies that process $P\sigma$ does not perform illegal actions w.r.t. δ. Because of the static inference, the definition of $match_{\delta}$ simply relies on the following variant of rule (M$_4$) in Table 5:

$$\frac{\pi \subseteq \delta(l')}{match_{\delta}(!u:\pi, l') = [l'/u]}$$

---

[1] This check prevents a malicious node l from forging capabilities by creating a new node with more powerful privileges (where, e.g., sending a malicious process that takes advantage of capabilities not owned by l).

Indeed, the static inference verifies that P performs over u at most the operations declared by π; hence, if δ enables the actions identified by π over l', then $P\sigma$ will never violate policy δ due to operations over l'.

By relying on static and dynamic typechecking, we can prove that the type system is *sound*, namely that well-typedness is an invariant of the operational semantics (*subject reduction*) and that well-typed nets are free from run-time errors, caused by misuse of access rights (*type safety*).

Let's now see the impact of type soundness in practice. The protection of P on-line publications can now be programmed very easily: to preserve data secrecy it suffices to assign the privilege $[l_R \mapsto \{r\}]$ only to the authorized nodes, and to preserve data integrity it suffices to assign the privilege $[l_R \mapsto \{i, o\}]$ only to the node associated to P (say a node with address l_P). Indeed, type soundness ensures that P's papers will be read only by processes running in authorized nodes, and that only processes running at l_P will be allowed to modify the repository l_R.

4.2 Dynamic Privileges Management

The above modeling of the publisher scenario satisfies the requirements that motivated our approach to type discipline μKLAIM. However, it is far from being realistic and usable, especially in e-commerce applications, because of its static nature. In this section, we show some simple modifications that enable programming dynamic privileges acquisition; this will allow us to deal with more flexible and sensitive applications of our theory. We conclude by sketching how privilege loss could be added to the picture; the interested reader is referred to [GP03c] for full details and additional examples.

The main characteristic of the revised theory is the possibility of programming privileges exchange; to this aim, we shall decorate localities in output actions with a *capability specification*, μ, expressing the conveyed privileges. Hence, tuple fields take now the form

$$f ::= e \quad | \quad \ell : \mu$$

Formally, μ is a partial function with finite domain from localities (and locality variables) to subsets of capabilities. Intuitively, action $\mathbf{out}(l : [l_1 \mapsto \pi_1, \ldots, l_m \mapsto \pi_m])@l'$ creates a tuple containing locality l that can be accessed only from localities $l_1, \ldots, l_m$; moreover, when the tuple will be retrieved from l_i, l_i's access policy will acquire the privilege $[l \mapsto \pi_i]$. To rule out simple capability forging, we must ensure that the privilege $[l \mapsto \pi_1 \cup \ldots \cup \pi_m]$ is really owned by the node executing the $\mathbf{out}$. This can be done through a revised tuple evaluation function $[\![\cdot]\!]_\delta$, whose most significant definition rule is

$$\frac{\mu = [l_1 \mapsto \pi_1, \ldots, l_m \mapsto \pi_m] \qquad \mu' = [l_1 \mapsto \pi_1 \cap \delta(l), \ldots, l_m \mapsto \pi_m \cap \delta(l)]}{[\![l : \mu]\!]_\delta = l : \mu'}$$

The operational rule for $\mathbf{out}$ now becomes

$$\frac{[\![\,t\,]\!]_\delta = et}{l::^\delta \textbf{out}(t)@l'.P \parallel l'::^{\delta'} P' \longmapsto l::^\delta P \parallel l'::^{\delta'} P' \parallel l'::\langle et\rangle}$$

In this new setting, the execution of actions **in** and **read** has two effects: replacing free occurrences of variables with localities/values (like before) and enriching the type of the node performing the action with the privileges granted along with the tuple. The new rule for **in** (the rule for **read** is similar) is:

$$\frac{match_l^\delta([\![\,T\,]\!]_\delta, et) = \langle \delta'', \sigma\rangle}{l::^\delta \textbf{in}(T)@l'.P \parallel l'::\langle et\rangle \longmapsto l::^{\delta[\delta'']} P\sigma \parallel l'::\textbf{nil}}$$

Function $match_l^\delta$ differs from $match_\delta$ in two aspects: it returns the substitution σ to be applied to the continuation process together with the privileges passed by (the producer of) the tuple to node l, and it typechecks $P\sigma$ by also considering such privileges. Its definition relies on the following variants of rules (M_3), (M_4) and (M_5) of Table 5:

$$match_l^\delta(l'\!:\mu, l'\!:\mu') = \langle [\,], \epsilon\rangle \qquad \frac{\pi \subseteq \delta(l') \cup \mu(l)}{match_l^\delta(!\,u\!:\pi, l'\!:\mu) = \langle [l' \mapsto \pi], [l'/u]\rangle}$$

$$\frac{match_l^\delta(F, f) = \langle \delta_1, \sigma_1\rangle \quad match_l^\delta(T, t) = \langle \delta_2, \sigma_2\rangle}{match_l^\delta(\,(F, T)\,,\,(f, t)\,) = \langle \delta_1[\delta_2], \sigma_1 \circ \sigma_2\rangle}$$

Since node $l::^\delta P$ can dynamically acquire privileges when P performs in/read actions, it is possible that statically illegal actions can become permissible at run-time. For this reason, if P intends to perform an action not allowed by δ, the static inference system cannot now reject the process, since the capability necessary to perform the action could in principle be dynamically acquired by l. In such cases, the inference system simply *marks* the action to require its dynamic checking. Hence, in the new setting the node $l::^{[l'\mapsto\{r\}]}$ **read**$(!u\!:\{o\})@l'.\textbf{out}(t)@l'$ turns out to be legal. Action **out**$(t)@l'$ can be marked and checked at run-time since, if u would be dynamically replaced with l', l will acquire the privilege $[l' \mapsto \{o\}]$ and the process running at l could proceed; otherwise, the process will be suspended. In this type system, the dynamic acquisition of privileges is exploited exactly for relaxing the static type checking and admitting nodes like l while requiring on (part of) them a dynamic checking.

The static semantics now is built up over the judgement $\delta \vdash_l P \triangleright P'$, where process P' is obtained from P by possibly marking some actions. Intuitively, it means that all the variables in P' are used according to their definition and, when P' is located at l, its unmarked actions are allowed by δ. Since the new static checker cannot reject anymore those processes intending to perform statically illegal actions, the rules for typing processes shown before must be slightly modified. Thus, e.g., the rule for typing **eval** actions becomes

$$\frac{\delta \vdash_l P \triangleright P'}{\delta \vdash_l \textbf{eval}(Q)@\ell.P \triangleright mark_\delta(\textbf{eval}(Q)@\ell).P'}$$

where $mark_\delta(\textbf{eval}(Q)@\ell)$ is $\underline{\textbf{eval}}(Q)@\ell$ if $e \notin \delta(\ell)$ and is **eval**$(Q)@\ell$ otherwise.

Once the syntax of processes has been extended to allow processes to contain marked actions, a net can be deemed *executable* if for each node $l::^\delta P$ it holds that $\delta \vdash_T P \triangleright P$ (i.e. if the net already contains all the necessary marks).

As far as the operational semantics is concerned, the rule for **eval** must be modified so that the process that is actually sent for execution is that resulting (if any) from the typechecking of the original incoming process, thus such a process contains all necessary marks. Moreover, for taking into account execution of marked actions, the following rules must be added to the previous ones

$$\frac{l' = tgt(a) \qquad cap(a) \in \delta(l') \qquad l::^\delta a.P \parallel l'::^{\delta'} Q \succ\!\!\longrightarrow N}{l::^\delta \underline{a}.P \parallel l'::^{\delta'} Q \succ\!\!\longrightarrow N}$$

$$\frac{l' = tgt(a) \qquad cap(a) \in \delta(l') \qquad l::^\delta a.P \parallel l'::\langle et\rangle \succ\!\!\longrightarrow N}{l::^\delta \underline{a}.P \parallel l'::\langle et\rangle \succ\!\!\longrightarrow N}$$

where $tgt(a)$ and $cap(a)$ denote, resp., the target locality and the capability associated to action a. In substance, these rules say that the marking mechanism acts as an in-lined security monitor by stopping the execution of marked actions whenever the privilege for executing them is missing. *Type soundness* still holds, but is now formulated in terms of executable nets.

By exploiting this more sophisticated type theory, the publisher example can be formulated by using the following net, that models both user and publisher behaviour:

$$l_U ::^{[l_U \mapsto \{i\}, l_P \mapsto \{o\}]}$$
$$\quad \mathbf{out}(\text{``Subsc''}, l_U : [l_P \mapsto \{o\}])@l_P.\mathbf{in}(\text{``Access''}, u : \{r\})@l_U.C \parallel$$
$$l_P ::^{[l_P \mapsto \{i\}, l_R \mapsto \{i,o\}]} *$$
$$\quad \mathbf{in}(\text{``Subsc''}, !u' : \{o\})@l_P.\mathbf{out}(\text{``Access''}, l_R : [u' \mapsto \{r\}])@u' \parallel$$
$$l_R ::^{[]} \langle paper1\rangle \mid \langle paper2\rangle \mid \ldots$$

Process $*P$ stands for $P|P|\ldots$ (i.e. the π-calculus *replication* operator) and can be easily encoded via process definitions. C represents the user usage of the on-line publications, thus it may contain operations like $\mathbf{read}(\ldots)@l_R$ that would be marked by the static inference. This setting is more realistic because the only privileges statically assigned are $[l_R \mapsto \{i, o\}]$ to l_P (to implement data integrity) and $[l_P \mapsto \{o\}]$ to allow the user l_U to require (by possibly paying a certain fee) the subscription to P's publications. It is then l_P that gives l_U the possibility of accessing l_R. Upon completion of the protocol, the net will be

$$l_U ::^{[l_U \mapsto \{i\}, l_P \mapsto \{o\}, l_R \mapsto \{r\}]} C \parallel l_R ::^{[]} \langle paper1\rangle \mid \langle paper2\rangle \mid \ldots \parallel$$
$$l_P ::^{[l_P \mapsto \{i\}, l_C \mapsto \{i,o\}, l_U \mapsto \{o\}]} *$$
$$\quad \mathbf{in}(\text{``Subscr''}, !u' : \{o\})@l_P.\mathbf{out}(\text{``Access''}, l_R : [u' \mapsto \{r\}])@u'$$

Notice that all processes eventually spawned at l_U are then enabled to use the privilege $[l_R \mapsto \{r\}]$.

We now comment on possible variations of the type theory. In real situations, a (mobile) process could dynamically acquire some privileges and, from time to time, decide whether it wants to keep them for itself or to share them with other processes running in the same environment, viz. at the same node. In our example, the user might just buy an 'individual licence'. Our framework can smoothly accommodate this feature, by associating privileges also to processes and letting them decide whether an acquisition must enrich their hosting node or themselves. Moreover, the subscription could have an expiration date, e.g., it could be an annual subscription. Timing information can easily be accommodated in the framework presented by simply assigning privileges a validity duration and by updating these information for taking into account time passing. Furthermore, 'acquisition of privileges' can be thought of as 'purchase of services/goods'; hence it would be reasonable that a process lose the acquired privilege once it uses the service or passes the good to another process. In our running example, this corresponds to purchasing the right of accessing P's publications a given number of times. A simple modification of our framework, for taking into account multiplicities of privileges and their consumption (due, e.g., to execution of the corresponding action or to cession of the privilege to another process), can permit to deal with this new scenario. Finally, the granter of a privilege could decide to revoke the privilege previously granted. In our example, P could prohibit l_U from accessing its publications because of, e.g., a misbehaviour or expiry of the subscription time (in fact, this could be a way of managing expiration dates without assigning privileges a validity duration). To manage privileges revocation we could annotate privileges dynamically acquired with the granter identity and enable processes to use a new 'revoke' operation.

4.3   Other Uses of Types

We conclude this short overview on KLAIM types for security by mentioning two variants. The first one enables a more efficient static checking (but is less realistic and heavier to deal with); the second one allows for a finer control of processes activities (but is more complicated). In both cases, a static type checker is exploited to minimize the number of run-time checks; type soundness is then formulated in terms of the corresponding notion of well-typedness.

The types for KLAIM originally proposed in [DFP99,DFPV00,DFP00] were functions mapping localities (and locality variables) into functions from sets of capabilities to types. A type of the form $[\ell \mapsto \pi \mapsto \delta]$ describes the intention of performing the actions corresponding to π at ℓ; moreover, it imposes constraint δ on the processes that could possibly be spawned at ℓ.

Thus, if $[l \mapsto \{e\} \mapsto \delta]$ is in the policy of node l', then processes running at l' can spawn over l code that typechecks with δ. This is required in order to enable the static inference to decide whether the spawned process can legally run at l or not. However, to make this possible, it must hold that δ is a subtype of l's type; hence, a global knowledge of node types is required. This can be reasonable for LANs while is hardly implementable in WANs, where usually nodes are under the control of different authorities. The type system presented in Section 4.1 is more realistic in that the static checker only need local information; however, it is less efficient because it requires a larger amount of dynamic checks.

Moreover, types can be *recursive*. Recursive types are used for typing migrating recursive processes like, e.g., $P \stackrel{\triangle}{=} \mathbf{in}(!x)@l.\mathbf{out}(x)@l'.\mathbf{eval}(P)@l''$. P can be typed by solving the recursive type equation $\delta = [l \mapsto \{i\} \mapsto \bot, l' \mapsto \{o\} \mapsto \bot, l'' \mapsto \{e\} \mapsto \delta]$, where $\bot$ denotes the empty type. However, notice that recursive processes do not necessarily have recursive types: e.g. process $Q \stackrel{\triangle}{=} \mathbf{in}(!x)@l.\mathbf{out}(x)@l'.Q$ has type $[l \mapsto \{i\} \mapsto \bot, l' \mapsto \{o\} \mapsto \bot]$.

In [GP03b] the type system of Section 4.1 has been refined to incorporate other real systems security features, i.e. granting different privileges to processes coming from different nodes and constraining the operations allowed over different tuples. Thus, for example, if l trusts l', then l security policy could accept processes coming from l' and let them accessing any tuple in its TS. If l' is not totally trusted, then l's security policy could grant processes coming from l', e.g., the capabilities for executing **in/read** only over tuples that do not contain classified data. To this aim, we let types to be functions from localities (and locality variables) into functions from localities (and locality variables) into sets of capabilities. Intuitively, the association $[l \mapsto l' \mapsto \pi]$ in the policy of node l'' enables processes spawned over l'' by (a process running at) node l to perform over l' the operations enabled by π. Capabilities are still used to specify the allowed process operations, but now they also specify the shape (i.e. number of fields, kind of each field, ...) of **in/out/read** arguments. For example, the capability $< i \ , \ \langle \text{"public"}, - \rangle >$ (where '−' is used to denote a generic template field) states that action $\mathbf{in}(T)$ is enabled only if T is made up of two fields and the first one is the string *"public"*. Thus, it enables the operations $\mathbf{in}(\text{"public"}, !x)@...$ and $\mathbf{in}(\text{"public"}, 3)@...$, while disables operations $\mathbf{in}(\text{"private"}, !x)@...$ and $\mathbf{in}(!x, !y)@...$.

5   HotKlaim

This section introduces *Higher-Order Typed* KLAIM (HOTKLAIM), and extension of system F [Gir72,Rey74] with primitives from KLAIM. The purpose of HOTKLAIM is to enhance KLAIM with general purpose features, namely the powerful abstraction mechanisms and types of system F, which are orthogonal to network-aware programming. These features allow to deal with highly parameterized mobile components and to dynamically enforce host security policies: types are metadata extracted at run-time and used to express trustiness guarantees. A further extension, called METAKLAIM, is described in [FMP03]. METAKLAIM supports the interleaving of computational activities with metaprogramming activities, like dynamic linking and assembling and customization of components, through the use of METAML-style *staging annotations* [TS00,MHP00].

HOTKLAIM borrows the computational paradigm from μKLAIM: a *net* is a collection of *nodes*, and each node is addressed by a *locality* and consists of a multi-set of active *processes* and passive *tuples*. In HOTKLAIM terms include localities, processes and tuples, while types include the types L and $(t_i | i \in m)$

of localities and tuples. There is no type for processes[2], because process actions can be performed by terms of any type. The primitives of HOTKLAIM take the following form:

- $spawn(e)$ activates a process (obtained from e) in a parallel thread. Thus $P|Q$ of μKLAIM corresponds to $spawn(\lambda_-: ().P); Q$.
- $new(e)$ creates a new locality l, activates a process (obtained from e) at l, and returns l. Thus $new(\lambda u: L.P)$ corresponds to the sequence of actions **newloc**(u).**eval**$(P)@u$ of μKLAIM.
- $output(l, e)$ adds the value of e to the tuple space (TS) at l ($output$ is non-blocking). Thus **out**$(t)@\ell.P$ of μKLAIM corresponds to $output(\ell, t); P$
- $input(l, p \Rightarrow e)$ accesses the TS located at l to fetch a value v matching p. If such a v exists, it is removed from the TS, and the variables $x!t$ declared in p are replaced within e by the corresponding values in v. Otherwise, the operation is suspended until one becomes available. Thus **in**$(T)@\ell.P$ of μKLAIM correspods to $input(\ell, T \Rightarrow P)$.

Remark 4. In KLAIM the variables declared in a template pattern have no type annotation, because there are only three *types* of variables (values $!x$, localities $!u$, and processes $!X$). In HOTKLAIM variables can have any type, thus the *input* primitive performs dynamic type-checking, to ensure that a matching v is consistent with the types of variables declared in the pattern. In KLAIM there is a primitive $eval(l, e)$ for activating a process at a remote locality l. This primitive for asynchronous process mobility has not been included in HOTKLAIM for the following reasons:

- *eval* relies on dynamic scoping (a potentially dangerous mechanism), which is not available in HOTKLAIM, since in a functional setting one can use (the safer mechanism of) parametrization.
- with *eval* a node may activate a process on another node, but the target node has no control over the incoming process. This can be a source of security problems. In particular, Local Type Safety (see below) fails, if *eval* is added.

In HOTKLAIM process mobility occurs only by "mutual agreement", i.e. a node can *output* a process abstraction in any TS, but the abstraction becomes an active process (at l) only if a process (at l) *inputs* it. Higher-order remote communication is essential to implement this form of mobility.   □

In the rest of this section, we will use the following notations and conventions.

- m, n range over the set N of natural numbers. Furthermore, $m \in$ N is identified with the set $\{i \in N | i < m\}$ of its predecessors.
- $FV(e)$ is the set of free variables in e. If E is a set of syntactic entities, then E_0 indicates the set of entities in E without free variables.
- $\bar{e}$ ranges over finite sequences of e. $\bar{e}: t$ is a shorthand for $e_i: t$ for each e_i in the sequence $\bar{e}$.

---
[2] One could identify processes with terms of type ().

Table 18. Syntax of types and terms.

Types $t \in \mathsf{T} ::= X \mid L \mid t_1 \to t_2 \mid (t_i \mid i \in m) \mid \forall X.t \mid U \Rightarrow t$
Contexts $\Gamma \in \mathsf{Ctx} ::= \emptyset \mid \Gamma, X \mid \Gamma, x\!:\!t$
Terms $e \in \mathsf{E} ::= x \mid l \mid \lambda x\!:\!t.e \mid e_1\ e_2 \mid \mathsf{fix}\ x\!:\!t.e \mid (e_i \mid i \in m) \mid \pi_j\ e \mid op\ e \mid \Lambda X.e \mid e\{t\} \mid p \Rightarrow e$
Patterns $p \in \mathsf{P} ::= x!t \mid\ = e \mid (p_i \mid i \in m)$

– $\mu(A)$ is the set of multisets with elements in A, and $\uplus$ is multiset union.

Table 18 summarizes the syntax of HOTKLAIM, which uses the following primitive categories

– a numerable set XT of *type variables*, ranged over by $X, \ldots$;
– a numerable set X of *term variables*, ranged over by $x, \ldots$;
– a numerable set L of *localities*, ranged over by $l, \ldots$;
– a finite set $\mathsf{Op} = \{spawn, new, output, input\}$ of *local operations*, ranged over by op.

The syntax of HOTKLAIM can be explained in terms of system F and KLAIM (in the following we assume that t, Γ, e, p respectively range over T, Ctx, E and P).

– From system F we borrow functional types $t_1 \to t_2$, abstraction $\lambda x\!:\!t.e$ and application $e_1\ e_2$, and polymorphic types $\forall X.t$, type abstraction $\Lambda X.e$ and instantiation $e\{t\}$.
– From KLAIM we borrow localities l of type L, tuples $(e_i \mid i \in m)$ of type $(t_i \mid i \in m)$, and the construct $p \Rightarrow e$ of type $U \Rightarrow t$, which performs pattern matching and dynamic type-checking on *untrusted* values deposited in a TS (in KLAIM this construct is bundled with the *input* primitive); the primitives *spawn*, *new*, *output* and *input* are among the local operations Op.
– Finally, we have recursive definitions $\mathsf{fix}\ x\!:\!t.e$ and projections $\pi_j\ e$.

In HOTKLAIM, we perform a dynamic type check, when we input an untrusted value from a TS, in order to ensure some trustiness guarantees. The type system of HOTKLAIM is relatively simple, and the guarantees we can express are limited. For instance, we cannot express constraints on the computational effects of a term, such as the ability to spawn new threads or to perform input/output. We circumvent this limitation by allowing only input of *global* values.

A term $e \in \mathsf{E}_0$ is **global** $\overset{\Delta}{\iff}$ it has no occurrences of *local* operations $op \in \mathsf{Op}$.

$$(1)$$

Thus the only way we can turn a global value v into a process (interacting with its environment) is by passing some local operations (possibly in customized form), in other words v must be a higher-order abstraction representing processes parameterized w.r.t. customized local operations.

Remark 5. The use of dynamic type dispatching in a distributed polymorphic programming language has been strongly advocated in [Dug99]. For simplicity, we have chosen not to include dynamic type dispatching in HOTKLAIM, but it would be a very appropriate extension. One might wonder whether $input(x!t{\Rightarrow}e)$ of HOTKLAIM is *semantically equivalent* to typecase _ of $(x{:}t)e$ of [ACPP91], [ACPR95]. In fact, they are different! To simplify the comparison we consider a type U of untrusted values, and replace the *input* primitive with a construct check _ against $(x!t)e$.

- The type U of untrusted values has the following introduction and elimination rules

$$\frac{\Gamma \vdash}{\Gamma \vdash \langle e \rangle : U} \qquad \frac{\Gamma \vdash v{:}U \qquad \Gamma, x{:}t \vdash e{:}t'}{\Gamma \vdash \text{check } v \text{ against } (x{:}t)e{:}t'}$$

  the reduction semantics is check $\langle v \rangle$ against $(x{:}t)e \longrightarrow e[v/x]$ provided $\emptyset \vdash v{:}t$, thus at run-time we have to check that v has type t (in the empty context).

- In [ACPP91,ACPR95] the type D of dynamics has similar introduction and elimination rules

$$\frac{\Gamma \vdash e{:}t}{\Gamma \vdash d(e{:}t){:}D} \qquad \frac{\Gamma \vdash v{:}D \qquad \Gamma, x{:}t \vdash e{:}t'}{\Gamma \vdash \text{typecase } v \text{ of } (x{:}t)e{:}t'}$$

  the reduction semantics is typecase $d(v{:}t'')$ of $(x{:}t)e \longrightarrow e[v/x]$ provided $t'' \equiv t$, thus at run-time we only need to check equality of types.

Therefore, the two mechanisms accomplish different useful tasks. For instance, if we have an untrusted dynamic value $\langle d(v{:}t) \rangle$, we must first check that $d(v{:}t){:}D$ (or equivalently that $v{:}t$), and only then we can compare t with other types to decide how to use v safely. $\qquad\square$

5.1   A Type System

The type system derives judgments of the following forms

- $\Gamma \vdash$, i.e. Γ is a well-formed context
- $\Gamma \vdash t$, i.e. t is a well-formed type
- $\Gamma \vdash e{:}t$, i.e. e is a well-formed term of type t

The declarations in a context Γ have the following meaning: X means that the type variable X ranges over types t, while $x{:}t$ means that the term variable x ranges over *values* of type t.

Table 19 gives the typing rules. They are standard, except rule **(case)**, which uses some auxiliary notation, namely a context $\Gamma(p)$ and a sequence $\bar{e}(p)$ of terms, defined by induction on $p \in \mathsf{P}$

$p \in \mathsf{P}$	$\Gamma(p) \in \mathsf{Ctx}$	$\bar{e}(p) \in \mathsf{E}^*$
$x!t$	$x{:}t$	$\emptyset$
$= e$	$x{:}L$	e
$(p_i \mid i \in m)$	$\Gamma(p_0), \dots, \Gamma(p_{m-1})$	$\bar{e}(p_0), \dots, \bar{e}(p_{m-1})$

Table 19. Type system.

$$\frac{}{\emptyset \vdash} \qquad \frac{\Gamma \vdash}{\Gamma, X \vdash} \; X \text{ fresh} \qquad \frac{\Gamma \vdash t}{\Gamma, x\!:\!t \vdash} \; x \text{ fresh} \quad X \quad \frac{\Gamma \vdash}{\Gamma \vdash X} \; X \in \Gamma \quad L \quad \frac{\Gamma \vdash}{\Gamma \vdash L}$$

$$\rightarrow \frac{\Gamma \vdash t_1 \quad \Gamma \vdash t_2}{\Gamma \vdash t_1 \rightarrow t_2} \qquad (\_) \; \frac{\Gamma \vdash t_i \quad i \in m}{\Gamma \vdash (t_i | i \in m)} \qquad \forall \; \frac{\Gamma, X \vdash t}{\Gamma \vdash \forall X.t} \qquad U{\Rightarrow} \; \frac{\Gamma \vdash t}{\Gamma \vdash U{\Rightarrow}t}$$

$$\text{var} \; \frac{\Gamma \vdash}{\Gamma \vdash x\!:\!t} \; x\!:\!t \in \Gamma \quad \text{loc} \; \frac{\Gamma \vdash}{\Gamma \vdash l\!:\!L} \quad \text{fun} \; \frac{\Gamma, x\!:\!t_1 \vdash e\!:\!t_2}{\Gamma \vdash \lambda x\!:\!t_1.e\!:\!t_1 \rightarrow t_2} \quad \text{app} \; \frac{\Gamma \vdash e_1\!:\!t_1 \rightarrow t_2 \quad \Gamma \vdash e_2\!:\!t_1}{\Gamma \vdash e_1\,e_2\!:\!t_2}$$

$$\text{fix} \; \frac{\Gamma, x\!:\!t \vdash e\!:\!t}{\Gamma \vdash \text{fix}\,x\!:\!t.e\!:\!t} \quad \text{tuple} \; \frac{\Gamma \vdash \quad \{\Gamma \vdash e_i\!:\!t_i \mid i \in m\}}{\Gamma \vdash (e_i | i \in m)\!:\!(t_i | i \in m)} \quad \text{proj} \; \frac{\Gamma \vdash e\!:\!(t_i | i \in m)}{\Gamma \vdash \pi_j\,e\!:\!t_j} \; j < m$$

$$\text{spawn} \; \frac{\Gamma \vdash e\!:\!() \rightarrow t}{\Gamma \vdash \text{spawn}\,e\!:\!()} \quad \text{new} \; \frac{\Gamma \vdash e\!:\!L \rightarrow t}{\Gamma \vdash \text{new}\,e\!:\!L} \quad \text{input} \; \frac{\Gamma \vdash e\!:\!(L,U{\Rightarrow}t)}{\Gamma \vdash \text{input}\,e\!:\!t} \quad \text{output} \; \frac{\Gamma \vdash e\!:\!(L,t)}{\Gamma \vdash \text{output}\,e\!:\!()}$$

$$\text{poly} \; \frac{\Gamma, X \vdash e\!:\!t}{\Gamma \vdash \Lambda X.e\!:\!\forall X.t} \quad \text{spec} \; \frac{\Gamma \vdash e\!:\!\forall X.t_2 \quad \Gamma \vdash t_1}{\Gamma \vdash e\{t_1\}\!:\!t_2[t_1/X]} \quad \text{case} \; \frac{\Gamma \vdash \overline{e}(p)\!:\!L \quad \Gamma, \Gamma(p) \vdash e\!:\!t}{\Gamma \vdash p{\Rightarrow}e\!:\!U{\Rightarrow}t}$$

5.2 Operational Semantics

A net $N \in \mathsf{Net} \overset{\Delta}{=} \mu(\mathsf{L} \times (\mathsf{E_0} + \mathsf{V_0} + \{\mathsf{err}\}))$ is a multi-set of pairs consisting of a locality l and either a process term e, or a value $\langle v \rangle$ in the TS, or err indicating that a process at l has crashed. The dynamics of a net is given by a relation $N \longmapsto N'$ defined in terms of two transition relations $e \overset{a}{\longmapsto} e'$ and $e \longmapsto \mathsf{err}$ for terms: err means that a process has crashed, this is different from node failure (that we do not model), and from a deadlocked process (e.g. a process that is waiting to input a tuple that never arrives). The transitions relations are defined in terms of evaluation contexts (see [WF94]) and reductions $r \overset{a}{\longrightarrow} e'$ (and $r \longrightarrow \mathsf{err}$).

Table 20 summarizes the syntactic categories for the operational semantics. Redexes are the subterms where rewriting takes place. Evaluation contexts identify which of the redexes in a term should be evaluated first, namely the hole $[]$ gives the position of such a redex.

In the following we let v, vp, r, E, a range over V, VP, R, EC and A, respectively.

Table 21 defines the reduction $\longrightarrow$ and uses an auxiliary function $match(p,v)$, which returns a closed substitution $\sigma\!:\!\mathsf{X} \overset{fin}{\to} \mathsf{V_0}$ or $fail$. Its definition is by induction on $p \in \mathsf{P}$. The base cases are:

p	$match(p,v)$	
$x!t$	$[v/x]$	if $\emptyset \vdash v\!:\!t$ and v global, otherwise $fail$
$= e$	$\emptyset$	if $v \equiv e \in \mathsf{L}$, otherwise $fail$

$match$ is used by $input$ for dynamic type checking of $global$ values (see (1), page 121).

We just comment on some of the reduction rules in Table 21 (the others are standard):

Table 20. Values, redexes and evaluation contexts.

Values	$V ::= l \mid \lambda x{:}t.e \mid (v_i \mid i \in m) \mid \Lambda X.e \mid vp{\Rightarrow}e$
Evaluated Patterns	$VP ::= x!t \mid\ = v \mid (vp_i \mid i \in m)$
Redexes	$R ::= v_1 v_2 \mid \text{fix } x{:}t.e \mid \pi_j\ v \mid op\ v \mid v\{t\}$
Evaluation Contexts	$EC ::= [\,] \mid Ee \mid v\ E \mid (\overline{v}, E, \overline{e}) \mid \pi_j\ E \mid op\ E \mid E\{t\} \mid Ep{\Rightarrow}e$
Evaluation Contexts	
for patterns	$Ep ::= (\overline{vp}, Ep, \overline{p}) \mid\ = E$
Actions	$A ::= \tau \mid l{:}e \mid s(e) \mid i(v)@l \mid o(v)@l$ with $e \in E_0$ and $v \in V_0$

Table 21. Reductions for actions and symbolic evaluation.

$$(\lambda x{:}t.e)\ v_2 \xrightarrow{\tau} e[v_2/x] \qquad\qquad v_1\ v_2 \longrightarrow \text{err} \quad \text{if } v_1 \not\equiv \lambda x{:}t.e$$

$$\pi_j\ (v_i \mid i \in m) \xrightarrow{\tau} v_j \quad \text{if } j < m \qquad \pi_j\ v \longrightarrow \text{err} \quad \text{if } v \not\equiv (v_i \mid i \in m) \text{ with } j < m$$

$$\text{fix } x{:}t.e \xrightarrow{\tau} e[\text{fix } x{:}t.e/x] \qquad\qquad -$$

$$spawn\ v \xrightarrow{s(v())} () \qquad\qquad\qquad -$$

$$new\ v \xrightarrow{l:(vl)} l \qquad\qquad\qquad -$$

$$output\ (l, v) \xrightarrow{o(v)@l} () \qquad\qquad output\ v \longrightarrow \text{err} \quad \text{if } v \not\equiv (l, v_1)$$

$$input\ (l, vp{\Rightarrow}e) \xrightarrow{i(v)@l} e\sigma$$
$$\qquad \text{if } match(vp, v) = \sigma \qquad input\ v \longrightarrow \text{err} \quad \text{if } v \not\equiv (l, vp{\Rightarrow}e)$$

$$(\Lambda X.e)\{t\} \xrightarrow{\tau} e[t/X] \qquad\qquad v\{t\} \longrightarrow \text{err} \quad \text{if } v \not\equiv \Lambda X.e$$

- The rules for *spawn*, *new*, *output* and *input* come from KLAIM.
- *input* requires pattern matching and dynamic type-checking of global values. Moreover, *input* may get stuck, e.g. $input(l, x!X{\Rightarrow}e)$ is stuck because there are no closed values of type X.
- All reductions to err correspond to type-errors.

The transition relation $\longmapsto$ is defined (in terms of $\longrightarrow$) by the following standard rules

$$\frac{r \xrightarrow{a} e'}{E[r] \xmapsto{a} E[e']} \qquad\qquad \frac{r \longrightarrow \text{err}}{E[r] \longmapsto \text{err}}$$

The relation $\rightarrowtail$ is defined (in terms of $\longmapsto$) by the following rules

$$\frac{e \longmapsto \text{err}}{N \uplus (l{::}e) \rightarrowtail N \uplus (l{::}\text{err})} \qquad\qquad \frac{e \xmapsto{\tau} e'}{N \uplus (l{::}e) \rightarrowtail N \uplus (l{::}e')}$$

$$\frac{e \xmapsto{i(v)@l_2} e'}{N \uplus (l_1{::}e) \uplus (l_2{::}\langle v \rangle) \rightarrowtail N \uplus (l_1{::}e') \uplus (l_2{::}())}$$

$$\frac{e \xmapsto{o(v)@l_2} e'}{N \uplus (l_1::e) \succ\!\!\longrightarrow N \uplus (l_1::e') \uplus (l_2::\langle v \rangle)} \qquad \frac{e \xmapsto{s(e_2)} e_1}{N \uplus (l::e) \succ\!\!\longrightarrow N \uplus (l::e_1) \uplus (l::e_2)}$$

$$\frac{e \xmapsto{l_2::e_2} e_1}{N \uplus (l_1::e) \succ\!\!\longrightarrow N \uplus (l_1::e_1) \uplus (l_2::e_2)} \quad l_2 \notin L(N) \cup \{l_1\}$$

where $L(N) \triangleq \{l \mid (l::\_) \in N\} \subseteq_{fin} \mathsf{L}$ is the set of localities in the net N. The rules have an obvious meaning, we just remark that the side condition in the last rule ensures freshness of l_2.

5.3   Type Safety

In order to express the type safety results we introduce two notions of well-formed net: one is *global*, the other is relative to a subset L of nodes.

Global: A net N is well-formed $\xleftrightarrow{\Delta}$ $(l::\mathsf{err}) \notin N$, and for every $(l::e) \in N$ exists t s.t. $\emptyset \vdash e:t$.

Local: A net N is well-formed w.r.t. $L \subseteq L(N) \xleftrightarrow{\Delta} (l::\mathsf{err}) \notin N$ when $l \in L$, and for every $(l::e) \in N$ with $l \in L$ exists t s.t. $\emptyset \vdash e:t$.

In the definition of well-formed net nothing is said about values $\langle v \rangle$ in a TS, since they are considered untrusted. In fact, processes can fetch such values only through the *input* primitive, which performs dynamic type-checking. Indeed, we have the following theorem about type safety:

If $N \succ\!\!\longrightarrow N'$, then
   Global: N well-formed implies N' well-formed
   Local: N well-formed w.r.t. L implies N' well-formed w.r.t. L

The type safety theorem then guarantees that a well-formed net will never give rise to type errors. Together with dynamic type checking performed with input operations, these imply that our type system can be used for protecting hosts from imported code, thus ensuring various kinds of host security properties (as in [YH99]).

Remark 6. The local type safety property is enforced by two features of HOTKLAIM: the dynamic type-checking performed by the input operation (namely *match*), which prevents ill-typed values in a TS to pollute well-typed processes; the absence of KLAIM's *eval* primitive, which would allow processes external to L to spawn ill-typed processes at a locality in L. For instance, with an *eval* primitive similar to a 'remote' *spawn* the following net transition would become possible

$$l_{bad}::eval(l_{good}, v_{bad}), l_{good}::\langle v \rangle \succ\!\!\longrightarrow l_{bad}::(), l_{good}::v_{bad}(), l_{good}::\langle v \rangle$$

where v_{bad} is any closed value such that $v_{bad}() \longmapsto \mathsf{err}$.   □

5.4   An Example: Nomadic Data Collector

We address the issue of protecting host machines from malicious mobile code. Consider a scenario where a user wants to assemble information about a specific item (e.g. the price of certain devices). Part of the behaviour of the user's application strictly depends on this information. However, there are some activities which are independent of it. The user's application exploits the mobility paradigm: a mobile component travels among hosts of the net looking for the required information. For simplicity, we assume that each node of the distributed database contain tuples either of the form (i,d), where i is the search key and d is the associated data, or of the form (i,l), where l is a locality where more data associated to i can be searched. We freely use ML-like notations for functions and sequential composition, and write fn x:t.e instead of $\lambda x{:}t.e$ and V X.t instead of $\forall X.t$.

```
L                      (* localities *)
type Key  = ...        (* authorization keys *)
type Data = ...
(* polymorphic types of local operations input, output, spawn *)
type I = V X. (L,U=>X) -> X
type O = V X. (L,X) -> ()
type S = V X. (() -> X) -> ()
(* polymorphic types of customized operations for input, output *)
type KI = Key -> I
type KO = Key -> O
(* process abstractions with security checks *)
type EnvK = (L,KI,KO,S)
type CAK = EnvK -> ()
```

The type CAK of (mobile) process abstractions is parameterized with respect to the locality where the process will be executed and the customized operations. In other words, the type EnvK can be interpreted as the network environment of the process. This environment must be fed with the information about the current location and its local operations. We want to emphasize that the customized operations for communication require an authorization key. In such a way, depending on the value of the key k (that below is checked by a function safe), the customized operation in' k could generate an actual input or () when the key does not allow to read anything. Customization of the output operation is done similarly.

```
fun in' (k:Key):I = if safe k then input else ()
```

We now discuss the main module of our mobile application: the nomadic data collector. Process abstraction pca(k,i,u) is the mobile process which retrieves the required information on the distributed database. The parameter k is an authorization key, i is a search key, and u is the locality where all data associated to i should be collected. The behavior of pca(k,i,u) is rather intuitive. After being activated, pca(k,i,u) spawns a process that perform a *local query* (which removes from the local database data associated to the search key i). Then the mobile process forwards the result of the query to the TS located at u, and sends copies of itself (i.e. of pca(k,i,u)) to localities that may contain data associated to i.

```
fun pca(k:Key, i:Data, u:L):CAK =
 fix ca:CAK. fn (self', in', out', spawn'):EnvK .
  spawn' {()} (() => fix p:().
      (in' k) {()} (self', (_=i, x!Data) => (out' k) {Data} (u,x)) ; p);
   fix q:(). (in' k) {()} (self', (_=i, l!L) => (out' k) {CAK} (l,ca)) ; q
```

The process abstraction pca(k,i,u) is instantiated and activated by process execute, which fetches values of type CAK, and activates them by providing a customized environment env

```
fun execute (self:L, env:EnvK):() =
 fix exec:(). input (self, X!CAK => spawn (() => X env) ; exec)
```

6   O'Klaim: An Object-Oriented Klaim

O'KLAIM is a linguistic integration of KLAIM with object-oriented features. The coordination part and the object-oriented part are orthogonal, so that, in principle, such an integration would work for any extension/restriction of KLAIM, from cKLAIM onward, and also for other calculi for mobility and distribution, such as *DJoin* [FGL+96]. O'KLAIM is built following the design of the core calculus MoMi (Mobile Mixins).

6.1   MoMi and O'Klaim

MoMi was introduced in [BBV02] and extended in [BBV03b]. The underlying motivating idea is that standard class-based inheritance mechanisms, which are often used to implement distributed systems, do not scale well to distributed contexts with mobility. MoMi's approach consists in structuring mobile object-oriented code by using mixin-based inheritance (a mixin is an incomplete class parameterized over a superclass, see [BC90,FKF98,ALZ03]); this fits the dynamic and open nature of a mobile code scenario. For example, a downloaded mixin, describing a mobile agent that must access some files, can be completed with a base class in order to provide access methods specific of the local file system. Conversely, critical operations of a mobile agent, enclosed in a down-loaded class, can be redefined by applying a local mixin to it (e.g., in order to restrict access to sensible resources, as in a *sand-box*)[3]. Therefore, MoMi is a combination of a core coordination calculus and an object-oriented mixin-based calculus equipped with types. The key rôle in MoMi's typing is played by a *subtyping* relation that guarantees safe, yet flexible and scalable, code communication, and lifts type soundness of local code to a global type safety property. In fact, we assume that the code that is sent around has been successfully compiled and annotated with its static type. When the code is received on a site (under the hypothesis that the local code has been successfully compiled, too), it is accepted only if its type is subtyping-compliant with the expected one. If the code

---

[3] A more complete example of use of mixins can be found in Section 7.2, implemented in the object-oriented version of X-KLAIM.

is accepted, it can be integrated with the local code under the guarantee of no run-time errors, and without requiring any further type checking of the whole code. MoMi's subtyping relation involves not only object subtyping, but also a form of class subtyping and mixin subtyping: therefore, subtyping hierarchies are provided along with the inheritance hierarchies. It is important to notice that we are not violating the design rule of keeping inheritance and subtyping separated, since mixin and class subtyping plays a pivotal role only during the communication, when classes and mixins become genuine run-time polymorphic values.

In synthesis, MoMi consists of:

1. the definition of an object-oriented "surface calculus" with types called SOOL (*Surface Object-Oriented Language*), that describes the essential features that an object-oriented language must have to write mixin-based code;
2. the definition of a subtyping relation on the class and mixin types of the above calculus, to be exploited dynamically at communication time;
3. a very primitive coordination language based on a synchronous send/receive mechanism, to put in practice the communication of the mixin-based code among different site.

O'KLAIM is the integration of SOOL and its subtyping (both described in the next section), within KLAIM, which offers a much more sophisticated, complete, and effective coordination mechanism than the toy one of MoMi.

6.2   Sool: Syntax, Types, and Subtyping

In this section we present the object-oriented part of O'KLAIM, called SOOL. SOOL is defined as a standard class-based object-oriented language supporting mixin-based class hierarchies via *mixin definition* and *mixin application*. It is important to notice that specific incarnations of most object-oriented notions (such as, e.g., functional or imperative nature of method bodies, object references, cloning, etc.) are irrelevant in this context, where the emphasis is on the structure of the object-oriented mobile code. Hence, we work here with a basic syntax of the kernel calculus SOOL (shown in Table 22), including the essential features a language must support to be O'KLAIM's object-oriented component.

SOOL expressions offer object instantiation, method call and mixin application; $\diamond$ denotes the mixin application operator. A SOOL value, to which an expression reduces, is either an object, which is a (recursive) record $\{m_i = f_i{}^{i \in I}\}$, or a class definition, or a mixin definition, where $[m_i = f_i{}^{i \in I}]$ denotes a sequence of method definitions, $[m_k : \tau_{m_k} \text{ with } f_k{}^{k \in K}]$ denotes a sequence of method redefinitions, and I, J and K are sets of indexes. Method bodies, denoted here with f (possibly with subscripts), are closed terms/programs and we ignore their actual structure. A mixin can be seen as an abstract class that is parameterized over a (super)class. Let us describe informally the mixin use through a tutorial example:

Table 22. Syntax of SOOL.

$$
\begin{array}{lll}
exp ::= & v & \text{(value)} \\
| & \text{new } exp & \text{(object creation)} \\
| & exp \Leftarrow m & \text{(method call)} \\
| & exp_1 \diamond exp_2 & \text{(mixin appl.)} \\
v ::= & \{m_i = f_i{}^{i \in I}\} & \text{(record)} \\
| & x & \text{(variable)} \\
| & \text{class } [m_i = f_i{}^{i \in I}] \text{ end} & \text{(class def)} \\
& \text{mixin} & \\
& \quad \text{expect}[m_i : \tau_{m_i}{}^{i \in I}] & \\
| & \quad \text{redef}[m_k : \tau_{m_k} \text{ with } f_k{}^{k \in K}] & \text{(mixin def)} \\
& \quad \text{def}[m_j = f_j{}^{j \in J}] & \\
& \text{end} &
\end{array}
$$

Table 23. Syntax of types.

$$
\begin{array}{ll}
\tau ::= & \Sigma \\
| & \text{class}\langle \Sigma \rangle \\
| & \text{mixin}\langle \Sigma_{new}, \Sigma_{red}, \Sigma_{exp} \rangle \\
\Sigma ::= & \{m_i : \tau_{m_i}{}^{i \in I}\}
\end{array}
$$

$M = \text{mixin}$
  $\text{expect } [n : \tau]$
  $\text{redef } [m_2 : \tau_2 \text{ with } \ldots \text{ next} \ldots]$
  $\text{def } [m_1 = \ldots n() \ldots]$
end

$C = \text{class}$
  $[n = \ldots$
  $m_2 = \ldots]$
end

$(\text{new } (M \diamond C)) \Leftarrow m_1()$

Each mixin consists of three parts:

1. methods defined in the mixins, like m_1;
2. *expected methods*, like n, that must be provided by the superclass;
3. *redefined methods*, like m_2, where *next* can be used to access the implementation of m_2 in the superclass.

The application $M \diamond C$ constructs a class, which is a subclass of C.

The set $\mathcal{T}$ of types is defined in Table 23. Σ (possibly with a subscript) denotes a record type of the form $\{m_i : \tau_{m_i}{}^{i \in I}\}$. As we left method bodies unspecified (see above), we must assume that there is a type system for the underlying part of SOOL to type method bodies and records. We will denote this type derivability with $\Vdash$. Rules for $\Vdash$ are obviously not specified, but $\Vdash$-statements are used as assumptions in other typing rules. The typing rules for SOOL values are in Table 24.

Mixin types, in particular, encode the following information:

1. record types Σ_{new} and Σ_{red} contain the types of the mixin methods (new and redefined, respectively);
2. record type Σ_{exp} contains the *expected* types, i.e., the types of the methods expected to be supported by the superclass;

Table 24. Typing rules for SOOL values.

$$\frac{}{\Gamma, x{:}\tau \vdash x{:}\tau}\,(proj) \qquad \frac{\Gamma \Vdash \{m_i = f_i{}^{i \in I}\}{:}\{m_i{:}\tau_{m_i}{}^{i \in I}\}}{\Gamma \vdash \{m_i = f_i{}^{i \in I}\}{:}\{m_i{:}\tau_{m_i}{}^{i \in I}\}}\,(rec)$$

$$\frac{\Gamma \vdash \{m_i = f_i{}^{i \in I}\}{:}\{m_i{:}\tau_{m_i}{}^{i \in I}\}}{\Gamma \vdash \mathsf{class}\,[m_i = f_i{}^{i \in I}]\ \mathsf{end}{:}\mathsf{class}\langle\{m_i{:}\tau_{m_i}{}^{i \in I}\}\rangle}\,(class)$$

$$\frac{\begin{array}{c}\Gamma, \bigcup_{i \in I} m_i{:}\tau_{m_i}, \bigcup_{k \in K} m_k{:}\tau_{m_k} \vdash \{m_j = f_j{}^{j \in J}\}{:}\{m_j{:}\tau_{m_j}{}^{j \in J}\} \\ \Gamma, \bigcup_{i \in I} m_i{:}\tau_{m_i}, \bigcup_{k \in K} m_k{:}\tau_{m_k}, \bigcup_{j \in J} m_j{:}\tau_{m_j}, \mathsf{next}{:}\tau_{m_r} \Vdash f_r{:}\tau'_{m_r} \quad \tau'_{m_r} <{:}\tau_{m_r} \quad \forall r \in K \\ Subj(\Sigma_{new}) \cap Subj(\Sigma_{exp}) = \emptyset \quad Subj(\Sigma_{new}) \cap Subj(\Sigma_{red}) = \emptyset \\ Subj(\Sigma_{red}) \cap Subj(\Sigma_{exp}) = \emptyset\end{array}}{\Gamma \vdash \begin{array}{l}\mathsf{mixin} \\ \quad \mathsf{expect}[m_i{:}\tau_{m_i}{}^{i \in I}] \\ \quad \mathsf{redef}[m_k{:}\tau_{m_k}\ \mathsf{with}\ f_k{}^{k \in K}] \\ \quad \mathsf{def}[m_j = f_j{}^{j \in J}] \\ \mathsf{end}\end{array} : \mathsf{mixin}\langle\Sigma_{new}, \Sigma_{red}, \Sigma_{exp}\rangle}\,(mixin)$$

where $\Sigma_{new} = \{m_j{:}\tau_{m_j}{}^{j \in J}\}$, $\Sigma_{red} = \{m_k{:}\tau_{m_k}{}^{k \in K}\}$, $\Sigma_{exp} = \{m_i{:}\tau_{m_i}{}^{i \in I}\}$

Table 25. Typing rules for SOOL expressions.

$$\frac{\Gamma \vdash exp{:}\{m_i{:}\tau_{m_i}{}^{i \in I}\} \qquad j \in I}{\Gamma \vdash exp \Leftarrow m_j{:}\tau_{m_j}}\,(lookup) \qquad \frac{\Gamma \vdash exp{:}\mathsf{class}\langle\{m_i{:}\tau_{m_i}{}^{i \in I}\}\rangle}{\Gamma \vdash \mathsf{new}\ exp{:}\{m_i{:}\tau_{m_i}{}^{i \in I}\}}\,(new)$$

$$\frac{\begin{array}{l}\Gamma \vdash exp_1{:}\mathsf{mixin}\langle\Sigma_{new}, \Sigma_{red}, \Sigma_{exp}\rangle \\ \Gamma \vdash exp_2{:}\mathsf{class}\langle\Sigma_b\rangle \\ \Sigma_b <{:} (\Sigma_{exp} \cup \Sigma_{red}) \\ Subj(\Sigma_b) \cap Subj(\Sigma_{new}) = \emptyset\end{array}}{\Gamma \vdash exp_1 \diamond exp_2{:}\mathsf{class}\langle\Sigma_b \cup \Sigma_{new}\rangle}\,(mixin\ app)$$

3. well typed mixins are well formed, in the sense that name clashes among the different families of methods are absent (the last three clauses of the (*mixin*) rule).

The typing rules for SOOL expressions are in Table 25.

Rule (*mixin app*) relies strongly on a subtyping relation $<{:}$. The subtyping relation rules depend obviously on the nature of the SOOL calculus we choose, but an essential constraint is that it must contain the *subtyping-in-width* rule for record types: $\Sigma_2 \subseteq \Sigma_1 \Rightarrow \Sigma_1 <{:} \Sigma_2$.

An extension of SOOL with *subtyping-in-depth* can be found in a preliminary form in [BBV03b]. Subtyping-in-depth offers a much more flexible communication pattern, but it complicates the object-oriented code exchange for problems similar to the "subtyping-in-depth versus override" matter of the object-based languages (see [AC96,BBV03b] for examples).

We consider $m{:}\tau_1$ and $m{:}\tau_2$ as distinct elements, and $\Sigma_1 \cup \Sigma_2$ is the standard record union. Σ_1 and Σ_2 are considered *equivalent*, denoted by $\Sigma_1 = \Sigma_2$, if they differ only for the order of their pairs $m_i{:}\tau_{m_i}$.

Table 26. Subtype on class and mixin types.

$$\frac{\Sigma' <: \Sigma}{\mathsf{class}\langle\Sigma'\rangle \sqsubseteq \mathsf{class}\langle\Sigma\rangle} \quad (\sqsubseteq\ class)$$

$$\frac{\Sigma'_{new} <: \Sigma_{new} \qquad \Sigma_{exp} <: \Sigma'_{exp} \qquad \Sigma'_{red} = \Sigma_{red}}{\mathsf{mixin}\langle\Sigma'_{new}, \Sigma'_{red}, \Sigma'_{exp}\rangle \sqsubseteq \mathsf{mixin}\langle\Sigma_{new}, \Sigma_{red}, \Sigma_{exp}\rangle} \quad (\sqsubseteq\ mixin)$$

In the rule (*mixin app*), Σ_b contains the type signatures of all methods supported by the superclass to which the mixin is applied. The premises of the rule (*mixin app*) are as follows:

i) $\Sigma_b <: (\Sigma_{exp} \cup \Sigma_{red})$ requires that the superclass provides all the methods that the mixin expects and redefines.
ii) $Subj(\Sigma_b) \cap Subj(\Sigma_{new}) = \emptyset$ guarantees that no name clash will take place during the mixin application.

Notice that the superclass may have more methods than those required by the mixin constraints. Thus, the type of the mixin application expression is a class type containing both the signatures of all the methods supplied by the superclass (Σ_b) and those of the new methods defined by the mixin (Σ_{new}).

The key idea of SOOL's typing is the introduction of a novel subtyping relation, denoted by $\sqsubseteq$, defined on class and mixin types. This subtyping relation is used to match dynamically the actual parameter's types against the formal parameter's types during communication. The part of the operational semantics of O'KLAIM, which describes communication formally, is presented in Section 6.5. The subtyping relation $\sqsubseteq$ is defined in Table 26; rule ($\sqsubseteq$ *class*) is naturally induced by the (width) subtyping on record types, while rule ($\sqsubseteq$ *mixin*): permits the subtype to define more 'new' methods; prohibits to override more methods; and enables a subtype to require less expected methods.

6.3 O'Klaim: Syntax

O'KLAIM processes are defined formally in Table 27. The reader may note that the operations of **in** (and **read**) and **out**, retrieving from and inserting into a tuple space, are relevant for our purpose (so they need to be modified accordingly), while net composition and the **newloc** operation are not (and therefore they are not discussed here, because they are the same as the ones of KLAIM). In order to obtain O'KLAIM, we extend the KLAIM syntax of tuples t (presented in Section 2.3) to include any object-oriented value v (defined in Table 22). In particular, formal fields are now explicitly typed (typing rules for typing O'KLAIM are in Section 6.4). Indeed, since types are crucial in O'KLAIM, the scope of process definitions is now made explicit by means of the construct $\mathsf{def}\,A(id_1\colon\tau_1,\ldots,id_n\colon\tau_n) = P$ in P', where also process formal parameters are explicitly typed. Actions **in**$(t)@\ell$ (and **read**$(t)@\ell$) and **out**$(t)@\ell$ can be used

Table 27. O'KLAIM process syntax (see Table 22 for the syntax of exp and v; types τ are defined in Table 23). **newloc** is not relevant in this context as it is the same of Section 2.3, so it is omitted.

$$
\begin{array}{lll}
P ::= & \mathbf{nil} & \text{(null process)} \\
 \mid & act.P & \text{(action prefixing)} \\
 \mid & P_1 \mid P_2 & \text{(parallel composition)} \\
 \mid & X & \text{(process variable)} \\
 \mid & A\langle arg_1, \ldots, arg_n \rangle & \text{(process invocation)} \\
 \mid & \mathbf{def}\, A(id_1 : \tau_1, \ldots, id_n : \tau_n) = P\, \mathbf{in}\ \ P' & \text{(process definition)} \\
 \mid & \mathbf{def}\ x = exp\ \mathbf{in}\ \ P & \text{(object-oriented expression)} \\
act ::= & \mathbf{out}(t)@\ell \ \mid \ \mathbf{in}(t)@\ell \ \mid \ \mathbf{read}(t)@\ell \ \mid \ \mathbf{eval}(P)@\ell \\
t ::= & f \ \mid \ f,t \\
f ::= & arg \ \mid \ !\, id : \tau \\
id ::= & x \ \mid \ X \\
arg ::= & e \ \mid \ P \ \mid \ \ell \ \mid \ v
\end{array}
$$

to move object-oriented code (together with the other KLAIM items) from/to a locality ℓ, respectively. Moreover, we add to KLAIM processes the construct **def** $x = exp$ **in** P in order to pass to the sub-process P the result of computing exp (for exp syntax see Table 22).

6.4 Typing for O'Klaim

Typing rules for processes are defined in Table 28. O'KLAIM type system is not concerned with access rights and capabilities, as it is instead the type system for KLAIM presented in Section 4. In the O'KLAIM setting, types serve the purpose of avoiding the "message-not-understood" error when merging local and foreign object-oriented code in a site. Thus, we are not interested in typing actions inside processes: from our perspective, an O'KLAIM process is well typed when it has type proc, which only means that the object-oriented code that the process may contain is well typed. O'KLAIM requires that every process is statically type-checked separately on its site and annotated with its type. In particular, every tuple item t_i that takes part in the information exchange (which may be an object-oriented value) must be decorated with type information, denoted by $t_i^{\tau_i}$ (see Table 30). The types of the tuples are built statically by the compiler: notice that only the types of formal arguments in the process definition **def** $A(id_1 : \tau_1, \ldots, id_n : \tau_n) = P$ **in** P' must be given explicitly by the programmer. In a process of the form $\mathbf{in}(!\, id : \tau)@\ell.P$, the type τ is used to statically type check the continuation P, where id is possibly used.

6.5 Operational Semantics for O'Klaim

The operational semantics of O'KLAIM involves two sets of rules. The first set of rules describes how SOOL object-oriented expressions reduce to values and is

Table 28. Typing rules for processes.

$$\frac{}{\Gamma, X\colon \mathsf{proc} \vdash X\colon \mathsf{proc}}\ (proj) \qquad\qquad \frac{}{\Gamma \vdash \mathbf{nil}\colon \mathsf{proc}}\ (nil)$$

$$a \equiv \mathbf{in}, \mathbf{read}, \mathbf{out} \quad \frac{\begin{array}{c}\Gamma \vdash \ell\colon \mathsf{loc} \\ \Gamma \vdash t_i\colon \tau_i \qquad i = 1, \ldots, n \\ \Gamma \cup \mathit{ftypes}(t_1, \ldots, t_n) \vdash P\colon \mathsf{proc}\end{array}}{\Gamma \vdash a(t_1, \ldots, t_n)@\ell.P\colon \mathsf{proc}}\ (receive)$$

$$\mathit{ftypes}(f, t) = \begin{cases} \{id\colon \tau\} \cup \mathit{ftypes}(t) & \text{if } f \equiv !id\colon \tau \\ \mathit{ftypes}(t) & \text{otherwise} \end{cases}$$

$$\frac{\Gamma \vdash Q\colon \mathsf{proc} \qquad \Gamma \vdash \ell\colon \mathsf{loc}}{\Gamma \vdash \mathbf{eval}(Q)@\ell.P\colon \mathsf{proc}}\ (\textsc{Eval})$$

$$\frac{\Gamma \vdash P_1\colon \mathsf{proc} \qquad \Gamma \vdash P_2\colon \mathsf{proc}}{\Gamma \vdash (P_1 \mid P_2)\colon \mathsf{proc}}\ (comp) \qquad \frac{\Gamma \vdash exp\colon \tau \qquad \Gamma, x\colon \tau \vdash P\colon \mathsf{proc}}{\Gamma \vdash \mathbf{def}\ x = exp\ \mathbf{in}\ P\colon \mathsf{proc}}\ (let)$$

$$\frac{\Gamma, id_1\colon \tau_1, \ldots, id_n\colon \tau_n \vdash P\colon \mathsf{proc}\ \Gamma, A(id_1\colon \tau_1, \ldots, id_n\colon \tau_n)\colon \mathsf{proc} \vdash P'\colon \mathsf{proc}}{\Gamma \vdash \mathbf{def}\,A(id_1\colon \tau_1, \ldots, id_n\colon \tau_n) = P\ \mathbf{in}\ P'\colon \mathsf{proc}}\ (defproc)$$

$$\frac{\Gamma \vdash A(id_1\colon \tau_1, \ldots, id_n\colon \tau_n)\colon \mathsf{proc} \qquad \Gamma \vdash arg_i\colon \tau_i' \quad \tau_i' <: \tau_i \quad i = 1, \ldots, n}{\Gamma \vdash A\langle arg_1, \ldots, arg_n\rangle\colon \mathsf{proc}}\ (proccall)$$

denoted by $\twoheadrightarrow$. We omit here most of the rules because they are quite standard; they can be found in [BBV03a]. However, we want to describe the rule concerning mixin application, that produces a new class containing all the methods which are added and redefined by the mixin and those defined by the superclass. The rule (*mixinapp*) is presented in Table 29. The function *override*, defined below and used by rule (*mixinapp*), takes care of introducing in the new class the overridden methods, and of binding the special variable *next* to the implementations provided by the super class in the mixin's redefined method bodies: these "old" method implementations are given a fresh name, denoted by $m_{i'}$. Dynamic binding is then implemented for redefined methods, and old implementations from the super class are basically hidden in the derived class, since they are given a fresh name (this is reflected in the X-KLAIM implementation, presented in Section 7.2).

Definition 2. *Given two method sets, ϱ_1 and ϱ_2, the result of override(ϱ_1, ϱ_2) is the method set ϱ_3 defined as follows:*

- *for all $m_i = f_i \in \varrho_2$ such that $m_i \neq m_j$ for all $m_j = f_j \in \varrho_1$, then $m_i = f_i \in \varrho_3$;*
- *for all $m_i = f_i \in \varrho_1$ such that $m_i = f_i' \in \varrho_2$, let $m_{i'}$ be a fresh method name: then $m_{i'} = f_i' \in \varrho_3$ and $m_i = f_i[m_{i'}/next] \in \varrho_3$.*

Table 29. The (*mixinapp*) operational rule.

$$
\cfrac{exp_1 \twoheadrightarrow \left(\begin{array}{l} \text{mixin} \\ \quad \text{expect}[m_i\!:\!\tau_{m_i}\ ^{i\in I}] \\ \quad \text{redef}[m_k\!:\!\tau_{m_k}\ \text{with}\ f_k\ ^{k\in K}] \\ \quad \text{def}[m_j = f_j\ ^{j\in J}] \\ \text{end} \end{array}\right) \qquad exp_2 \twoheadrightarrow \text{class}\ [m_l = f_l\ ^{l\in L}]\ \text{end}}{exp_1 \diamond exp_2 \twoheadrightarrow \left(\begin{array}{l} \text{class} \\ \quad [m_j = f_j\ ^{j\in J}]\ \cup \\ \quad override([m_k = f_k\ ^{k\in K}], [m_l = f_l\ ^{l\in L}]) \\ \text{end} \end{array}\right)}
$$

Table 30. Additional matching rules (with proc <: proc).

$$
\cfrac{match(\tau, \tau_i)}{match(!id\!:\!\tau, t_i^{\ \tau_i})}
$$

$$
match(\tau_1, \tau_2) = \begin{cases} \tau_1 \sqsubseteq \tau_2 & \text{if } \tau_1 \text{ and } \tau_2 \text{ are mixin or class types} \\ \tau_1 <: \tau_2 & \text{otherwise} \end{cases}
$$

Notice that name clashes among methods during the application will never take place, since they have already been solved during the typing of mixin application.

The second set of rules for O'KLAIM concerns processes and it is a simple extension of the operational semantics of KLAIM, presented in Section 2.3. Notice that the O'KLAIM's operational semantics must be defined on typed (compiled) processes, because the crucial point is the dynamic matching of types. Indeed, an **out** operation adds a tuple decorated with a (static) type to a tuple space. Conversely, a process can perform an **in** action by synchronizing with a process which represents a matching typed tuple. To this aim, the standard matching predicate for tuples, *match* (Table 5), is extended with an additional rule presented in Table 30.

The additional matching rule uses the static type information, delivered together with the tuple items, in order to dynamically check that the received item is correct with respect to the type of the formal field, say τ. Therefore, an item is accepted if and only if is subtyping-compliant with the expected type of the formal field. Informally speaking, one can accept any class containing more resources than expected. Conversely, any mixin with weaker requests about methods expected from the superclass can be accepted. Note that the subtyping checking is analogous to the one we would perform in a sequential language where mixins and classes could be passed as parameters to methods. In a sequential setting, this dynamic checking might look as a burden, but in a distributed mobile setting the burden seems well-compensated by the added flexibility in communications. Finally, in order to obtain the full O'KLAIM's

Table 31. The *(def)* operational rule.

$$\frac{exp \twoheadrightarrow v}{\ell ::_\rho \text{ def } x = exp \text{ in } P \succ\!\!\longrightarrow \ell ::_\rho P[v/x]} \ (def)$$

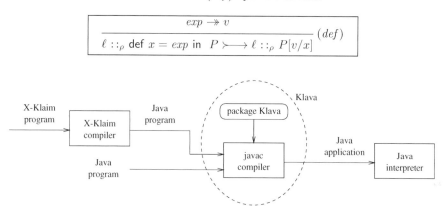

Fig. 1. The framework for X-KLAIM.

operational semantics, we must add a rule for def $x = exp$ in P to KLAIM's operational semantics. The additional rule is presented in Table 31. This rule relies on the reduction relation for object-oriented expressions $\twoheadrightarrow$. No further modification to the semantics of KLAIM is required.

Type safety of the communication results from the (static) type soundness of local and foreign code; there is no need of additional type-checking after a communication takes place. Therefore, we can reuse most of the meta-theory of MoMi (presented in [BBV03a]) to prove O'KLAIM's soundness. This shows the modularity of our approach. A complete proof of a "global soundness property" for O'KLAIM in the spirit of the one proved for MoMi is in progress.

In Section 7.2, an implementation of O'KLAIM in X-KLAIM is sketched. The reader should have noticed that O'KLAIM was left parametric with respect to the object-oriented language underlying SOOL, but a working implementation of O'KLAIM necessitates of: a coordination language; and a language underneath SOOL. Therefore, it is important to notice that X-KLAIM enriched with object-oriented features (following SOOL's design) plays the double role of the coordination language, and of the object-oriented language underneath SOOL (i.e., this means essentially that method bodies are expressed in X-KLAIM).

7   The Programming Language X-Klaim

X-KLAIM (*eXtended* KLAIM) is an experimental programming language that extends KLAIM with a high level syntax for processes: it provides variable declarations, enriched operations, assignments, conditionals, sequential and iterative process composition.

The implementation of X-KLAIM is based on KLAVA, a Java package that provides the run-time system for X-KLAIM operations, and on a compiler, which translates X-KLAIM programs into Java programs that use KLAVA. The structure of the KLAIM framework is outlined in Figure 1. X-KLAIM can be used to write the higher layer of distributed applications while KLAVA can be seen both as a middleware for X-KLAIM programs and as a Java framework for programming according to the KLAIM paradigm. With this respect, by using KLAVA directly, the programmer is able to exchange, through tuples, any kind of Java object, and implement a more fine-grained kind of mobility. X-KLAIM and KLAVA are available on line at `http://music.dsi.unifi.it`. KLAVA is briefly described in [BDFP98] and presented in detail in [BDP02,Bet03].

Remark 7. In [Tuo99] a similar approach has been adopted for `Klada` that is an `Ada95` implementation of a KLAIM-based prototype language. The main peculiarity of `Klada` regards the treatment of dynamic evolving nets. In particular, implementing the **newloc** primitive requires the use of remote access type objects of `Ada95` and the introduction of a unique globally shared name manager.

□

X-KLAIM syntax is shown in Table 32. We just describe the more relevant features. Local variables of processes are declared in the **declare** section of the process definition. Standard base types are available (**str**, **int**, etc...) as well as X-KLAIM typical types, such as **loc** for locality variables, **process** for process variables and **ts**, i.e., tuple space, for implementing data structures by means of tuple spaces, e.g. lists, that can be accessed through standard tuple space operations. Finally, comments start with the symbol **#**.

A locality variable can be initialized with a string that will correspond to its actual value. We distinguish between two kinds of localities (see the remark 1 in Section 2.3): *logical localities* are symbolic names for nodes (the distinct logical locality, **self**, can be used by processes to refer to their execution node); *physical localities* are identifiers through which nodes can be uniquely identified within a net and must have the form <IP_address>:<port>. Thus, a physical locality variable has to be initialized with a string corresponding to an Internet address. The type **loc** represents a generic locality, without specifying whether it is logical or physical, while **logloc** (resp. **phyloc**) represents a logical (resp. physical) locality. A simple form of subtyping is supplied for locality variables in that **logloc** <: **loc** and **phyloc** <: **loc**. Logical localities that are used as "destination" are evaluated automatically, i.e., if the locality used after the @ is a logical one, it is first translated to a physical locality. Conversely, when tuples are evaluated, locality names resolution does not take place automatically: it has to be explicitly invoked by putting the operator ∗ in front of the locality that has to be evaluated:

l := ∗output; # *retrieve the physical locality associated to output*
out(∗output)@self; # *insert the physical locality associated to output*

Apart from standard KLAIM operations, X-KLAIM also provides non-blocking version of the retrieval operations, namely **readp** and **inp**; these act like **read** and **in**, but, in case no matching tuple is found, the executing process does not block but `false` is returned. Indeed, **readp** and **inp** can be used where a boolean expression is expected. These variants, used also in some versions of Linda [CG89], are useful whenever one wants to search for a matching tuple in

Table 32. X-KLAIM process syntax. Syntax for other standard terms is omitted.

RecProcDefs	::= **rec** id formalparams procbody
	| **rec** id formalparams **extern**
	| RecProcDefs ; RecProcDefs
formalParams	::= [paramlist]
paramlist	::= ϵ | id : type | **ref** id : type | paramlist , paramlist
procbody	::= declpart **begin** proc **end**
declpart	::= ϵ | **declare** decl
decl	::= **const** id := expression
	| **locname** id
	| **var** idlist : type
	| decl ; decl
idlist	::= id | idlist , idlist
proc	::= KAction | **nil**
	| id := expression | **var** id : type | proc ; proc
	| **if** boolexp **then** proc **else** proc **endif**
	| **while** boolexp **do** proc **enddo**
	| **forall** Retrieve **do** proc **enddo**
	| procCall | **call** id | (proc) | **print** exp
KAction	::= **out**(tuple)@id | **eval**(proc)@id | Retrieve
	| **go**@id | **newloc**(id)
Retrieve	::= Block | NonBlock
Block	::= **in**(tuple)@id | **read**(tuple)@id
NonBlock	::= **inp**(tuple)@id | **readp**(tuple)@id | Block **within** numexp
boolexp	::= NonBlock | *standard bool exp*
tuple	::= expression | proc | ! id | tuple , tuple
procCall	::= id (actuallist)
actuallist	::= ϵ | expression | proc | id | actuallist , actuallist
expression	::= * expression | *standard exp*
id	::= *string*
type	::= **int** | **str** | **loc** | **logloc** | **phyloc** | **process** | **ts** | **bool**

a tuple space with no risk of blocking. For instance, **readp** can be used to test whether a tuple is present in a tuple space.

Furthermore, a *timeout* (expressed in milliseconds) can be specified for **in** and **read**, through the keyword **within**; the operation is then a boolean expression that can be tested to determine whether the operation succeeded:

if in(!x, !y)@l **within** 2000 **then** ... **else** ... **endif**

Time-outs can be used when retrieving information for avoiding that processes block due to network latency bandwidth or to absence of matching tuples.

It is often useful to iterate over all elements of a tuple space matching a specific template. However, due to the inherent nondeterministic selection mechanism of pattern matching a subsequent **read** (or **readp**) operation may repeatedly return the same tuple, even if several other tuples match. For this reason

X-KLAIM provides the construct **forall** that can be used for iterating actions through a tuple space by means of a specific template. Its syntax is:

forall Retrieve **do** proc **enddo**

The informal semantics of this operation is that the loop body "proc" is executed each time a matching tuple is available. Even duplicate tuples are repeatedly retrieved by the **forall** primitive; it is however guaranteed that each tuple is retrieved only once. Notice however that the tuple space is not blocked when the execution of the **forall** is started, thus this operation is not atomic: the set of tuples matching the template can change before the command completes. A locked access to such tuples can be explicitly programmed. Our version of **forall** is different from the one proposed in [BWA94] and is similar to the **all** variations of retrieval operations in *PLinda* [AS92].

Data structures can be implemented by means of the data type **ts**; a variable declared with such type can be considered as a tuple space and can be accessed through standard tuple space operations, apart from **eval** that would not make sense when applied to variables of type **ts**. Furthermore **newloc** has a different semantics when applied to a variable of type **ts**: it empties the tuple space. Then, **forall** can be used to iterate through such data structures.

eval(*P*)@*l* starts the process *P* on the node at locality *l*; *P* can be either a process name (and its arguments):

eval(P("foo", 10))@l

or the code (i.e., the actions) of the process to be executed:

eval(**in**(!i)@self; **out**(i)@l2)@l

Processes can also be used as tuple fields, such as in the following code:

out(P("foo", 10), **in**(!i)@self; **out**(i)@l2)@l

However, in this case, these processes are not started automatically at *l*: they are simply inserted in its tuple space. They can be retrieved (e.g., by another process executing at *l*) and explicitly evaluated:

in(!P1, !P2)@self;
eval(P1)@self;
eval(P2)@self

Thus, basically, **eval** provides *remote evaluation* functionalities, while **out** can be used to implement the *code on-demand* paradigm.

X-KLAIM also provides *strong mobility* by means of the action **go**@*l* [BD01] that makes an agent migrate to *l* and resume its execution at *l* from the instruction following the migration action. Thus in the following piece of code an agent retrieves a tuple from the local tuple space, then it migrates to the locality *l* and inserts the retrieved tuple into the tuple space at locality *l*:

in(!i, !j)@self;
go@l;
out(i, j)@self

Table 33. X-Klaim node syntax.

```
NodeDefs     ::= ε | nodes nodedefs endnodes
ProcDefs     ::= ε | RecProcDefs
nodedefs     ::= id ::·{ environment } nodeoptions nodeprocdefs
             | nodedefs ; nodedefs
environment  ::= ε | id ∼ id | environment , environment
nodeprocdefs ::= procbody | nodeprocdefs || nodeprocdefs
nodeoptions  ::= class id | port num
```

Also I/O operations in X-Klaim are implemented as tuple space operations. For instance the logical locality *screen* can be attached (mapped) to the output device. Hence, operation **out**("foo\n")@*screen* corresponds to printing the string "foo\n" on the screen. Similarly, the locality *keyboard* can be attached to the input device, so that a process can read what the user typed with a **in**(!s)@*keyboard*. Further I/O devices, such as files, printers, etc., can also be handled through the locality abstraction.

A process can execute only on a Klava node since in Klaim nodes are the execution engines. The syntax for defining a node in X-Klaim is in Table 33. A node is defined by specifying its name (*id*), its allocation environment, some options (described later) and a set of processes running on it. An allocation environment contains the mapping from logical localities to physical localities of the form

logical_locality_variable ∼ physical_locality_constant

thus it also implicitly declares the logical locality variables for all the processes defined in the node. Processes defined in a node have the same syntax of Table 32 but they do not have a name, since these processes are visible and accessible only from within the node where they were defined and not in the whole program. Basically the processes defined in a node correspond to the `main` entry point in languages such as Java and C.

With the option **class** it is possible to specify the actual Java class that has to be used for this node, and the option **port** can be used to specify the Internet port where the node is listening. Remember that, together with the IP address of the computer where the node will run, the port number defines the physical locality of the node.

Now we show a programming example dealing with mobility, implemented in X-Klaim, namely, a *news gatherer*, that relies on mobile agents for retrieving information on remote sites. We assume that some data are distributed over the nodes of an X-Klaim net and that each node either contains the information we are searching for, or, possibly, the locality of the next node to visit in the net. This example is inspired by the one of [DFP98].

The agent *NewsGatherer* first tries to read a tuple containing the information we are looking for, if such a tuple is found, the agent returns the result back home; if no matching tuple is found within 10 seconds, the agent tests whether

```
rec NewsGatherer[ item : str, retLoc : loc ]
  declare
    var itemVal : str ;
    var nextLoc : loc ;
    var again : bool
  begin
    again := true;
    while again do
      if read( item, !itemVal )@self within 10000 then
        go@retLoc;
        print "found " + itemVal;
        again := false;
      else
        if readp( item, !nextLoc )@self then
          go@nextLoc
        else
          go@retLoc;
          print "search failed";
          again := false
        endif
      endif
    enddo
  end
```

Listing 1: X-KLAIM implementation of a news gatherer using strong mobility.

a link to the next node to visit is present at the current node; if such a link is found the agent migrates there and continues the search, otherwise it reports the failure back home. The implementation of this agent exploiting strong mobility (by means of the migration operation **go**) is reported in Listing 1.

7.1 Connectivity Actions

X-KLAIM relies on the hierarchical model of OPENKLAIM, presented in Section 2.4. Thus, it also provides all the primitives for explicitly dealing with node connectivity. Consistently with the hierarchical model of KLAIM such actions can be performed only by *node coordinators*.

The syntax of node coordinators is shown in Table 34, and is basically the same of standard X-KLAIM processes (Table 32) apart from the new privileged actions. We briefly comment these actions:

– **login**(*loc*) logs the node where the node coordinator is executing at the node at locality *loc*; **logout**(*loc*) logs the node out from the net managed by the node at locality *loc*. **login** returns **true** if the login succeeds and **false** otherwise.
– **accept**(*l*) is the complementary action of **login** and indeed, the two actions have to synchronize in order to succeed; thus a node coordinator on the server node (the one at which other nodes want to log) has to execute **accept**. This action initializes the variable *l* to the physical locality of the node that is

Table 34. X-KLAIM node coordinator syntax. This syntax relies on standard process syntax shown in Table 32.

```
NodeCoordinator ::= rec NodeCoordDef
NodeCoordDef    ::= nodecoord id formalparams declpart nodecoordbody
                  | nodecoord id formalparams extern
nodecoordbody   ::= begin nodecoordactions end
nodecoordaction ::= standard process action | login( id ) | logout( id )
                  | accept( id ) | disconnected( id ) |
                                            disconnected( id , id )
                  | subscribe( id , id ) | unsubscribe( id , id )
                  | register( id , id ) | unregister( id )
                  | newloc( id ) | newloc( id , nodecoordactions )
                  | newloc( id , nodecoordactions , num , classname )
                  | bind( id , id ) | unbind( id )
                  | dirconnect( id ) | acceptconn( id )
```

logging. **disconnected**(l) notifies that a node has disconnected from the current node; the physical locality of such node is stored in the variable l. **disconnected** also catches connection failures. Notice that both **accept** and **disconnected** are blocking in that they block the running process until the event takes place. Instead, **logout** does not have to synchronize with **disconnected**.

- **subscribe**(*loc, logloc*) is similar to **login**, but it also permits specifying the logical locality (*logloc* is an expression of type **logloc**) with which a node wants to become part of the net coordinated by the node at locality *loc*; this request can fail also because another node has already subscribed with the same logical locality at the same server. **unsubscribe**(*loc, logloc*) performs the opposite operation. Notice that, in OPENKLAIM (Section 2.4), these operations are not part of the syntax of the dialect, but they are derived operations; in the implementation we preferred to supply them as primitives.
- **register**(*pl, ll*), where *pl* is a physical locality variable and *ll* is a logical locality variable, is the complementary action of **subscribe** that has to be performed on the server; if the subscription succeeds *pl* and *ll* will respectively contain the physical and the logical locality of the subscribed node. The association $pl \sim ll$ is automatically added to the allocation environment of the server. **unregister**(*pl, ll*) records the unsubscriptions.

bind(*logloc, phyloc*) allows to dynamically modify the allocation environment of the current node: it adds the mapping *logloc* $\sim$ *phyloc*. On the contrary, **unbind**(*logloc*) removes the mapping associated to the logical locality *logloc*. **newloc** is a privileged action and is supplied in three forms in order to make programming easier: apart from the standard form that only takes a locality variable, where the physical locality of the new created node is stored, also the form **newloc**(*l, nodecoordinator*) is provided. Since **newloc** does not automatically logs the new created node in the net of the creating node, this second

```
rec nodecoord SimpleLogin[ server : loc ]
  begin
    if login( server ) then
      print "login successful";
      out("logged", true)@self
    else
      print "login failed!"
    endif
  end

rec nodecoord SimpleLogout[ server : loc ]
  begin
    in("logged", true)@self;
    logout(server);
    print "logged off."
  end
```

```
rec nodecoord SimpleAccept[]
  declare
    var client : phyloc
  begin
    # waiting for clients...
    accept(client);
  end

rec nodecoord SimpleDisconnected[]
  declare
    var client : phyloc
  begin
    # waiting for disconnections...
    disconnected(client);
  end
```

Listing 2: An example showing **login** and **logout** (left) and the corresponding **accept** and **disconnected**.

form allows to install a node coordinator in the new node that can perform this action (or other privileged actions). Notice that this is the only way of installing a node coordinator on another node: due to security reasons, node coordinators cannot migrate, and cannot be part of a tuple. In order to provide better programmability, this rule is slightly relaxed: a node coordinator can perform the **eval** of a node coordinator, provided that the destination is self. Finally the third form of **newloc** takes two additional arguments: the port number where the new node is going to be listening and the (Java) class of the new node.

7.2   Object-Oriented Features

The object-oriented part of X-KLAIM, based on O'KLAIM (described in Section 6.3), is shown in Table 35 and it is to be considered complementary to the one shown in Table 32. So, the syntax of X-KLAIM processes is extended with object-oriented operations, and basically the syntax of method bodies is the same of the one of an X-KLAIM process (apart from the **return** statement). The syntax of X-KLAIM is extended in order to include mixins, classes, the mixin application operation <>, objects, the object instantiation operation **new**, and the method call, and, by consequence, the Java code generated by the compiler will interact, apart from KLAVA, also with momi (a Java package implementing the virtual machine for MoMI). It is important to remark that the package momi is independent from the specific mobile code framework (e.g., KLAVA, in our case). Class and mixin fields are always considered *private* and **this** is used to refer to the host object.

Class and mixin names, that are used for specifying a type (e.g., **object** id, **class** id, **mixin** id) in a variable or parameter declaration, are only a shortcut for their actual interface. Thus, when performing type checking and structural subtyping, internally, the compiler replaces a class (resp. mixin) name with the

Table 35. X-Klaim syntax for MoMi features. Symbols of the shape *xxxs*, such as "parameters" and "arguments", are intended as (possibly empty) lists of *xxx*, separated by the appropriate separator.

```
       class ::= class id { declare fields } methods end
       mixin ::= mixin id { declare fields } mixinmethods end
       field ::= const id := expression
             |   locname id
             |   var idlist : type
        type ::= xklaimtype | object id | class id | mixin id
      method ::= id ( parameters ) { : type } { localvars }
                                  begin methodactions end
 mixinmethod ::= (def | redef | expect ) method
methodaction ::= processaction | return exp
         exp ::= xklaimexp | new exp | exp <> exp | methodcall
processaction ::= xklaimaction | methodcall
  methodcall ::= exp . id ( arguments ) | next ( arguments )
```

corresponding class (resp. mixin) type. This enables a remote site, for instance, to ask for a class providing specific methods with specific types, without any requirements on the name of such a class. The same obviously holds for mixins. Obviously there must be some types on which all nodes that want to exchange object-oriented code have to agree upon, and by default these are the basic types.

An object can be declared as follows:

var my_obj : object C

that declares `my_obj` as an object of a class with the interface of C. Thus it can be assigned also an object of a class whose interface is a subtype of the one of C, as hinted above.

Class and mixins names can be used as expressions for creating objects, for specifying a type (as in the above declaration) and for delivering code to a remote site. Higher-order variables of kind class and mixin can be declared similarly:

var my_class : **class** C;
var my_mixin : **mixin** M

The above declarations state that `my_class` (`my_mixin`) represents a class (mixin) with the same interface of C (M). Once initialized, these variables can be used where class and mixin names are expected:

my_class := C;
my_obj := **new** my_class; # *same as new C*
my_obj := **new** (my_class <> M); # *provided that the application is well–typed*
my_mixin := M;
my_obj := **new** (my_class <> my_mixin); # *same as above*

An object declaration such as

var my_obj : object M

is correct even when M refers to a mixin definition. This does not mean that an object can be instantiated from a mixin directly; however, such a declared object can be instantiated with a class created via the application of M to a (correct) superclass:

my_obj = **new** (M <> C)   *# OK, provided the application is well typed*

Indeed, the declared object will be considered as having the same interface of the mixin M, that is the interface of a class having all the defined, redefined and expected methods of M.

One of the most interesting feature of MoMI is the ability of sending classes and mixins as mobile code as shown in the following example. We assume that a site provides printing facilities for local and mobile agents. The access to the printer requires a driver that the site itself has to provide to those that want to print, since it highly depends on the system and on the printer. Thus, the agent that wants to print is designed as a mixin, that expects a method for actually printing, `print_doc`, and defines a method `start_agent` through which the execution engine can start its execution. The actual instance of the printing agent is instantiated from a class dynamically generated by applying such mixin to a local superclass that provides the method `print_doc` acting as a wrapper for the printer driver.

However the system is willing to accept any agent that has a compatible interface, thus any mixin that is a subtype to the one used for describing the printing agent. Thus any client wishing to print on this site can send a mixin that is subtyping compliant to the one expected. In particular such a mixin can implement finer printing formatting capabilities.

Listing 3 presents a possible implementation of the printing client node (on the left) and of the printer server node (on the right). The printer client sends to the server a mixin `MyPrinterAgent` that respects (it is a subtype of) the mixin that the server expects to receive, `PrinterAgent` (not shown here). In particular this mixin will print a document on the printer of the server after preprocessing it. On the server, once the mixin is received, it is applied to the local (super)class `LocalPrinter`, and an object (the agent) is instantiated from the resulting class, and started so that it can actually print its document. The result of the printing task is then retrieved and sent back to the client.

We observe that the sender does not actually know the mixin name `PrinterAgent`: it only has to be aware of the mixin type expected by the server (remember that in X-Klaim class and mixin definition names are only shortcut for their actual types). Furthermore, the sent mixin can also define more methods than those specified in the receiving site, thanks to the mixin subtyping relation (Table 26). This adds a great flexibility to such a system, while hiding these additional methods to the receiving site (since they are not specified in the receiving interface they are actually unknown statically to the compiler), and also avoiding dynamic name clashes.

```
# this is the mixin actually sent to the remote site
# MyPrinterAgent <: PrinterAgent
mixin MyPrinterAgent
  expect print_doc(doc : str) : str;
  def start_agent() : str
  begin
    return
    this.print_doc(this.preprocess("my document"))
  end;
  def preprocess(doc : str) : str
  begin
    return "preprocessed(" + doc +")"
  end
end

rec SendPrinterAgent[server : loc]
  declare
    var response : str;
    var sent_mixin : mixin MyPrinterAgent
  begin
    print "sending printer agent to " + server;
    sent_mixin := MyPrinterAgent;
    out(sent_mixin)@server;
    in(!response)@server;
    print "response is " + response
  end
```

```
# the following class provides print_doc, so a PrinterAgent can be
# applied to it. Notice that it also provides another method, init()
# that is ignored by the mixin
class LocalPrinter
  print_doc(doc : str) : str
  begin
    # real printing code omitted :-)
    return "printed " + doc
  end;
  init()
  begin
    nil # foo init
  end
end

rec ReceivePrinterAgent[]
  declare
    var rec_mixin : mixin PrinterAgent;
    var result : str
  begin
    print "waiting for a PrinterAgent mixin...";
    in(!rec_mixin)@self;
    print "received " + rec_mixin;
    result := (new rec_mixin <> LocalPrinter).start_agent();
    print "result is " + result;
    out(result)@self
  end
```

Listing 3: The printer agent example (above: the sender site - the printer client, below: the receiver site - the printer server).

8   Conclusions

The work on KLAIM began in 1995 with the aim of combining the work on process algebras with localities and the one based on asynchronous generative communication mechanisms. The idea was that of building on the clean modelling of concurrency achieved with process algebras and on the success of the Linda coordination model [DP96]. Moreover, it was prompted by the intuition that network aware programming was calling for new languages and paradigms that would consider localities as first-class citizens, that should be dynamically created and handled via appropriate scoping rules [DFP97]. Since then, a lot of work has been done, also by other groups, by trying to enrich the model and the linguistic primitives to face the new challenges posed by the continuously evolving scenario of global computing.

In this paper we have tried to give a brief account on the work on KLAIM, by privileging the foundational aspects. We have thus presented a series of variants of the languages aiming, on one hand, at finding the appropriate tool for understanding and modelling processes behaviour over evolving wide area networks and, on the other hand, at finding the appropriate linguistic constructs to actually design and develop applications for such a challenging environment. We have also described programming logics for proving properties of widely distributed programs and prototype implementations of the proposed abstractions.

We want to conclude by saying that we do not see this as the end of our work on this topics, convinced as we are, that much work remains to be done and that the model and the language for network aware programming is still far to come, and that for sure will not be KLAIM. But, we hope that some of the ideas outlined here will help the search.

References

AC96.   M. Abadi and L. Cardelli. *A Theory of Objects*. Springer, 1996.

ACPP91.   M. Abadi, L. Cardelli, B. Pierce, and G. Plotkin. Dynamic typing in a statically typed language. *ACM Transactions on Programming Languages and Systems*, 13(2):237–268, April 1991.

ACPR95.   M. Abadi, L. Cardelli, B. Pierce, and D. Remy. Dynamic typing in polymorphic languages. *Journal of Functional Programming*, 5(1):111–130, January 1995.

AFH99.   K. Arnold, E. Freeman, and S. Hupfer. *JavaSpaces Principles, Patterns and Practice*. Addison-Wesley, 1999.

ALZ03.   D. Ancona, G. Lagorio, and E. Zucca. Jam - designing a java extension with mixins. *ACM Transaction on Programming Languages and Systems*, 2003. To appear.

AS92.   B. G. Anderson and D. Shasha. Persistent Linda: Linda + Transactions + Query Processing. In J. P. Banatre and D. Le Metayer, editors, *Proc. of Research Directions in High–Level Parallel Programming Languages*, volume 574 of *LNCS*, pages 93–109. Springer, 1992.

BBV02.   L. Bettini, V. Bono, and B. Venneri. Coordinating Mobile Object-Oriented Code. In F. Arbarb and C. Talcott, editors, *Proc. of Coordination Models and Languages*, number 2315 in LNCS, pages 56–71. Springer, 2002.

BBV03a.   L. Bettini, V. Bono, and B. Venneri. MoMi - A Calculus for Mobile Mixins. Manuscript, 2003.

BBV03b.   L. Bettini, V. Bono, and B. Venneri. Subtyping Mobile Clasees and Mixins. In *Proc. of Foundation of Object Oriented Languages (FOOL10)*, 2003.

BC90.   G. Bracha and W. Cook. Mixin-based inheritance. In *Proc. OOPSLA '90*, pages 303–311, 1990.

BCC01.   M. Bugliesi, G. Castagna, and S. Crafa. Reasoning about security in mobile ambients. In *Concur 2001*, number 2154 in LNCS, pages 102–120. Springer, 2001.

BD01.   L. Bettini and R. De Nicola. Translating Strong Mobility into Weak Mobility. In G. P. Picco, editor, *Mobile Agents*, number 2240 in LNCS, pages 182–197. Springer, 2001.

BDFP98.   L. Bettini, R. De Nicola, G. Ferrari, and R. Pugliese. Interactive Mobile Agents in X-KLAIM. In P. Ciancarini and R. Tolksdorf, editors, *Proc. of the 7th Int. IEEE Workshops on Enabling Technologies: Infrastructure for Collaborative Enterprises (WETICE)*, pages 110–115, Stanford, 1998. IEEE Computer Society Press.

BDL03.   L. Bettini, R. De Nicola, and M. Loreti. Formulae meet programs over the net: a framework for correct network aware programming. submitted for pubblication, available at http://music.dsi.unifi.it/, 2003.

BDP02.   L. Bettini, R. De Nicola, and R. Pugliese. KLAVA: a Java Package for Distributed and Mobile Applications. *Software — Practice and Experience*, 32:1365–1394, 2002.

Bet03.   L. Bettini. *Linguistic Constructs for Object-Oriented Mobile Code Programming & their Implementations*. PhD thesis, Dip. di Matematica, Università di Siena, 2003. Available at http://music.dsi.unifi.it.

BLP02.   L. Bettini, M. Loreti, and R. Pugliese. An Infrastructure Language for Open Nets. In *Proc. of ACM SAC 2002, Special Track on Coordination Models, Languages and Applications*, pages 373–377. ACM, 2002.

BMR97.   S. Bistarelli, U. Montanari, and F. Rossi. Semiring-based constraint satisfaction and optimization. *Journal of the ACM*, 44(2):201–236, March 1997.

BWA94.   P. Butcher, A. Wood, and M. Atkins. Global Synchronisation in Linda. *Concurrency: Practice and Experience*, 6(6):505–516, 1994.

Car99.   L. Cardelli. Abstractions for Mobile Computation. In Vitek and Jensen [VJ99], pages 51–94.

CCR96.   S. Castellani, P. Ciancarini, and D. Rossi. The ShaPE of ShaDE: a coordination system. Technical Report UBLCS 96-5, Dip. di Scienze dell'Informazione, Univ. di Bologna, Italy, 1996.

CG89.   N. Carriero and D. Gelernter. How to Write Parallel Programs: A Guide to the Perplexed. *ACM Computing Surveys*, 21(3):323–357, 1989.

CG00.   L. Cardelli and A.D. Gordon. Mobile ambients. *Theoretical Computer Science*, 240(1):177–213, 2000. An extended abstract appeared in *Proceedings of FoSSaCS '98*, number 1378 of LNCS, pages 140-155, Springer, 1998.

CGZ01.   G. Castagna, G. Ghelli, and F. Zappa Nardelli. Typing mobility in the seal calculus. In *Concur 2001*, number 2154 in LNCS, pages 82–101. Springer, 2001.

CMC99.   M. Scott Corson, Joseph P. Macker, and Gregory H. Cirincione. Internet-based mobile ad hoc networking. *Internet Computing*, 3(4), 1999.

CTV+98.   P. Ciancarini, R. Tolksdorf, F. Vitali, D. Rossi, and A. Knoche. Coordinating multiagent applications on the WWW: A reference architecture. *IEEE Transactions on Software Engineering*, 24(5):362–366, 1998.

CV99.   G. Castagna and J. Vitek. Seal: A framework for secure mobile computa-
            tions. In H. Bal, B. Belkhouche, and L. Cardelli, editors, *Internet Program-
            ming Languages*, number 1686 in LNCS, pages 47–77. Springer, 1999.
Deu01.   D. Deugo. Choosing a Mobile Agent Messaging Model. In *Proc. of ISADS
            2001*, pages 278–286. IEEE, 2001.
DFM⁺03.   R. De Nicola, G. Ferrari, U. Montanari, R. Pugliese, and E. Tuosto. A for-
            mal basis for reasoning on programmable qos. In *International Symposium
            on Verification – Theory and Practice – Honoring Zohar Manna's 64th
            Birthday*, LNCS. Springer-Verlag, 2003.
DFP97.   R. De Nicola, G. Ferrari, and R. Pugliese. Locality based Linda: Program-
            ming with explicit localities. In Michel Bidoit and Max Dauchet, editors,
            TAPSOFT '97: Theory and Practice of Software Development, volume 1214
            of *LNCS*, pages 712–726. Springer-Verlag, 1997.
DFP98.   R. De Nicola, G. Ferrari, and R. Pugliese. KLAIM: a Kernel Language for
            Agents Interaction and Mobility. *IEEE Transactions on Software Engineer-
            ing*, 24(5):315–330, 1998.
DFP99.   R. De Nicola, G. Ferrari, and R. Pugliese. Types as Specifications of Access
            Policies. In Vitek and Jensen [VJ99], pages 117–146.
DFP00.   R. De Nicola, G. Ferrari, and R. Pugliese. Programming Access Control:
            The Klaim Experience. In C. Palamidessi, editor, *Proc. of the 11th Inter-
            national Conference on Concurrency Theory (CONCUR'00)*, volume 1877
            of *LNCS*, pages 48–65. Springer-Verlag, 2000.
DFPV00.   R. De Nicola, G. Ferrari, R. Pugliese, and B. Venneri. Types for Ac-
            cess Control. *Theoretical Computer Science special issue on Coordination*,
            240(1):215–254, 2000.
DL02.   R. De Nicola and M. Loreti. A Modal Logic for Mobile Agents. *ACM
            Transactions on Computational Logic*, 2002. To appear. Available at
            `http://music.dsi.unifi.it/`.
DP96.   R. De Nicola and R. Pugliese. A process algebra based on linda. In P. Cian-
            carini and C. Hankin, editors, *Proceedings of the First International Confer-
            ence on Coordination Models and Languages (COORDINATION'96)*, vol-
            ume 1061 of *Lecture Notes in Computer Science*, pages 160–178. Springer,
            1996.
Dug99.   D. Duggan. Dynamic typing for distributed programming in polymorphic
            languages. *ACM Transactions on Programming Languages and Systems*,
            21(1):11–45, 1999.
DWFB97.   N. Davies, S. Wade, A. Friday, and G. Blair. Limbo: a tuple space based
            platform for adaptive mobile applications. In *Int. Conference on Open Dis-
            tributed Processing/Distributed Platforms (ICODP/ICDP'97)*, 1997.
FGL⁺96.   C. Fournet, G. Gonthier, J. J. Levy, L. Maranget, and D. Remy. A Calculus
            of Mobile Agents. In U. Montanari and V. Sassone, editors, *Proc. of 7th
            Int. Conf. on Concurrency Theory (CONCUR'96)*, volume 1119 of *LNCS*,
            pages 406–421. Springer-Verlag, 1996.
FKF98.   M. Flatt, S. Krishnamurthi, and M. Felleisen. Classes and mixins. In *Proc.
            POPL '98*, pages 171–183, 1998.
FMP03.   G. Ferrari, E. Moggi, and R. Pugliese. MetaKlaim: A type safe multi-stage
            language for global computing. *Mathematical Structures in Computer Sci-
            ence*, 2003.
FMSS02.   G. Ferrari, C. Montangero, L. Semini, and S. Semprini. Mark, a reasoning
            kit for mobility. *Automated Software Engineering*, 9:137–150, 2002.

FPV98.   A. Fuggetta, G. Picco, and G. Vigna. Understanging code mobility. *IEEE Transactions on Software Engineering*, 24(5):342–361, 1998.

Gel85.   D. Gelernter. Generative Communication in Linda. *ACM Transactions on Programming Languages and Systems*, 7(1):80–112, 1985.

Gel89.   D. Gelernter. Multiple Tuple Spaces in Linda. In J.Hartmanis G. Goos, editor, *Proceedings, PARLE '89*, volume 365 of *LNCS*, pages 20–27, 1989.

Gir72.   J.-Y. Girard. *Interprétation fonctionelle et élimination des coupures dans l'arithmétique d'ordre supérieur*. Thèse de doctorat d'etat, University of Paris VII, 1972.

GP03a.   D. Gorla and R. Pugliese. Behavioural equivalences for distributed and mobile systems. Research report, Dipartimento di Sistemi e Informatica, Università di Firenze, 2003. Available at
           `http://rap.dsi.unifi.it/~pugliese/DOWNLOAD/bis4klaim.pdf`.

GP03b.   D. Gorla and R. Pugliese. Enforcing Security Policies via Types. In *Proc. of the 1st International Conference on Security in Pervasive Computing (SPC'03)*, LNCS. Springer-Verlag, 2003.

GP03c.   D. Gorla and R. Pugliese. Resource access and mobility control with dynamic privileges acquisition. Research report, Dipartimento di Sistemi e Informatica, Università di Firenze, 2003. Available at
           `http://rap.dsi.unifi.it/~pugliese/DOWNLOAD/muklaim-full.pdf`.
           An extended abstract appeared in *Proceedings of ICALP'03*, LNCS, Springer, 2003.

HM85.   M. Hennessy and R. Milner. Algebraic Laws for Nondeterminism and Concurrency. *Journal of the ACM*, 32(1):137–161, January 1985.

HR02.   M. Hennessy and J. Riely. Resource access control in systems of mobile agents. *Information and Computation*, 173(1):82–120, 2002.

Lor02.   M. Loreti. *Languages and Logics for Network Aware Programming*. PhD thesis, Università di Siena, 2002. Available at
           `http://music.dsi.unifi.it`.

LRVD99.   X. Leroy, D. Rémy, J. Vouillon, and D. Doligez. The Objective Caml system, documentation and user's guide. `http://caml.inria.fr/ocaml/htmlman/`, 1999.

MHP00.   The MetaML Home Page, 2000. Provides source code and documentation online at
           `http://www.cse.ogi.edu/PacSoft/projects/metaml/index.html`.

MPW92.   R. Milner, J. Parrow, and J. Walker. A Calculus of Mobile Processes, I and II. *Information and Computation*, 100(1):1–40, 41–77, 1992.

MR98.   P.J. McCann and G-C. Roman. Compositional programming abstraction for mobile computing. *IEEE Transactions on Software Engineering*, 24(2):97–110, 1998.

Ora99.   Oracle. Oracle 9*i*AS application server lite web page. In *http://www.oracle.com/*, 1999.

OZ99.   A. Omicini and F. Zambonelli. Coordination for internet application development. *Autonomous Agents and Multi-agent Systems*, 2(3):251–269, 1999. Special Issue on Coordination Mechanisms and Patterns for Web Agents.

PMR99.   G.P. Picco, A.L. Murphy, and G.-C. Roman. LIME: Linda Meets Mobility. In D. Garlan, editor, *Proc. of the 21st Int. Conference on Software Engineering (ICSE'99)*, pages 368–377. ACM Press, 1999.

PR98.   A.S. Park and P. Reichl. Personal Disconnected Operations with Mobile Agents. In *Proc. of 3rd Workshop on Personal Wireless Communications, PWC'98*, Tokyo, 1998.

Rey74.   J.C. Reynolds. Towards a theory of type structure. In *Proceedings Colloque sur la Programmation, Paris*, volume 19 of *Lecture Notes in Computer Science*, pages 408–425, New York, NY, june 1974. Springer-Verlag. Extension of typed lambda calculus to user-defined types and polymorphic functions.

Row98.   A. Rowstron. WCL: A web co-ordination language. *World Wide Web Journal*, 1(3):167–179, 1998.

SMH00.   F.B. Schneider, G. Morrisett, and R. Harper. A language-based approach to security. In *Informatics: 10 Years Ahead, 10 Years Back. Conference on the Occasion of Dagstuhl's 10th Anniversary*, number 2000 in Lecture Notes in Computer Science, pages 86–101. Springer-Verlag, 2000.

Sun99.   Sun Microsystems. Javaspace specification. available at: http://java.sun.com/, 1999.

TS00.   W. Taha and T. Sheard. MetaML: Multi-stage programming with explicit annotations. *Theoretical Computer Science*, 248(1-2), 2000.

Tuo99.   E. Tuosto. An ada95 implementation of a network coordination language with code mobility. In M. G. Harbour and J. A. de la Puente, editors, *Intl. Conference on Reliable Software Technologies - Ada-Europe'99*, volume 1622 of *LNCS*, pages 199–210, Santander, Spain, June 1999. Springer-Verlag.

VJ99.   J. Vitek and C. Jensen, editors. *Secure Internet Programming: Security Issues for Mobile and Distributed Objects*, number 1603 in LNCS. Springer-Verlag, 1999.

WF94.   A.K. Wright and M. Felleisen. A syntactic approach to type soundness. *Information and Computation*, 115(1):38–94, 1994.

WMLF98.   P. Wyckoff, S. McLaughry, T. Lehman, and D. Ford. TSpaces. *IBM Systems Journal*, 37(3):454–474, 1998.

WS99.   M. Wand and I. Siveroni. Constraint systems for useless variable elimination. In *In proceedings of the ACM Symposium on Principles of Programming Languages (POPL)*, pages 291–302, 1999.

YH99.   N. Yoshida and M. Hennessy. Assigning types to processes. CogSci Report 99.02, School of Cognitive and Computing Sciences, University of Sussex, UK, 1999.

Ambient Calculi with Types: A Tutorial

Elio Giovannetti⋆

Dipartimento di Informatica, Università di Torino
Corso Svizzera 185, 10149 Torino, Italy
elio@di.unito.it

Abstract. A tutorial introduction to the key concepts of ambient calculi and their type disciplines, illustrated through a number of systems proposed in the last few years, such as Mobile Ambients, Safe Ambients, Boxed Ambients, and other related calculi with types.

1 Introduction

1.1 Basics of Calculi for Mobility

In the last few years a new conceptual dimension of computing has emerged, for which an adequate theoretical foundation is being searched: space and movement in space.

A huge amount of computational entities distributed worldwide, exchanging data, moving from one location to another, interacting with each other (either cooperatively or competitively), gives rise to a global computing activity. Computation has therefore to be abstractly described as something that develops not only in time and in memory space, either sequentially (λ-calculus) or as a dynamic set of concurrent processes (π-calculus), but also in a wide geographical and administrative space. The well-established theoretical models of concurrency and communication were then to be augmented with the handling of distribution and mobility.

One of the earliest proposals was the *Distributed π-calculus* (Dπ) [19], which extended π-calculus [23, 22] with the notions of a *location* and of movement between locations. In Dπ all processes and channels are *located* in named immobile locations, and may individually migrate from one location to another through an action go m (where m is a location name). The structure of locations is flat (no nesting), and communication is purely local, through named (typed) channels. Remote communication is therefore to be achieved via process movement coupled with local input-output.

Several other distributed process calculi were originated; an extensive and comparative account of them is given in [12]. This tutorial concentrates on later systems derived from the *Calculus of Mobile Ambients* (MA) [8] which, already included in that review, is indeed a sort of junction and turning point between two related strands of research.

⋆ Partially supported by MURST Cofin'01 NAPOLI Project and by EU within the FET - Global Computing initiative, project DART IST-2001-33477.

The calculus of MA, also building upon the concurrency paradigm represented by the π-calculus, was the first to introduce the notion of a mobile location or *ambient*. Its extreme simplicity and elegance, along with its expressive power, is presumably the reason of its immediate success and its widespread acceptance, in the following few years, as the new basic theoretical paradigm for mobile computing.

Ambients may move in and out of other ambients, driven by their internal processes; they therefore have a tree structure of nestings, which may dynamically change.

Ambients are thus themselves processes; as a matter of fact, from a formal point of view the syntactic category *ambient* does not exist: there are only *ambient names* $m, n, \ldots$, and the construct $m[P]$ represents a process consisting of an ambient named m containing the process P. Thus $m[P]$ and P are in the same syntactic category, *process*. The content P generally consists of a parallel composition of processes, some of which may in turn be ambients.

In MA, and in all ambient calculi subsequently introduced, there are therefore two main forms of processes, which we will respectively call (for lack of a better term) *naked processes* (or *lightweight processes*) and *ambient-processes* (or *heavyweight processes*).

The former are unnamed lists of actions[1] $\mathrm{act}_1.\mathrm{act}_2 \ldots \mathrm{act}_m$ to be executed sequentially, generally in concurrency with other processes: they can perform communication and drive their containers through the spatial hierarchy, but cannot individually go from one ambient to another (differently from $D\pi$-processes).

The latter, of the form $m[P]$, are named containers of concurrent processes: they can enter and exit other ambients, driven by their internal processes, but cannot directly perform communication. Unlike in $D\pi$, distinct subterms of the form $m[\ldots]$ with the same m represent distinct ambients with the same name: $m[P] \mid m[Q]$ is not equivalent to $m[P \mid Q]$. The term $m[P]$ can therefore be used to model a named process, with however the essential difference that its name is not unique.

Communication, in the original MA calculus, is purely local, with no channels; which is tantamount to the existence of one anonymous channel in each ambient (in fact, when process calculi are coded in ambient calculi, channels are coded by ambients). What may be communicated is either an ambient name, or a capability (i.e., an argument of the form $\mathrm{op}\,m$, where op may be in, out, or any other mobility primitive possibly introduced), or a sequence of capabilities.

In summary, disregarding polyadic communication for the sake of simplicity, the portion of syntax common to most ambient calculi is:

$Term ::= M \mid P$

$M, N ::= n \mid x \mid \mathsf{in}\, M \mid \mathsf{out}\, M \mid M . M'$

$P, Q \quad ::= 0 \mid M . P \mid P \mid Q \mid (\nu n)P \mid \,!P \mid M[P] \mid (x)P \mid \langle M \rangle$

---

[1] Actions in a broad sense, including input and output; besides, a sequence of actions may end with an ambient-process creation $m[P]$, or with a forking into different parallel processes.

The two syntactic categories of terms are *messages*, denoted by M, N, ..., and *processes*, denoted by P, Q,.... The difference between names n and variables x is inessential: ambient names can be formally viewed as variables that are free or are bound by the ν-binder (but not by the input binder)[2].

With the two *mobility actions* in m and out m a process respectively drives the enclosing ambient into a sibling ambient named m or out of a parent ambient named m, as specified by the reduction rules:

$$n[\texttt{in } m.\, P\,|\,Q]\,|\,m[R] \rightarrow m[n[P\,|\,Q]\,|\,R]$$
$$m[n[\texttt{out } m.\, P\,|\,Q]\,|\,R] \rightarrow n[P\,|\,Q]\,|\,m[R]$$

This kind of mobility has been called *subjective*, since the migration command originates from within the migrating ambient itself[3].

In contrast, *objective* mobility would be one by which an external process orders an ambient to move, e.g., via a possible construct [8] move m in n whose reduction rule would be:

$$\textsf{move } m \textsf{ in } n.\, R\,|\,m[P]\,|\,n[Q] \;\rightarrow\; R\,|\,n[m[P]\,|\,Q]$$

Another kind of primitive is often considered as a possible objective move, namely a construct of the form $\textsf{spawn}(m, P)$, with the reduction rule:

$$\textsf{spawn}(m, P)\,|\,m[Q] \;\rightarrow\; m[P\,|\,Q]$$

The process executing such action spawns a new process in the ambient m, thus, in a sense, sending P into m. For example, through $\textsf{spawn}(m, n[P])$ the ambient-process $n[P]$ is sent by an outside process (the one performing the spawning action) into the ambient m, in contrast with the subjective moves in and out where the moving command comes from the ambient-process' inside.

This classification is however debatable: if the $\textsf{spawn}$ construct is written as go $m.P$, and consequently the very same reduction rule is written as

$$\textsf{go } m.P\,|\,m[Q] \;\rightarrow\; m[P\,|\,Q]$$

the syntax suggests the view that go $m.P$ is a process that subjectively moves to m and there continues as P, thus modelling some primitives for mobile-agent programming, where a running procedure may stop at a certain point, migrate to another location, and there resume execution.

In calculi where lightweight processes are unnamed and there is no notion of a process unique identifier, it seems to be a matter of taste whether in the term $\alpha.P$ the subterm P is to be considered a different process from $\alpha.P$ or merely its continuation.

---

[2] Of course, not every free variable can be considered an ambient name: a free variable in prefix position, such as x in $x.P$, cannot.

[3] The terminology "subjective/objective" for migration was introduced by Cardelli and Gordon [8].

Such "objective" primitives cannot be encoded in a context-free way by MA primitives; they can however be emulated, in a context-dependent way, for specific ambients.

The rule for communication in ambient calculi is similar to the one of π-calculus, without channel names:

$$(x)P \mid \langle M \rangle \quad \rightarrow \quad P\{x := M\}$$

Observe that asynchronicity is, as usual, simply obtained by the syntactic constraint that an output cannot prefix a process but may only occur as the last operation. Input is blocking for the sequential process that performs it, of course.

The complete operational semantics consists, analogously to π-calculus, of *basic* reduction rules like the ones above, supplemented by a set of contextual reduction rules, and by the definition of a structural congruence relation $\equiv$, which allows redexes to be formed by trivial syntactic restructuring of terms.

The contextual reduction rules are:

$$P \rightarrow Q \Rightarrow n[P] \rightarrow n[Q]$$
$$P \rightarrow Q \Rightarrow (\nu n)P \rightarrow (\nu n)Q$$
$$P \rightarrow Q \Rightarrow P \mid R \rightarrow Q \mid R$$
$$P' \equiv P,\ P \rightarrow Q,\ Q \equiv Q' \Rightarrow P' \rightarrow Q'$$

The structural congruence is defined as the least reflexive, transitive and symmetric relation which is a congruence, makes the operator $\mid$ commutative, associative and with 0 as zero element, and is closed w.r.t. to the following rules (where $fn(P)$ denotes the set of free names of P, defined in the standard way):

1. $!P \equiv P \mid !P$;
2. $(M.M').P \equiv M.(M'.P)$;
3. $(\nu m)0 \equiv 0$; $n \neq m \Rightarrow (\nu m)(\nu n)P \equiv (\nu n)(\nu m)P$;
4. $m \notin fn(P) \Rightarrow P \mid (\nu m)Q \equiv (\nu m)(P \mid Q)$; $n \neq m \Rightarrow n[(\nu m)P] \equiv (\nu m)n[P]$.

The construct $(\nu n)P$ for name scoping limits a name's visibility to a portion of the whole system; however, owing to rules 3 and 4 of structural congruence, such portion may change dynamically by effect of communication, exactly as in π-calculus (the well-known phenomenon of scope extrusion).

For example, in the system represented by the term $n[(\nu m)\langle m \rangle \mid R] \mid p[(x)P]$ the secret name m is initially known only by the process $(\nu m)\langle m \rangle$ at the location n; owing to scope extrusion and communication, it then becomes known in the whole system: $(\nu m)(n[R] \mid p[P\{x := m\}])$. Of course, one can always assume that m does not occur in R and P, since otherwise it suffices to perform an α-renaming of m; like any binder, the ν-construct really creates a *new* fresh name, different from all those existing before.

Ambient names, capabilities and sequences of capabilities may be communicated from one process to another, similar to passwords that permit certain actions to be performed. Since there is no construct allowing to extract the name m from the expressions in m, out m, etc. or to extract a subexpression M from an expression M', it is possible for a process to propagate, instead of an ambient's full name, which grants unrestricted power over it, only a particular capability (or sequence of capabilities) for that ambient. For example, if the redex $\langle \mathsf{out}\, m \rangle \mid (x)P$ is reduced, the process P acquires the capability of driving its enclosing ambient out of m, but not the one of making it re-enter m.

On the other hand, the identification of the source for in n (i.e., the common enclosing ambient), and of the destination for out n, which is the ambient enclosing n, are implicit. In this way an ambient, if it has the capability of going out of its surrounding ambient n, is able to do it in whatever environment the ambient n ends up: which may be considered to be safe, since ambients are "closed" entities (in MA they may actually be opened, but only by the host ambient).

Following this view, an ambient named Ulysses may come out of the horse into Troy but may only take a harmless walk in the city (unless, in MA, some Trojan opens Ulysses' ambient to let out the real destroying process).

1.2 Types

Differently from λ-calculus, ambient calculi are usually presented as typed calculi, in the limited sense that the definitions of their respective term languages rely on typing to keep (untyped) syntaxes and operational semantics as simple as possible: instead of two categories of variables along with two corresponding versions of the communication primitives, one for ambient names and the other for capabilities, only one kind of constructs and variables is introduced; thus meaningless terms can be defined, or can be created by communication of wrong categories. For example, one may obtain an ambient whose name is an action, or viceversa an action consisting of an ambient name: $\langle \mathsf{in}\, m \rangle \mid (x)x[P] \;\to\; (\mathsf{in}\, m)[P]$, or $\langle m \rangle \mid (x)x\,.\,P \;\to\; m\,.\,P$.

Such anomaly is then eliminated by a simple type system where the two syntactic categories become two message types: ambients and capabilities. The fact that ambient calculi, though inheriting from process calculi the usual constructs for process composition and communication, do not have (named) channels, has an important consequence: since the reduction rules do not contain types, the above undesired reductions may only be ruled out by ensuring that input and output actions of different types can never coexist in a situation where they may synchronize with each other.

To this end, each ambient has to be assigned one type, the so-called topics of conversation, and all processes within it may only talk and listen about this topics, i.e., communicate messages of this type (since an ambient, as we observed, may be viewed as an anonymous local channel available to all its processes). If we indicate by $\mathsf{amb}(T)$ the type of ambients where the topics of conversation is a suitably defined type T, and by $\mathsf{proc}(T)$ the type of processes that perform communication of type T, the basic rules, which are found (possibly with appropriate variations) in most systems, are then:

$$\text{AMB} \;\frac{\Gamma \vdash M : \mathsf{amb}(T) \quad \Gamma \vdash P : \mathsf{proc}(T)}{\Gamma \vdash m[P] : \mathsf{proc}(S)} \qquad \text{PAR} \;\frac{\Gamma \vdash P : \mathsf{proc}(T) \quad \Gamma \vdash Q : \mathsf{proc}(T)}{\Gamma \vdash P\,|\,Q : \mathsf{proc}(T)}$$

The *environment* Γ is, as usual, a set or a sequence of assumptions of the form $\xi{:}W$, with ξ variable or ambient name.

In the original MA, only local input-output is possible: therefore in the AMB rule's conclusion the process $m[P]$ may be assigned any (process) type, since an ambient-process cannot perform any communication and may therefore be safely put in any ambient. In other systems, where forms of inter-ambient communication are allowed, some constraints on the type of the conclusion have to be introduced, as we will see.

The type of a process P is of course determined by P's input and output operations, which must be all of the same type W; as a starting point for the derivations a null process axiom is necessary, as usual. The rule for the ν-binder is analogous to the one for the input binder. The resulting rules are therefore:

$$\text{INPUT}\ \frac{\Gamma, x{:}W \vdash P : \mathsf{proc}(W)}{\Gamma \vdash (x{:}W)P : \mathsf{proc}(W)} \qquad \text{OUTPUT}\ \frac{\Gamma \vdash M : W}{\Gamma \vdash \langle M \rangle : \mathsf{proc}(W)}$$

$$\text{NULL}\ \frac{(\Gamma \text{ is a well-formed env.})}{\Gamma \vdash 0 : \mathsf{proc}(T)} \qquad \text{AMB-RES}\ \frac{\Gamma, m{:}\mathsf{amb}(S) \vdash P : \mathsf{proc}(T)}{\Gamma \vdash (\nu m{:}\mathsf{amb}(S))P : \mathsf{proc}(T)}$$

where we anticipate the distinction between message types W and communication types T, which is completely useless here but will be required in all the subsequent development of the tutorial, starting from next section.

In a system with only local communication, the in and out mobility primitives do not unleash any new possibility of communication; in the absence of any other mobility primitive, their typing rules would trivially be:

$$\text{IN}\ \frac{\Gamma \vdash M : \mathsf{amb}(S)}{\Gamma \vdash \mathsf{in}\ M : \mathsf{cap}} \qquad \text{OUT}\ \frac{\Gamma \vdash M : \mathsf{amb}(S)}{\Gamma \vdash \mathsf{out}\ M : \mathsf{cap}}$$

$$\text{PATH}\ \frac{\Gamma \vdash M_1 : \mathsf{cap} \quad \Gamma \vdash M_2 : \mathsf{cap}}{\Gamma \vdash M_1.M_2 : \mathsf{cap}} \qquad \text{PREF}\ \frac{\Gamma \vdash M : \mathsf{cap} \quad \Gamma \vdash P : \mathsf{proc}(T)}{\Gamma \vdash M.P : \mathsf{proc}(T)}$$

The remaining rules (variable, replication) needed to complete the type system are straightforward.

Since most ambient calculi allow communication of ambient names and capabilities (or paths) but not of processes, the message type W can only be of the forms $\mathsf{amb}(T)$ and cap. Summarizing, a minimal type syntax would be:

Trm ::= *term type*
    W message type
    Proc   process type

Proc ::= $\mathsf{proc}(T)$ type of processes performing communication of type T

W ::= *message type*
    $\mathsf{amb}(T)$ type of ambient names where the topics of conversation is T
    cap type of capabilities

T, S ::= W communication of messages of type W

Examples of types are:

- amb(cap), the type of ambients where capabilities may be exchanged;
- amb(amb(cap)), the type of ambients wherein names of ambients of type amb(cap) are exchanged;
- proc((amb(cap)), the type of processes that communicate names of ambients of type amb(cap);
- etc.

Remark the different roles played, in any type system for ambients, respectively by ambient types and process types. Ambients are names, therefore an ambient's typing always immediately results from an assumption; on the contrary, a process is a term of an arbitrary syntactic complexity, which is reflected in the complexity of the typing derivation, from assumptions on names and variables.

In general, a typing $m{:}A$ means that the property A is assumed to hold for any occurrence of a subterm of the form $m[P]$ within the term representing the global program. If such term is well typed, then we may be sure that the property actually holds and will keep holding during the computation – if the type system, as usual, verifies the subject reduction.

1.3   Ambient Interaction and Remote Communication

With only the primitives above illustrated, no interaction between different ambients would be possible, and ambient mobility itself would be completely useless; some other construct is therefore needed. The choice of the mechanisms for ambient interaction and remote communication is what characterizes the different versions of ambient calculi, strongly determining their nature.

In the original MA, a third mobility construct is provided: open m . P, which opens an ambient named m, i.e., dissolves its boundary thus directly exposing the contained processes; the corresponding reduction rule is:

$$\text{open } m.\,P \mid m[Q] \;\rightarrow\; P \mid Q$$

In the calculus of Boxed Ambients [5], on the other hand, the open capability is replaced by forms of inter-ambient communication between parent and children. In the $\mathbf{M}^3$ calculus [15] a form of individual mobility of lightweight processes is provided, analogous to the one in Dπ. All these different mechanisms of course require extensions and modifications of the skeletal type system delineated above.

Remote communication is achieved either by ambient movement followed by opening (in MA), or by movement and parent-children communication (in Boxed Ambients), or by lightweight mobility (in $\mathbf{M}^3$).

In MA, for example, mobile processes must be represented by ambient-processes; communication between them is represented by the exchange of other ambient-processes of usually shorter life, which have their boundaries dissolved by an open action so as to expose their internal lightweight processes performing the input-output proper.

In MA and in many other ambient calculi an ambient-process $m[P]$ is thus a general-purpose construct, intended to uniformly model many different sorts of things, at different levels of granularity: physical and virtual locations, sub-networks, administrative and security domains, mobile physical devices, mobile agents and processes, messages or packets exchanged over the network, etc.: this in agreement with the foundational character of such formalisms.

The tutorial continues by examining a certain number of particular calculi and type systems suitable to exemplify some of the main ideas in this research area, with no pretension of exhaustiveness or of giving a general overview of the field.

Section 2 achieves the account of the Calculus of Mobile Ambients proper, by considering its distinguishing features w.r.t. successive variants, and by showing how it introduced the fundamental ideas of mobility types and ambient groups.

Section 3 describes the extension with co-capabilities, first introduced in the Calculus of Safe Ambients [20] and later adopted by several other proposals; it also expounds in some detail the original type system for Safe Ambients, which motivated the extension.

In Section 4 a completely different type discipline for the same calculus is considered, namely the Secure Safe Ambients [3, 4], as an example of fine-grained types used for a kind of static flow analysis.

Sections 5 and 6 are devoted to the approach inaugurated by Boxed Ambients [5], consisting in dropping the open capability while providing for parent-children communication. In particular, Section 6 shows how this approach may be combined [21] with some of the previous ideas (groups, mobility types), and illustrates the benefits of the extended use of a non-trivial subtyping.

Finally, an overview of some of the other significant systems and results is found in Section 7, which is followed by a few lines of conclusion.

In order to be able to compare the different systems and make immediately visible their differences and their similarities, we will adopt throughout the tutorial a uniform notation, particularly for types. That will often imply the usage of concrete syntaxes not coinciding (or only partially coinciding) with the ones of the original papers.

2   Mobile Ambients

As recalled in the introduction, MA are characterized by the presence of the open primitive. Its complete syntax (for the untyped calculus) is therefore:

$$M, N ::= n \mid x \mid \text{in } M \mid \text{out } M \mid \text{open } M \mid M. M'$$
$$P, Q ::= 0 \mid M. P \mid P \mid Q \mid (\nu n)P \mid !P \mid M[P] \mid (x)P \mid \langle M \rangle$$

The basic reduction rules are:

$$n[\text{in } m. P \mid Q] \mid m[R] \rightarrow m[n[P \mid Q] \mid R]$$
$$m[n[\text{out } m. P \mid Q] \mid R] \rightarrow n[P \mid Q] \mid m[R]$$
$$\text{open } m. P \mid m[Q] \rightarrow P \mid Q$$
$$(x)P \mid \langle M \rangle \rightarrow P\{x := M\}$$

While the in and out operations are dual of each other, open does not possess an inverse operation proper. It provides a form of *objective* collective migration, since it has the effect of moving all the processes (either heavyweight or lightweight) contained in an ambient into its parent ambient.

It is worth mentioning that the sub-calculus of MA consisting of the only mobility primitives, without communication (but with open), has been proved in the original paper [8] to be Turing-complete.

2.1 Communication Types

The presence of the open capability requires the type syntax and typing rules to be modified w.r.t. to the minimal system shown in the introduction. Since the opening action dissolves an ambient's boundary and merges its content with the parent's one, the two concerned ambients must have the same topics of conversation; the type of open m must therefore record the internal topics of m, which requires capability types to be of the form $cap(T)$.

With this, however, the definitions of type expressions become mutually recursive, and a basis is needed to start the inductive construction of types (in place of the atomic type cap of subsect. 1.2). In order to keep the calculus pure, such basic type is suitably chosen as a topics called shh, characterizing ambients where no communication occurs.

Types T of topics are thus not totally coinciding with message types W, since shh cannot be a message type, i.e., it cannot type an input variable or an output expression. Message and communication types therefore become:

W ::= *message type*
         $amb(T)$ names of ambients where the topics of conversation is T
         $cap(T)$ capabilities compatible with the topics T, i.e., which
                      do not open ambients, or open ambients with topics T

T, S ::= *communication type (or exchange type, or topics of conversation)*
         shh   no communication
         W communication of messages of type W

Examples of types are $amb(shh)$, $cap(shh)$, $amb(amb(shh))$, $amb(cap(shh))$, etc.

The in and out actions, not triggering any communication, may be assigned any capability type. The typing rules for actions and action composition and prefixing therefore are:

$$\text{IN} \frac{\Gamma \vdash M : amb(S)}{\Gamma \vdash in\ M : cap(T)} \qquad \text{OUT} \frac{\Gamma \vdash M : amb(S)}{\Gamma \vdash out\ M : cap(T)} \qquad \text{OPEN} \frac{\Gamma \vdash M : amb(T)}{\Gamma \vdash open\ M : cap(T)}$$

$$\text{PATH} \frac{\Gamma \vdash M_1 : cap(T) \quad \Gamma \vdash M_2 : cap(T)}{\Gamma \vdash M_1.M_2 : cap(T)}$$

$$\text{PREF} \frac{\Gamma \vdash M : cap(T) \quad \Gamma \vdash P : proc(T)}{\Gamma \vdash M.P : proc(T)}$$

The other rules are unchanged. The type system was originally presented in [9].

2.2   Ambient Groups and Mobility Types

Groups and Group Restriction. A refinement of the archetypical system sketched in the previous subsection is presented in [7], where the notion of a *group* of ambients is introduced.

A first motivation for groups is the possibility of an increased control over ambient-name propagation, through the use of group restriction. Syntactically, groups are merely names G occurring as further constituents of ambient types, whose syntax is now (using, for uniformity, a slightly different notation from the original) $\mathsf{amb}(G, T)$: the type of ambients of topics T and group G. Process types, on the other hand, are still of the form $\mathsf{proc}(T)$, with no specification of a group. The syntax allows the existence of distinct types for distinct ambients "belonging" to the same group.

The typing rules reported in the previous subsection are almost unaffected, except for the obvious replacement of $\mathsf{amb}(T)$ with the new form. For example, the ambient rule becomes:

$$\text{AMB}\ \frac{\Gamma \vdash M : \mathsf{amb}(G, T) \quad \Gamma \vdash P : \mathsf{proc}(T)}{\Gamma \vdash m[P] : \mathsf{proc}(S)}$$

However, the syntax of the calculus itself is modified, with the introduction of the restriction on groups, written as $(\nu G)P$. This kind of restriction, which concerns ambient *types* instead of ambient names, allows to limit the extension of the scope extrusion for ambient names, and thus to better preserve name secrecy.

As a matter of fact, the new construct does not affect the operational semantics (the reduction rule is $P \to Q \Rightarrow (\nu G)P \to (\nu G)Q$), but it makes types more inherent in the calculus. Group names might be viewed as type variables of a *kind* $\mathbb{G}$ (the class of all possible groups) which, being the only kind, may be omitted. The corresponding natural typing rule is:

$$\text{G-RES}\ \frac{\Gamma, G : \mathbb{G} \vdash P : \mathsf{proc}(T) \quad G \notin freegroups(T)}{\Gamma \vdash (\nu G)P : \mathsf{proc}(T)}$$

where it must be observed that, in MA, environments are sequences (not sets), and group names may be used in environment assumptions only after being explicitly declared. In a different and less formal style, where environments are sets, and group names need not be explicitly declared, the rule could be written as:

$$\text{G-RES}\ \frac{\Gamma \vdash P : \mathsf{proc}(T) \quad G \notin freegroups(T) \quad G \ does\ not\ occur\ in\ \Gamma}{\Gamma \vdash (\nu G)P : \mathsf{proc}(T)}$$

We recalled in the introduction (subsect. 1.1) that in the original MA if a well-typed process $P = (\nu m \!:\! \mathsf{amb}(\mathsf{shh}))(\langle m \rangle \,|\, Q)$ is present in a system represented by a larger term, then the scope of the restriction, initially limited to P, may be dynamically extended through communication and mobility, and the name m, initially not known outside P, may be transmitted arbitrarily far. Thus an initially secret name may be inadvertently given away by poor programming.

On the contrary, a well-typed process of the form $(\nu G)(\nu m\!:\!\mathsf{amb}(G,\mathsf{shh}))P$, in whatever context it's placed, is guaranteed not to give away the name m, since group restriction, by hiding an essential constituent – the group G – of the *type* of the secret name, forbids in any other process even the definition of a well-typed input construct $(x\!:\!\mathsf{amb}(?,\mathsf{shh}))Q$ able to receive that name. At the same time, the possibility of scope extrusion also for group names ensures that group restriction "does not impede mobility of ambients that are enclosed in the initial scope of fresh groups but later move away" [7].

Finally, observe that a process of the form $(\nu G)(\nu n\!:\!\mathsf{amb}(G,T))\langle n\rangle$ is not well typed: the restriction on the group name G cannot be performed, since G occurs in the type $\mathsf{proc}(\mathsf{amb}(G,T))$ of the process one would like to restrict. Neither is well-typed the process $(\nu G)m[\,(\nu n\!:\!\mathsf{amb}(G,\mathsf{shh}))\langle n\rangle\,]$: though the type of $m[\,(\nu n\!:\!\mathsf{amb}(G,\mathsf{shh}))\langle n\rangle\,]$ may be freely chosen not to contain G, any such typing may only be derived w.r.t. an environment where G occurs in the type assumed for m, in contradiction with the rightmost premiss of the typing rule.

Mobility Types. As first argued in [7], since types are supposed to maintain key invariants of programs, and ambient calculi are explicitly designed to model mobile code, type systems for ambients should naturally be able to express properties related to mobility.

In [7] a type system for MA is defined, which tracks ambient opening and ambient movement, and thus makes apparent the second reason for the introduction of groups: the will to express properties regarding an ambient's movements w.r.t. other ambients though avoiding *dependent types*, i.e., types dependent on values, notoriously delicate to handle.

For example, as observed in [7], if through a typing one wants to declare that the ambient m has the property of being able to enter the ambient n, one should write $m\!:\!CanEnter(n)$, where the type depends on the value n. Groups allow to avoid this situation, by acting as intermediaries between types and values: one reformulates the above property as the more general statement that the ambient m may enter the ambients of group G and that n is an ambient of G, and therefore writes the two typings $m\!:\!CanEnter(G)$, $n\!:\!\mathsf{amb}(G)$.

The types introduced in [7] and the properties they denote, if we disregard polyadic communication and objective moves (also present in the calculus), are the following:

$$
\begin{array}{lll}
 & G_1, G_2, \ldots & \text{groups (group names)}\\
\mathscr{C}, \mathscr{O} ::= & \{G_1,\ldots,G_k\} & \text{finite sets of group names}\\[4pt]
Trm ::= & & \text{\textit{term type}}\\
 & Proc & \text{process type}\\
 & W & \text{message type}\\[4pt]
Proc ::= & \mathsf{proc}(\mathscr{C},\mathscr{O},T) & \text{type of processes whose communication is of type } T,\\
 & & \text{able to drive ambients in and out of ambients of}\\
 & & \text{groups } \mathscr{C}, \text{ and to open ambients of groups } \mathscr{O}
\end{array}
$$

W	$::=$	*message type*

$\quad\quad$ $\mathsf{amb}(G, \mathscr{C}, \mathscr{O}, T)$ $\quad$ type of ambients of group G, which may be driven
$\quad\quad\quad\quad\quad\quad\quad\quad\quad\quad\quad\quad$ in and out of ambients of groups $\mathscr{C}$,
$\quad\quad\quad\quad\quad\quad\quad\quad\quad\quad\quad\quad$ wherein ambients of groups $\mathscr{O}$ may be opened,
$\quad\quad\quad\quad\quad\quad\quad\quad\quad\quad\quad\quad$ and wherein communication is of type T

$\quad\quad$ $\mathsf{cap}(\mathscr{C}, \mathscr{O}, T)$ $\quad$ type of capabilities that may be in processes which:
$\quad\quad\quad\quad\quad\quad\quad\quad\quad\quad\quad\quad$ drive ambients in and out of ambients of groups $\mathscr{C}$,
$\quad\quad\quad\quad\quad\quad\quad\quad\quad\quad\quad\quad$ open ambients of groups $\mathscr{O}$,
$\quad\quad\quad\quad\quad\quad\quad\quad\quad\quad\quad\quad$ perform communication of type T.

$T, S ::=$		*communication type (or exchange type)*
	shh	no communication
	W	communication of messages of type W

In the concrete syntax used in [7] group sets are written $\mathbf{G}, \mathbf{H}$; process types $\mathsf{proc}(\mathscr{C}, \mathscr{O}, T)$ and capability types $\mathsf{cap}(\mathscr{C}, \mathscr{O}, T)$ are both indicated by the notation $^\frown\mathbf{G}, {}^\circ\mathbf{H}, T$; ambient types $\mathsf{amb}(G, \mathscr{C}, \mathscr{O}, T)$ are written $G[^\frown\mathbf{G}, {}^\circ\mathbf{H}, T]$; the triple $^\frown\mathbf{G}, {}^\circ\mathbf{H}, T$ is called an *effect* and is possibly denoted by F.

With the new types the ambient rule obviously becomes (omitting, here and in the following, the well-formedness requirements for types):

$$\text{AMB} \quad \frac{\Gamma \vdash M : \mathsf{amb}(G, \mathscr{C}, \mathscr{O}, T) \quad \Gamma \vdash P : \mathsf{proc}(\mathscr{C}, \mathscr{O}, T)}{\Gamma \vdash m[P] : \mathsf{proc}(\mathscr{C}', \mathscr{O}', T')}$$

The rules for the capabilities formally express the informal meanings described above. The in m and out m actions make the containing ambient cross the boundary of m, which is an ambient of group G; therefore G must be in the groups $\mathscr{C}'$ "crossable" by the ambients where the action takes place:

$$\text{IN-OUT} \quad \frac{\Gamma \vdash m : \mathsf{amb}(G, \mathscr{C}, \mathscr{O}, T) \quad G \in \mathscr{C}'}{\Gamma \vdash \mathsf{in/out}\ m : \mathsf{cap}(\mathscr{C}', \mathscr{O}', T')}$$

Analogously, in the case of open m the group G of m must be in the groups $\mathscr{O}'$ of ambients that may be opened within the ambient where the action is executed. Moreover, since the open m dissolves the boundary of m, the type of the opener process must be the same as the processes in m, i.e., $\mathscr{C}' = \mathscr{C}, \mathscr{O}' = \mathscr{O}, T' = T$. In conclusion:

$$\text{OPEN} \quad \frac{\Gamma \vdash m : \mathsf{amb}(G, \mathscr{C}, \mathscr{O}, T) \quad G \in \mathscr{O}}{\Gamma \vdash \mathsf{open}\ m : \mathsf{cap}(\mathscr{C}, \mathscr{O}, T)}$$

Hence the rule must require that if an ambient is openable then all ambients of its group may be opened inside it; in other words, if an ambient n may be opened within m, processes internal to n must have the same rights as those in m: among them, the one of opening n itself (i.e., all ambients of its group).

This has the pleasant side-effect that a type $\mathsf{amb}(G, \mathscr{C}, \mathscr{O}, T)$ specifies whether the ambient is openable or not, depending on whether G is or is not contained in $\mathscr{O}$. The form of the rules, however, also has the consequence that, recursively, an ambient must have the same capabilities of any ambient where it can stay, at any level of nesting (within a chain of openable ambients).

A quantity of other type disciplines for MA, for variations of MA and for other ambient calculi have been proposed, particularly in the latest years, and some of them will be reviewed in the next sections. The original calculus, however, equipped with the above sketchily reported type system and supplemented by a modal spatial and temporal logic [10] in which to express and study program properties, has become one of the well-established paradigms for mobile computing, and a natural basis for any study in this area.

3 Safe Mobile Ambients

3.1 Coactions

The calculus of *Safe Mobile Ambients* (SA) [20] is obtained from MA by adding to the three mobility actions three corresponding *coactions*: $\overline{\text{in}}\ m$, $\overline{\text{out}}\ m$, $\overline{\text{open}}\ m$, with the consequent modification of the three related reduction rules; for an action $op\ m$ to take place (with $op = \text{in, out, open}$), it is necessary that the ambient m gives its consent, through the simultaneous execution of the corresponding coaction, as follows:

$$n[\text{in}\ m.\ P_1 \mid P_2] \mid m[\overline{\text{in}}\ m.\ Q_1 \mid Q_2] \rightarrow m[n[P_1 \mid P_2] \mid Q_1 \mid Q_2]$$
$$m[n[\text{out}\ m.\ P_1 \mid P_2] \mid \overline{\text{out}}\ m.\ Q_1 \mid Q_2] \rightarrow n[P_1 \mid P_2] \mid m[Q_1 \mid Q_2]$$
$$\text{open}\ n.\ P \mid n[\overline{\text{open}}\ n.\ Q_1 \mid Q_2] \rightarrow P \mid Q_1 \mid Q_2$$

Movement therefore always results from a handshaking between the migrating ambient and the exited or entered ambient. The open primitive, requiring now the agreement of the ambient to be opened, loses its character of purely objective move.

All the other constructs and rules are unchanged, with the exception, irrelevant here, that replication (the construct !P) is replaced by recursion (with the construct rec $X.P$), and consequently the equivalence rule $!P \equiv P \mid !P$ is replaced by the obvious unfolding reduction rule.

An ambient's behaviour results both from the subjective control exerted by the enclosed processes, as in MA, and from the consent given by the ambient where the coaction is consumed. In particular, in dissolving an ambient the open and $\overline{\text{open}}$ primitives play a completely symmetric role: the coaction might be viewed as a self-open action, whose coaction is the open.

Observe that a MA-like behaviour for an ambient n may be obtained in the obvious way [20] by placing inside n the processes $!\overline{\text{in}}\ n$, $!\overline{\text{out}}\ n$, $!\overline{\text{open}}\ n$ (where !P is here intended as a shorthand for rec $X.(P \mid X)$).

The introduction of the coactions is explicitly motivated by the aim of eliminating *grave interferences*, i.e., situations where "the activity of a process is damaged or corrupted because of the activities of other processes" [20].

Such situations may arise, in MA, when an expression intended to model a particular real-world process or system is put in a context that models a possible reality different from the one first envisaged. This is due to the fact that mutually exclusive reductions are possible which represent semantically contrasting behaviours, as in the following examples taken from [20]:

$$\text{open } n \mid n[\text{in } m.\, P] \mid m[Q] \quad \rightarrow \quad \begin{cases} \text{in } m.\, P \mid m[Q] \\ \text{open } n \mid m[n[P] \mid Q] \end{cases}$$

$$h[n[\text{in } m.\, P \mid \text{out } h.\, R] \mid m[Q]] \quad \rightarrow \quad \begin{cases} h[m[n[P \mid \text{out } h.\, R] \mid Q]] \\ n[\text{in } m.\, P \mid R] \mid h[m[Q]] \end{cases}$$

In the first example, the ambient n may either be dissolved, or migrate into m (where its opening may become impossible); in the second, n may exit its parent h or else enter its sibling m. In either example the two different reducts are certainly non-equivalent w.r.t. any reasonable notion of equivalence, and it's hard to imagine a real-world situation modelled by a nondeterministic choice between two so contrasting behaviours.

However, because of the kind of nondeterminism inherent in MA, it is difficult to avoid that these situations may arise when running a "MA program", particularly when plugging a MA module into a (maybe unforeseen) MA context. The above examples are therefore more likely to represent unintended behaviours coming with those intentionally specified: i.e., programming errors.

The result is the difficulty of designing MA systems provably correct (w.r.t. the specifications) in all contexts; which of course is also the difficulty of designing protocols and algorithms for security that be guaranteed free from loopholes.

With coactions, each ambient may decide whether, at a given instant, it may accept a sibling ambient coming in, or whether it may let out a contained ambient. Observe however that, in the reduction rules, the argument of the coaction is the same as the one of the action: the name of the authorizing, not of the authorized ambient. The handshaking for in and out is therefore not symmetric: an ambient cannot directly authorize one ambient of a given name to come in or to go out.

On the other hand, the above remarked symmetry of the two opening constructs changes the potentially dangerous character of the original open into a much more manageable operation.

3.2 Types for Characterizing Single-Threaded Ambients

The type system is based on the same general scheme as that for MA; however, not using groups, it may only express, w.r.t. mobility, the binary property of being immobile or not: $\text{amb}(I, T)$ is the type of immobile ambients of topics T, while $\text{amb}(B, T)$ is the type of *basic* (i.e., unconstrained) ambients. This is in contrast with the more expressive MA group system where immobility is only a particular case among many possible mobility types: an ambient is immobile if the $\mathscr{C}$ component of its type is empty. It is as there were only two predefined groups, B and I, instead of all those definable by the programmer.

Subject reduction guarantees that if an ambient m is typed as immobile, no process $m[P]$ will ever come out of the enclosing ambient or enter a sibling ambient, though the enclosing ambient may be free to move (immobility is relative to the surrounding ambient). Of course, an unconstrained ambient does not necessarily move, only it cannot be guaranteed to be immobile.

The distinguishing feature of the SA type system, which differentiates it from most other ambient systems, is however the expression of the *single-threadedness* property.

A *single-threaded* (ST) ambient is one where "at any moment at most *one* process may have the control thread and may therefore use a capability" [20]; a ST process is the corresponding notion for processes, so that a term of the form $m[P]$, with m ST, is well-typed iff P is ST. More precisely, a ST ambient or process is one in which at any reduction step there is, among those not nested in subambients, at most one unguarded action or coaction, i.e., an action or coaction in initial prefix position, ready for execution.

This does not forbid that in internal subambients other actions be concurrently performed (for example, if an open is executed, at least the matching $\overline{\text{open}}$ must be consumed!). Moreover, as stated above, only the execution of a capability represents a step of the thread of computation; an input or output operation, though also being a computational activity, is not in itself considered a step of an individual thread, since it is not a "control" action affecting an ambient's movement or dissolution; it may however find itself inserted in a thread, between or after actions, as in out $m.(x)$in $n.P$ or in out $n.\langle M \rangle$ (in which cases, as we will see, it may transfer the thread).

In a ST ambient, therefore, communication between processes (not holding the control) is allowed concurrently with the control thread, as for example in the term:

$$[\,\text{out } m.\text{in } n \mid \langle k \rangle \mid (x)x[P]\,]$$

where the thread is defined by the process that drives the ambient out of m into n; communication between the other two processes is performed in concurrency (simulated by interleaving), but it is not considered to define a distinct thread.

Within a ST ambient the thread may pass from one sequential process to another through the opening of an ambient, whereby a newly exposed process catches the control, as in the following example adapted from [20]:

$$n[\,\text{open } m.\langle M \rangle \mid m[\overline{\text{open}}\, m.\text{in } k.\text{in } h\,]\,] \mid k[\,h[\ldots]\,] \;\rightarrow\; n[\,\langle M \rangle \mid \text{in } k.\text{in } h\,] \mid k[\,h[\ldots]\,]$$

In the ambient n the single thread is initially held by the sequential process performing the open; after this action the process only has to perform an output, and therefore relinquishes the thread to the process in $k.$in h, which will drive n into k and h.

The thread may also pass from one process to another through communication: an input-output operation cannot give rise to a thread but it may transmit one, as in the following example again taken from [20]:

$$n[\,\text{in } h.\langle M \rangle \mid (x)x.Q\,] \mid h[\,\overline{\text{in}}\, h.R\,] \;\rightarrow\; \rightarrow\; h[\,R \mid n[M.Q]\,]$$

The thread of n is initially held by in $h.\langle M \rangle$, which after executing the in passes the capability M to the process $(x)x.Q$; the latter, by turning itself into $M.Q$, immediately activates M itself and so takes hold of the thread.

Ambient types are thus the following (where again the original syntax, rather different, is adapted to the tutorial's uniform notation):

Amb	$::=$	$\mathsf{amb}(bi, T)$	ordinary ambients of topics T, with mobility bi
		$\textsc{st-amb}(th, Tt)$	single-threaded ambients of *single-threaded topics* Tt, whose opening exposes a process with *thread-property* th
T	$::=$	shh	no communication
		W	communication of type W
Tt	$::=$	shh	no communication
		$\textsc{st-msg}(th, W)$	communication of type W, with thread-property th
bi	$::=$	B	the property of being a mobile and openable ambient, (which however cannot be opened in an I-ambient);
		I	the property of being an ambient that cannot be moved nor opened, and wherein no ambient may be opened
th	$::=$	$\uparrow$	holding or carrying the thread
		$\dagger$	not holding or not carrying the thread

An ambient of type $\textsc{st-amb}(\uparrow, Tt)$ is a ST-ambient whose opening exposes a process taking the thread; an ambient of type $\textsc{st-amb}(\dagger, Tt)$ is a ST-ambient whose opening exposes processes not taking the thread.

Observe that Tt, the communication type of ST ambients, is different from the one of ordinary ambients: the type $\textsc{st-msg}(\uparrow, W)$ indicates communication where messages carry the thread, while $\textsc{st-msg}(\dagger, W)$ is communication where messages do not carry the thread.

Process and capability types have corresponding forms:

$$Proc ::= \mathsf{proc}(bi, T) \mid \textsc{st-proc}(th, T)$$
$$Cap ::= \mathsf{cap}(bi, T) \mid \textsc{st-cap}(th, T)$$

where $\textsc{st-proc}(th, T)$ is the type of ST processes holding or not holding the thread, according to whether $th = \uparrow$ or $th = \dagger$; $\textsc{st-cap}(th, T)$ is the type of an action that, when performed, leaves its continuation with thread right th.

During a computation, the condition for a ST process of being owner of the thread is only defined up to some indetermination: at a given step a ST process surely holds the thread if it has one unguarded capability (i.e., it is ready to perform a control instruction), or if it is an output process passing the thread, or if it had the thread in the previous step (i.e., it is the derivative of a process holding the thread in the previous reduction step) and no other parallel ST process now holds the thread. In the other cases, it may be assumed as having or not having the thread, with the constraints that at most one among all the parallel components of a ST process may own the thread, and that the process P consisting of the whole content of a ST ambient $m[P]$ must own the thread.

Thus, for example, in a process $P = (x)0 \mid (y)(z)0$ either the component $(x)0$ or the component $(y)(z)0$ or none of them may be assumed as thread owner.

However, if P in turn is in parallel with a process surely owning the thread, say out m, this forces the third alternative ("none of them"); if on the other hand P is the whole content of a ST ambient m, like in the term $m[P]$, the choice must be on one of the first two possible assumptions.

The typing rules, as usual, formally define the above described meanings. The fundamental rule that links the assumed ambient's behaviour to its content is the same as in MA:

$$\text{BI-AMB}\ \frac{\Gamma \vdash m : \mathsf{amb}(bi, T) \quad \Gamma \vdash P : \mathsf{proc}(bi, T)}{\Gamma \vdash m[P] : Proc}$$

$$\text{ST-AMB}\ \frac{\Gamma \vdash m : \text{ST-}\mathsf{amb}(th, Tt) \quad \Gamma \vdash P : \text{ST-}\mathsf{proc}(\uparrow, Tt)}{\Gamma \vdash m[P] : Proc}$$

The absence of explicit subtyping with a subsumption rule imposes that each kind of process may only stay in the corresponding kind of ambient, for example a process typed as ST or immobile (that is, good for staying in immobile ambients) cannot go into a basic ambient. There is however in the system an implicit subtyping: the simultaneous applicability of different rules and the usual polymorphism of 0 allow to assign different types to a same term. In particular, a process typed as ST may, at certain conditions (no free recursion variables, process not holding the thread, unthreaded or silent communication), also be typed as basic or immobile.

Also observe that in the rule ST-AMB the process P, consisting of the whole content of the ST ambient m, hence with no other concurrent processes in m, must forcedly have the (single) thread. This is not in contradiction with the fact that m may be an ambient not catching the thread on opening: when m is opened, P – which has the thread – must execute a $\overline{open}$, but its continuation, exposed in the surrounding ambient, need not hold the thread (for example, it may create an ambient $n[Q]$, or perform unthreaded communication, or just die); in such case the control is kept by the process originally in the enclosing ambient.

Singleness is naturally expressed by the rules for parallel composition, where at most one of the components may hold the thread:

$$\text{ST-PAR1}\ \frac{\Gamma \vdash P_1 : \text{ST-}\mathsf{proc}(\uparrow, Tt) \quad \Gamma \vdash P_2 : \text{ST-}\mathsf{proc}(\dagger, Tt)}{\Gamma \vdash P_1 \mid P_2 : \text{ST-}\mathsf{proc}(\uparrow, Tt)}$$

$$\text{ST-PAR2}\ \frac{\Gamma \vdash P_1 : \text{ST-}\mathsf{proc}(\dagger, Tt) \quad \Gamma \vdash P_2 : \text{ST-}\mathsf{proc}(\uparrow, Tt)}{\Gamma \vdash P_1 \mid P_2 : \text{ST-}\mathsf{proc}(\uparrow, Tt)}$$

$$\text{ST-PAR3}\ \frac{\Gamma \vdash P_1 : \text{ST-}\mathsf{proc}(\dagger, Tt) \quad \Gamma \vdash P_2 : \text{ST-}\mathsf{proc}(\dagger, Tt)}{\Gamma \vdash P_1 \mid P_2 : \text{ST-}\mathsf{proc}(\dagger, Tt)}$$

An output process $\langle M \rangle$, if it is a process with thread-carrying communication, must hold the thread, i.e., it must be the continuation of a control process, now ready to pass the capability M to some other process which is going to immediately use it and thus to catch in turn the thread. With non-thread-carrying communication, the output may have or not have the thread (depending on the process of which it is the continuation).

An input process $(x)P$, on the other hand, is only required (in the rule's premiss) that its continuation P does or does not hold the thread depending on whether the message carries it or doesn't. An input process waiting for a thread-carrying message is of course not (yet) holding the thread. The rules therefore are:

$$\text{ST-OUTP1} \quad \frac{\Gamma \vdash M : W}{\Gamma \vdash \langle M \rangle : \text{ST-proc}(\uparrow, \text{ST-msg}(\uparrow, W))}$$

$$\text{ST-OUTP2} \quad \frac{\Gamma \vdash M : W}{\Gamma \vdash \langle M \rangle : \text{ST-proc}(th, \text{ST-msg}(\dagger, W))}$$

$$\text{ST-INP} \quad \frac{\Gamma, x:W \vdash P : \text{ST-proc}(th, \text{ST-msg}(th, W))}{\Gamma \vdash (x:W).P : \text{ST-proc}(th', \text{ST-msg}(th, W))}$$

The other possibly thread-passing event is described by one of the open rules: when a ST ambient is opened within another ST ambient, the thread is kept or relinquished by the old process respectively if the newly exposed process catches it or doesn't:

$$\text{ST-OPEN1} \quad \frac{\Gamma \vdash m : \text{ST-amb}(th, Tt)}{\Gamma \vdash \text{open } m : \text{ST-cap}(th^{-1}, Tt)} \qquad \text{where } \uparrow^{-1} \text{ is } \dagger \text{ and conversely.}$$

The reason why this rule, if expressed in words as above, sounds tautological, is that it actually *defines* the meaning of the component th of types $\text{ST-amb}(th, Tt)$.

The rules for the other constructs are generally more standard, though many of them present different cases corresponding to the different kinds of ambients (mobile, immobile, single-threaded). For example, the in and out primitives can never be inserted in a process staying in an immobile ambient; if they are inserted in a process in a ST ambient, by definition they hold the thread:

$$\text{BI-INOUT} \quad \frac{\Gamma \vdash m : Amb}{\Gamma \vdash \text{in/out } m : \text{cap}(\mathsf{B}, T)} \qquad \text{ST-INOUT} \quad \frac{\Gamma \vdash m : Amb}{\Gamma \vdash \text{in/out } m : \text{ST-cap}(\uparrow, Tt)}$$

The corresponding coactions, on the other hand, being exercised not in the driven ambients but in those where they are moved to or from, may stay in immobile ambients too:

$$\text{BI-COINOUT} \quad \frac{\Gamma \vdash m : \text{amb}(bi, T)}{\Gamma \vdash \overline{\text{in/out}} \, m : \text{cap}(bi, S)} \qquad \text{ST-COINOUT} \quad \frac{\Gamma \vdash m : \text{ST-amb}(th, Tt)}{\Gamma \vdash \overline{\text{in/out}} \, m : \text{ST-cap}(\uparrow, Tt')}$$

In conclusion, the type system for SA is a rather complex construction, which expresses and checks properties not easily found in other systems for ambients. Immobile and ST types allow to define algebraic laws for a behavioural equivalence consisting of a barbed congruence; this is only possible owing to the synchronous character of the movement interactions, which is obtained with the introduction of coactions, and is a distinguishing feature of SA, originally motivating its development.

4   Secure Safe Ambients

Elimination of grave interferences may also be considered a natural basis for the explicit handling of security, which has been from the start one of the major concerns of the ambient paradigm. It is therefore not casual that the calculus of SA – if not its type system – has been successively chosen as the one for which to define type disciplines directly addressing this issue.

Among them, *Secure Safe Ambients* (SSA) [3, 4] are paradigmatic even from the name. Only the SA mobility sub-calculus is considered, without communication; the type system uses groups, more appropriately called (security) *domains*; capability types are of the fine-grained forms in G, out G, etc., where G is a group (domain) name; process types have three components respectively representing, for a process P, "the effects that can be observed at the level of the ambient enclosing P, at the level of P itself, and within P, whenever P is of the form $m[P']$" [3, 4].

Most interestingly, and unlike most other systems, the type of an ambient m is basically the type of an $m[P]$ process, not the type of P (though of course related to it). The ambient rule is therefore completely different from the usual one, where the type of a well-typed process $m[P]$ can be any process, unrelated with the types of m and P.

Recast into our notation, the type syntax of SSA is the following (where of course there is no message type and thus the only term types are process types):

ambient type:
$G_1, G_2, \ldots$ groups (group names)

capability type (or action type):
$Cap ::= op\ G$ type of the capabilities $op\ m$, with m ambient of group G
where $op ::= \text{in} \mid \overline{\text{in}} \mid \text{out} \mid \overline{\text{out}} \mid \text{open} \mid \overline{\text{open}}$

$\mathscr{C}_+, \mathscr{C}_0, \mathscr{C}_- ::= \{Cap_1, \ldots, Cap_k\}$ finite sets of capability types

process type:
$Proc ::= \text{proc}(\mathscr{C}_+, \mathscr{C}_0, \mathscr{C}_-)$ type of the processes that are allowed to execute:
actions of types $\mathscr{C}_+$ synchronizing with *up-level* processes,
actions of types $\mathscr{C}_0$ synchronizing with *same-level* processes,
actions of types $\mathscr{C}_-$ synchronizing with *down-level* processes.

ambient group type:
$\text{gr}(Proc)$ type of groups whose ambients m are such that
any process $m[P]$ is of type $Proc$

The notations $\mathscr{C}_+$ and $\mathscr{C}_-$ are to be considered abbreviations respectively for $\mathscr{C}_{+1}$ and $\mathscr{C}_{-1}$, so that the three components of a process type are $\mathscr{C}_\eta$, with $\eta = +1, 0, -1$.

An environment consists of two parts: a set Γ of group typing assumptions and a set E of ambient typing assumptions:

$$Env ::= \Gamma; E \quad \text{where} \quad \Gamma ::= \varnothing \mid \Gamma, G{:}\text{gr}(Proc) \quad E ::= \varnothing \mid E, m{:}G$$

A natural notion of subtyping as set inclusion may be defined:

$$\mathsf{proc}(\mathscr{C}_+, \mathscr{C}_0, \mathscr{C}_-) \leq \mathsf{proc}(\mathscr{C}'_+, \mathscr{C}'_0, \mathscr{C}'_-) \quad \text{if} \quad \mathscr{C}_+ \subseteq \mathscr{C}'_+ \ \& \ \mathscr{C}_0 \subseteq \mathscr{C}'_0 \ \& \ \mathscr{C}_- \subseteq \mathscr{C}'_-$$

The SSA type system is implicitly based on the notion of a process being able to execute an action, in the sense of the static flow analysis: a process P is *able to execute an action* α or *to exercise a capability* α if the static analysis described below does not exclude that such action may be executed during a possible evolution of P. As usual, the analysis cannot guarantee that there actually is a possible evolution where the action is indeed executed.

Such notion, for capabilities occurring in the process' (initial) expression, is independent from the context, which would appear existentially quantified in a natural definition of the property: if P_Δ (where Δ is a label that identifies a node in the syntax tree of P) is an occurrence in P of an action α, the process P is said to be able to execute P_Δ if there exists a suitable context $\mathcal{C}[\,]$ such that in a possible reduction sequence of $\mathcal{C}[P]$ the action is executed.

For example, a process P of the form $op\,m.P'$ is able to (immediately) execute the action $op\,m$, in the sense that if P is inserted in an appropriate context $\mathcal{C}[\,]$, the "execution" of the action $op\,m$ is a possible (first) reduction step of $\mathcal{C}[P]$; in particular, the process P *immediately exhibits* the capability $op\,m$.

Inductively, if the process P' is able to execute an action β, then the process $P = \alpha.P'$ is also able to execute the action β (though not immediately), since by inserting P in an appropriate context $\mathcal{C}[\,]$, β may be "executed" in a step of a possible reduction sequence of $\mathcal{C}[P]$.

Also, if P or Q is able to execute an action α, so is the parallel composition $P\,|\,Q$ (and if the action is *immediate* for P or Q, so is for $P\,|\,Q$).

On the other hand, the process $\mathsf{open}\,m.P$, if it executes $\mathsf{open}\,m$ by synchronizing with the process $m[\overline{\mathsf{open}}\,m.Q]$, unleashes all the actions executable by Q, which are not action occurrences in P. Of course, it would be meaningless to state that the process $\mathsf{open}\,m.P$ can execute any imaginable action just because one can always take a context $[\,]\,|\,m[\overline{\mathsf{open}}\,m.Q]$ with Q doing such action.

Rather, the notion of ability to execute an action must be made dependent on assumptions on the ambients' behaviours. For example, if one assumes that any process of the form $m[Q]$ may execute the action $\overline{\mathsf{open}}\,m$ and the action α, then $\mathsf{open}\,m.P$ is able to execute the action α.

Besides, as a consequence of the opening mechanism, (some) capabilities exhibited by a process P enclosed in an ambient m have to be also taken into account as capabilities of the process $m[P]$.

For example, the process $m[\overline{\mathsf{open}}\,m.P\,|\,Q]$ after executing $\overline{\mathsf{open}}\,m$ (through synchronization with an external $\mathsf{open}\,m$) continues as $P\,|\,Q$, and therefore may execute all the actions executable by this process. On the other hand, in a term like $m[n[\mathsf{open}\,q\,|\,Q]]\,|\,P]$, the action $\mathsf{open}\,q$, though being executable by the ambient-process of boundary n, is not executed by the top term, for which it is an invisible action with no effect in its context. The notion of a relative *level* at which a process executes an action is therefore necessary.

The actions in, $\overline{\mathsf{in}}$, out, $\overline{\mathsf{open}}$ operate at one level up – or level $+1$ – w.r.t. themselves, since their respective synchronizing actions must be located in a parent or sibling ambient of the one immediately containing them; in contrast, open and $\overline{\text{out}}$ operate at their own level, or level 0, since they synchronize with actions found in a subambient of the ambient immediately containing them.

If $m[P]$ is an ambient-process where P executes an action at one of the above two levels, such execution must be viewed as also being performed by the process $m[P]$, but one level down.

In conclusion, a process may be able to execute an action at one of three different (relative) levels, *up, same level* (as itself), *down*, or $+1, 0, -1$, where actions at level -1 may be executed only by processes of the form $m[Q]$ or compositions of them. We introduce here the notation $A \vdash P \downarrow^\eta \alpha$ to denote the fact that with the set A of assumptions the process P is able to execute at level η the action α; we rely however on the above informal description without going into the details of a formal definition.

In A we write assumptions of the form $m \downarrow^\eta \alpha$, meaning that any process of the form $m[P]$ is such that $m[P] \downarrow^\eta \alpha$. Moreover, we assume that sets of assumptions satisfy some closure constraints, for example:

$$\{n \downarrow^0 \text{ out } m, \ m \downarrow^0 \overline{\text{out}} \ m, \ n \downarrow^\eta \alpha\} \subseteq A \quad \Rightarrow \quad m \downarrow^\eta \alpha \in A$$
$$\{n \downarrow^0 \text{ open } m, \ m \downarrow^0 \overline{\text{open}} \ m, \ m \downarrow^\eta \alpha\} \subseteq A \quad \Rightarrow \quad n \downarrow^\eta \alpha \in A$$
$$\{n \downarrow^0 \text{ in } m, \ m \downarrow^0 \overline{\text{in}} \ m\} \subseteq A \quad \Rightarrow \quad m \ bounds \ n \ in \ A$$

where $m \ bounds \ n \ in \ A \triangleq \begin{cases} n \downarrow^\eta \alpha \in A \ \Rightarrow \ m \downarrow^{\eta-1} \alpha \in A, \text{ for } \eta = 0, +1; \\ n \downarrow^0 \overline{\text{open}} \ n \in A \ \& \ n \downarrow^\eta \alpha \in A \ \Rightarrow \ m \downarrow^\eta \alpha \in A. \end{cases}$

The first constraint says that if ambients named n are permitted to go out of ambients named m, then m is responsible for whatever may be done by n (a process $m[Q]$, by letting out an ambient-process $n[P]$, unleashes execution of $n[P]$ actions at its own level). The second constraint states that if an ambient is responsible for an action open m, and m lets itself be opened, then n is also accountable for whatever action m is allowed to perform. The third constraint, more complex, is needed for the in capability: if an ambient n is allowed to go into another ambient m, then m must be able to perform, at a level decreased by 1, all the actions performed by n at the two upper levels; if moreover the ambient m allows its boundary to be dissolved, then n must be able to do whatever action n is able to execute.

For example, in the term $P \equiv p[m[\text{in } n.Q] \mid n[\overline{\text{in}} \ n.R]]$ the action in n is executed at level $+1$ by the process in $n.Q$, at level 0 by the process $m[\text{in } n.Q]$, at level -1 by the top process P. Observe that in n is for P a "visible" internal action that varies the number of its immediate subambients. If one inserts P into another ambient t, for example by forming the term $t[P \mid P']$, then the process $t[P \mid P']$ is not considered to be executing in n, since this action does not change the number of the immediate subambients of t, at whose level the execution remains therefore completely invisible.

As another example, in the term $m[\text{open } n.P]$ the capability open n is exhibited at level 0 by the process open $n.P$, at level -1 by the whole term. As an example of non-immediate capability (from [3]), the process $m[\overline{\text{in}} \ m.\text{open } n]$ is able to execute the actions $\overline{\text{in}} \ m$ and open n; the same process, taken as a subterm of the parallel composition $m[\overline{in}\ m.\mathsf{open}\ n]\ |\ n[in\ m.\overline{\mathsf{open}}\ n.in\ p]$, also exhibits the capability in p, since in such context it reduces to $m[in\ p]$.

There is an important well-formedness constraint on process types: if a process of type *Proc* wants to open (ambients of type) G', and G' lets itself be opened (by $\overline{\mathsf{open}}\ G'$), then *Proc* must possess all the capability types of G'. Group environments Γ must satisfy closure constraints corresponding to the ones on the sets of assumptions A, with groups instead of ambients.

The meaning of process and group types, hinted at by the synthetic descriptions given with the syntax, is a specification of the types of capabilities that a process can exercise. The judgement $\Gamma; E \vdash P\colon \mathsf{proc}(\mathscr{C}_+, \mathscr{C}_0, \mathscr{C}_-)$ states that, with the group type assumptions Γ and the ambient type assumptions E:

- $\mathscr{C}_+$ is the set of action types that P is able to execute at level $+1$, i.e., through synchronization with processes contained in the ambient one level up w.r.t. to the one where it lives, possibly in a nested ambient (but not in its own ambient);
- $\mathscr{C}_0$ is the set of action types that P is able to execute at level 0, i.e., through synchronization with processes contained (with possible nesting) in the very ambient wherein P is located;
- $\mathscr{C}_-$ is the set of action types that P is able to execute at level -1, i.e., through synchronization with processes located in one of the subambients of P itself; as remarked above, this is possible only if P is of the form $m[Q]$.

Synthetically, one has $op\ G \in \mathscr{C}_\eta$ if and only if $A \vdash P \downarrow^\eta op\ m$ holds for an m such that $m{:}G \in E$, with assumptions A "agreeing" with $\Gamma; E$ (where the notion of "agreeing" can be appropriately defined). For example [3]:

- $\Gamma; m\colon G_m \vdash in\ m\,.\,P\colon \mathsf{proc}(\mathscr{C}_+, \mathscr{C}_0, \mathscr{C}_-) \implies in\ G_m \in \mathscr{C}_+$
- $\Gamma; m\colon G_m \vdash n[in\ m\,.\,P]\colon \mathsf{proc}(\mathscr{C}_+, \mathscr{C}_0, \mathscr{C}_-) \implies in\ G_m \in \mathscr{C}_0$
- $\Gamma; m\colon G_m \vdash \overline{out}\ m\,.\,P\colon \mathsf{proc}(\mathscr{C}_+, \mathscr{C}_0, \mathscr{C}_-) \implies \overline{out}\ G_m \in \mathscr{C}_0$
- $\Gamma; m\colon G_m \vdash n[\mathsf{open}\ m\,.\,P]\colon \mathsf{proc}(\mathscr{C}_+, \mathscr{C}_0, \mathscr{C}_-) \implies \mathsf{open}\ G_m \in \mathscr{C}_-$

These informal meanings are formally expressed by the typing rules for actions:

$$\mathrm{ACT}_{op}\ \frac{\Gamma; E \vdash m{:}G \quad \Gamma; E \vdash P{:}\mathsf{proc}(\mathscr{C}_+, \mathscr{C}_0, \mathscr{C}_-) \quad op\ G \in \mathscr{C}_+}{\Gamma; E \vdash op\ m.P\colon \mathsf{proc}(\mathscr{C}_+, \mathscr{C}_0, \mathscr{C}_-)} \quad op = in, \overline{in}, out, \overline{\mathsf{open}}$$

$$\mathrm{ACT}_{op}\ \frac{\Gamma; E \vdash m{:}G \quad \Gamma; E \vdash P{:}\mathsf{proc}(\mathscr{C}_+, \mathscr{C}_0, \mathscr{C}_-) \quad op\ G \in \mathscr{C}_0}{\Gamma; E \vdash op\ m.P\colon \mathsf{proc}(\mathscr{C}_+, \mathscr{C}_0, \mathscr{C}_-)} \quad op = \overline{out}, \mathsf{open}$$

The assumption $G\colon \mathsf{gr}(Proc)$ in Γ states that, for any assumption $m{:}G$ in E, any process of the form $m[P]$ is assumed to have type *Proc*, i.e., it may at most execute, at the three levels, actions of types specified by *Proc*.

As a consequence, the condition for a process $m[P]$ to be well-typed is that the actions exhibited by P give rise to actions exhibited by $m[P]$ that respect the constraints imposed by the type of the group G of m.

To this end, observe that since η-level capabilities of the process P, with $\eta = 0, 1$, become capabilities at the level $\eta - 1$ for $m[P]$, the same must hold for capability types: if P has type $\mathsf{proc}(\mathscr{C}_+,\mathscr{C}_0,\mathscr{C}_-)$, the elements of $\mathscr{C}_+$ and $\mathscr{C}_0$ become elements respectively of the components $\mathscr{C}_0'$ and $\mathscr{C}_-'$ of the type $\mathsf{proc}(\mathscr{C}_+',\mathscr{C}_0',\mathscr{C}_-')$ of $m[P]$.

Besides, if $\mathscr{C}_0$ contains the element $\overline{\mathsf{open}}\,G$, then the process P allows the boundary m of $m[P]$ to be dissolved: therefore all the actions executable by P become also executable by $m[P]$: i.e., $\mathsf{proc}(\mathscr{C}_+,\mathscr{C}_0,\mathscr{C}_-) \le \mathsf{proc}(\mathscr{C}_+',\mathscr{C}_0',\mathscr{C}_-')$.

In conclusion, the process type that constitutes the group type of G must *bound* the type of P, according to the following definition:

$$\Gamma, G : \mathsf{proc}(\mathscr{C}_+',\mathscr{C}_0',\mathscr{C}_-') \vdash G \text{ bounds } \mathsf{proc}(\mathscr{C}_+,\mathscr{C}_0,\mathscr{C}_-) \triangleq$$

$$\mathscr{C}_+ \subseteq \mathscr{C}_0' \ \& \ \mathscr{C}_0 \subseteq \mathscr{C}_-' \ \& \ (\overline{\mathsf{open}}\,G \in \mathscr{C}_0 \Rightarrow \mathsf{proc}(\mathscr{C}_+,\mathscr{C}_0,\mathscr{C}_-) \le \mathsf{proc}(\mathscr{C}_+',\mathscr{C}_0',\mathscr{C}_-'))$$

If such relation holds, $m[P]$ is well-typed, with the type $Proc'$ specified by the ambient group type. The typing rule is then:

$$\text{AMB} \ \frac{\Gamma \vdash G{:}\mathsf{gr}(Proc') \quad E \vdash m{:}G \quad \Gamma;E \vdash P{:}Proc \quad \Gamma \vdash G \text{ bounds } Proc}{\Gamma;E \vdash m[P]: Proc'}$$

The other rules are standard. Owing to the presence of subtyping, an alternative is possible: either, as in [3], the rule NULL assigns to the null process the minimal type, and an explicit subsumption rule is introduced (where, as in the sequel, process types are always understood as well-formed):

$$\text{NULL} \ \frac{}{\Gamma;E \vdash 0 : \mathsf{proc}(\varnothing,\varnothing,\varnothing)} \qquad \text{SUB} \ \frac{\Gamma;E \vdash P{:}Proc \quad Proc \le Proc'}{\Gamma;E \vdash P{:}Proc'}$$

or, as in [4], the rule NULL assigns to the null process any type, and then subsumption holds as an admissible rule:

$$\text{NULL} \ \frac{}{\Gamma;E \vdash 0 : Proc}$$

It should be intuitively clear that, given a term P and assumptions $\Gamma;E$, if the term is typable under these assumptions, then among all the types assignable to P there exists a minimal type, which is a sort of principal type for P (w.r.t. $\Gamma;E$).

The type system may be easily presented in a form that only assigns such minimal type: one just needs to eliminate the subsumption rule while keeping the minimal "empty" typing for the null process, and moreover writing the other rules so that they build the type in the conclusion by putting together the minimal types in the premises. For example:

$$\text{ACT-1} \ \frac{\Gamma;E \vdash P: \mathsf{proc}(\mathscr{C}_+,\mathscr{C}_0,\mathscr{C}_-) \quad E \vdash m:G \quad op \in \{\mathsf{in},\overline{\mathsf{in}},\mathsf{out},\overline{\mathsf{open}}\}}{op\ m.P: \mathsf{proc}(\mathscr{C}_+ \cup \{op\ G\},\mathscr{C}_0,\mathscr{C}_-)}$$

Of course, the rule

$$\text{PAR} \ \frac{\Gamma;E \vdash P: Proc \quad \Gamma;E \vdash Q: Proc}{\Gamma;E \vdash P\,|\,Q: Proc}$$

becomes

$$\text{PAR} \ \frac{\Gamma; E \vdash P: Proc \quad \Gamma; E \vdash Q: Proc'}{\Gamma; E \vdash P \mid Q: Proc \cup Proc'}$$

where $\text{proc}(\mathscr{C}_+, \mathscr{C}_0, \mathscr{C}_-) \cup \text{proc}(\mathscr{C}'_+, \mathscr{C}'_0, \mathscr{C}'_-) \triangleq \text{proc}(\mathscr{C}_+ \cup \mathscr{C}'_+, \mathscr{C}_0 \cup \mathscr{C}'_0, \mathscr{C}_- \cup \mathscr{C}'_-)$.

More importantly, the system enjoys a property of principal *typing* in the sense of [28]: given a process P and a set E of assignments of groups to ambients, there exists a minimal typing consisting of a group environment Γ and a process type *Proc* such that:

$$\Gamma; E \vdash P{:}Proc \ \ \& \ \ (\Gamma'; E \vdash P{:}Proc' \ \Rightarrow \ \Gamma \leq \Gamma' \ \& \ Proc \leq Proc')$$

where the ordering over group environments is suitably defined by pointwise extension to them of the type ordering over process types. A type reconstruction algorithm that computes such typing is given.

A classical example showing the system's expressiveness is the detection of a Trojan horse's attack. Let Ulysses, the horse and Troy with Priam's palace be modelled by the following processes:

$$
\begin{aligned}
Ulysses &= ulys[\text{in } horse . \text{out } horse . \text{in } pal . \textit{Kill}]\\
Horse &= horse[\overline{\text{in}} \ horse . \text{in } troy . \text{out } troy]\\
Troy &= troy[\overline{\text{in}} \ troy . Q \mid pal[\overline{\text{in}} \ pal . P]]
\end{aligned}
$$

The whole mythic situation is the process $Ulysses \mid Horse \mid Troy$. Suppose the assignment of groups to ambients is $horse: G^{horse}$, $pal: G^{pal}$, etc. If one only looks at the horse's capabilities by inspecting the *Horse* term, nothing dangerous shows up. On the contrary, in SSA the myth is well-typed only w.r.t. (an environment containing) the assumption $G^{horse}: \text{gr}(\text{proc}(\mathscr{C}^h_+, \mathscr{C}^h_0, \mathscr{C}^h_-))$ with in $G^{pal} \in \mathscr{C}^h_0$. The type of the horse ambient group immediately signals that some process under horse's "responsibility" has the capability of entering Priam's palace.

As is apparent even from the form of types, the mobility properties described by the SSA system are much finer than in most type systems for ambients; what is performed is actually a static flow analysis. Consequently, if the "declarative" meaning of types may look less straightforward than in other systems, in return they are amenable to a comparison with precise dynamic notions of behaviour, leading to significant safeness results.

A dynamic characterization is one obtained by means of the reduction relation, in contrast with static characterizations, formulated by means of induction on term structure. The notion of a process P *exhibiting a capability* α *at level* η *in the context* $\mathcal{C}[\ ]$ is defined in [3, 4], as a dynamic counterpart of the static notion of *being able to execute an action*; it will be indicated here by the pictorial notation $\mathcal{C}[P \Downarrow^\eta \alpha]$.

The definition is rather technical; intuitively, $\mathcal{C}[P \Downarrow^\eta \alpha]$ holds if there is an evolution of $\mathcal{C}[P]$ that eventually generates a *residual* of P *immediately exhibiting* α, where the immediate exhibition of a capability is what we called, in the static characterization, *immediate* ability to execute it.

Of course, the two characterizations cannot be equivalent; however, a type safeness result states that if $\Gamma; E \vdash \mathcal{C}[P] : Proc$ and $\Gamma; E \vdash P : \text{proc}(\mathscr{C}_+, \mathscr{C}_0, \mathscr{C}_-)$, i.e., the context $C[\,]$ (filled with P) respects the type environment that types P, then every (type of) capability dynamically *exhibited* by P in the context $C[\,]$ is recorded (at the right level) in the type of P:

$$C[P \Downarrow^\eta op \ m] \ \& \ m{:}G \in E \ \Rightarrow \ op \ G \in \mathscr{C}_\eta$$

For example (from [3, 4]), the process $m[\overline{\text{in}} \ m.\text{open} \ n]$ is able to execute the actions $\overline{\text{in}} \ m$ and open n; the same process, taken as a subterm of the parallel composition $m[\overline{\text{in}} \ m.\text{open} \ n] \mid n[\text{in} \ m.\overline{\text{open}} \ n.\text{in} \ p]$, also exhibits the capability in p, since in such context it reduces to $m[\text{in} \ p]$.

The papers [3, 4] also define a powerful language, based on SSA, for expressing security properties, and present a distributed version of SSA featuring a typed reduction relation that allows to check security even in ill-typed contexts, in a precise analogy with the security mechanisms of the Java Virtual Machine.

Another type discipline for ensuring security properties in SA is presented in [16, 2], also based on a group approach, where however groups become (partially ordered) security levels, and an ambient at a security level s can only be traversed or opened by ambients at security levels greater or equal to s.

5 Boxed Ambients

5.1 Inter-ambient Communication instead of open

Boxed Ambients (BA) [5] are another ambient calculus derived from MA, where the open primitive is dropped, and its absence is compensated by the possibility of communication[4] across one ambient boundary, between parent and children.

To this purpose, upward and downward input-output primitives are provided, beside the usual communication constructs of MA; inter-ambient communication is achieved by synchronizing a local input or output with an across-the-boundary complementary operation. Of course, downward communication requires the name of the child ambient addressed, while in the upward direction the parent, being implicit, does not need to be named.

More precisely, the possibility of atomically forwarding an input request – or dropping an output – into the enclosing ambient or into a named enclosed ambient is obtained through the constructs $(x)^\eta P$ and $\langle M \rangle^\eta P$, where $\eta = M, \uparrow$: M is an ambient name or a variable standing for an ambient name, the symbol $\uparrow$ denotes communication with the parent.

An output dropped across a boundary can be collected by a local input in the other ambient; symmetrically, an input request across a boundary can collect a local output in the other ambient. For example, a message may be passed from child to parent (i.e., from a process in an ambient m to a process in the ambient enclosing m) by synchronizing a local output in m with a downward input in the parent, or by an upward output in m with a local input in the parent; analogously is obtained the reverse communication.

---

[4] inspired by the *Seal* calculus [11].

Direct communication between sibling ambients is not possible: it must be mediated by communication with the parent.

All the above is formally stated by the reduction rules:

$$
\begin{aligned}
&(\textit{local commun.}) &&(x)P \mid \langle M \rangle Q \rightarrow P\{x := M\} \mid Q\\
&(\textit{input from child}) &&(x)^n P \mid n[\,\langle M \rangle Q \mid R\,] \rightarrow P\{x := M\} \mid n[\,Q \mid R\,]\\
&(\textit{input from parent}) &&\langle M \rangle P \mid n[\,(x)^{\uparrow} Q \mid R\,] \rightarrow P \mid n[\,Q\{x := M\} \mid R\,]\\
&(\textit{output to child}) &&\langle M \rangle^n P \mid n[\,(x)Q \mid R\,] \rightarrow P \mid n[\,Q\{x := M\} \mid R\,]\\
&(\textit{output to parent}) &&(x)P \mid n[\,\langle M \rangle^{\uparrow} Q \mid R\,] \rightarrow P\{x := M\} \mid n[\,Q \mid R\,]
\end{aligned}
$$

Observe that each of two untagged communication primitives inherited from MA occurs three times in the set of rules, i.e., both in the intra-domain and in the inter-domain communication. Such instructions are therefore not, as in MA, purely local input/output primitives, rather they are forms of undirected input or output, in contrast with the directed communication requests represented by the tagged versions.

This implies a certain supplementary amount of nondeterminism: an undirected input may synchronize either with a local output or with an output from (a process in) a child or parent ambient (i.e., across one boundary); the analogous holds for undirected output.

The six communication primitives are redundant, as remarked above: for example, an input by an ambient from a parent's output may be performed either as an undirected input from a directed output, or as a directed input from an undirected output. The two different implementations, however, are not equivalent, since the respective synchronizations take place in different ambients and are therefore subject to different possible "interferences".

As a matter of fact, in [5] the natural alternative is also discussed in which communication primitives inherited from MA keep their purely local character, and communication across a boundary must be directed from both sides. The reduction rules for the tagged primitives then become:

$$
\begin{aligned}
&(x)^n P \mid n[\,\langle M \rangle^{\uparrow} Q \mid R\,] \rightarrow P\{x := M\} \mid n[\,Q \mid R\,]\\
&\langle M \rangle^n P \mid n[\,(x)^{\uparrow} Q \mid R\,] \rightarrow P \mid n[\,Q\{x := M\} \mid R\,]
\end{aligned}
$$

This solution "provides ambients with full control of the exchanges they may have with their children" [5], but in turn it makes difficult the modelling of other kinds of communication protocols easily implemented by the original BA primitives (such as the possibility for an ambient to broadcast a message to any entering agent, like mobile phone companies do whenever a cell-phone crosses a national border).

The absence of the open operation implies that ambients, once activated, live forever (since there is no way of destroying them); in any realistic situation a garbage collection is therefore needed to dispose of ambients no longer involved in any potential computation.

5.2   Synchronous vs. Asynchronous Communication

Differently from MA and SA, communication is synchronous, which is simply expressed in the syntax by the fact that the output primitive is now a prefix $\langle M \rangle P$ exactly like input, also blocking its continuation. Asynchronous communication, which has convincingly been argued to be the main form of communication in mobile and distributed computing [6], may of course be considered a special case of synchronous communication where the process performing the output has a null continuation.

In [5], however, various other possible versions of the calculus w.r.t. the issue of synchronous vs. asynchronous communication are discussed, especially in relation with typing. In particular, a calculus is considered where the reduction rules for directed output are replaced by asynchronous versions, and a new reduction rule for undirected output is introduced:

$$
\begin{aligned}
&(\textit{asynch. undirected output}) && \langle M \rangle P \rightarrow \langle M \rangle \mid P \\
&(\textit{asynch. output to child}) && \langle M \rangle^n P \mid n[\,Q\,] \rightarrow P \mid n[\,\langle M \rangle \mid Q\,] \\
&(\textit{asynch. output to parent}) && n[\,\langle M \rangle^\uparrow P \mid Q\,] \rightarrow \langle M \rangle \mid n[\,P \mid Q\,]
\end{aligned}
$$

If the rules for input are kept unchanged, their overlapping with the asynchronous version of undirected output gives rise to a form of nondeterminism in communication, which may be performed either in one step atomically, or in two steps. For example:

$$
\langle M \rangle P \mid n[\,(x)^\uparrow Q \mid R\,] \quad \rightarrow \quad \begin{cases} P \mid n[\,Q\{x := M\} \mid R\,] \\ \langle M \rangle \mid P \mid n[\,(x)^\uparrow Q \mid R\,] \rightarrow \cdots \end{cases}
$$

This phenomenon may be avoided by adopting an asynchronous version of the input rules too, consisting of input instructions that only accept asynchronous (i.e., non-prefix) outputs:

$$
\begin{aligned}
&(x)P \mid \langle M \rangle \rightarrow P\{x := M\} \\
&(x)^n P \mid n[\langle M \rangle \mid Q] \rightarrow P\{x := M\} \mid n[Q] \\
&\langle M \rangle \mid n[\,(x)^\uparrow Q \mid R\,] \rightarrow n[\,Q\{x := M\} \mid R\,]
\end{aligned}
$$

Every communication is then carried out following a two-step protocol, always with the intermediation of the form $\langle M \rangle$ which may be interpreted as an ambient's memory cell.

5.3   Types

The extended communication mechanism gives rise to the basic difference of type systems for BA w.r.t. those with only local communication: for each ambient or process the topics of conversation now are two: the local topics, and the parent's topics; they do not need be the same. In this way, the parent may exchange values of its local type with its children (which are all required to have the same upward topics), but in addition the parent may exchange values of different types with different children, using its downward primitives.

For instance, using extra atomic types just for the sake of the example, suppose b is an ambient whose topics is bool, which encloses ambients r of topics real, s of topics string and t of topics toy, as in $b[P \mid n[Q] \mid s[S] \mid t[R]]$. The four different possibilities of communication may be exemplified as follows:

- $P = (x)P_1$, $Q = \langle\text{true}\rangle^\uparrow Q_1$, $S = \langle\text{false}\rangle^\uparrow S_1$, $R = \langle\text{false}\rangle^\uparrow R_1$;
  processes Q, S, R, located in the children ambients, pass booleans to P, located in the parent;
- $P = \langle\text{true}\rangle P_1$, $Q = (x)^\uparrow Q_1$, $S = (y)^\uparrow S_1, \ldots$
  parent passes booleans to children;
- $P = (x)^r (y)^s P_1 \mid (z)^t P_2$, $Q = \langle 3.14 \rangle$, $S = \langle\text{"hi Mom!"}\rangle$, $R = \langle\text{ball}\rangle$
  children pass respectively reals, strings and toys to parent;
- $P = \langle 2.71\rangle^r \langle\text{"hi Sally!"}\rangle^s \mid \langle\text{ball}\rangle^t$, $Q = (x)Q_1$, $S = (y)S_1$, $R = (z)R_1$
  parent passes respectively reals, strings and toys to children.

Ambient and process types thus have two components; on the other hand, owing to the absence of open, capability types have only one component: which however has a completely different meaning w.r.t. MA and SA.

In those systems $\text{cap}(T)$ is the type of the open capabilities which open ambients of topics T; as we saw, the type T must be the same as the one of the ambient where the capability is exercised; in and out actions may be assigned any (capability) type.

Here there is no opening, hence no "openable topics" as a component of the capability type; instead, communication with the parent requires that an ambient m is only allowed to stay within – and therefore to be driven into – those ambients whose (local) topics is the same as m's upward communication type. While in MA and SA the type $\text{cap}(T)$ records the topics T of the ambients m occurring in open m constructs, in BA it must record the topics T of the ambients whereinto the in and out operations may drive the ambients in which they are exercised.

Finally, observe that ambient and process types do not need to record children's topics, as this information is available locally to each child.

The type syntax is then the following:

W	::=		message type
		Amb	ambient type
		Cap	capability type

$Proc$ ::=	$\text{proc}(T, S)$	processes performing local communication of type T and upward communication of type S, able to drive ambients into ambients of local topics S
Amb ::=	$\text{amb}(T, S)$	ambients having T as local topics and S as upward topics, therefore allowed to stay within ambients of local topics S
Cap ::=	$\text{cap}(S)$	capabilities that drive ambients of upward topics S into ambients of local topics S

T, S	::=		type of topics, i.e., type of communication
		shh	no communication
		W	communication of messages of type W

The above described meanings of capability types are translated into the introduction rules for $\mathsf{cap}(T)$. If within m the local topics of conversation is T, while within m's parent the topics is S, then the action $\mathsf{in}\ m$, which turns its own ambient into a child of m, must be performed by a process talking T upward; $\mathsf{out}\ m$, which turns its own ambient into a sibling of m, must be performed by a process "upward-talking" S. Moreover, silent communication, i.e., absence of input and output, is compatible with any type of communication: a silent process may safely participate to a conversation in whatever topics. The rules therefore are:

$$\frac{\Gamma \vdash m : \mathsf{amb}(T,S)}{\Gamma \vdash \mathsf{in}\ m : \mathsf{cap}(T)} \qquad \frac{\Gamma \vdash m : \mathsf{amb}(T,S)}{\Gamma \vdash \mathsf{out}\ m : \mathsf{cap}(S)} \qquad \frac{\Gamma \vdash m : \mathsf{amb}(T,S)}{\Gamma \vdash \mathsf{in/out}\ m : \mathsf{cap}(\mathsf{shh})}$$

As already remarked, superposition between rules – in this case between the third rule and the first two – is a form of implicit subtyping. In all ambient calculi, therefore, $\mathsf{shh} \leq T$ is a natural form of subtyping, which should be implicitly or explicitly present in the type system. In BA the explicit formulation is chosen and the rules are rewritten as:

$$\text{IN}\ \frac{\Gamma \vdash m : \mathsf{amb}(T,S)\quad T' \leq T}{\Gamma \vdash \mathsf{in}\ m : \mathsf{cap}(T')} \qquad \text{OUT}\ \frac{\Gamma \vdash m : \mathsf{amb}(T,S)\quad S' \leq S}{\Gamma \vdash \mathsf{out}\ m : \mathsf{cap}(S')}$$

The rules for prefix and ambient are easily obtained from the above informal definitions:

$$\text{PREF}\ \frac{\Gamma \vdash M : \mathsf{cap}(S)\quad \Gamma \vdash P : \mathsf{proc}(T,S)}{\Gamma \vdash M.P : \mathsf{proc}(T,S)}$$

$$\text{AMB}\ \frac{\Gamma \vdash m : \mathsf{amb}(T,S)\quad \Gamma \vdash P : \mathsf{proc}(T,S)}{\Gamma \vdash m[P] : \mathsf{proc}(S,S')}$$

the component S of the capability type is the process' upward topics; the fundamental rule AMB is only modified w.r.t. MA to take into account upward communication: from the typing of m in the premiss, S is the local topics of the m-enclosing ambient, which by definition is the ambient enclosing the process $m[P]$; hence S is the type of local conversation $m[P]$ may be engaged in.

The other rules for processes are standard, but to be able to exploit the relation $\mathsf{shh} \leq T$ one has to extend subtyping to process types and introduce for them a subsumption rule:

$$\text{PROC-SUBTYPING:}\ \mathsf{proc}(\mathsf{shh}, S) \leq \mathsf{proc}(T, S)$$

$$\text{PROC-SUBSUM:}\ \frac{\Gamma \vdash P : Proc\quad Proc \leq Proc'}{\Gamma \vdash P : Proc'}$$

Observe that subtyping does not apply to upward communication: an upward-silent process is not a process that may safely drive its surrounding ambient into whatever ambient, since it may take with it a parallel process of an incompatible type. The rules for the six forms of input-output are as expected from the definition.

In BA, owing to the two-level input-output, mobility is closely connected with (and constrained by) communication, and – differently from basic MA and SA systems – the basic type system here briefly presented already expresses and checks mobility properties. The subtyping $\mathsf{shh} \leq T$ is further exploited in a system's refinement called *moded typing*, where the silent and non-silent phases of process execution are expressed at a finer grain, and typed mobility is enhanced.

6   Mobility Types with Subtyping for Boxed Ambients

A sophisticated type system for BA is the one presented in [21], which adds to the system described in the previous subsection mobility types and groups, in conformity with the paradigm of [7]. Subtyping is explicitly introduced both on communication and mobility, with suitable subsumption rules, and is for the first time extensively used in a type system for ambients, to achieve greater expressive power and flexibility. For brevity, the system will be referred to as MSBA[5] in the sequel.

As in [7], in MSBA an ambient type consists of, besides local and upward communication types, a group name G and two group sets $\mathscr{E}$ and $\mathscr{D}$, which have a similar role to the one played by $\mathscr{C}$ in [7].

In MA, however (as described in subsect. 2.2), the set $\mathscr{C}$ records which ambients an ambient may *cross*, i.e., which destination an ambient may be driven into by an in action, or which source an ambient may be driven out of by an out action. In MSBA, on the other hand, the presence of upward communication and the consequent need, for its correctness, of always knowing which is the ambient's parent, imposes that also in the case of out the system must keep track of which destination the ambient is driven into.

The component $\mathscr{D}$ therefore records the groups of all the ambients where an ambient can stay, either because created in one such ambient, or because driven downward into it (by an in action) or upward into it (by an out action).

The source ambient of the out action is also recorded, though not in the type of the driven ambient, but in the one of the source ambient, in the form of the set $\mathscr{E}$ of groups of ambients that may exit it.

A further component of the ambient type, written (following the authors' notation) as a subscript of the type constructor, consists of a subset χ of the set $\{\mathsf{i}, \mathsf{o}, \mathsf{c}, \mathsf{r}, \mathsf{w}\}$. It indicates "what the ambient name can be used for" [21], i.e., in what kinds of syntactic constructs it may turn up as an argument (possibly by variable instantiation).

More precisely, the meaning of the typing $m\colon \mathsf{amb}_\chi(\dots)$ is, for each of the possible elements of χ:

- i: the name m may be used in actions in m, i.e., m is an ambient that may be entered by other ambients through its outer boundary;
- o: the name m may be used in actions out m, i.e., m is an ambient which other ambients may come out of;

---

[5] "Mobility types with Subtyping for BA", or "Merro-Sassone's BA".

c: the name m may be used in ambient constructions of the form $m[P]$, i.e., there may indeed be an ambient (i.e., an ambient-process) named m;

r: the name m may be used as a tag in downward input $(x{:}W)^m$, i.e., m is an ambient within which its parent may read;

w: the name m may be used as a tag in downward output $\langle N \rangle^m$, i.e., m is an ambient within which its parent may write.

Groups and types are thus the following, if we do not consider, for the moment, the form of communication types and how they relate to message types:

$G_1, G_2, \ldots$ group names
$\mathscr{D}, \mathscr{E}, \mathscr{S}, \ldots$ sets of group names
$\mathfrak{U}$ universal set of group names

$Trm ::=$		*term type*
	$Proc$	process type
	W	message type
$W \quad ::=$		message types
	Amb	ambient types
	Cap	capability types
$Proc ::= \mathsf{proc}(G, \mathscr{D}, T, S)$		processes that can stay in ambients of group G, can drive them into ambients of groups $\mathscr{D}$, perform local communication of type T, and upward communication of type S
$Amb ::= \mathsf{amb}_\chi(G, \mathscr{E}, \mathscr{S}, T, S)$		ambients of group G, which can be argument of actions in $\chi \subseteq \{\mathsf{i}, \mathsf{o}, \mathsf{c}, \mathsf{r}, \mathsf{w}\}$, allow ambients of groups in $\mathscr{E}$ to exit, are allowed to stay in ambients of groups in $\mathscr{S}$, where local communication is of type T, and upward communication is of type S
$Cap ::= \mathsf{cap}(G, \mathscr{D}, S)$		capabilities that can be exercised in ambients of group G with upward communication S, and can drive them into ambients of groups $\mathscr{D}$

Hence the meaning of the typing $P\colon \mathsf{proc}(G, \mathscr{D}, T, S)$ is:

the process P may stay in ambients of group G, may drive by means of in and out actions its enclosing ambient (of group G) into any ambient of groups $\mathscr{D}$, may perform local communication of type T and upward communication of type S.

The meaning of the typing $m : \mathsf{amb}_\chi(G, \mathscr{E}, \mathscr{S}, T, S)$ is:

m is an ambient name of group G and it can be used in operations χ; ambients of groups $\mathscr{E}$ may go out of m (i.e., of a process $m[P]$) driven by an *out* action, any ambient-process $m[P]$ may be enclosed in ambients of groups $\mathscr{S}$, local communication within m is of type T, upward communication is of type S.

Environments are, as in [7], lists of assumptions the forms $G{:}\mathbb{G}$ (meaning G is a group) and $\xi{:}W$, where ξ is a variable or an ambient name. In the examples of rules we will adopt the less formal style where lists are replaced by sets and group declarations are omitted, in agreement with what observed in subsect. 2.2.

The form of communication types is another interesting feature of MSBA. Following the approach of [27, 29], a process' message type is split into an input and an output type, which respectively are the type of the messages the process may receive and the one of the messages it may send.

This allows in input-output a subtyping polymorphism analogous to the standard one by which the type of a procedure's actual parameter may be a subtype of the formal parameter's type: a process may accept a message whose type is a subtype of the expected one, so that two processes do not need to have exactly the same message type to be able to communicate; it is sufficient that the output type is a subtype of the input.

A communication type (in π-calculus or in an ambient calculus) thus also consists of an input type W_I and an output type W_O, with $W_O \leq W_I$; for example, if int is a subtype of real, it would be perfectly safe for an ambient to host processes that perform int output and real input.

One naturally defines a subtyping relation between communication types, covariant w.r.t. the output type and contravariant w.r.t. input, in a not surprising analogy with function types:

$$\leq\text{-IO} \quad \frac{W_I' \leq W_I \qquad W_O \leq W_O'}{\mathsf{io}(W_I, W_O) \leq \mathsf{io}(W_I', W_O')}$$

This approach encompasses the simple subtyping between shh and message types, described in previous sections: if one completes the set of message types with a universal type $\top$ and an empty type $\bot$, which respectively are the top and bottom of the message type order, then the type shh of silent ambients becomes, as shown in the following, merely a particular pair of input and output types, losing its character of a special communication type distinct from any message type.

Observe that, since any type W is a subtype of $\top$, any output of an expression, whatever its type W, is also an output of type $\top$. Any process is therefore a process of output type $\top$.

On the other hand, since $\bot$ is the empty (not the unit!) type, there is no possible expression M of such type, i.e., no possible output of type $\bot$. A process of output type $\bot$ is a process that cannot perform any output.

Dually, input of the universal type, i.e., of an expression of a no further specified type, is possible only if the process does not use its input (except possibly in re-sending it out again). In particular, a process that performs no input may be assumed to be of input type $\top$; as a matter of fact, this is the only case in which a process is assigned such type, since input variables of type $\top$ are not permitted in the actual system. Of course, a process of input type $\top$ may be put in parallel with outputs of any type W, in agreement with the fact that, being $W \leq \top$ for any W, the condition $W_O \leq W_I$ is then satisfied.

On the other hand, a process $(x{:}W)P$ waiting for an element of a type W can, by that, also wait forever for a non-existing element of the empty type. Therefore, any process is also a process of input type $\bot$.

Summarizing, the meanings of a process' top and bottom message types are:

$$\bot = \text{any input} = \text{no output} \qquad \top = \text{no input} = \text{any output}$$

As noted above, the extended message type that includes $\bot$ and $\top$ is sensibly not allowed as a variable type, but it's only used as input or output process type. The syntax that links communication types with message types is therefore:

$$\begin{aligned} T & ::= \text{io}(W_I, W_O) \\ W_I, W_O & ::= \bot \mid W \mid \top \end{aligned}$$

The subtyping rule for the extended message type is, as stated above:

$$\leq\text{-MSG} \; \frac{}{\bot \leq W \leq \top}$$

The type shh of silent ambients (and silent processes) is simply the type $\text{io}(\top, \bot)$ of ambients and processes with no input and no output, which is the bottom communication type. Other special types are, for each W:

$\text{io}(W, \bot) = W$ input, no output: everybody wants to listen W, nobody talks;
$\text{io}(\top, W) = $ no input, W output: everybody talks W, but nobody listens.

Ambients with this kind of contents were already allowed by the previous communication type system. Two really new, though rather peculiar, situations are those corresponding to two particular top elements in the partial order of communication types:

$\text{io}(\top, \top) = $ no input, any output: everybody can talk of any topics,
      but since nobody is listening, this is perfectly safe;
$\text{io}(\bot, \bot) = $ any input, no output: everybody can wait for messages of any type,
      but since nobody is talking, there is no risk of not understanding.

To be able to have in message types a subtyping relation not limited to the singular cases involving $\top$ and $\bot$, subtyping must be extended to capability and process types, obviously using set inclusion in case of set components:

$$\leq\text{-GRP} \; \frac{\mathscr{S}_0 \subseteq \mathscr{S}_1}{\mathscr{S}_0 \leq \mathscr{S}_1 \leq \mathcal{U}} \qquad \leq\text{-CAP} \; \frac{\mathscr{S}_0 \leq \mathscr{S}_1 \quad S_0 \leq S_1}{\text{cap}(G, \mathscr{S}_0, S_0) \leq \text{cap}(G, \mathscr{S}_1, S_1)}$$

$$\leq\text{-PROC} \; \frac{\mathscr{D}_0 \leq \mathscr{D}_1 \quad T_0 \leq T_1 \quad S_0 \leq S_1}{\text{proc}(G, \mathscr{D}_0, T_0, S_0) \leq \text{proc}(G, \mathscr{D}_1, T_1, S_1)}$$

For example, if a process drives its enclosing ambient into ambients of groups G, G', of course it can also stay in an ambient allowed to be driven into ambients of groups G, G', G''. The universe of groups $\mathcal{U}$ allows "to express, for instance, the type $\text{amb}_\chi(G, \mathscr{E}, \mathcal{U}, T, S)$ of ambients that can stay everywhere" [21].

Ambient subtyping is obviously contravariant w.r.t. the χ component: if an ambient name is usable, say, for the set $\{\mathtt{i},\mathtt{o},\mathtt{r}\}$ of operations (i.e., in, out and input), then it is certainly usable for any subset of it.

On the other hand, if an ambient is assumed to be allowed to stay in a certain set of (groups of) ambients, it is not allowed to stay in a superset of it, otherwise no constraint at all could be definable on ambient mobility; but also, it cannot be assumed to be able to stay in only a subset of it, otherwise on the basis of that assumption it could be placed where it should not. Analogous considerations hold for all the other components of an ambient type, whose subtyping has therefore to be kept invariant w.r.t. them:

$$\leq\text{-AMB}\ \frac{\chi' \subseteq \chi}{\mathsf{amb}_\chi(G,\mathscr{E},\mathscr{S},T,S) \leq \mathsf{amb}_{\chi'}(G,\mathscr{E},\mathscr{S},T,S)}$$

Subtyping is exploited by the introduction of an explicit subsumption rule:

$$\text{SUB}\ \frac{\Gamma \vdash term : Trm \quad Trm \leq Trm'}{\Gamma \vdash term : Trm'}$$

where, of course, a term is either a process or a capability.

The other rules of the system formally express the informal meanings of types described above. For example, the typing rules for capabilities are (possibly using the underscore in a Prolog-like manner to indicate components whose forms are immaterial, i.e., single-occurrence metavariables):

$$\text{IN}\ \frac{\Gamma \vdash M : \mathsf{amb}_{\mathtt{i}}(G,\_,\_,T,\_)}{\Gamma \vdash \mathsf{in}\ M : \mathsf{cap}(G',\{G\},T)} \qquad \text{OUT}\ \frac{\Gamma \vdash M : \mathsf{amb}_{\mathtt{o}}(\_,\mathscr{E},\mathscr{S},\_,S) \quad G' \in \mathscr{E}}{\Gamma \vdash \mathsf{out}\ M : \mathsf{cap}(G',\mathscr{S},S)}$$

The reading of the IN rule is: if M is an ambient of group G usable as argument of in and with local topics T, then the action in M may stay in an ambient of any group G'; the group G of the ambient M, into which the action drives its enclosing ambient, must be in the possible "destination" groups $\mathscr{D}$ of the capability; the local topics of M must be the same as the upward topics of the capability's enclosing ambient, since this is going to have M as a new parent. Observe that the second component of the type in the conclusion is the minimal one, since any larger type is given by subsumption.

The reading of the OUT rule is analogous. If M is an ambient usable for out with upward topics S, the capability out M may be exercised within an ambient of any group G', provided the ambient M lets G'-ambients out, i.e., $G' \in \mathscr{E}$; observe that in this case the component of the ambient type cannot be simply given in the form $\{G'\}$, for the very reason that subsumption does not hold between ambient types. Also, since out m drives its enclosing ambient into M's parent, the $\mathscr{D}$ component of the capability type must coincide with the $\mathscr{S}$ component of the type of M, and the upward topics of the process exercising the capability must coincide with M's upward topics.

The prefix and parallel rule state, as usual, that a process' type basically is the common type of all the capabilities and input-output operations present in the process; subsumption here ensures that all these types do not need to be identical, provided they can be subsumed by a common process type.

$$\text{PREF}\ \dfrac{\Gamma \vdash M\colon \mathsf{cap}(G, \mathscr{D}, S) \quad \Gamma \vdash P\colon \mathsf{proc}(G, \mathscr{D}, T, S)}{\Gamma \vdash M.P\colon \mathsf{proc}(G, \mathscr{D}, T, S)}$$

$$\text{PAR}\ \dfrac{\Gamma \vdash P\colon \mathit{Proc} \quad \Gamma \vdash Q\colon \mathit{Proc}}{\Gamma \vdash P \,|\, Q\colon \mathit{Proc}}$$

Rather standard is also the ambient rule:

$$\text{AMB}\ \dfrac{\Gamma \vdash M\colon \mathsf{amb_c}(G, \mathscr{E}, \mathscr{S}, T, S) \quad \Gamma \vdash P\colon \mathsf{proc}(G, \mathscr{S}, T, S) \quad G' \in \mathscr{S}}{M[P]\colon \mathsf{proc}(G', \varnothing, S, \mathsf{shh})}$$

where however the ambient name must be usable for construction, and the ambients whereinto $M[P]$ may be driven must be a subset of the set of ambients where it can stay: but subsumption allows to replace inclusion with equality (between respectively the third an the second component of M's and P's type). Invariance of ambient types ensures that if an ambient requires its content to be of a certain type, an ambient with a smaller type can do as well, but the ambient's type is fixed.

The NULL rule assigns to the null process the minimum type:

$$\text{NULL}\ \dfrac{}{0 : \mathsf{proc}(G, \varnothing, \mathsf{shh}, \mathsf{shh})}$$

As an example of communication rule we can consider untagged input:

$$\text{INPUT}\ \dfrac{\Gamma, x{:}W \vdash P : \mathsf{proc}(G, \mathscr{D}, \mathsf{io}(W_I, W_O), S) \quad W_I \le W}{\Gamma \vdash (x{:}W)P : \mathsf{proc}(G, \mathscr{D}, \mathsf{io}(W_I, W_O), S)}$$

The other communication rules are similar.

In [21] an extension of MSBA is also presented, for a variant of BA, called Safe Boxed Ambients, where coactions similar to those of SA are added. In order to keep track of coactions, an additional component is needed in ambient, process and capability types: the set of (groups of) ambients which an ambient may contain, or which a process or capability allows to enter its enclosing ambient.

For the coaction mechanism to fit smoothly with the BA type system, the $\overline{\mathsf{out}}$ coaction has to be defined in a different way than in SA: since in BA one must check the destination ambient for the out too, the co-capability $\overline{\mathsf{out}}\, n$, in agreement with that, must be exercised in the ambient where n exits into, not the one which n leaves.

7   Other Types of/for MA

Though much research in ambient typing has concentrated on mobility and security, more sophisticated disciplines concerned with only the communication aspect of MA have also been devised. In particular, in [1] a system is proposed for a MA calculus enriched with the basic features of functional programming languages (λ-abstraction and application, if-then-else) and with the $\overline{\text{open}}$ capability. Its type structure is very rich, and process types are more appropriately called *behaviours* to distinguish them from the more traditional ambient and action types.

Basic process behaviours are communication types analogous to those of the previous subsections, of the forms $o(W), i(W)$, respectively indicating output and input of type W; but, built from these, general behaviours (i.e., general process types) b are of such forms as $b_1.b_2$, the behaviour of all processes that first exhibit behaviour b_1 then behaviour b_2, or the type of all processes that first have type b_1 then type b_2; the notation $b_1 \mid b_2$ indicates the type of processes that behave like a parallel composition of processes of types b_1 and b_2; etc.

An atomic behaviour diss, recording the occurrence of the ambient-dissolving coaction $\overline{\text{open}}$, is also needed; another basis for the inductive construction of behaviours is the type ϵ of processes which exhibit no traceable action, and is therefore assignable to the null process.

The basic typing rules, respectively corresponding to null process, input and output, therefore are, if we neglect polyadic communication:

$$\frac{}{\Gamma \vdash 0 : \epsilon} \qquad \frac{\Gamma, x : W \vdash P : b}{\Gamma \vdash (x)P : i(W).b} \qquad \frac{\Gamma \vdash M : W}{\Gamma \vdash \langle M \rangle : o(W)}$$

Ambient types, of the form $\mathsf{amb}(b, b')$ represent, as usual, the type b of processes an ambient is allowed to contain (plus the type b' of the process it unleashes when opened). Since action prefixing transforms a process into another process, capability types are viewed as a kind of type functions transforming a behaviour into another behaviour; the full notion of type function not being needed, capability types $\mathsf{cap}(b_{\llcorner\lrcorner})$ merely consist of behaviour contexts $b_{\llcorner\lrcorner}$, i.e., "behaviours with a hole", which is filled in the prefix rule:

$$\frac{\Gamma \vdash M : \mathsf{cap}(b_{\llcorner\lrcorner}) \quad \Gamma \vdash P : b'}{\Gamma \vdash M.P : b_{\llcorner}b'_{\lrcorner}}$$

Since the type system does not handle mobility, the only non-empty-context rules are those for open and $\overline{\text{open}}$:

$$\frac{\Gamma \vdash m : \mathsf{amb}(b, b')}{\Gamma \vdash \mathsf{in/out}\, m : \mathsf{cap}(\llcorner\lrcorner)} \qquad \frac{\Gamma \vdash m : \mathsf{amb}(b, b')}{\Gamma \vdash \mathsf{open}\, m : \mathsf{cap}(b' \mid \llcorner\lrcorner)} \qquad \frac{\Gamma \vdash m : \mathsf{amb}(b, b')}{\Gamma \vdash \overline{\mathsf{open}}\, m : \mathsf{cap}(\mathsf{diss}.\llcorner\lrcorner)}$$

The rule for parallel composition is trivial, in agreement with the definition of parallel behaviour:

$$\frac{\Gamma \vdash P_1 : b_1 \quad \Gamma \vdash P_2 : b_2}{\Gamma \vdash P_1 \mid P_2 : b_1 \mid b_2}$$

The type system, differently from most of the other ones, is given a (trace) semantics which, being so fine-grained, is a first step towards a model for the calculus itself. A subtyping relation is defined semantically on this type model.

As should be clear, the main motivation of [1] is that of permitting the so-called *orderly* polymorphism, whose absence is actually a strong limitation of ordinary ambient typings. Here an ambient is no more a boring place where there is always the same topics of conversation, and a process is no more a monomaniac guy always talking the same subject; on the contrary, a process may first have a type (of conversation) and then a different one, and the type system checks that this happens at the same time for all those enclosed in the same ambient, so that no message non-understanding is possible. For such type changes to work, i.e., for subject reduction, an explicit subsumption rule (holding both for behaviours and for the other types) is necessary.

In an related area, but with a completely different purpose, is the work of [13, 14]. The goal is the construction of a model for an ambient calculus starting from the definition of a suitable type system, in the well-established tradition of filter models. In particular, [13] defines a type system – whence a model – for a pure version of MA without communication primitives, while [14] does the same for the whole *public* calculus (i.e., the calculus without restriction). Actually, the latter considers an extended version of MA (with synchronous output $\langle M \rangle P$) where communication is formally higher-order, in the sense that messages consist of full processes instead of capabilities.

Models are theories in which for two programs or processes to be identified it does not suffice that their respective executions satisfy a same set of key invariants, like being immobile, or single-threaded, or always outputting integer values; but they really have to "behave the same", according some suitable definition of an externally observable behaviour.

Moreover, recalling that a sound model is fully abstract w.r.t. a behavioural equivalence if does not discriminate *more*, it must be noticed that for the models built in [13, 14] full abstraction, though not holding for ordinary MA, is recovered by the addition of a self-open primitive, akin to the acid considered by Cardelli.

In filter models, which are based on an elegant application of the Stone duality, two terms are identified if and only if they may be assigned the same types; therefore a type system built for this purpose must be much more fine-grained than even the one above-mentioned of [1]: the type of a term really has to capture, with a limited abstraction, the information on all its possible interactions, i.e., all its possible reductions in all possible contexts.

Process types for full (asynchronous higher-order) MA are (omitting the self-open):

$$T, T' := \quad \omega \mid \text{in } m.T \mid \text{out } m.T \mid \text{open } m.T$$
$$\mid \text{i}(T^-).T \mid \text{o}(T^-).T \mid m[T] \mid T \mid T' \mid T \wedge T'$$

where T^- are *simple* types, i.e., not containing the $\wedge$ operator. As is apparent, types are almost copies of terms, with only input variables and output values abstracted away, and are analogous to those of [1]; however, w.r.t. them they have different, dual meanings. The type in $m.T$ is not, like in [1] and in the usual behavioural type systems, the type of all processes that first surely perform the action in m and then behave as specified by T; instead, it is the type of all processes that *may* perform the action in m and then behave as specified by T, in one of their possible executions; similarly, $T \mid T'$ is the type of processes that *may* behave like the parallel composition of processes of types T and T', and so on.

In other words, while in traditional programming-oriented type systems a process (or more generally a nondeterministic program) has a given type if *all* its executions satisfy the invariant described by the type, in model-oriented type systems a process may be assigned a given type if *there exists* at least one execution satisfying the invariant. In the first case the process *must* behave as specified by T (*must*-nondeterminism, universal quantification on reduction paths), in the second it may (*may*-nondeterminism, existential quantification).

Crucial, in this regard, is the role played by the conjunction: the type $T \wedge T'$ is the type of every term for which there exists a reduction path satisfying T *and* there exists a (generally different) path satisfying T'. Thus each term has many different types, corresponding to all its possible reductions.

Finally, the most striking feature, from a programmer's point of view, is that this kind of systems does not have the subject reduction property, but just the opposite: the subject expansion. Execution, by choosing an actual path among the many possible, decreases the set of branching possibilities, and therefore the set of types it can be assigned; hence, their intersection, which is the minimal type, becomes larger. The null process 0 has only the type ω, which is the greatest type, representing the trivially true property holding for every process.

8   Conclusion

The tutorial started from Cardelli and Gordon's calculus and from its first type system, purely dealing with communication and constituting the minimal typing without which, in a sense, the calculus itself does not have a full meaning (presence of "error terms").

Then it tried to show how this original core has been extended in different directions either by introducing richer types without modifying the calculus, or by extending or modifying the calculus so as to make it possible to define more expressive types. To sum up, the most meaningful points are: the major role played by the expression of properties concerning ambient movements (not surprisingly, given the very name and scope of the original MA); the introduction of the group technique for avoiding dependent types; types for enhanced communication flexibility, where the interplay between communication and mobility, inherent in the ambient paradigm, is in some cases so tight that the extension actually concerns both, as in BA; types for security.

New type disciplines for expressing and checking other classes of invariants are continuously emerging (for example those accounting for resource allocation and consumption, in a not unlimited world [18]) thus opening new directions of research, though staying away from the witty definition that "a type is whatever is put at the right-hand-side of the colon" (U. de' Liguoro).

It is also fair to say that ambient calculi have been strongly criticized as a possible foundation for global and mobile computing, since the atomicity of mobility actions, of course essential in their definitions, seems to be very difficult to implement in a distributed setting (which is the relevant case), as remarked in [26]. If, for example, an ambient m wants to perform an in n action, then, as explained in [26,17], first it must be checked whether there is a sibling ambient named n, then the actual transfer of m must be performed; which requires that either the involved ambients be locked (in case of synchronous implementations) so as to avoid that in the meanwhile for example the ambient n moves somewhere else, or a complex message mechanism must be set up (in asynchronous implementations, like [17]).

On the other hand, the implementation of Safe Ambients reported in [25] separates the logical structure of an ambient system from its physical distribution, so that "ambients cease to be meaningful abstractions for the control of the physical distribution of computations" [26].

Nevertheless, it is fitting to conclude this tutorial by mentioning one of the latest offsprings of Mobile Ambients, again counting Cardelli among its authors: the *Bio-Ambients* [24], intended to model some important aspects of biomolecular systems, which are clearly immune from the above criticism. In this way, with the help of life sciences, Mobile Ambients are maybe going to find a new unhindered life[6].

Acknowledgement

This tutorial originates from the study developed in the Mikado EU project on domain-oriented models for global computing, and is based on material, revised and expanded, I prepared for some of the first-year deliverables. I thank all the members of Mikado involved in the preparation of deliverables for the many helpful discussions both at the meetings and via e-mail.

I thank Michele Bugliesi for kindly answering all my questions about Secure Safe Ambients and providing many clarifications.

Special thanks to Mariangiola Dezani and Mario Coppo for first suggesting me to write this tutorial, then discussing its content, carefully reading the drafts, suggesting improvements, pointing out necessary corrections, and helping in many ways.

References

1. T. Amtoft and A. J. Kfoury and S. M. Pericas-Geertsen. What are Polymorphically Typed Ambients? In *ESOP 2001*, volume 2028 of LNCS, pages 206–220. Springer-Verlag, 2001.

---

[6] It is interesting to observe that the new calculus adopts a kind of action-coaction mechanism similar to the one of Safe Ambients, and adopts a parent-children communication similar to what proposed in (some versions of) Boxed Ambients, supplemented with (local and) inter-siblings communication; it replaces the open with a merge primitive, equally powerful but more appropriate for modelling bio-molecular systems (it merges two ambients into one). Finally, communication takes place through channels, like in π-calculus and Dπ.

2. F. Barbanera, M. Dezani-Ciancaglini, I. Salvo, and V. Sassone. A type inference algorithm for secure ambients. In *TOSCA'01*, volume 62 of ENTCS. Elsevier, 2002.

3. M. Bugliesi, G. Castagna. Secure Safe Ambients. In *POPL '01*, pages 222–235. ACM Press, 2001.

4. M. Bugliesi, G. Castagna. Behavioural Typing for Safe Ambients. *Computer Languages*, 28(1), pages 61–99. Elsevier, 2002.

5. M. Bugliesi, G. Castagna, and S. Crafa. Boxed ambients. In *TACS 2001*, volume 2215 of LNCS, pages 38–63. Springer-Verlag, 2001.

6. L. Cardelli. Abstractions for mobile computations. In *Secure Internet Programming: Security Issues for Mobile and Distributed Objects*, volume 1603 of LNCS, pages 51–94. Springer-Verlag, 1999.

7. L. Cardelli and G. Ghelli and A. D. Gordon. Types for the Ambient Calculus. *Information and Computation*, 177, pages 160–194. Elsevier, 2002.

8. L. Cardelli and A. D. Gordon. Mobile ambients. In *FOSSACS'98*, volume 1378 of LNCS, pages 140–155. Springer-Verlag, 1998.
   Expanded version in *Theoretical Computer Science*, Special Issue on Coordination, 240(1), June 2000, pages 177–213.

9. L. Cardelli and A. D. Gordon. Types for mobile ambients. In *POPL'99*, pages 79–92. ACM Press, 1999.

10. L. Cardelli and A. D. Gordon. Anytime, anywhere. Modal logics for mobile ambients. In *POPL'00*, pages 365–377. ACM Press, 2000.

11. G. Castagna, G. Ghelli, and F. Zappa Nardelli. Typing Mobility in the Seal Calculus. In *CONCUR 2001*, volume 2154 of LNCS, pages 82–101. Springer-Verlag, 2001.

12. I. Castellani. Process algebras with localities. In *Handbook of Process Algebra*, pages 945–1045. North-Holland, 2001.

13. M. Coppo and M. Dezani-Ciancaglini. A fully abstract model for mobile ambients. In *TOSCA'01*, volume 62 of ENTCS. Elsevier, 2001.

14. M. Coppo and M. Dezani-Ciancaglini. A fully abstract model for higher-order mobile ambients. In *VMCAI'02*, volume 2294 of LNCS, pages 255–271. Springer-Verlag, 2002.

15. M. Coppo, M. Dezani-Ciancaglini, E. Giovannetti, and I. Salvo. M^3: Mobility types for mobile processes in mobile ambients. In *CATS 2003*, volume 78 of ENTCS. Elsevier, 2003.

16. M. Dezani-Ciancaglini and I. Salvo. Security types for safe mobile ambients. In *ASIAN'00*, volume 1961 of LNCS, pages 215–236. Springer-Verlag, 2000.

17. C. Fournet, J.-J. Lévy and A. Schmitt. An Asynchronous, Distributed Implementation of Mobile Ambients. In *IFIP TCS 2000*, volume 1872 of LNCS, pages 348–364. Springer-Verlag, 2000.

18. J. C. Godskesen, T. Hildebrandt, V. Sassone. A Calculus of Mobile Resources. In *CONCUR 2002*, volume 2421 of LNCS, pages 272-287. Springer-Verlag, 2002.

19. M. Hennessy and J. Riely. Resource access control in systems of mobile agents (extended abstract). In *HLCL'98*, volume 16(3) of ENTCS, pages 1–15. Elsevier, 1998.

20. F. Levi and D. Sangiorgi. Controlling interference in ambients. In *POPL 2000*, pages 352–364. ACM Press, 2000.

21. M. Merro and V. Sassone. Typing and subtyping mobility in boxed ambients. In *CONCUR'02*, volume 2421 of LNCS, pages 304–320. Springer-Verlag, 2002.

22. R. Milner. The polyadic π-calculus: A tutorial. In *Logic and Algebra of Specification*, volume 94 of *NATO ASI Series F: Computer and Systems Sciences*, pages 203–246. Springer-Verlag, 1993.

23. R. Milner, J. Parrow, and D. Walker. A calculus of mobile processes, parts 1-2. *Information and Computation*, 100(1), pages 1–77, 1992.

24. A. Regev, E. M. Panina, W. Silverman, L. Cardelli, E. Shapiro. BioAmbients: An Abstraction for Biological Compartments. *Theoretical Computer Science*, to appear. Elsevier, 2003.

25. D. Sangiorgi and A. Valente. A distributed abstract machine for Safe Ambients. In *ICALP'01*, volume 2076 of LNCS, pages 408-420. Springer-Verlag, 2001.

26. J.-B. Stefani. A Calculus of Kells. In *2nd Workshop on Foundations of Global Computing*. To appear, 2003.

27. N. Yoshida and M. Hennessy. Assigning Types to Processes. *Information and Computation*, 173, pages 82-120. Elsevier, 2002.

28. J. Wells. The essence of principal typings. *ICALP'02*, volume 2380 of LNCS, pages 913–925. Springer-Verlag, 2002.

29. P. Zimmer. Subtyping and Typing Algorithms for Mobile Ambients. In *FOS-SACS'00*, volume 1784 of LNCS, pages 375-390. Springer-Verlag, 2000.

Facets of Security

Dieter Gollmann

Microsoft Research
Roger Needham Building
J J Thomson Avenue
Cambridge CB3 0FB, United Kingdom
diego@microsoft.com

Abstract. The force that drives fundamental changes in security is change in the use of information technology. To show how the environment impinges on security requirements and the selection of security mechanisms we compare familiar closed systems and emerging open systems. We illustrate how specific features of a given communications network influence security design and security analysis, and examine whether the new challenges we are facing in security should be described as issues of trust. Recommendations on directions in security research conclude the paper, with the development of suitable conceptual frameworks as a main objective.

1 Introduction

Too often, work on security is driven by existing security mechanisms ("security technology") or by standard assumptions about the security goals that ought to be achieved. Such approaches treat security as an issue that can be studied and realized in isolation from other aspects of the particular system one is dealing with. However, security requirements primarily depend on the application and only in the second instance on the technology currently deployed. The statement from [27]:

> It is a frequently overlooked fact that security policies are established "independent of the use of computers" [23].

may not be strictly true in all cases, but in the context of global computing we should start by looking at the applications envisaged for the new computing environment to understand the nature of the security requirements we have to address.

When examining the reasons for insufficient security in current systems, the complexity of systems and a lack of attention to security are often listed among the prime causes. Rigorous design methodologies and in particular the use of formal methods are suggested as remedies. Indeed, the use of formal methods has a long history in computer security as illustrated by work on the Multics operating system in the 1970s [3], and by 1980 sufficient progress had been made to convince some that security was a solved problem.

C. Priami (Ed.): GC 2003, LNCS 2874, pp. 192–202, 2003.
© Springer-Verlag Berlin Heidelberg 2003

However, their hopes were disappointed and formal methods are at best only part of the solution. Before we can contemplate a formal analysis of a system we have to understand and properly formalize the desired security goals, and we need a faithful model of the system under analysis. Again, this observation is by no means novel but deserves to be re-iterated. We quote from [26]:

> However, the formal analysis process is largely one of working within the rules of a formal system that achieves its results by manipulating uninterpreted symbols. Extensive review of the meanings and implications of the tautologies produced by this process is needed before a supportable conclusion can be drawn on the relevance and applicability of such results. Equally important, the scope of the formal findings as well as the assumptions on which they are based need to be understood.

At worst, formal methods are misleading. Methods geared to standard security goals or making standard assumptions about communications networks may point to "attacks" that are meaningless in the given setting or may create a false sense of security when they fail to check novel security goals. Already at a technical level changes in protocol goals may be missed. For example, the formal analysis of the IKE protocol in [20] did check agreement on keys but not on the full security association (including the choice of cryptographic algorithm) and missed an attack later described in [28] whereby an intruder interferes in a protocol run and alters the choice of security association.

Our aim is to identify and illustrate general issues that should be considered when defining research directions for security in global computing. Section 2 contrasts some of the essential features of the "closed" environments traditional computer security concepts have emerged from and rely on with the realities of the "open" environments that are often the focus of security research today. Section 3 employs authentication as an example to show how manifold and changeable the meaning of fundamental security concepts can be. Section 4 takes a problem from Mobile IPv6 security to show how specific network aspects can influence the design of security protocols. Section 5 examines whether we need trust to solve security problems in emerging applications. Section 6 concludes with recommendations on research directions.

2   The Environment

Technical security measures tend to rely on features of the environment they are deployed in to be effective. When the environment changes familiar mechanisms may become ineffective. We will illustrate this observation by contrasting the mechanisms and the assumptions underpinning security in closed and open environments.

2.1   Closed Environments

Security research originated in closed organisations like research laboratories or university departments. In such organisations, users have identities (company

ID, student ID), can be physically located, and are subject to the authority of other entities in the organisation (managers, heads of department). Assumptions specific to closed environments underpin many familiar approaches to security. In traditional computer security,

- security policies refer to user identities; access control consists of authentication (checking who you are) and authorisation (checking whether you have the necessary access rights) [18].
- access control defends against attacks by outsiders; principals are "honest" as stated by Needham [22]: If they [principals] were people they were honest people; if they were programs they were correct programs.
- auditing is used to detect attacks by insiders: "If you break the rules we can get hold of you".

The anthropomorphic metaphor that principals are "honest" should not be misinterpreted as a general expectation that people within the organisation are honest. This metaphor is simply being used to state that certain security mechanisms do not address threats from insiders. It is also the case that some verification methods, e.g. the BAN logic of authentication [6], explicitly make this very assumption. Obviously, any conclusion drawn from an analysis by such a method is only valid in environments that match the assumptions made.

2.2   Open Environments

For the purpose of this paper, open environments are characterized by the absence of strict lines of authority. In the extreme case, parties may join and leave the system on their own terms. Some ad-hoc networks fit this description [19]. As another example, consider parties joining together in a virtual organisation where there is some agreement between partners but no entity has real authority over the others.

Our emphasis is on organisational structures. In this respect, our concerns are different from those in open systems security as commonly understood in network security, where we often have closed environments connected by open networks. For security, the move to open environments has a number of implications.

- User identities may be of little value. Names are useful locally [8] but in an open environment we may deal with users we have not known previously, whose name (identity) does not appear in any security policy, and who may be outside the reach of any authority we are able to invoke.
- Security policies use attributes other than identity. Java security [13] and .NET security [17] have been moving to code-based (evidence based) access control for some time.
- There need not be a central authority for setting policies, e.g. in ad-hoc networks or in peer-to-peer networks.
- There need not be a central point for making access control decisions.
- There is no boundary between inside and outside so the enemy is within by default. Principals need not be honest.

If security policies no longer refer to user identities and if authentication checks who you are, we have access control without authentication. Incidentally, if authorisation checks that your identity appears in an access control list and if security policies are completely encoded in certificates, we have access control without authorisation.

As we see, even the language we use to discuss security is geared to closed environments and starts to fail us when we move to new settings. The general challenge today is to expose closed system assumptions that are inappropriate in open environments, both in the security mechanisms we are familiar with and in the (formal) analysis methods at our disposal.

3 Properties – A Case Study

To illustrate how established security concepts can get in the way of understanding the issues at hand or may have to be re-adjusted when the environment changes we take a look at authentication.

3.1 Entity Authentication

The brief explanation of authentication given in section 2.1 captures one traditional usage, i.e. verifying a claimed identity. In communications systems, a claimed identity is often verified for the purpose of setting up a secure session, so authenticating verifies "whom you are talking to". The term *peer entity authentication* captures this meaning.

> Peer entity authentication: The corroboration that a peer entity in an association is the one claimed. This service is provided for use at the establishment of, or at times during, the data transfer phase of a connection to confirm the identities of one or more of the entities connected to one or more of the other entities [9].

When cryptographic keys are established to create a secure session, today's convention refers to *key establishment* rather than to authentication. On the other hand, *entity authentication* is now used in a way that does not refer to sessions at all.

> Entity authentication mechanisms allow the verification, of an entity's claimed identity, by another entity. The authenticity of the entity can be ascertained only for the instance of the authentication exchange [15].

The current cryptologic terminology can be found in [21]. More comments on the development of the terminology for authentication are given in [12]. Approaches for formally capturing authentication have been examined in [10,11].

3.2   Data Origin Authentication

For individual messages, *data integrity* and *data origin authentication* are relevant security goals. The following definitions are given in [9].

> Data integrity: The property that data has not been altered or destroyed in an unauthorized manner.

> Data origin authentication: The corroboration that the source of data received is as claimed.

In a communications system, can we have one without the other? If the sender's identity (address) is an integral part of a message, a spoofed message should not be accepted as genuine. To check the integrity of a message we would also have to verify its origin. Secondly, if messages pass through a completely insecure network, we can only rely on evidence provided by the sender to verify that a message has not been altered in transit. For both reasons data integrity is subsumed by data origin authentication. Conversely, for data origin authentication we have to verify that a message is unchanged. Hence, data integrity and data origin authentication can be viewed as equivalent, a view taken for example in [21, page 359].

However, in an open environment where the identities of other parties are unknown the sender's identity may not be an integral part of a message. Furthermore, if we do not assume that the network is completely insecure, we might conclude that a message is received exactly as it was sent if a sufficient number of *independent witnesses* can vouch for this fact. Of course, in turn we may have to rely on other witnesses that confirm the witness statements. In this setting we can have data integrity without data origin authentication.

Once we know more about the structure of a network, we not only can ask about the identity of a party we are communicating with but also about its location in the network. Authentication could thus refer to identity or to location. Note that the two parts of an IPv6 address are a unique identity and topological network information.

4   Communication Models – Case Study

When modelling communications in an insecure network we often assume that the enemy is in complete control of the network and can alter, suppress, replay and insert messages. This worst-case scenario does not consider the internal structure of the network. However, in a concrete application we may have a network where more restrictive assumptions about an attacker's ability to compromise traffic can sensibly be made. Security mechanisms may be able to exploit the internal structure of the network and verification methodologies have to be able to capture this structure.

In open environments it may actually be more relevant to model scenarios where nodes are corrupt but communications cannot be interfered with than to

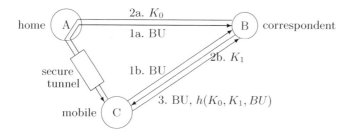

Fig. 1. Binding updates in Mobile IPv6.

model the familiar closed world where honest principals (nodes) communicate over an insecure medium.

As a case study, we sketch security issues related to location management in Mobile IPv6. Each *mobile node* has an address in its *home network*. Messages sent to this home address are routed to the mobile node via a secure tunnel. For more efficient communications, a mobile node can inform a *correspondent node* about its current location by performing a *binding update*. We have thus three channels, with different security characteristics (Fig. 1).

– Mobile ↔ home: the mobile node and its home network have a prearranged security association, which they can use to create a secure IP tunnel to transfer messages.
– Correspondent ↔ home: uses the wired Internet.
– Mobile ↔ correspondent: unprotected radio channel.

The overall security requirement is that mobile IP should not weaken IP. The attackers considered include mobile nodes lying about their identity or their location. An attacker can use its own location as the victim's current address in a fraudulent binding update to hijack a connection or give the victim's address as its own location to mount a denial-of-service attack. Attackers also include eavesdroppers listening to traffic on the radio links used by the mobile node, but not someone who is in a position to intercept both channels used by the correspondent.

In the protocol given in [2], where also a detailed explanation of its design rationale can be found, the mobile node first sends a binding update (BU) request to the correspondent, directly over the radio channel and via the home agent (messages 1a and 1b). The correspondent replies to both BU requests independently, sending a key K_0 to the mobile node via the home address of the mobile node and a second key K_1 directly to the claimed current location (messages 2a and 2b). The mobile node needs both keys to authenticate the binding update (message 3) using a message authentication code (keyed hash function h). In the threat model chosen, it is admissible to send keys in the clear on the channels from the correspondent.

5   Trust

As programs like the Global Computing Initiative are exploring novel ways of using information and communications technology, it comes as no surprise when established security paradigms are found to be wanting. New problems require new solutions and it has become fashionable to treat new security problems as issues of *trust*. If the term *security* is associated with the old technologies then indeed something new is needed but we have argued above that a narrow focus on technology is mistaken, although quite common.

If we use security in its general meaning, we can investigate areas where new approaches are needed, and ponder whether trust is a good description for the problems we identify. We will now discuss a number of emerging security issues that have been associated with trust.

5.1   Trust as Access Right

In access control, we have already observed the shift from identity-based access control to code-based access control. Code-based access control has sometimes been described as "code trust". Code running with high privileges is often called "trusted", code running with low privileges "untrusted", and code in between "semi-trusted" or "partially trusted". In this usage trust characterizes the access rights (permissions) given to a piece of code, not the reasons why they were given. To add to the confusion, in other places "trusted" is used to indicate that code originates from a "trusted party".

As part of the shift from closed to open environments we may want to deploy access control schemes where several parties contribute to an access decision, in contrast to the familiar centralized enforcement of security policies. Such distributed and more flexible schemes have become known as *trust management systems* [5,4]. These systems do not manage "trust" in an intuitive anthropomorphic meaning but the specific access rights and policies of a given application. As an aside, note that Digital Rights Management systems do not manage "rights" as the term is understood in legal theory but permissions [25]. For example, in the legal terminology fair use is a right but the "right" to copy a file is a permission.

5.2   Trust as Contract

A party engaged in a collaborative project may need to give its partners access to some of its resources. In terms of access control, a security policy stating who is entitled to access which resource has to be defined and enforced. Sometimes, these policies are described as capturing trust relationships between partners. In most commercial collaborations the security policy will capture a well defined contractual relationship, in which case trust is a contract.

When parties interact that are not regulated by a common policy, they will apply their own local policies while negotiating which permissions to give to the other party. The interests of the two parties need not coincide and the term *multilateral security* has been coined to describe situations where independent security policies should be applied simultaneously, see e.g. [24]. The process of negotiating permissions acceptable to both parties has been described in the literature as *trust negotiation*. In this case, "trust" are permissions that are required or granted, possibly conditional on receiving other permissions in return.

5.3 Trust and Risk

Lack of trust is also the frequent explanation why customers are slow to take up e-commerce and other e-services, and one finds definitions like:

> Trust is the user's willingness to risk time, money, and personal data on a website.

It may be possible to increase trust by limiting the risks users are taking in on-line transactions. So-called trust enabling technologies like digital signatures and Public Key Infrastructures may actually have the opposite effect if they are used in a way where users incur unlimited liabilities.

It is furthermore an interesting psychological question to identify the factors that increase trust. It is, however, doubtful whether the security technologies mentioned above will be a major contributor for members of the general public.

5.4 Trust as a Placeholder

We have already collected too many different notions to use trust as an overarching security principle, and there are many more around. Within one technical community, trust may have a specific precise definition so there will be no ambiguity in internal discussions. There is, however, no clear causal relationship between the different aspects of trust. On occasion some notions are related, in other circumstances there may be no such link. In the end, trust is mostly used as a placeholder to indicate a security issue we have yet to fully understand.

6 Conclusions and Recommendations

In any area of research, progress is closely tied to the development of a language in which the concerns at hand can be clearly expressed. The current language of information security was conceived in the 1980s and earlier, and is strongly influenced by the applications and computer systems of that time. Familiar terminology thus does not capture "security" per se but security from one particular historic angle.

Security is a moving target. Hence, a new domain like global computing has to examine whether canonical security requirements are actually relevant and whether current concepts serve the purpose of clearly expressing the new security challenges we encounter. Quite likely our language will have to develop to encompass new facets of security. At the same time, fashionable but ill-defined new terms do not help our cause.

"Trust" is today the prime example for such a term. Trust is overloaded with various technical meanings, which individually may be precise enough but collectively are too diverse to contribute to a clear understanding of security. Moreover, trust has emotional connotations relating to human relationships, which can get in the way of understanding how a technical system works, or create expectations that by technical means we can make people feel in certain ways about new technologies. We can take the emergence of trust in current security discussions as an indicator that new approaches are necessary. Within technical communities, we can use precisely defined concepts we call trust, but have to take care to distinguish our usage from other technical definitions and from colloquial meanings of the word.

In access control a shift away from identity-based systems geared towards monolithic organisations is under way. Provisions for code-based access control are already part of commercial products. Various proposals for versatile languages for expressing security policies exist, see e.g. [7]. Certificate-based trust management schemes demonstrate how distributed access control schemes can be implemented. In these areas, a major impulse for research has to come from practical experiences in using these ideas that can provide the points of reference for further theoretical work.

In communications security, there is less a need for new general primitives but for security solutions tailored to concrete networks. Established views on the design of security protocols may become a liability in this process. For example, a well-known *prudent engineering practice* in protocol design calls for the names of principals to be included in all messages to prevent protocol messages from being used out of context [1]. However, including the name of the correspondent in a signed message conflicts with *plausible deniability*[1], a privacy requirement now considered for the IKEv2 key management protocol [16].

Security requirements can conflict as in the case just mentioned. Priorities will depend on the actual application. For this very reason, security protocols that defend against a very powerful attacker are not necessarily "more secure" than those that defend against a limited threat. A seemingly stronger solution may have side-effects that tip the balance against it in comparison to a less ambitious protocol.

In security analysis we have to beware of the dangers of abstraction. Analysis with respect to traditional security properties and general models can easily miss its target and have little impact on the security of the new systems we are designing. To repeat the remarks from the start of this paper, security is not an add-on that can be dealt with in separation from the system under design. Experience has shown that defining security properties is difficult and error prone. Security terminology is constantly evolving and adapting to new scenarios. It is a major challenge to find suitable concepts for discussing security in the setting of global computing.

---

[1] Two parties can communicate without anyone being able to prove that they did have a conversation, even with the collusion of one of the parties [14].

References

1. Martín Abadi and Roger Needham. Prudent engineering pratice for cryptographic protocols. In *Proceedings of the 1994 IEEE Symposium on Research in Security and Privacy*, pages 122–136, 1994.
2. Tuomas Aura, Michael Roe, and Jari Arkko. Security of Internet location management. In *Proceedings of the 18th Annual Computer Security Applications Conference*, pages 78–87, December 2002.
3. David Bell and Leonard LaPadula. Secure computer system: Unified exposition and Multics interpretation. Technical Report ESD-TR-75-306, The MITRE Corporation, Bedford, MA, 1975.
4. Matt Blaze, Joan Feigenbaum, John Ioannidis, and Angelos D. Keromytis. The KeyNote Trust-Management System Version 2, September 1999. RFC 2704.
5. Matt Blaze, Joan Feigenbaum, and Jack Lacy. Decentralized trust management. In *Proceedings of the 1996 IEEE Symposium on Security and Privacy*, pages 164–173, 1996.
6. Michael Burrows, Martín Abadi, and Roger Needham. A logic of authentication. *DEC Systems Research Center*, Report 39, revised February 22 1990.
7. John DeTreville. Binder, a logic-based security language. In *Proceedings of the 2002 IEEE Symposium on Security and Privacy*, pages 105–113, 2002.
8. Carl M. Ellison, Bill Frantz, Butler Lampson, Ron Rivest, Brian M. Thomas, and Tatu Ylonen. *SPKI Certificate Theory*, September 1999. RFC 2693.
9. International Organisation for Standardization. *Basic Reference Model for Open Systems Interconnection (OSI) Part 2: Security Architecture*. Genève, Switzerland, 1989.
10. Dieter Gollmann. What do we mean by entity authentication? In *Proceedings of the 1996 IEEE Symposium on Security and Privacy*, pages 46–54, 1996.
11. Dieter Gollmann. Authentication by correspondence. *IEEE Journal on Selected Areas in Communications*, 21(1):88–95, January 2003.
12. Dieter Gollmann. Analysing security protocols. In A. Abdallah, editor, *Formal Aspects of Security, LNCS 2629*. Springer Verlag, to appear.
13. Li Gong. *Inside Java 2 Platform Security*. Addison-Wesley, Reading, MA, 1999.
14. Dan Harkins, Charlie Kaufman, Tero Kivinen, Stephen Kent, and Radia Perlman. *Design Rationale for IKEv2*, February 2002. Internet Draft, draft-ietf-ipsec-ikev2-rationale-00.txt.
15. International Organization for Standardization. *Information technology – Security techniques – Entity authentication mechanisms; Part 1: General model*. Genève, Switzerland, September 1991. ISO/IEC 9798-1, Second Edition.
16. Charlie Kaufman. *Internet Key Exchange (IKEv2) Protocol*, January 2003. Internet Draft, draft-ietf-ipsec-ikev2-04.txt.
17. Brian LaMacchia, Sebastian Lange, Matthew Lyons, Rudi Martin, and Kevin Price. *.NET Framework Security*. Addison Wesley Professional, 2002.
18. Butler Lampson, Martín Abadi, Michael Burrows, and Edward Wobber. Authentication in distributed systems: Theory and practice. *ACM Transactions on Computer Systems*, 10(4):265–310, November 1992.
19. Silja Mäki and Tuomas Aura. Towards a survivable security architecture for ad-hoc networks. In B. Christiansen et al., editor, *Security Protocols, 9th International Workshop, Cambridge, LNCS 2467*, pages 63–73. Springer Verlag, 2002.
20. Catherine A. Meadows. Analysis of the Internet Key Exchange protocol using the NRL Protocol Analyzer. In *Proceedings of the 1999 IEEE Symposium on Security and Privacy*, pages 216–231, 1999.

21. Alfred J. Menezes, Paul C. van Oorschot, and Scott A. Vanstone. *Handbook of Applied Cryptography*. CRC Press, Boca Raton, FA, 1997.
22. Roger Needham. Keynote address: The changing environment (transcript of discussion). In B. Christiansen et al., editor, *Security Protocols, 7th International Workshop, Cambridge, LNCS 1796*, pages 1–5. Springer Verlag, 2000.
23. US Department of Defense. *DoD Trusted Computer System Evaluation Criteria*, 1985. DOD 5200.28-STD.
24. Kai Rannenberg. How much details and negotiations can users handle? In F. Cuppens et al., editor, *ESORICS 2000, LNCS 1895*, pages 37–54. Springer Verlag, 2000.
25. Pamela Samuelson. DRM {and, or, vs.} the Law. *Communications of the ACM*, 46(4):41–45, April 2003.
26. Marvin Schaefer. Symbol security condition considered harmful. In *Proceedings of the 1989 IEEE Symposium on Security and Privacy*, pages 20–46, 1989.
27. Daniel F. Sterne. On the buzzword "Security Policy". In *Proceedings of the 1991 IEEE Symposium on Research in Security and Privacy*, pages 219–230, 1991.
28. Jianying Zhou. Fixing a security flaw in IKE protocols. *Electronics Letters*, 35(13):1072–1073, June 1999.

A Study about Trade-Off between Performance and Security in an Internet Audio Mechanism

Alessandro Aldini[1] and Roberto Gorrieri[2]

[1] Istituto di Scienze e Tecnologie dell'Informazione
Università di Urbino, Italy
aldini@sti.uniurb.it
[2] Dipartimento di Scienze dell'Informazione
Università di Bologna, Italy
gorrieri@cs.unibo.it

Abstract. We study the nature of the relationship between performance measures and privacy guarantees in the case study of an adaptive protocol for the secure transmission of real-time audio over the Internet. The analysis is conducted on a process-algebraic description of the audio mechanism by following a methodology that allows the modeler to (*i*) employ the noninterference approach to information flow theory for the analysis of security requirements, and (*ii*) derive performance measures obtained through markovian analysis techniques. The main result we present is that the analysis of performance properties helps to estimate the effectiveness (and to find a related countermove) of an attack that is captured by the security analysis.

1 Introduction

The analysis of Quality of Service (QoS) properties and of security conditions are two important problems that arise in the modeling phase of computer systems, especially when dealing with applications working over public, untrusted networks and with strict functional and performance requirements [SDS01]. In this paper, we focus on the potential relationship between these two aspects in the context of a protocol for audio communications over IP, developed in a software tool called BoAT [RGPSB01,AGR01,AMR03,AGR03]. We chose this case study because the success of voice over IP services strictly depends on their capability of coping with unforeseeable environment constraints, typical of public wide area networks, such as variable queueing delays, packet loss, and lack of security guarantees. In particular, BoAT aims at providing an audio quality that is comparable to that of the circuit-switched telephone system, and a security level comparable to that of a private channel, by following two main strategies. On the one hand, BoAT employs a mechanism that adaptively adjusts the playout of the received audio packets to the fluctuating network delays in order to offer at the receiving site the same audio quality as that produced at the sending site under any scenario. The core of such a mechanism is represented by a handshaking protocol, which is used to exchange estimations of the traffic conditions between

C. Priami (Ed.): GC 2003, LNCS 2874, pp. 203–228, 2003.

the involved parties. A simulative comparison between this novel mechanism and other existing adaptive algorithms revealed that BoAT succeeds in offering an adequate QoS [ABGR01]. On the other hand, BoAT employs a cryptographic protocol, which adopts a lightweight securing mechanism based on the use of a stream cipher (see, e.g., [Schn96]) and of a sequence of secret keys needed to secure the conversation. The brief lifetime of each secret key (which is exchanged in the same handshaking packets used by the adaptive playout algorithm and is used by the stream cipher to encrypt few hundreds of bytes only) is the main feature of BoAT that strengthens the robustness of the cryptographic algorithm against cryptanalysis attacks. Moreover, as experimental studies have emphasized [AGR01,AGR03], such an approach suffers a computational overhead that is quite negligible with respect to other securing tools proposed in the literature.

The formal analysis we conduct in this paper aims at studying the effectiveness of the securing mechanism of BoAT in the light of the considerations above. The results we obtain have a twofold interest. On the one hand, the security analysis reveals an attack by an adversary that tries to intercept all the handshaking packets containing the secret keys, thus blocking the re-keying mechanism. On the other hand, the performance analysis shows that the throughput of the playout control algorithm, expressed in terms of number of audio packets delivered (and played out) per sec, and the throughput of the privacy infrastructure, expressed in terms of number of secret keys exchanged per sec, are strictly coupled. In particular, by analyzing the relation between these two measures, we can estimate the privacy level of the system and possibly detect the attack described above. Moreover, it is worth noting that the results of the same formal analysis help not only to reveal the weaknesses of the audio protocol but also to single out and evaluate a strategy that makes it vain the attack of the adversary.

The study is conducted on a formal description of BoAT expressed in a probabilistic process algebra [BA03]. Timed, probabilistic, and stochastic extensions of process algebras (see, e.g., [HHHMR94,HS95,BDG98]) have been introduced that formally describe both functional and performance aspects on the same system model, in order to bridge the gap between formal verification and quantitative validation. In this setting, the novelty of our approach is that both performance related properties and information flow security properties can be evaluated on the same system model. From a performance standpoint, we can derive a Discrete Time Markov Chain from the algebraic specification of BoAT and then we can evaluate steady-state based performance measures (expressible by attaching rewards to actions) through markovian analysis techniques [Ber99]. Such an analysis is automatically conducted with the software tool TwoTowers [BCSS98]. From a security viewpoint, the same system model is analyzed by employing a probabilistic extension [ABG02] of the noninterference approach [GM82,FG95] to the information flow theory.

The rest of the paper is organized as follows. In Sect. 2, we briefly recall BoAT and its main features. In Sect. 3, we describe the probabilistic process-algebraic framework based on which we conduct the analysis. Then, in Sect. 4 we present the algebraic specification of BoAT and we report on the results obtained by analyzing such a model. Finally, in Sect. 5 some conclusions terminate the paper.

2   A Secure Real-Time Audio Protocol: BoAT

In this section, we briefly describe BoAT, an adaptive protocol proposed for the trusted, private transmission of real-time audio over public networks like the Internet [RGPSB01,AGR01,AMR03,AGR03].

On the one hand, BoAT provides an adaptive control mechanism that supports quality guarantees of Internet voice software in spite of highly fluctuant transmission delay variation and packet loss. The goal of providing a synchronous playout of audio packets at the receiving site is typically achieved by buffering the received audio packets and by delaying their playout time in order to compensate for variable network delays. With respect to other adaptive audio algorithms (see, e.g., [Schu92,HSK98]), BoAT dynamically adapts the playout delays to the network traffic conditions assuming neither the existence of an external mechanism for maintaining an accurate clock synchronization between the sender and the receiver, nor a specific distribution of the end-to-end transmission delays experienced by the audio packets.

On the other hand, BoAT embodies a privacy infrastructure that provides authentication of the two involved parties, secrecy and integrity of the protocol data and of the audio conversation. This is obtained with a minimal per-packet communication overhead that does not jeopardize the performance guaranteed by the adaptive playout mechanism.

Succinctly, the core of the mechanism of BoAT is based on a three way handshake protocol periodically performed during the conversation between the sender and the receiver. Thanks to such a packet exchange, usually performed once a second, the two parties obtain (*i*) an estimation (called Δ) of the *upper bound* for the packet transmission delay experienced during the audio communication, and (*ii*) a new secret key used to secure the conversation.

A correct estimation of Δ represents the key factor for the success of the playout control mechanism. Indeed, Δ directly influences the talkspurt playout delay, which is dynamically set at the receiving site from one talkspurt to the next one on the basis of the result of the handshaking phase. A description of such a mechanism is as follows. The sender begins the synchronization policy by sending a *probe* packet timestamped with the time value t_s shown by its own clock. At the reception of this packet, the receiver sets its own clock to t_s and sends immediately back a *response* packet timestamped with the same value t_s. Upon receiving the response packet, the sender checks if it is related to the last *probe* message sent to the receiver and, in such a case, computes the value of the round trip time (RTT) by subtracting the value of the timestamp t_s from the current value of its local clock. At that moment, the difference between the sender clock and the receiver clock is equal to an unknown quantity (say t_0), which may range from a theoretical lower bound of 0 (i.e., all the RTT has been consumed on the way back from the receiver to the sender), and a theoretical upper bound of RTT (i.e., all the RTT has been consumed during the transmission of the *probe* packet). The final packet of the handshaking phase sent by the sender to the receiver is an *installation* packet, with attached the calculated RTT value and the timestamp t_s. Upon receiving this packet, the receiver sets the time of its local clock, by subtracting from the current value of its local clock the value of the transmitted RTT. At that moment, the difference between the sender clock and the receiver clock is equal to a value given by $\Delta = t_0 + RTT$, where Δ ranges in the interval $[RTT, 2 \times RTT]$, depending on the unknown value of t_0, that in turn may range in the interval $[0, RTT]$. Usually, the installation of a new clock value at the receiving site does not occur during a talkspurt since it may artificially alter the comprehension of the conversation. Therefore, the *install* message is not sent as soon as the *response* packet is received; instead, it is sent during a silence period. Finally, the last step of the handshaking protocol is given by the transmission of a timestamped *acknowledgement* packet from the receiver to the sender. At the end of the protocol, the difference between the sender clock and the receiver clock represents the estimate of an upper bound for the transmission delay that is used to dynamically adjust the playout delay and the buffer size. In particular, each audio packet is timestamped with the value of the sender clock at its generation instant, and such a value also represents the playout instant that must be scheduled by the receiver. Hence, a maximum transmission delay equal to the difference between the two clocks is left to each audio packet to arrive at the receiver in time for its playout. The reader interested in more details and proofs concerning this adaptive playout control mechanism should refer to [RGPSB01,ABGR01].

The other goal of the handshaking protocol is to provide privacy of the audio communication. This is done as follows. A preliminary authentication phase is carried out by the two parties before the conversation (e.g., by resorting to a digital signature scheme). During this step, the trusted parties agree on a secret key, which is used to encrypt the packet exchange of a first handshaking phase that precedes the audio communication. Then, during each handshaking phase i, the authenticated parties agree on a session key K_i (e.g., exchanged in the *install* packet). Whenever the three-way handshake has a positive outcome, K_i is the session key used by a stream cipher to secure the subsequent chunk of conversation. Since the handshaking protocol is periodically started during the conversation, a sequence of keys $\{K_i\}_{i \in \mathbb{N}}$ is generated, where each key has a lifetime equal to the time between two consecutive synchronizations. Details related to such a protocol and to the securing algorithm can be found in [AGR01,AGR03].

Summing up, the synchronization policy is periodically repeated throughout the whole conversation. In particular, in order for the proposed policy to adaptively adjust to the highly fluctuant network conditions, the above mentioned synchronization technique is first carried out prior to the beginning of the conversation, and then repeated about once a second thus preventing the two clocks (possibly equipped with different clock rates) from drifting apart. The proposed protocol guarantees that (*i*) both playout delay and buffer size are always proportioned to the traffic conditions, and (*ii*) the brief lifetime of each session key makes it harder any cryptanalysis attack conducted by an adversary (see, e.g., [BSW00], where it is shown that a few seconds of conversation are enough to complete a cryptanalysis attack against a stream cipher).

3   A Process-Algebraic Framework

3.1   The Probabilistic Calculus

Basic process algebras (and their extensions) are specification languages used to describe in a compositional way the behavior of concurrent systems in order to formally derive their functional (and non-functional) properties. The basic elements of any process algebra are the actions, which in our calculus are syntactically divided into output actions and input actions, and the algebraic operators, which in our calculus are equipped with probabilistic information. The model of probabilities we adopt is a mixture of the generative and reactive approaches of [GSS95]. In particular, we assume the output actions behaving as *generative* actions (a generative process autonomously decides, on the basis of a probability distribution, which action will be executed and how to behave after such an event) and the input actions behaving as *reactive* actions (a reactive process internally reacts to the choice of the action type, say a, performed by the environment, on the basis of a probability distribution associated with the reactive actions of type a it can perform).

Formally, $AType$ is the set of visible action types, ranged over by $a, b, \ldots$. For each visible action type a, we distinguish the (generative) output action a and the (reactive) input action a_*. The set of actions is denoted by Act, ranged over by $\pi, \pi', \ldots$, including the input and the output actions with type in $AType$, and the special action τ, representing the internal, unobservable action. We point out that τ behaves as a generative action, because it expresses an autonomous internal move, which does not react to external stimuli. The set $\mathcal{L}$ of process terms is generated by the syntax:

$$P ::= \underline{0} \mid \pi.P \mid P +^p P \mid P \|_S^p P \mid P \backslash L \mid P/_a^p \mid A$$

where $S, L \subseteq AType$, $a \in AType$, and $p \in]0, 1[$. The set $\mathcal{L}$ is ranged over by $P, Q, \ldots$. Constants A are used to specify recursive systems. In general, when defining an algebraic specification, we assume a set of constants defining equations of the form $A \overset{\triangle}{=} P$ to be given. In the following, we restrict ourselves to the set of finite state, closed, guarded terms of $\mathcal{L}$, which we call processes [Mil89].

As usual in security models, we distinguish among high-level visible actions and low-level visible actions by defining two disjoint sets $AType_H$ of high-level types and $AType_L$ of low-level types, which form a covering of $AType$, such that the output action a and the input action a_* are high- (low-) level actions if $a \in AType_H$ ($a \in AType_L$). Finally, we say that P is a high-level process if all actions syntactically occurring in the action prefix operators within P are high-level actions.

Now, we informally describe the semantics of the operators and the probabilistic model through some examples (for a formal presentation the reader should refer to [ABG02]).

Example 1. Let us consider the system

$$Writer \parallel^{p}_{\{produce\}} Buffer,$$

described as the interaction of two processes, *Writer* and *Buffer*. The communication interface $\{produce\}$ says that the two processes interact by synchronously executing actions of type *produce*. Each other local action is asynchronously executed by the two processes. Probability p is the parameter of a probabilistic scheduler that, in each system state, decides which of the two processes must be scheduled, i.e. *Writer* with probability p and *Buffer* with probability $1-p$. Now, let us detail each component in isolation. Process *Writer* repeatedly produces new items:

$$Writer \overset{\Delta}{=} produce.Writer +^{q} \tau.Writer.$$

The alternative choice operator "$\_ +^{q} \_$" says that process *Writer* can either produce a message (action *produce*) with probability q, or stay idle (action τ) with probability $1 - q$, and afterwards behaving as the same process *Writer*. The actions *produce* and τ are *generative*, hence the process itself autonomously decides, on the basis of a probability distribution guided by parameter q, which action will be executed and how to behave after such an event (see Fig. 1(a), showing the labeled transition system associated to process *Writer* in isolation). Process *Buffer*, instead, is ready to accept new incoming items or it stays idle:

$$Buffer \overset{\Delta}{=} (produce_{*}.discard.Buffer +^{r} produce_{*}.store.Buffer) +^{r'} \tau.Buffer.$$

The two actions $produce_{*}$ are *reactive*, hence the process reacts internally to the choice of the action type *produce*, performed by its environment, on the basis of a probability distribution associated with the reactive actions of type *produce* it can perform. Whenever the action type *produce* is chosen by the environment, process *Buffer* reacts by choosing either the first action $produce_{*}$ with probability r and then discarding the message (action *discard*), or the second action $produce_{*}$ with probability $1-r$ and then storing the message (action *store*). Alternatively, if process *Buffer* is not accepting items from the environment, the internal action τ is repeatedly executed to model the idle periods of the buffer. The choice between the input actions $produce_{*}$ and such an internal event is nondeterministic (parameter r' is not considered), because the execution of an action $produce_{*}$ is entirely guided by the external environment (see Fig. 1(b), showing the labeled transition system associated to process *Buffer* in isolation).

According to the considerations above, the two processes interact in the composed system as follows. If process *Writer* decides to perform the action *produce*, then process *Buffer* reacts by executing one of its $produce_{*}$ actions. In the initial state of our example (see Fig. 1(c)), the system executes a move of process *Writer* with probability p: it executes either the internal move τ with probability $p \cdot (1 - q)$, or the move *produce* with probability $p \cdot q$ (with probability

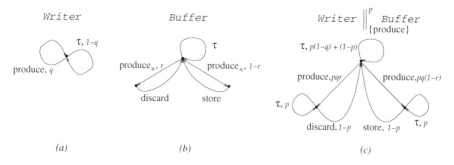

Fig. 1. Labeled transition systems associated to different process terms. Transitions are labeled with an action and a probability, which is equal to 1 if omitted.

$p \cdot q \cdot r$ it executes a *produce* action synchronized with the first reactive action of process *Buffer* and with probability $p \cdot q \cdot (1 - r)$ a *produce* action synchronized with the second reactive action of process *Buffer*). On the other hand, the system may schedule with probability $1 - p$ the process *Buffer* by executing its internal action τ (that gets the *entire* probability $1 - p$ associated to process *Buffer*). Afterwards, if, e.g., the winning action is the action *produce* leading to term $Writer \parallel_{\{produce\}}^{p} store.Buffer$, then the system executes either the action *store* with probability $1 - p$, thus reaching the initial state again, or the action τ of process *Writer* (which gets the *entire* probability p associated to process *Writer*, since it is the only generative action of the left-hand process enabled by the system).

Example 2. Let us consider the system

$$Job \parallel_{S}^{q} Scheduler,$$

where processes *Job* and *Scheduler* interact by synchronizing on actions in the set $S = \{schedule, end\}$. We now detail the several components and their interactions. Process *Job* repeatedly produces new jobs:

$$Job \stackrel{\Delta}{=} schedule.end_{*}.Job.$$

Whenever the synchronizing generative action *schedule* is executed, which models a new job passed to the scheduler component, process *Job* waits for the termination of the job, which is signalled via a synchronization through the reactive action end_{*}, and then behaves as the same process *Job*. Term *Scheduler* is in turn composed of two communicating processes:

$$Scheduler \stackrel{\Delta}{=} (Fetch \parallel_{\{pass\}}^{q'} Exec)/_{pass}^{p}$$

which model a pipeline whose components sequentially execute the received job:

$$Fetch \stackrel{\Delta}{=} schedule_{*}.\tau.pass.Fetch$$

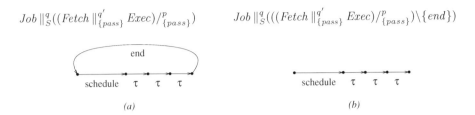

Fig. 2. Labeled transition systems associated to the models of Example 2.

fetches a new job (action $schedule_*$), does an internal computation, and then passes the control (action $pass$) to term

$$Exec \overset{\Delta}{=} pass_*.\tau.end.Exec,$$

which in turn does some internal computation and then communicates the result by synchronizing with process Job (action end). The hiding operator "$\_/^p_{pass}$" turns the action $pass$, resulting from the synchronization between processes $Fetch$ and $Exec$, into the action τ. This is because the activity modeled by the action $pass$ represents an internal computation of term $Scheduler$, which should not be observable by an external component like process Job.

In the initial state of our example, the synchronizing action $schedule$ (expressing the communication between processes Job and $Fetch$) is the only generative action executable by the system, therefore it gets the entire probability 1 to be performed. Moreover, note that process $Exec$ is blocked since the action $pass_*$ cannot synchronize. By following the same considerations, we then execute a sequence of τ actions representing the computations of term $Scheduler$, followed by the action end leading to the initial state again (see Fig. 2(a)). As a consequence, since probabilistic choices among concurrent processes are never to be performed, parameters q and q', which guide the probabilistic parallel execution of processes Job, $Fetch$, and $Exec$, never come into play. Moreover, parameter p is not meaningful (we will shortly explain its use). Now, let us assume that a malfunction prevents the scheduler from informing process Job that the current job has been completed. This behavior can be modeled with the restriction operator "$\_\backslash L$" by changing the system as follows:

$$Job \,\|^q_S (Scheduler \backslash \{end\}),$$

where term $Scheduler$ is prevented from executing actions of type end. Therefore, in term $end_*.Job \,\|^q_S (((Fetch \,\|^{q'}_{\{pass\}} end.Exec)/^p_{pass}) \backslash \{end\})$, which is reachable from the initial state by executing the sequence of actions $schedule\,\tau\,\tau\,\tau$, the synchronization on the action of type end is not enabled. Since the composed system does not enable other actions that can get the probability of the restricted action end, the system deadlocks with probability 1 (see Fig. 2(b)).

The two examples above put in evidence some features of our probabilistic calculus.

As far as the CSP-like communication policy is concerned, in any binary synchronization at most one generative action can be involved and, in such a case, the result is a generative action of the same type. Instead, in case two reactive actions of type a synchronize, then the result is again a reactive action of type a. We recall that the actions belonging to the communication interface are constrained to synchronize, while all the other actions are locally and independently executed by the processes that compose the system.

As far as the probabilistic model is concerned, the following comments are in order. Probabilistic choices among generative actions (among reactive actions of the same type) are fully probabilistic, while in each other case the choice is completely nondeterministic. This is essentially due to the fact that the reactive actions are underspecified since they are guided by the environment behavior. As a consequence, the parameters that probabilistically guide the choices come into play if and only if a probabilistic choice is really to be performed. Some further details are in order in case of the parallel operator $P \parallel_S^p Q$:

- since the execution of some generative actions of P can be prevented in $P \parallel_S^p Q \ (P \backslash L)$, the probabilities of executing the remaining generative actions of P are proportionally redistributed (similarly for Q), as shown both in Example 1 and in Example 2 (note that this is a standard approach when restricting actions in the generative model [GSS95]);
- in case of synchronizing generative actions a of P, their probability is distributed among the multiple actions a obtained by synchronizing with reactive actions a_* executable by Q, according to the probability the actions a_* are chosen in Q (symmetrically for Q), as shown in Example 1;
- in case both P and Q can execute some synchronizing actions $a_* \in S$, then $P \parallel_S^p Q$ can execute some actions a_*: the probability of each action a_* executable by $P \parallel_S^p Q$ is the product of the probabilities of the two actions a_* (one of P and one of Q) that are involved in the synchronization.

We point out that in each system state of a process term, the sum of the probabilities of the generative actions (reactive actions of a given type a), if there are any, is always equal to 1.

A final remark is in order for the hiding operator $P/_a^p$, which turns reactive and generative actions of type a into τ actions. Parameter p expresses the probability that actions τ obtained by hiding actions a_* of P are executed with respect to the generative actions previously enabled by P. Hence, p guarantees that the hiding operator does not introduce nondeterminism among generative actions. Instead, parameter p is not used when hiding generative actions (like in Example 2), since the choice among generative actions is already probabilistic. Here, we do not detail the semantics of such an operator when hiding reactive actions, since this particular case does not arise in our case study.

In the rest of the paper we use the following abbreviations. We assume parameter p to be equal to $\frac{1}{2}$ whenever it is omitted from any probabilistic operator. Moreover, when it is clear from the context, we use the abbreviation P/S, with $S = \{a_1, \ldots, a_n\} \subseteq AType$, to denote the expression $P/_{a_1 \ldots a_n} = P/_{a_1} \cdots /_{a_n}$.

3.2   Security Analysis

Unauthorized disclosure of information in multi-level security systems can be revealed by verifying whether the several components of the system fail to protect a confidential, high-level information by leaking it to a public, unclassified, low-level user. Nondeterministic approaches to the information flow theory analyze such a kind of interference by studying the effect of the confidential activities on the public view of the system behavior (see, e.g., [McL90,FG95]). Anyway, two main problems arise when considering an approach based on pure nondeterminism. On the one hand, such a binary, qualitative notion of information leakage turns out to be too restrictive in several real systems, where high level interferes with low level all the time [RMMG01] and the effort of the designer consists of minimizing such a kind of undesirable interactions. On the other hand, the analysis of nondeterministic security properties is not appropriate to reveal those interferences that are not solely nondeterministic, since they may depend on additional information, like probabilities and time [Gra92]. Along this line, in [ABG02] we have proposed a probabilistic extension to the nondeterministic information flow theory of [FG95] based on the probabilistic process algebra surveyed above, which is intended to:

- capture those information flows which are not observable in a purely nondeterministic setting;
- deal with the general case where the tolerance for information leakage is given by a quantitative estimate expressed by probabilistic measures.

The analysis of a given security property, say SP, in a process algebraic setting roughly consists of:

1. deriving two models from the algebraic specification of the system at hand;
2. checking the semantic equivalence between such derived models.

The definition of the submodels to be compared depends on the definition of SP. One of the most intuitive properties described in [ABG02] is the Probabilistic Bisimulation Nondeducibility on Composition property ($PBNDC$), which informally says that the probabilistic low-level view of a system P in isolation is not to be altered when considering the potential interactions of P with the high-level activities offered by the external environment. The definition of $PBNDC$ is formalized as follows.

Definition 1. $P \in PBNDC$ if and only if

$$P \backslash ATypeH \approx_{PB} ((P \parallel^p_{\{h_1,\ldots,h_n\}} \Pi)/^{q_1}_{h_1} \ldots /^{q_n}_{h_n}) \backslash ATypeH$$

$\forall\, p, q_1, \ldots, q_n \in]0, 1[, \ \forall \{h_1, \ldots, h_n\} \subseteq ATypeH,$ and $\forall$ high-level process Π.

Term $P \backslash ATypeH$, where the high-level actions are prevented, models the low-level behavior of the system P in isolation, i.e. without high-level interactions with the environment. Term $((P \parallel^p_{\{h_1,\ldots,h_n\}} \Pi)/^{q_1}_{h_1} \ldots /^{q_n}_{h_n}) \backslash ATypeH$ models, from the low-level standpoint, the behavior of P when interacting, through the communication interface $\{h_1, \ldots, h_n\}$, with the high-level activities offered by the external environment, represented by any process Π (enabling high-level actions only) put in parallel with P. Finally, $\approx_{PB}$ is the equivalence relation, called weak probabilistic bisimulation [ABG02], which is a probabilistic version (inspired by [BH97]) of the classical weak bisimulation of [Mil89]. If the two views of the system are indistinguishable from the standpoint of an external observer that can access the low-level part only, then no unwanted information leakage occurs and the system is considered to be secure.

3.3   Performance Analysis

As far as the temporal aspect is concerned, we now describe an interpretation of the probabilistic process algebra in the context of discrete time [Bra02,BA03], i.e. where time is represented by a sequence of discrete steps, like in Discrete Time Markov Chains (DTMCs), and the duration of each step is given by a fixed time unit. In such a framework, the parallel composition operator we adopt allows (*i*) processes with different *probabilistic advancing speeds* (mean number of actions executed per time unit) to be modeled, and (*ii*) several processes based on different time units to be composed in parallel by preserving their temporal behavior.

In our discrete time setting, $P \|_S^p Q$ models a system where p $(1-p)$ is the probabilistic advancing speed of P (Q), i.e., at each system state a *probabilistic scheduler* schedules for execution an action of P with probability p and an action of Q with probability $1-p$. Now, on the basis of the mean action frequency or, in other words, of the time unit adopted by each process in isolation, we can adequately calculate a global time unit for the composed model and a suitable probabilistic parameter for the parallel operator in such a way that each process preserves its mean action frequency. More precisely, $P \|_S^p Q$ can be interpreted as being a description of the actual concurrent execution of two processes P and Q specified with respect to different action durations. This is done as follows. If f_P is the mean action frequency in process P (i.e. each action takes time $1/f_P$ on average to be executed) and f_Q is the mean action frequency in process Q, the mean action frequency of the parallel composition of P and Q is $f = f_P + f_Q$. Therefore, the time unit for $P \|_S^p Q$ is $u = 1/(f_P + f_Q)$. Now, given that p is the probabilistic advancing speed of P, the mean action frequency of P with respect to u is given by $p/u = p \cdot f$. Therefore, if we take $p = f_P/f = f_P/(f_P + f_Q)$, it follows that the mean action frequency of P within $P \|_S^p Q$ is f_P. Similarly, the action frequency $1-p$ of Q with respect to u is $1-p = f_Q/f = f_Q/(f_P + f_Q)$.

Such an approach holds under the restriction that in each system state reachable from $P \|_S^p Q$, a probabilistic choice between P and Q guided by parameter p is to be performed. Then, from the labeled transition system associated to a fully specified process (i.e., not enabling nondeterministic choices), we can derive a DTMC (by discarding types from transition labels), on which we can apply standard techniques to evaluate performance measures of interest. Finally, we point out that if we are interested in evaluating steady state based performance measures (which are expressible by attaching rewards to actions), the approach described above provides an exact solution even if the advancing speeds are considered to be exact instead of probabilistic [BA03].

As we will show in the next section, we employ such an approach to model the temporal behavior of each component of the audio protocol specification.

4   Performance and Security Analyses of BoAT

In a previous work [ABGR01] we conducted a simulative analysis on an algebraic specification of BoAT (based on the process algebra $EMPA_{gr}$ [Ber99]) to get some performance measures related to the QoS offered by the adaptive play-out control algorithm. The reason for resorting to $EMPA_{gr}$ was its expressive power given by a set of features, such as probabilities, priorities, and value-passing. However, the results of such an analysis were limited to the functional and performance properties of BoAT. In this section, we employ the approach described in Sect. 3 in order to formally evaluate also the security level of BoAT.

4.1   The Algebraic Specification of BoAT

In this section, we introduce the algebraic specification of BoAT based on the calculus presented in Sect. 3. To this aim, we resort to the following assumptions. Since all packets are encrypted with secret keys that are not known by external parties, we abstract away from the cryptosystem used within the protocol and we just model the packet exchange. Moreover, for the sake of simplicity, we take into consideration the half-duplex part of the communication during which the so-called *sender* talks and the so-called *receiver* listens.

In Table 1 we show the model of a sender which repeatedly transmits audio packets and periodically performs the three-way handshaking protocol[1]. Process *Sen* models the situation in which a new handshaking phase is to be started: the output action *prepare_packet* expresses the transmission of an audio packet, the output action *prepare_probe* represents the transmission of the first message of the handshaking phase, and the output action *idle_S* denotes the inactivity periods of the sender during which no packets are sent out, e.g. due to a temporary overloaded channel. As far as the reactive behavior is concerned, process *Sen* is ready to accept messages coming from the receiving site. Since we just model the part of the communication during which the sender talks and the receiver listens, the only messages originated by the receiving site can be those related to the handshaking protocol, i.e. *response* messages and *ack* messages. In particular, in process *Sen* the reception of a *response* message, modeled by the input action *trans_response_**, refers to an old unsuccessful handshaking phase. Therefore, it is simply ignored (note that the action of type *trans_response* does not cause a change of state). Similarly, in process *Sen*, *ack* packets related to previous synchronization protocols are not expected to be received. In this case,

---

[1] We will discuss the values of the parameters associated to the operators in the next section, where we will consider the temporal behavior of the system.

Table 1. BoAT – Model of the sending site.

$$
\begin{aligned}
Sen &\stackrel{\Delta}{=} ((prepare\_packet.Sen +^{0.96} prepare\_probe.Sen') + \\
&\quad idle\_S.Sen) + (trans\_response_*.Sen + ignore\_ack_*.Sen) \\
Sen' &\stackrel{\Delta}{=} ((prepare\_packet.Sen' +^{0.96} prepare\_probe.Sen') + \\
&\quad idle\_S.Sen') + (trans\_response_*.Sen'' + ignore\_ack_*.Sen') \\
Sen'' &\stackrel{\Delta}{=} (((prepare\_packet.Sen'' +^{in} prepare\_install.Sen''') +^{0.96} \\
&\quad prepare\_probe.Sen') + idle\_S.Sen'') + \\
&\quad (trans\_response_*.Sen'' + ignore\_ack_*.Sen'') \\
Sen''' &\stackrel{\Delta}{=} ((\tau.Sen''' +^{s} prepare\_packet.Sen'''') +^{0.96} \\
&\quad prepare\_probe.Sen') + (trans\_response_*.Sen''' + trans\_ack_*.Sen) \\
Sen'''' &\stackrel{\Delta}{=} ((prepare\_packet.Sen'''' +^{0.96} prepare\_probe.Sen') + \\
&\quad idle\_S.Sen'''') + (trans\_response_*.Sen'''' + trans\_ack_*.Sen)
\end{aligned}
$$

we model the reception of an ack message via the input action of type *ignore_ack*, which denotes an *ack* packet received and discarded by the sender (i.e., related to a failed synchronization). In case of successful completion of the handshaking protocol, we will use the action type *trans_ack*. The motivation for such an explicit distinction is that we will be interested in quantifying failed and successful handshaking phases.

When a new *probe* message is transmitted, the sender waits for a *response* message from the receiver in term Sen'. Note that, in each term of the sender model, we allow a new synchronization phase to be started via the execution of the action *prepare_probe*, which leads to term Sen', since the original audio protocol discards those handshaking phases that (*i*) are not completed within a second (e.g. due to sudden spikes in end-to-end delays), and (*ii*) are deadlocked because of some lost handshaking packets. With respect to term Sen, in term Sen' the reception of a *response* message through the input action $trans\_response_*$ expresses the completion of the first step of the handshaking protocol after which the sender prepares an *install* packet to be sent in term Sen''.

After the execution of the action *prepare_install*, the sender waits for the final ack from the receiver in term Sen'''. Since usually the *install* packet is sent during a silence period, term Sen''' models the inactivity phase of the sender by repeatedly executing an internal action τ. Alternatively, the execution of the action *prepare_packet*, which leads to term Sen'''', represents the termination of the idle period and the beginning of a new talkspurt. For both terms Sen''' and Sen'''' the execution of the action *trans_ack* represents the final step of a three-way handshake completed with success, whose effect is that the initial state Sen is reached again.

We now describe a (possible) model for the receiver and for the channel (see Table 2). As far as the network is concerned, since we concentrate on the half-duplex audio communication between the sender and the receiver, we explicitly model the channel that transmits packets from the sending site to the receiving

Table 2. BoAT – Model of a perfect channel and of the receiving site.

$$
\begin{aligned}
Ch \;&\stackrel{\Delta}{=}\; prepare\_packet_*.For\_packet + \\
&\quad prepare\_probe_*.For\_probe + \\
&\quad prepare\_install_*.For\_install + \\
&\quad idle\_R_*.Ch \\
For\_packet \;&\stackrel{\Delta}{=}\; trans\_packet_*.Ch + idle\_S_*.For\_packet \\
For\_probe \;&\stackrel{\Delta}{=}\; trans\_probe_*.Ch + idle\_S_*.For\_probe \\
For\_install \;&\stackrel{\Delta}{=}\; trans\_install_*.Ch + idle\_S_*.For\_install \\[2mm]
Rec \;&\stackrel{\Delta}{=}\; (trans\_probe.Rec' + trans\_install.Rec'') + \\
&\quad (trans\_packet.Rec + idle\_R.Rec) \\
Rec' \;&\stackrel{\Delta}{=}\; trans\_response.Rec \\
Rec'' \;&\stackrel{\Delta}{=}\; trans\_ack.Rec + ignore\_ack.Rec \\[2mm]
BoAT \;&\stackrel{\Delta}{=}\; Sen \parallel_S^p (Ch \parallel_R Rec) \\
S \;&\stackrel{\Delta}{=}\; \{prepare\_packet, prepare\_probe, prepare\_install, \\
&\quad trans\_response, trans\_ack, ignore\_ack, idle\_S\} \\
R \;&\stackrel{\Delta}{=}\; \{trans\_packet, trans\_probe, trans\_install, idle\_R\}
\end{aligned}
$$

site. Instead, the packets originated by the receiver and destined to the sender are directly passed between these two terms, so that we abstract away from the related channel.

Term Ch is a fully reactive process modeling a perfect channel that does not lose packets and is always ready to accept packets originated by the sender. The action $idle\_R_*$ is enabled to inform the receiver that currently no packet is ready to be delivered. Once a packet is transmitted from the sender to the channel, term Ch passes the control to one of terms For_packet, For_probe, or $For\_install$, which are in charge of forwarding the packet to the receiver. In each of these terms, the channel is not ready to accept further packets from the sender, so that the action $idle\_S_*$ is enabled to inform the sender of such a situation.

Term Rec models a receiver that either is idle (and repeatedly executes action $idle\_R$) or accepts any arriving packet. If a handshaking packet is delivered, term Rec passes the control to one of the following terms: term Rec' transmits a _response_ message in case a _probe_ packet has been received; term Rec'' transmits an _ack_ message in case an _install_ packet has been received.

Finally, in Table 2 we also report the overall system $BoAT$, expressing the parallel execution of the three models specified so far, together with the related communication interfaces.

4.2   Security Analysis of BoAT

From a security standpoint, we want to verify if the handshaking protocol (which is the core of the securing mechanism of BoAT) is robust against external attacks.

To this aim, in order to apply the methodology described in Sect. 3 we have to single out the high-level actions and the low-level ones, so that the high and low behaviors of the system can be specified.

According to an approach proposed in [FGM00] for the analysis of noninterference properties of cryptographic protocols, the high level expresses the external, possibly dishonest environment, where the intruders act in order to interfere with the activities of the protocol. Hence, it is reasonable to assume that all actions that are used to model the protocol, which interacts with the environment, are high-level actions. Instead, the low-level actions are extra observable actions that we include into the protocol specification in order to observe the properties of the protocol itself.

In the context of our case study, we have to add some low-level actions that allow an external low-level observer to analyze the behavior of the three-way handshake, that is the core of the protocol under analysis. We point out that the successful execution of a handshaking phase starts with the transmission of a *probe* message and terminates with the reception of an *ack* message. Therefore, if we include in the sender model a low-level action **init_synch** immediately after the execution of each action of type *prepare_probe*, and a low-level action **end_synch** immediately after the execution of each action of type *trans_ack*, a low-level observer may infer the result of any handshaking phase and potentially realize that an adversary is trying to interfere with the synchronization policy. As an example, term *Sen* of Table 1 should be changed as follows (similarly for the other ones):

$$Sen \stackrel{\Delta}{=} ((prepare\_packet.Sen +^{0.96} prepare\_probe.\textbf{init\_synch}.Sen') + idle\_S.Sen) + (trans\_response_*.Sen + ignore\_ack_*.Sen).$$

In the following, we denote by Sen_l the sender model enriched with the low-level actions as specified above. Now, we are ready to apply the methodology described in Sect. 3 for the security analysis of BoAT. Since we are assuming that both participants have been previously authenticated, potential interferences may come from the channel only. Therefore, the security property we intend to check can be informally defined as follows.

BoAT is secure if and only if the execution of the protocol without external interferences is invariant with respect to the execution of the protocol in an untrusted channel possibly under the control of the adversary.

On the one hand, we observe that term *BoAT* of Table 2 expresses the execution of the protocol without interferences. Indeed, we recall that term *Ch* of Table 2 models a perfect, private channel with no intruders. Therefore, it follows that the low-level view of the system in the sense specified above is expressed by term $BoAT_l \stackrel{\Delta}{=} (Sen_l \|_S^P (Ch \|_R Rec))/(S \cup R)$, where all the high-level actions denoting the protocol activities are hidden.

On the other hand, if we assume that the network is under the control of the adversary, then we have to consider the system for any model of the communi-

cation channel, which may include external attacks. Therefore, we can formalize
the security property in a $PBNDC$ style as follows[2]:

$$BoAT_l \backslash AType_H \approx_{PB} ((Sen_l \|_S^q (Ch' \|_R^{q'} Rec))/_{\mathbf{s} \cdot \mathbf{r}}^{\mathbf{P}}) \backslash AType_H$$

$\forall q, q' \in]0,1[$, $\forall \mathbf{p} \in Seq_{]0,1[}^{|S \cup R|}$ and $\forall$ high-level process Ch'.

The formula above says that the low-level view of $BoAT_l$ in isolation is to be
the same as that observed when the sender and the receiver perform their protocol steps by transmitting their packets over an untrusted (potentially controlled
by the adversary) channel (modeled by any high-level term Ch', which may include dishonest strategies). Note that in $BoAT_l \backslash AType_H$ the final restriction on
the set $AType_H$ is redundant, since in term $BoAT_l$ the high-level actions are
either hidden (if they result from a synchronization) or restricted by the parallel
operators (if they cannot synchronize).

The low view of term $BoAT_l$ consists of a sequence of actions **end_synch**,
each one preceded by at least one action **init_synch**. This correctly represents
the expected behavior of BoAT, which periodically starts a new handshaking
phase (denoted by action **init_synch**) and each of these phases may be completed with success (denoted by action **end_synch**).

If we take into consideration only the possible behaviors of the system[3], then
the low behavior of BoAT is not altered if we consider intruders that interfere
by capturing some of the transmitted packets (replace, e.g., term Ch' by term
Ch_lossy of Table 3). In fact, even if an adversary blocks some handshaking packets, the observable low-level view is given by a sequence of actions **end_synch**,
each one preceded by at least one action **init_synch**. On the other hand, it is easy
to see that a denial-of-service attack conducted by an adversary (which eavesdrops the channel and discards each transmitted packet – consider, e.g., term
Ch_blind of Table 3) is the only kind of attack that is responsible for altering
the expected low view of the system. In fact, in such a case, the low-level action
end_synch is never enabled. However, if we take into consideration the probabilistic information, we observe that the probability of observing the successful
handshakes (with respect to those that fail) depends on the probabilistic behavior of the intruder. For instance, if the considered channel is term Ch_lossy
of Table 3, then the probability of observing the low-level action **end_synch**
depends on parameters d_a, d_p, and d_i, which probabilistically model the loss
percentage of audio packets, probe packets, and install packets, respectively.

Based on these considerations, we conclude that $BoAT$ does not satisfy the
security property. Now, we are interested in estimating how the security level of
BoAT is affected by the adversary strategy. More precisely, we want to evaluate
if the honest participants are able to detect any external attack and how to

---

[2] Given $S \subseteq AType$, $\mathbf{s}$ denotes the sequence, in alphabetic order, of types contained in
S, while $\mathbf{s} \cdot \mathbf{s}'$ denotes the catenation of the two sequences $\mathbf{s}$ and $\mathbf{s}'$; we also denote
by Seq_D^k the set of k-length sequences with domain D.

[3] We can apply the noninterference theory for nondeterministic processes if we ignore
the probabilistic information reported in the algebraic specification of BoAT.

Table 3. Some models of possible channels.

$$
\begin{aligned}
Ch\_lossy \;&\overset{\Delta}{=}\; (prepare\_packet_*.Ch\_lossy +^{d_a} prepare\_packet_*.For\_packet) + \\
&\quad ((prepare\_probe_*.Ch\_lossy +^{d_p} prepare\_probe_*.For\_probe) + \\
&\quad\; (prepare\_install_*.Ch\_lossy +^{d_i} prepare\_install_*.For\_install)) + \\
&\quad idle\_R_*.Ch\_lossy \\
For\_packet \;&\overset{\Delta}{=}\; trans\_packet_*.Ch\_lossy + idle\_S_*.For\_packet \\
For\_probe \;&\overset{\Delta}{=}\; trans\_probe_*.Ch\_lossy + idle\_S_*.For\_probe \\
For\_install \;&\overset{\Delta}{=}\; trans\_install_*.Ch\_lossy + idle\_S_*.For\_install \\[6pt]
Ch\_blind \;&\overset{\Delta}{=}\; ((prepare\_packet_*.Ch\_blind + prepare\_probe_*.Ch\_blind) + \\
&\quad (prepare\_install_*.Ch\_blind + idle\_R_*.Ch\_blind))
\end{aligned}
$$

behave in such a case. To this aim, we pass to the performance model of BoAT in order to derive performance measures of interest.

4.3   Mixed Performance/Security Analysis of BoAT

Before introducing the performance model of BoAT, we specify the kind of attack whose effects we are interested in evaluating. Since we concentrate on the half-duplex part of the audio communication from the sender to the receiver, we take into consideration all possible attacks performed by an adversary that eavesdrops (and possibly captures) the packets generated by the sending site. Moreover, we consider the preliminary authentication phase preceding the audio conversation as a secure step. Therefore, since all packets are enriched with timestamps and encrypted with secret keys, we consider forgery, authentication and replication attacks by any external party as not meaningful. Instead, an adversary can try to conduct a cryptanalysis attack in order to compromize the privacy of the conversation. Since the secrecy level of BoAT trusts on the short duration of each session key (about a second of conversation, i.e. the time between two consecutive handshaking phases), and the robustness of the stream cipher used by BoAT may depend on the quantity of data encrypted with the same key (see, e.g., [BSW00]), then the probability of cracking a session key increases if several consecutive handshaking protocols fail, because in such a case the same key is used to encrypt several seconds of conversation. With this in view, a strategy for a dishonest adversary consists of intercepting and blocking the packets of the handshaking protocol, in order to weaken the secrecy condition of BoAT by extending the lifetime of each session key.

In the previous section, we have described a model of the channel (see the fully reactive term Ch_lossy of Table 3) that expresses such a kind of attack. More precisely, it is easy to verify that, from the viewpoint of a low-level external observer, the probabilistic behavior of term Ch_lossy (expressed by parameters d_a, d_p, and d_i only) within the overall system is responsible for affecting the probability distribution of the successful handshakes. In this section, we quantify the difference between the behavior of the system without intruders and the behavior of the system under the attack specified by term Ch_lossy. To this end, we first pass to a performance model by considering the temporal behavior of processes Sen and Rec, and then we analyze the composed system $((Sen \parallel_S^P (Ch\_lossy \parallel_R Rec))/(S \cup R)) \backslash ATDpe_H$, by varying the probabilistic behavior of term Ch_lossy. Note that the two limiting scenarios are represented by (i) the channel that blocks all the transmitted packets (see term Ch_blind of Table 3), and (ii) the channel that forwards each transmitted packet (see term Ch of Table 2). The goal of our analysis is the evaluation of the throughput of the handshaking protocol (i.e. the mean number of handshakes completed with success per time unit) for each adversary strategy between the two limiting scenarios. In the following, we show how to model the temporal behavior of each component according to the features of BoAT specified in [ABGR01,RGPSB01].

As far as the sender model is concerned, we consider a sending site that produces 25 audio packets per sec. To this end, the time unit we adopt for process Sen is 40 ms, i.e. each action of term Sen takes 40 ms on average to be executed or, equivalently, the mean action frequency of term Sen is 25 actions per sec. Moreover, we assume that the time between two consecutive handshaking phases is about 1 sec. The probabilistic parameters shown in Table 1 exactly reflect such temporal assumptions. In particular, since action $prepare\_probe$ has to be executed once a second on average and the mean action frequency for process Sen is 25 actions per sec, in each discrete step the action to be executed is $prepare\_probe$ with probability $1/25 = 0.04$ and $prepare\_packet$ with probability $1 - 0.04 = 0.96$. If such actions are enabled in the composed system, then the action $idle\_S$ is not; on the contrary, if such actions are not enabled, then the action $idle\_S$ is performed with probability 1.

In term Sen'', the probability 0.96 of sending a packet different from a $probe$ message has to be distributed between the two possible events: the transmission of either an audio packet or an $install$ message. Since the $install$ message is not sent as soon as the $response$ message is received, but only during a silence period, we employ parameter in to express the probability of executing the action $prepare\_packet$ with respect to the action $prepare\_install$. In practice, as parameter in increases, the probability of being in a talkspurt increases as well. Since experimental studies show that the duration of a silence period is about the 30% of the duration of a talkspurt [HSK98,ABGR01], in the following we assume $in = 0.7$, meaning that the probability of transmitting the $install$ message (instead of an audio packet) is equal to 30%.

In term Sen''', parameter s expresses the probability of being in a silence period between two consecutive talkspurts. More precisely, the duration of the inactivity phase of the sender is probabilistically modeled according to a Bernoulli distribution with parameter s: the sender either stays in its idle period with probability $s \cdot 0.96$ or starts a new talkspurt with probability $(1-s) \cdot 0.96$. If the sender is not allowed to send packets (i.e. actions $prepare\_packet$ and $prepare\_probe$ are not enabled), the action τ expressing the idling period is executed with probability 1. As far as the experimental scenario is concerned, we assume $s = 0.7$, namely in term Sen''' we start a new talkspurt (instead of staying idle) with probability 30%.

As far as the receiving site is concerned, the time unit adopted for term Rec is 1 ms, i.e. each action of term Rec takes 1 ms on average to be executed or, equivalently, the mean action frequency of term Rec is 1000 actions per sec. This choice expresses the fact that the receiving site is always ready to accept packets and, if necessary, to immediately send back a handshaking packet.

As far as the overall system is concerned, we now compute the global time unit u and the parameters of the probabilistic parallel operators for the composed system $((Sen \|_S^p (Ch\_lossy \|_R Rec))/(S \cup R)) \backslash AType_H$. The global time unit u is the inverse of the global action frequency of the composed system, which in turn is equal to 25 (i.e., the action frequency of term Sen) + 1000 (see term Rec) = 1025 actions per sec. Note that the process modeling the channel is completely reactive (that means we abstract away from the transmission delays experienced along the channel), so that it does not express a process with its own advancing speed. Moreover, we also have that in each system state both processes Sen and Rec can execute at least a generative action. Hence, parameter p represents the advancing speed of term Sen within the overall system and is given by the ratio of the action frequency of term Sen over the global action frequency of the composed system, i.e. $p = 25/1025 \approx 0.02439$.

From the algebraic specification of the composed system we can derive a DTMC, since the related labeled transition system is fully specified in the sense that all the choices are fully probabilistic or, in other words, reactive actions are never enabled. Therefore, in order to obtain steady state based performance measures, we adequately attach rewards to actions and we analyze the related DTMC. To this end, we resorted to the software tool TwoTowers [BCSS98], which has been extended to support the generative-reactive approach of our probabilistic calculus. Such a tool also implements the algebraic reward based method needed to specify and derive performance measures. On the one hand, we evaluate the throughput of the handshaking protocol at the sending site, i.e. the number of handshaking phases completed with success, expressed in terms of occurrences of actions of type $trans\_ack$. This is done by attaching a reward equal to 1 to the action $trans\_ack$ and a reward equal to 0 to each other action. On the other hand, we also evaluate the throughput for the receiver, i.e. the number of audio packets arrived at the receiving site, in terms of occurrences of actions of type $trans\_packet$, by attaching a reward equal to 1 to the above action and a reward equal to 0 to each other action.

The performance results we are going to present have been obtained by varying the probabilistic behavior of the channel model. As we have shown, an adversary that is interested in extending the lifetime of each session key tries to intercept and discard the handshaking packets. Given that all packets are encrypted, an adversary cannot distinguish the audio packets from the handshaking packets originated by the sender. Hence, in a first scenario we assume that an intruder can just try to randomly discard some of the transmitted packets. In particular, we vary from 0% to 100% the percentage of packets captured and blocked along the channel by the dishonest intruder. The extreme value 0% corresponds to the behavior modeled by term Ch of Table 2, while the extreme value 100% corresponds to the behavior modeled by term Ch_blind of Table 3. For each other value, we consider term Ch_lossy and, by assuming $d_a = d_p = d_i$ (expressing the probability of discarding audio, probe, and install packets, respectively), we vary such parameters from 0 to 1.

In Fig. 3 we show the tradeoff between the percentage of packets discarded by an adversary that eavesdrops the channel and the throughput at the sending site in terms of occurrences of actions of type $trans\_ack$, which expresses the completion with success of the handshaking phase. As an expected result, the number of synchronizations completed in a second decreases as the percentage of lost packets tends to 1. In particular, in case of a perfect and private channel, the audio protocol completes about 0.866 handshaking phases per sec. For a loss rate less than 10% such a throughput is still tolerable (greater than 0.7 phases completed per sec), but as the loss rate increases (20% and more) the throughput rapidly converges under 0.5 phases completed per sec, i.e. less than one synchronization every 2 sec. In particular, in Fig. 3 we also show the tolerable area beyond which the number of successful synchronizations is so low that (i) the estimated playout delay cannot represent an accurate evaluation of the current state of the channel [HSK98,RGPSB01], and (ii) the lifetime of each session key is noticeably greater than 1 sec. The main result that we derive from such an experiment is that the probabilistic behavior of the environment (adversary) affects the throughput of the three-way handshake protocol as measured by the sender. Similarly, we can infer the effect of the adversary behavior on the receiving site. In Fig. 4 we show the tradeoff between the percentage of packets discarded by an adversary that eavesdrops the channel and the throughput at the receiving site in terms of occurrences of actions of type $trans\_packet$. Once again, the number of packets received in a second decreases as the percentage of lost packets tends to 1. In Fig. 4 we also report the area denoting the performance that is desired by the authenticated parties, in the sense that beyond such an area (i.e., for loss rates greater than 10%) the quality of the perceived audio dramatically jeopardizes the comprehension of the conversation [RGPSB01,ABGR01].

The analysis conducted above clearly shows that each change in the probabilistic behavior of the (hostile) environment is reflected upon the performance behavior of BoAT as measured by the honest participants. Such an information can be exploited in order to quantify the risk for the encrypted data to be cracked by a dishonest third party. By comparing Fig. 3 and Fig. 4 we observe that an intruder that captures packets in a random way affects the performance of both audio packet throughput at the receiving site and handshaking throughput at the sending site. If the behavior of the intruder makes both throughputs come out from the tolerable area, the honest participants decide to cut off the communication due to the scarce QoS. If this is not the case, the throughputs maintain high values and, as a consequence, both audio quality and data secrecy are not compromized.

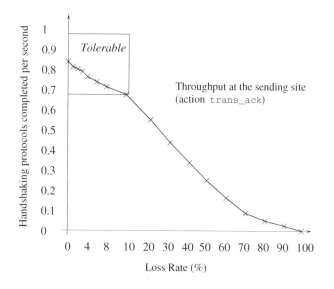

Fig. 3. Handshaking protocol throughput.

A more interesting result can be obtained by dealing with a clever adversary that somehow is able to intercept the handshaking packets transmitted by the sender. If this is the case, the intruder attack can make the throughput of the handshaking protocol decreased, without substantially altering the audio packet throughput at the receiving site. For instance, an adversary may try to exploit the fact that the *install* packet is sent during a silence period in order to intercept and block such a handshaking packet. However, this attack can be easily avoided by a sender that generates and transmits encrypted dummy packets during the silence phases between consecutive talkspurts, so that the adversary cannot detect the *install* packet. Alternatively, an intruder may try to guess the instant in which the *probe* packet is transmitted by the sender. Such a strategy can cause serious damage to the security level of the audio protocol if exactly 1 sec passes between the transmission of two consecutive *probe* messages, as in the original proposal of BoAT. Indeed, by assuming such a behavior of the sending site, the intruder can get a good approximation of the transmission time of the *probe* messages by eavesdropping the conversation from the beginning.

With this in view, here we evaluate the trade-off between the throughput of the synchronization protocol and the capability of the intruder of guessing the *probe* packets. To this end, we make the following assumptions. Supposed that the ith handshaking phase starts approximately i sec after the beginning of the conversation, we assume the instant of the transmission of the related *probe* message to follow a gaussian distribution with mean value i and standard deviation *dev*. By varying parameter *dev* and by fixing the width of the temporal interval around time i within which the intruder discards all the transmitted packets, we employ the normal distribution tables [Bey90] to measure the probability for the intruder of stopping exactly the *probe* message (such a probability is assigned to

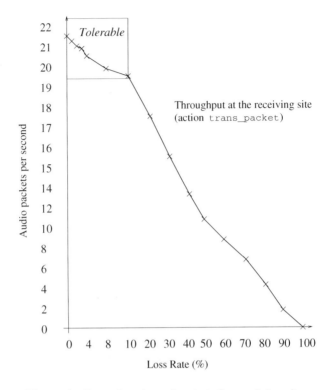

Fig. 4. Audio packet throughput at the receiving site.

parameter d_p of term *Ch_lossy* of the algebraic specification). In a first scenario, we assume that the intruder discards 5 packets transmitted around time i, by covering a time interval of 160 ms. If one of them is the *probe* packet, then the percentage of lost audio packets (modeled by parameter d_a) is 16%. In a second scenario, we assume that the intruder discards 3 packets only, by covering a time interval of 80 ms. This corresponds to $d_a = 8\%$. Finally, parameter d_i, which models the percentage of lost *install* packets, is set to 0, because the transmission instant of such a packet is out of the time interval within which the adversary captures packets.

In Fig. 5, we show the results that derive from the analysis of the BoAT specification where the term modeling the channel is changed according to the behavior above. We point out that the throughput of the handshaking protocol is computed exactly as explained in case of Fig. 3. The curves are obtained by varying the probability for the intruder of guessing the *probe* message according to different values of parameter *dev*, which varies from 25 to 400 ms. A low value of the standard deviation *dev* means that the approximation made by the intruder is accurate with high probability, because the ith *probe* packet is indeed transmitted around time i, while a high value of *dev* means that the intruder has a lower chance of guessing the *probe* message. Hence, by increasing parameter *dev* the throughput of the handshaking protocol tends to its limiting

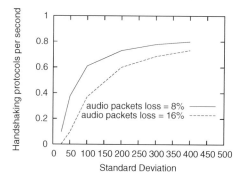

Fig. 5. Trade-off between handshaking protocol throughput and intruder strategy.

value 0.866, which represents the case in which no packets are stopped by the intruder. In the first scenario, i.e. when the intruder discards 5 packets per sec, we observe that for a standard deviation dev less than 100 ms, the throughput of the handshaking protocol rapidly converges to values corresponding to a lifetime of each session key noticeably greater than 5 sec (instead of 1 sec as expected by the protocol), which in many cases is more than enough to crack the session key and the encrypted data (see, e.g., [BSW00]). Anyway, in such a scenario we also have that the audio packet loss measured at the receiving site is about 16%, which represents a limiting performance typical of highly overloaded channels. Therefore, the audio communication will be likely terminated by the participants because of such a poor QoS. Instead, in the second scenario, i.e. when the intruder discards 3 packets per sec, the audio packet loss measured at the receiving site is about 8%, which is a performance acceptable by the honest participants. In spite of this, a clever intruder can reduce the throughput of the handshaking protocol up to about 0.096 and, even in case of parameter dev equal to 50 ms, the lifetime of each session key is about three times the expected value.

The unwanted behavior described above can be avoided by implementing a version of BoAT proposed in [AGR01], which suggests to vary, during the conversation lifetime, the time interval between two consecutive handshaking phases. More precisely, in order to make difficult for the intruder a precise evaluation of the time instant in which the *probe* message is sent, we introduce a random factor in the computation of such a time instant. To this end, we can employ the results of the formal analysis conducted above in order to evaluate the relationship between the choice of such a random factor and the number of expected successful handshaking phases. In particular, instead of sending the ith *probe* message exactly i sec after the beginning of the conversation, we could decide to send such a packet at a time instant sampled according to a gaussian distribution with mean value i and standard deviation dev. The choice of parameter dev affects the handshaking protocol throughput and, as a consequence, the lifetime of each session key and the secrecy level of the audio protocol. By following the results depicted in Fig. 5, it is easy to see that a value of parameter dev greater than 200 ms is more than enough to guarantee a throughput of the handshaking protocol that falls in the tolerable area put in evidence in Fig. 3, independently of the behavior of any clever intruder.

The mixed security/performance analysis revealed that an attack that aims at weakening the session keys can be easily prevented by changing the algorithm followed by the sending site to originate the *probe* messages. We conclude by observing that the effectiveness of such an attack and the related countermove cannot be viewed if we just employ a nondeterministic approach to the information flow theory. This is because in a nondeterministic setting we can reveal a denial-of-service attack only, while we have seen that the analysis of the performance behavior of BoAT is needed to give a quantitative estimate of the capability of a probabilistic adversary of compromizing the secrecy level of the audio communication.

5   Conclusion

We conclude by summarizing the two main results presented in this paper. On the one hand, we have emphasized that a nondeterministic approach is not enough to analyze the security level of real systems for which a quantitative estimate of the unwanted information flows is more significant. On the other hand, we have seen that performance behavior and security level can be tightly connected. To formally evaluate such a relation, an approach that allows both aspects to be described and analyzed on the same model is needed.

Finally, it is worth noting that in this paper we have considered a secrecy property whose analysis should help the modeler to reveal unwanted conditions in which cryptanalysis attacks can be successfully completed. We did not explicitly modeled the weaknesses of the keys by evaluating, e.g., the probability of guessing a message encrypted through a session key with a certain lifetime. To do this, we intend to extend our process algebraic approach in order to deal with cryptographic operations and imperfect cryptography.

Acknowledgement

We are grateful to Marco Roccetti, developer of BoAT, for his suggestions and comments. This work has been partially funded by Progetto MEFISTO (Metodi Formali per la Sicurezza e il Tempo) and supported by the DEGAS (Design Environments for Global Applications) project funded by the IST Programme, FET Proactive Initiative on Global Computing.

References

AMR03.   A. Aldini, A. Amoroso, M. Roccetti. A Secure Protocol for Voice-Operated E-Commerce Systems over IP Networks. *Int. Journal of Pure and Applied Mathematics* 4(2):121-142, Academic Publications, 2003.

ABGR01.   A. Aldini, M. Bernardo, R. Gorrieri, M. Roccetti. Comparing the QoS of Internet Audio Mechanisms via Formal Methods. *ACM Transactions on Modelling and Computer Simulation* 11(1):1-42, ACM Press, 2001.

ABG02.   A. Aldini, M. Bravetti, R. Gorrieri. A Process-algebraic Approach for the Analysis of Probabilistic Non-interference. *Journal of Computer Security*, to appear.

AGR01.   A. Aldini, R. Gorrieri, M. Roccetti. An Adaptive Mechanism for Real-time Secure Speech Transmission over the Internet. In *2nd IP-Telephony Workshop (IP-Tel'01)*, H. Schulzrinne ed., pp. 64-72, 2001.

AGR03.   A. Aldini, R. Gorrieri, M. Roccetti. On Securing Real Time Speech Transmission over the Internet: An Experimental Study. *EURASIP Journal on Applied Signal Processing*, Special Issue on Digital Audio for Multimedia Communications, Hindawi Publishing Corporation, to appear.

BH97.   C. Baier, H. Hermanns. Weak Bisimulation for Fully Probabilistic Processes. In *9th Int. Conf. on Computer Aided Verification (CAV'97)*, *LNCS* 1254:119-130, Springer, 1997.

Ber99.   M. Bernardo. Theory and Application of Extended Markovian Process Algebra. *Ph.D. Thesis*, University of Bologna, Italy, 1999. ftp://ftp.cs.unibo.it/pub/techreports/

BCSS98.   M. Bernardo, W.R. Cleaveland, S.T. Sims, W.J. Stewart. TwoTowers: A Tool Integrating Functional and Performance Analysis of Concurrent Systems. In *Joint Int. Conf. on Formal Description Techniques for Distributed Systems and Communication Protocols and Protocol Specification, Testing, and Verification (FORTE-PSTV'98)*, pp. 457-467, Kluwer, 1998.

BDG98.   M. Bernardo, L. Donatiello, R. Gorrieri. A Formal Approach to the Integration of Performance Aspects in the Modeling and Analysis of Concurrent Systems. *Information and Computation* 144:83-154, 1998.

Bey90.   W.H. Beyer. Standard Probability & Statistics Tables & Formulae. Boca Raton, FL: CRC Press, 1990.

BSW00.   A. Biryukov, A. Shamir, D. Wagner. Real Time Cryptanalysis of A5/1 on a PC. In *Fast Software Encryption Workshop*, LNCS 1978, Springer, 2000.

Bra02.   M. Bravetti. Specification and Analysis of Stochastic Real-Time Systems. *Ph.D. Thesis*, University of Bologna (Italy), 2002. ftp://ftp.cs.unibo.it/pub/techreports/

BA03.   M. Bravetti, A. Aldini. Discrete Time Generative-reactive Probabilistic Processes with Different Advancing Speeds. *Theoretical Computer Science* 290(1):355-406, 2003.

FG95.   R. Focardi, R. Gorrieri. A Classification of Security Properties. *Journal of Computer Security* 3(1):5-33, 1995.

FGM00.   R. Focardi, R. Gorrieri, F. Martinelli. Non Interference for the Analysis of Cryptographic Protocols. In *27th Int. Colloquium on Automata, Languages and Programming (ICALP'00)*, LNCS 1853:354-372, Springer, 2000.

GSS95.   R.J. van Glabbeek, S.A. Smolka, B. Steffen. Reactive, Generative and Stratified Models of Probabilistic Processes. In *Information and Computation* 121:59-80, 1995.

GM82.   J.A. Goguen, J. Meseguer. Security Policy and Security Models. In *Symposium on Security and Privacy (SSP'82)*, pp. 11-20, IEEE CS Press, 1982.

Gra92.   J. W. Gray III. Toward a Mathematical Foundation for Information Flow Security. In *Journal of Computer Security* 1:255-294, 1992.

HSK98.   V. Hardman, M.A. Sasse, I. Kouvelas. Successful Multi-Party Audio
            Communication over the Internet. *Communications of the ACM* 41:74-
            80, 1998. http://www-mice.cs.ucl.ac.uk/multimedia/software/rat/
HS95.   P. Harrison, B. Strulo. Stochastic Process Algebra for Discrete Event
            Simulation. In *Quantitative Methods in Parallel Systems, ESPRIT Basic
            Research Series*, pp. 18-37, Springer, 1995.
HHHMR94.   H. Hermanns, U. Herzog, J. Hillston, V. Mertsiotakis, M. Rettelbach.
            Stochastic Process Algebras: Integrating Qualitative and Quantitative
            Modelling. In *7th Conf. on Formal Description Techniques (FORTE'94)*,
            pp. 449-451, Chapman & Hall, 1994.
McL90.   J. McLean. Security Models and Information Flow. In *IEEE Symposium
            on Research in Security and Privacy*, pp. 180-189, 1990.
Mil89.   R. Milner. *Communication and Concurrency*, Prentice Hall, 1989.
RGPSB01.   M. Roccetti, V. Ghini, G. Pau, P. Salomoni, M. E. Bonfigli, Design and
            Experimental Evaluation of an Adaptive Playout Delay Control Mecha-
            nism for Packetized Audio for Use over the Internet. *Multimedia Tools
            and Appl., an Int. Journal* 14(1):23-53, Kluwer Academic Publ., 2001.
RMMG01.   P.Y.A. Ryan, J. McLean, J. Millen, V. Gligor. Non-interference: who
            needs it? In *14th Computer Security Foundations Workshop (CSFW'01)*,
            pp. 237-238, IEEE CS Press, 2001.
Schn96.   B. Schneier. *Applied Cryptography, 2nd Edition*, John Wiley & Sons,
            1996.
Schu92.   H. Schulzrinne. Voice Communication across the Internet: a Network
            Voice Terminal. *Tech. Rep.*, University of Massachusetts, Amherst (MA),
            1992. http://www.cs.columbia.edu/~hgs/rtp/nevot.html
SDS01.   R. Steinmetz, J. Dittman, M. Steinebach (Eds.). *Communications and
            Multimedia Security Issues of the New Century*, Kluwer Academic Pub-
            lishers, 2001.

Performance Evaluation for Global Computation

Linda Brodo[1], Pierpaolo Degano[2], Stephen Gilmore[3],
Jane Hillston[3], and Corrado Priami[4]

[1] Istituto Trentino Cultura – IRST
Via Sommarive 18, I-38050 Povo (Trento), Italy
brodo@itc.it
[2] Dipartimento di Informatica
Università di Pisa
F.Buonarroti 2, I-56127 Pisa, Italy
degano@di.unipi.it
[3] Laboratory for Foundations of Computer Science
The University of Edinburgh
Edinburgh EH9 3JZ, Scotland
{stg,jeh}@lfcs.ed.ac.uk
[4] Università di Trento
Dipartimento di Informatica e Telecomunicazioni
Via Sommarive 14, I-38050 Povo (Trento), Italy
priami@dit.unitn.it

Abstract. Global computing applications co-ordinate distributed computations across widely-dispersed hosts. Such systems present formidable design and implementation challenges to software developers and synchronisation, scheduling and performance problems come to the fore. Complex systems such as these can benefit from the application of high-level performance analysis methods founded on timed process algebras. In this paper we compare the use of two such approaches, the PEPA nets and EOS methods, illustrating our presentation with the example of modelling Web services.

1 Introduction

Our main concern here is comparing existing process algebraic primitives against the needs arising when modelling global applications with a view to determining their run-time performance. Communication and especially mobility are possibly the two main features characterising global computing. There are different approaches to their representation. One widely-studied approach represents mobility implicitly through the communication of links. A name n, representing a communication channel, is passed to an agent that now becomes connected through n to all the agents that know the link n. In this way the topology of the interconnecting network varies while the (distributed) computation goes on. The typical representative of this class is the well-known π-calculus [16].

An alternative approach to representing mobility and communication is taken by the PEPA nets formalism, which combines the process algebra PEPA with

C. Priami (Ed.): GC 2003, LNCS 2874, pp. 229–253, 2003.

a Petri net infrastructure [9]. In this formalism, which can be regarded as a high-level Petri net formalism, *places* are process algebra contexts and *tokens* are process algebra components. Mobility is modelled explicitly by the firing of a transition in the Petri net which has the result of a component moving from one place to another. Communication is restricted to be local and is modelled by the usual process algebra communication between components. We have previously studied the relationship between PEPA nets and the π-calculus, by translating a subset of the PEPA nets formalism into the stochastic π-calculus [2]. The objective of performance evaluation is to analyse the dynamic behaviour of a system and predict performance *indices* or *measures* such as throughput, utilisation or response time. A performance prediction may be useful at specification time both when the system implementation is known and when the specification is not connected to any particular implementation. In the first case analysis can suggest potential technical improvements of the implementation. In the second case many implementations can be imagined for the same specification and this could give hints in choosing the more adequate implementation. If a process algebra model is to be used for this purpose certain aspects of the behaviour of the model must be quantified. For example, in classical process algebras alternative behaviours are modelled by a non-deterministic choice. However from such a model no predictions about the likelihood of differing behaviours can be made. Therefore when the objective is performance evaluation, non-deterministic choice is replaced by probabilistic choice. Similarly, in the dynamic behaviour of a system the durations of actions (or equivalently the delays between events) are important and must be incorporated into the model.

Many probabilistic and timed extensions of process algebras have appeared in the literature in the last 15 years, however the most prevalent approach taken in performance evaluation is exemplified by PEPA [11]. In this language all actions have an associated duration which is specified by a random variable, governed by a negative exponential distribution. In PEPA probabilistic choice is not modelled explicitly; when more than one activity is possible it is assumed that the activities race in the sense that each draws from the corresponding distribution function to obtain a duration for this instance of the activity. The activity with the shorter duration sample is the one which will be performed first, thus "winning the race". In practice, since all durations are governed by a negative exponential distributions, the relative probability of activities in competition can be derived by a simple formula. The stochastic π-calculus [18] adopts similar constructs.

In this way, our process algebra models can be used to generate a Continuous Time Markov Chain (CTMC) which can be solved to obtain a steady state probability distribution from which performance measures can be derived. In recent work we have extended PEPA to allow the durations of activities to be defined via functions rather than explicitly [13, 12]. In the context of global computing this means that the duration of an activity can depend on the state of other components. In PEPA nets, again the target representation for performance analysis is a CTMC, and so both process algebra transitions, and Petri net firings have an associated duration which is negative exponentially distributed. As previously conflicts may be solved by the race policy but it is also possible to assign different priorities to different Petri net transitions, giving some firings priority over others [9].

In the EOS approach [6], the transition labels are enhanced so that they record the application of inference rules. The designer of the application under analysis can define evaluation functions that determine the rates of transitions, by inspecting enhanced labels, as these represent the low level routines performed by the run-time support to execute the transition itself. Since the rates are also affected by the target architecture, its peculiarities will also affect the evaluation functions, the parameters of which are then the enhanced labels and the architectural details [17].

Structure of this paper: The paper is organized as follows. In the next section we describe our running example of Web services. Section 3 recalls the basics of PEPA nets, while Sect. 4 introduces the PEPA nets semantics and shows how performance analysis can be carried out on the running example. Section 5 describes the EOS approach on the π-calculus and shows how it can be used to perform a quantitative analysis of the Web service system. Finally, we draw some conclusions.

2   Example: Modelling Web Services

Web services provide a technological platform which enables global computation. In a Web services architecture clients and services are loosely coupled and geographically distributed. Services are obtained by discovery from registries and directories. Web service descriptions specify the interfaces and locations of services. Method invocation and transport of data are performed by asynchronous message passing. The computing platform is heterogeneous and architecture-neutral. The implementation platform is also heterogeneous; web service clients may be implemented in a different implementation language from the service application. All of the above qualities typify global computation: distributed computations across heterogenous platforms utilising discovery services to effect remote evaluation.

Another typical quality of global computations is that they take place across administrative domains. In consequence they must coordinate communication and evaluation across different security contexts. Firewalls are used in distributed systems to safeguard systems against attack, preventing unrestricted communication between remote sites. Their presence is a necessity but one which causes problems for some communications protocols. Web services however are accessed by HTTP. The use of the HTTP protocol virtually eliminates the complications caused by firewalls.

Web services achieve global accessibility in practice by adherance to open standards which are widely supported and used. Both communication protocols and data formats are standardised. Web services are globally positioned by giving each a unique Uniform Resource Identifier (URI). Clients and services in a Web services architecture exchange XML-encoded messages using the standard SOAP protocol. The use of XML for data carriage provides an abstraction barrier over the language-dependent in-memory data formats used in application programs. The SOAP protocol provides a high-level transport and may itself be layered over native network protocols such as SMTP or HTTP. A special-purpose language WSDL (Web Services Description Language) exists for describing interface "contracts" between Web service provider and client.

Web services applications incorporate many significant practical advances over previous generations of distributed systems technology. One cost of their considerable advantages is that they are resource-intensive systems. Web services include many layers of encapsulation which would not be needed in traditional binary communication protocols. Service lookup is an overhead, as is XML-encoding. The XML language itself is a verbose, human-readable encoding format which is engineered for clarity, not for compactness. This has the consequence that XML-encoded method calls are weighty data items which incur significant transmission costs. The use of the HTTP protocol is another overhead. Network reliability, host availability problems and distributed system faults further degrade performance. For these reasons, Web services provide a highly appropriate example for performance modelling techniques such as those presented in this paper.

Process algebras are excellent tools for modelling Web services because they naturally support peer-to-peer architectures. The co-operator/co-operand style of process algebras allows an intuitive encoding of control flow logics such as callbacks. A process algebra which provides direct support for location-awareness is an added benefit. This provides the right conceptual modelling concepts to represent mobile code systems ranging from the asynchronous remote procedure call method provided by Web services to more complex configurations as embodied in the remote evaluation, code-on-demand or mobile agent paradigms.

3 PEPA Nets

PEPA nets extend the PEPA [11] stochastic process algebra by connecting individual PEPA models together as the places of a coloured stochastic Petri net. PEPA components travel from place to place as the tokens of the net.

A PEPA net differentiates between two types of change of state. We refer to these as *firings* of the net and *transitions* of PEPA components. Each are special cases of PEPA activities. Transitions of PEPA components will typically be used to model small-scale changes of state as components undertake activities. Firings of the net will typically be used to model large-scale changes of state such as context switches, breakdowns and repairs, one thread yielding to another, or a mobile software agent moving from one network host to another.

A firing in a PEPA net causes the transfer of one token from one place to another. The token which is moved is a PEPA component, which causes a change in the subsequent evaluation both in the source (where existing cooperations with other components now can no longer take place) and in the target (where previously disabled cooperations are now enabled by the arrival of an incoming component which can participate in these interactions). Firings have global effect because they involve components at more than one place in the net.

A transition in a PEPA net takes place whenever a transition of a PEPA component can occur (either individually, or in cooperation with another component). Components can only cooperate if they are resident in the same place in the net. The PEPA net formalism does not allow components at different places in the net to cooperate on a shared activity. An analogy is with message-passing distributed systems without shared-memory where software components on the same host can exchange information without incurring a communication overhead but software components on different hosts cannot. Additionally we do not allow a firing to coincide with a transition which is shared, i.e. it is not possible for two components in one place to cooperate *and* transfer to another place as an atomic action. Thus transitions in a PEPA net have local effect because they involve only components at one place in the net. Maintaining this strict distinction between firings and transitions is essential in order to provide the separation into macro- and micro-step state changes that we are seeking to represent.

Each place has a distinct alphabet for transitions and firings, meaning that the same action type cannot be used for both. Thus there can be no ambiguity between such micro- and macro-scale transitions.

A PEPA net is made up of PEPA *contexts*, one at each place in the net. A context consists of a number of *static* components (possibly zero) and a number of *cells* (at least one). Like a memory location in an imperative program, a cell is a storage area to be filled by a datum of a particular type. In particular in a PEPA net, a cell is a storage area dedicated to storing a PEPA component. The components which fill cells can circulate as the tokens of the net. In contrast, the static components cannot move.

We use the notation $Q[\_]$ to denote a context which could be filled by the PEPA component Q or one with the same alphabet. If Q has derivatives Q' and Q'' only and no other component has the same alphabet as Q then there are four possible values for such a context: $Q[\_]$, $Q[Q]$, $Q[Q']$ and $Q[Q'']$. $Q[\_]$ enables no transitions. $Q[Q]$ enables the same transitions as Q. $Q[Q']$ enables the same transitions as Q'. $Q[Q'']$ enables the same transitions as Q''. As usual with PEPA components we require that the component has an ergodic definition so that it is always possible to return to a state which one has previously reached. This has as a consequence that if Q' is a derivative of Q then it is also the case that Q is a derivative of Q', for any Q and Q'.

The introduction of contexts requires an extension to the syntax of PEPA. This extension is presented in Table 1.

For any token component its action type set can be partitioned in distinct subsets corresponding to transitions and firings respectively. For a component Q we will denote these sets by $\mathcal{A}_t(Q)$ and $\mathcal{A}_f(Q)$, where $\mathcal{A}_t(Q)$ is the set of local transitions currently enabled in Q and $\mathcal{A}_f(Q)$ is the set of firings currently enabled for Q. Note that for a firing to be enabled the token must enable the corresponding activity, it must be in a place connected to a net-level transition

Table 1. The syntax of PEPA extended with contexts.

$$N ::= D^+ M \qquad \text{(net)}$$

(definitions and marking)

$M ::= (M_\mathbf{P}, \ldots)$	(marking)	$D ::= I \stackrel{def}{=} S$	(component defn)
$M_\mathbf{P} ::= \mathbf{P}[C, \ldots]$	(place marking)	$\mid \ \mathbf{P}[C] \stackrel{def}{=} P[C]$	(place defn)
		$\mid \ \mathbf{P}[C, \ldots] \stackrel{def}{=} P[C] \bowtie_L P$	(place defn)

(marking vectors)   (identifier declarations)

$S ::= (\alpha, r).S$	(prefix)	$P ::= P \bowtie_L P$	(cooperation)	$C ::= \text{`\_'}$	(empty)
$\mid \ S + S$	(choice)	$\mid \ P/L$	(hiding)	$\mid \ S$	(full)
$\mid \ I$	(identifier)	$\mid \ P[C]$	(cell)		
		$\mid \ I$	(identifier)		

(sequential components)   (concurrent components)   (cell term expressions)

---

of the same type and there must be an empty cell at the output place of the transition of the correct token type.

We use capitalised names to denote PEPA components (such as P and Q) and lowercase for PEPA transitions (such as a and b). We use bold capitalised names for PEPA net places (such as $\mathbf{P_1}$ and $\mathbf{P_2}$) and bold lowercase for PEPA net firings (such as $\mathbf{a}$ and $\mathbf{b}$).

3.1 Markings in a PEPA Net

The *marking* of a classical Petri net records the number of tokens which are resident at each place in the net. Since the tokens of a classical Petri net are indistinguishable it is sufficient to record their number and one could present the marking of a Petri net with places P_1, P_2 and P_3 as $(P_1 : 2, P_2 : 1, P_3 : 0)$. If an ordering is imposed on the places of the net a more compact representation of the marking can be used. Place names are omitted and the marking can be written using vector notation thus, $(2, 1, 0)$.

For a PEPA net, we can denote a marking by $(\mathbf{P_1}[Q], \mathbf{P_2}[\_], \mathbf{P_3}[\_])$ (the token at place $\mathbf{P_1}$ is in state Q; the other places have no tokens). In general, a context may have more than one parameter, to be filled by PEPA components of different types. We denote the ith component of a marking M by M_i. For example, $(\mathbf{P_1}[Q], \mathbf{P_2}[\_], \mathbf{P_3}[\_])_1$ is $\mathbf{P_1}[Q]$.

It is simple to define a function to count the number of tokens in a PEPA net term and this function proves to be useful in practice.

$$\text{tokens}(P) = 0$$
$$\text{tokens}(P[\_]) = 0$$
$$\text{tokens}(P[P']) = 1$$
$$\text{tokens}(P \bowtie_L Q) = \text{tokens}(P) + \text{tokens}(Q)$$
$$\text{tokens}(P/L) = \text{tokens}(P)$$

3.2 Net-Level Transitions in a PEPA Net

Transitions at the net-level of a PEPA net are labelled in a similar way to the labelled multi-transition system which records the unfolding of the state space of a PEPA model. A labelling function ℓ maps transition names into pairs of names such as (α, r) where it is possible that $\ell(t_i) = \ell(t_j)$ but $t_i \neq t_j$. The first element of a pair (α, r) specifies an *activity* which must be performed in order for a component to move from the input place of the transition to the output place. The activity type records formally the activity which must be performed if the transition is to fire. The second element is an exponentially-distributed random variable which quantifies the *rate* at which the activity can progress in conjunction with the component which is performing it.

As an example, suppose that Q is a component which is currently at place $\mathbf{P_1}$ and that it can perform an activity α with rate r_1 to produce the derivative Q'. Further, say that the net has a transition between $\mathbf{P_1}$ and $\mathbf{P_2}$ labelled by (α, r_2). If Q performs activity α in this setting it will be removed from $\mathbf{P_1}$ (leaving behind an empty cell) and Q' will be deposited into $\mathbf{P_2}$ (filling an empty cell there).

3.3 Net Structure of a PEPA Net

The class of nets that we currently use for modelling the net structure of a PEPA net is restricted to *structural state machines,* i.e. nets whose transitions can have only one input place and one output place. This means that we can represent conflicts at the net level, while synchronisations are not allowed. This is consistent with the fact that PEPA components cannot cooperate on a shared activity when they are resident in different places.

It is usual with coloured Petri nets to associate functions with arcs, offering a generalisation of the usual, basic "functions" offered by arc multiplicities. In PEPA nets the arc functions are implicit. The modification of a token which takes place when it is fired is wholly specified by the action type of the firing, the definition of the token and the semantics. Furthermore, although we allow multiple tokens within net places, only one token can move at each firing. Thus arc multiplicities greater than one are not allowed.

4 Semantics

The PEPA language is formally defined by a small-step operational semantics. In order to describe the firing rule for PEPA nets formally we need a relational operator which is to be used to express the fact that there exists a particular

transition in the net superstructure. This operator must have the properties that
it identifies the source and target of the transition and that it records the activity
which is to be performed in order for a component to cross this transition, moving
from the source to the target. We use the notation

$$\mathbf{P_1} \xrightarrow{(\alpha, r)} \mathbf{P_2}$$

to capture the information that there is a transition connecting place $\mathbf{P_1}$ to
place $\mathbf{P_2}$ labelled by (α, r). This relation captures static information about the
structure of the net, not dynamic information about its behaviour. We could
describe the net structure in a PEPA net using a list of such declarations but
the more familiar graphical presentation of a net presents the same information
in a more accessible way.

Definition 1. *A PEPA net $\mathcal{N}$ is a tuple $\mathcal{N} = (\mathcal{P}, \mathcal{T}, I, O, \ell, \pi, \mathcal{C}, D, M_0)$ such
that*

- $\mathcal{P}$ *is a finite set of places;*
- $\mathcal{T}$ *is a finite set of net transitions;*
- $I : \mathcal{T} \to \mathcal{P}$ *is the input function;*
- $O : \mathcal{T} \to \mathcal{P}$ *is the output function;*
- $\ell : \mathcal{T} \to (\mathcal{A}_f, \mathbb{R}^+ \cup \{\top\})$ *is the labelling function, which assigns a PEPA activity ((type, rate) pair) to each transition. The rate determines the negative
  exponential distribution governing the delay associated with the transition;*
- $\pi : \mathcal{A}_f \to \mathbb{N}$ *is the priority function which assigns priorities (represented by
  natural numbers) to firing action types;*
- $\mathcal{C} : \mathcal{P} \to P$ *is the place definition function which assigns a PEPA context,
  containing at least one cell, to each place;*
- D *is the set of token component definitions;*
- M_0 *is the initial marking of the net.*

The semantic rules for PEPA nets are provided in Table 2. The Cell rule con-
servatively extends the PEPA semantics to define that a cell which is filled by a
component Q has the same transitions as Q itself. A healthiness condition on the
rule (also called a *typing judgement*) requires a context such as $Q[\_]$ to be filled
with a component which has the same alphabet as Q. We write $Q =_a Q'$ to state
that Q and Q' have the same alphabet. There are no rules to infer transitions
for an empty cell because an empty cell enables no transitions.

The Transition rule states that the net has local transitions which change
only a single component in the marking vector. This rule also states that these
transitions agree with the transitions which are generated by the PEPA semantics (including the extension for contexts). Recall that the transition and firing
alphabets of any place must be distinct.

The Firing rule takes one marking of the net to another marking by performing a PEPA activity and moving a PEPA component from the input place to the
output place. This has the effect that two entries in the marking vector change
simultaneously.

Table 2. Additional semantic rules for PEPA nets.

Cell:

$$\frac{Q' \xrightarrow{(\alpha,\, r)} Q''}{Q[Q'] \xrightarrow{(\alpha,\, r)} Q[Q'']} \quad (Q =_a Q')$$

Transition:

$$\frac{M_{\mathbf{P}} \xrightarrow{(\alpha,\, r)} M'_{\mathbf{P}}}{(\ldots, M_{\mathbf{P}}, \ldots) \xrightarrow{(\alpha,\, r)} (\ldots, M'_{\mathbf{P}}, \ldots)} (\alpha \in \mathcal{A}_t)$$

Enabling:

$$\frac{Q \xrightarrow{(\alpha,\, r_1)} Q' \quad \mathbf{P_i} \xrightarrow{(\alpha,\, r_2)} \mathbf{P_j}}{(.., \mathbf{P_i}[.., Q, ..], .., \mathbf{P_j}[.., -, ..], ..) \xrightarrow{(\alpha,\, R)}_{\pi(\alpha)} (.., \mathbf{P_i}[.., -, ..], .., \mathbf{P_j}[.., Q', ..], ..)} (\alpha \in \mathcal{A}_f)$$

Firing:

$$\frac{M \xrightarrow{(\alpha,\, r)}_n M' \quad M \xrightarrow{(\beta,\, s)}_m M''}{M \xrightarrow{(\alpha,\, r)} M'} (n \geq m)$$

4.1   The Net Bisimulation Relation

In this section we define a bisimulation relation for PEPA nets called *net bisimulation*. This relation is important both in theory and in practice. In the evolution of the state space of a model by our tool we only store states up to net bisimulation, i.e. we carry out automatic aggregation over equivalent states. This provides a dramatic reduction in the state space of the model under certain conditions.

Our relation is defined in the style of Larsen and Skou [14], based on a conditional transition rate between *markings*, rather than the strong equivalence relation of PEPA which considers the transition rates between components. The *conditional transition rate* from marking M to marking M' via action type α, denoted $q(M, M', \alpha)$, is the sum of the activity rates labelling arcs connecting the corresponding nodes in the derivation graph which are labelled by the action type α. The *total conditional transition rate* from a marking M to a set of markings E is defined as

$$q[M, E, \alpha] = \sum_{M' \in E} q(M, M', \alpha)$$

Definition 2. *An equivalence relation over markings,* $\mathcal{R} \subseteq M \times M$, *is a net bisimulation if whenever* $(M, M') \in \mathcal{R}$ *then for all* $\alpha \in \mathcal{A}$ *and for all equivalence classes* $E \in M/\mathcal{R}$,

$$q[M, E, \alpha] = q[M', E, \alpha]$$

4.2   PEPA Net Model of a Web Service

In modelling our Web services example as a PEPA net we first identify three components: *Client*, *WebService* and *SOAPmessage*. We begin with the simplest

of these, the *SOAPmessage*. The lifecycle of this component is that it is built
using a message composition API, then launched over the network and then read
using an XML parser. This leads to another message which is the continuation
of the lifetime of this component. This component plays the role of passive
data in our application so in its description it leaves unspecified ($\top$) the rates
at which these actions are performed, allowing the cooperating partner in the
synchronisation to determine these rates.

$$SOAPmessage \stackrel{def}{=} (compose\_message, \top).$$
$$(\textbf{launch}, \top).$$
$$(read\_message, \top).SOAPmessage$$

A *Client* divides its time between local computation, the details of which we do
not model here, and Web services interactions. When the client comes to a phase
in its local computation where it realises that it needs to use a Web service it
interacts with the discovery service to obtain a specification of the service. It then
composes a SOAP message to send to the service. The communication with the
remote Web service is asynchronous so the client returns to its local computation,
anticipating that a reply will come later. When a message is returned from the
service the client will read it and make use of the results in the remainder of its
computation.

$$Client \stackrel{def}{=} (local\_computing, r_l).Client$$
$$+ (discover, r_d).Client_1$$
$$Client_1 \stackrel{def}{=} (compose\_message, r_c^C).Client_2$$
$$Client_2 \stackrel{def}{=} (local\_computing, r_l).Client_2$$
$$+ (read\_message, r_r^C).Client$$

The lifetime of a Web service is modelled as a simple loop. Web services requests
are received and read; these lead to the execution of a Web service and the
composition of a message to return the results.

$$WebService \stackrel{def}{=} (read\_message, r_r^S).WebService_2$$
$$WebService_2 \stackrel{def}{=} (transact\_service, r_s).WebService_3$$
$$WebService_3 \stackrel{def}{=} (compose\_message, r_c^S).WebService$$

The places of the net specify that there is a cell (a storage place) for a SOAP
message at the client side and at the Web service side. The message synchronises
on composition and reading activities.

$$P_1[s] \stackrel{def}{=} SOAPmessage[s] \bowtie_L WebService$$
$$P_2[s] \stackrel{def}{=} SOAPmessage[s] \bowtie_L Client$$
$$\text{where } L = \{ compose\_message, read\_message \}$$

The initial marking of the net places a token on the client side, in its initial
state: $(P_1[\_], P_2[SOAPmessage])$.

Firing the operational semantics of the example generates the state space
depicted in Fig. 1 with the transition system given in Fig. 2. By erasing activity
names from the labelled transition system we obtain the CTMC given in Fig. 3.

As a concrete illustration of numerical evaluation take $r_d = r_m = 17.03$, $r_c^C = r_r^S = r_c^S = r_r^C = 3.28$ and $r_s = 1.10$. The value of r_l is immaterial because the self-loops on states which are visible at the process algebra level are not represented at the Markov chain level. In the Markov chain representation we are concerned with balancing flow into a state against flow out of a state, so self-loops have no role.

Denote the infinitesimal generator matrix of the CTMC in Fig 3 by $\mathbf{Q}$. As usual, we solve $\boldsymbol{\pi}\mathbf{Q} = \mathbf{0}$ subject to $\sum \boldsymbol{\pi} = 1$ giving (0.025, 0.132, 0.025, 0.132, 0.394, 0.132, 0.025, 0.132).

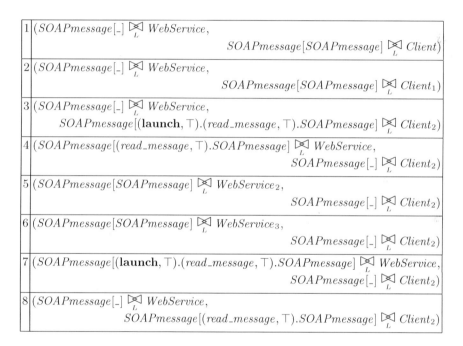

Fig. 1. Reachable state space of the PEPA nets Web services model shown as the markings of (P_1, P_2).

4.3   Using Logic to Specify Performance Measures

We now explain how to specify performance measures of interest with respect to a PEPA net model by using a probabilistic modal logic. The appropriate logic for PEPA nets is one which can specify performance measures over the places of the net, and has the capability of expressing requirements on tokens in addition to requirements on the transitions and firings of the net.

We introduce the PML_ν logic by means of a two-level grammar which separates the specification of place formulae and token formulae from the specification of transition and firing activities. Behaviour at the transition and firing level is captured by formulae of a sub-logic, PML_μ.

1	$-(local\_computing, r_l) \rightarrow$		1
1	$-(discover, r_d) \rightarrow$		2
2	$-(compose\_message, r_c^C) \rightarrow$		3
3	$-(local\_computing, r_l) \rightarrow$		3
3	$-(\textbf{launch}, r_m) \rightarrow$		4
4	$-(read\_message, r_r^S) \rightarrow$		5
4	$-(local\_computing, r_l) \rightarrow$		4

5	$-(transact\_service, r_s) \rightarrow$		6
5	$-(local\_computing, r_l) \rightarrow$		5
6	$-(compose\_message, r_c^S) \rightarrow$		7
6	$-(local\_computing, r_l) \rightarrow$		6
7	$-(\textbf{launch}, r_m) \rightarrow$		8
7	$-(local\_computing, r_l) \rightarrow$		7
8	$-(local\_computing, r_l) \rightarrow$		8
8	$-(read\_message, r_r^C) \rightarrow$		1

Fig. 2. The transition system of the Web services example.

$$1 \xrightarrow{r_d} 2 \xrightarrow{r_c^C} 3 \xrightarrow{r_m} 4$$
$$r_r^C \uparrow \qquad\qquad\qquad \downarrow r_r^S$$
$$8 \xleftarrow{r_m} 7 \xleftarrow{r_c^S} 6 \xleftarrow{r_s} 5$$

Fig. 3. The CTMC of the Web services example.

This separation of PML_ν formulae from PML_μ formulae enforces a syntactic restriction on the allowable terms in the logic whereby places cannot refer to the local state at another place. This reflects the global computing idiom that it is impossible to know the global state of the system. This restriction also strongly supports the PEPA nets modelling rule which forbids communication between components at different places in the net, as in distributed systems without shared memory.

We present the sub-logic PML_μ first. The constant true is represented by tt. Conjunction and negation are denoted as usual. The term ∇_α represents the inability of a process to perform an α action. The diamond operator specifies an activity α, a rate μ, and a succeeding formula which is to be satisfied by all one-step α-derivatives. The accumulated rate of these α activities must be at least μ. We use ϕ, ϕ_1, ϕ_2, ..., to range over PML_μ formulae.

$$\phi ::= \texttt{tt}$$
$$| \quad \neg\phi$$
$$| \quad \phi_1 \wedge \phi_2$$
$$| \quad \nabla_\alpha$$
$$| \quad \langle\alpha\rangle_\rho \phi$$

The meaning of the PML_μ connectives is given by reference to the transition relation of the PEPA net semantics. We require an addition simple auxilliary definition:

Definition 1 Let S be a set of states. $P \stackrel{(\alpha,\lambda)}{\Longrightarrow} S$ if for all successors $P' \in S$, $P \stackrel{\alpha}{\longrightarrow} P'$, and $\sum\{r : P \stackrel{(\alpha,r)}{\longrightarrow} P', P' \in S\} = \lambda$.

Now let P be a model of a PEPA net process. Then

$$P \models_\mu \mathtt{tt}$$
$$P \models_\mu \neg\phi \qquad \text{iff } P \not\models_\mu \phi$$
$$P \models_\mu \phi_1 \wedge \phi_2 \text{ iff } P \models_\mu \phi_1 \wedge P \models_\mu \phi_2$$
$$P \models_\mu \nabla_\alpha \qquad \text{iff } P \xrightarrow{\alpha}\!\!\!\!\!/$$
$$P \models_\mu \langle\alpha\rangle_\rho\phi \text{ iff } P \xRightarrow{(\alpha,\lambda)} S \text{ for some } \lambda \geq \rho, \text{ and for all } P' \in S, P' \models_\mu \phi.$$

It is convenient to introduce a number of derived operators. These add no expressive power to the logic but they shorten the statement of realistic performance measures in PML_μ.

$$\mathtt{ff} \overset{def}{=} \neg\mathtt{tt}$$
$$[\alpha]_\rho\phi \overset{def}{=} \neg\langle\alpha\rangle_\rho\neg\phi$$
$$\Delta_\alpha \overset{def}{=} \neg\nabla_\alpha$$
$$\phi_1 \vee \phi_2 \overset{def}{=} \neg((\neg\phi_1) \wedge (\neg\phi_2))$$

The PML_ν logic has as atomic propositions all of the formulae of PML_μ. In addition it has conjunction and negation, place formulae and token formulae. We use $\psi, \psi_1, \psi_2, \ldots$, to range over PML_ν formulae.

$$\psi ::= \phi$$
$$| \quad \neg\psi$$
$$| \quad \psi_1 \wedge \psi_2$$
$$| \quad P_i[\phi]$$
$$| \quad \#P_i \sim n$$

where $\sim = \{ =, \neq, <, \leq, >, \geq \}$.

The meaning of PML_ν formulae ($\models_\nu$) is defined in terms of the meaning of PML_μ formulae ($\models_\mu$) and the token counting function for PEPA nets. Let M be a marking of a PEPA net. Then,

$$M \models_\nu \phi \qquad \text{iff } M \models_\mu \phi$$
$$M \models_\nu \neg\psi \qquad \text{iff } M \not\models_\nu \psi$$
$$M \models_\nu \psi_1 \wedge \psi_2 \text{ iff } M \models_\nu \psi_1 \wedge M \models_\nu \psi_2$$
$$M \models_\nu P_i[\phi] \qquad \text{iff } M_i \models_\mu \phi$$
$$M \models_\nu \#P_i \sim n \text{ iff } \mathrm{tokens}(M_i) \sim n.$$

4.4   Selecting States of the Web Services Model

Performance measures characterising the long-run behaviour of the system are calculated from the computation of the probability of being in selected subsets of the states of the system.

We now use PML_ν to characterise some of the states of the Web services PEPA net model, illustrating its use as a specification language for performance measures.

The first value which we might wish to quantify is the *next-read probability*. This is the probability that one of the components of the model can read a message as its next action. We related this formula to the concrete subset of states of the Web services model as shown below:

$$\|\Delta_{read\_message}\| = \{4, 8\}$$

A slightly more specialised quantity is the *server next-read probability*. This is the probability that the Web service component can read a message as its next action. Again we relate a PML_{ν} formula to a subset of the state space, in this case this just turns out to be just a single state.

$$\|P_1[\Delta_{read\_message}]\| = \{4\}$$

As a final example we can specify the *blocking probability*. This describes the cases where a Web services request message is being processed at the server side and the client is delayed awaiting the reply, performing local computation only. For the present simple example, there are many ways to express this property some of which would also be applicable in a more complex, multi-threaded version of the model. The most direct expressions seem to come from stating the number of tokens at one of the places.

$$\|\#P_1 = 1\| = \|\#P_2 = 0\| = \{4, 5, 6, 7\}$$

5   Enhanced Operational Semantics

In this section we survey Degano and Priami's enhanced operational semantics (EOS for short) [5]. EOS is built upon operational semantics by enriching labels of transitions with the (partial) encodings of their proofs. By exploiting this information, different descriptions of process behaviour can be mechanically derived, thus expressing both quantitative and qualitative aspects [6]. Here, we shall concentrate on a quantitative description that enables us to measure the performance of global applications, specified in the π-calculus [16, 15].

We first recall below the EOS semantics of the π-calculus and then the stochastic interpretation of the enriched labels of the transitions. We shall then consider the web service example introduced in Section 3.

Definition 3. *Let $\mathcal{N}$ be a countable infinite set of names which is ranged over by $a, b, \ldots, x, y, \ldots$ with $\tau \notin \mathcal{N}$. We also assume a set $\mathcal{A}$ of agent identifiers ranged over by $A, A_1, \ldots$. Processes (denoted by $P, Q, R, \ldots \in \mathcal{P}$) are built from names according to the syntax*

$$P ::= \mathbf{0} \mid \pi.P \mid (\nu x)P \mid P|P \mid P + P \mid A(y_1, \ldots, y_n)$$

where π may be either $x(y)$ for input, or $\bar{x}y$ for output (where x is the subject, singled out by a function sbj and y the object, singled out by a function obj) or τ for silent moves. The order of precedence among the operators is the order (from left to right) listed above. Hereafter, the trailing $\mathbf{0}$ will be omitted.

Table 3. Structural congruence for the π-calculus.

$(\nu\, x)(\nu\, x')T \equiv (\nu\, x')(\nu\, x)P$	$A(\tilde{y}) \equiv P, \; if \; A(\tilde{y}) \stackrel{def}{=} P$
$(\nu x)(T_0 \vert T_1) \equiv ((\nu\, x)T_0) \vert T_1, \; if \; x \notin fn(T_1)$	$(\nu\, x)\mathbf{0} \equiv \mathbf{0}$

The process $\mathbf{0}$ can perform no actions. The prefix π is the first atomic action that the process $\pi.P$ can perform. The input $x(y)$ binds the occurrences of the variable y in the prefixed process P. Roughly, a name will be received on the channel x and it will substitute the free occurrences of the placeholder y in P. The output prefix $\overline{x}\, z$ sends the name z along the channel x without binding z. In the process $(\nu\, x)P$, the restriction operator $(\nu\, x)$ creates a new (unique) name x whose scope is P. The operator $\vert$ defines the parallel composition of processes. In the composition $P_1 \vert P_2$ the two processes act independently and they may communicate if they share a common channel name. The summation operator defines the non deterministic choice: $P_1 + P_2$ behaves either as P_1 or as P_2. For each agent identifier A there is a unique defining equation of the form $A(\tilde{y}) \stackrel{def}{=} P$, where $\tilde{y}$ is a list of distinct parameters which are the free names of the process P. Each occurrence of an agent identifier $A(\tilde{z})$ will be replaced by the process P, substituting the list of formal parameters $\tilde{y}$ by the list of actual parameters $\tilde{z}$. Here we assume that the processes associated to agent identifiers contain no parallel operators, *i.e.* have sequential behaviour.

We enrich the labels of transitions with tags that record the rules applied in their derivation and we call the new labels *proof terms*. We also define a function ℓ that maps proofs terms to standard labels.

Definition 4 (proof terms). *Let* $\vartheta \in \{\vert\vert_0, \vert\vert_1, +_0, +_1\}^*$. *Then the set* Θ *of proof terms (with metavariable* θ*) is defined by the following syntax*

$$\theta ::= \vartheta\mu \; \vert \; \vartheta\langle\vert\vert_0\vartheta_0\mu_0, \vert\vert_1\vartheta_1\mu_1\rangle$$

with $\mu_i = x(z)$ *iff* μ_{1-i} *is either* $\overline{x}z$ *or* $\overline{x}(z)$, *for* $i \in \{0, 1\}$.
    Function $\ell : \Theta \to Act$ *is defined as*

$$\ell(\theta\mu) = \mu; \quad \ell(\vartheta\langle\vert\vert_0\vartheta_0\mu_0, \vert\vert_1\vartheta_1\mu_1\rangle) = \tau.$$

Here, we only consider tags that record the occurrences of the parallel and summation operators, as they suffice for the present treatment. A more detailed definition is in [19] that uses tags for all the other π-calculus operators.

The enhanced operational semantics is defined by the inference rules in Tab. 4, assuming the minimal congruence, induced by α-congruence and by the rules in Tab. 3. Note that the $\vert$ and $+$ operators are no longer commutative and associative, and $\mathbf{0}$ is not the neutral element.

An Interpretation of the Proof Terms. Since the parallel operator has no congruence rules, we can interpret sequences of parallel tags as abstract addresses that uniquely identify sequential subprocesses. For example, consider the process

Table 4. Proved Transition system of the π-calculus.

$$Act : \mu.P \xrightarrow{\mu} P$$

$$Sum_0 : \frac{P \xrightarrow{\theta} P'}{P + Q \xrightarrow{+_0\theta} P'} \qquad\qquad Par_0 : \frac{P \xrightarrow{\theta} P'}{P|Q \xrightarrow{\|_0\theta} P'|Q}, bn(\ell(\theta)) \cap fn(Q) = \emptyset$$

$$Sum_1 : \frac{Q \xrightarrow{\theta} Q'}{P + Q \xrightarrow{+_1\theta} Q'} \qquad\qquad Par_1 : \frac{Q \xrightarrow{\theta} Q'}{P|Q \xrightarrow{\|_1\theta} P|Q'}, bn(\ell(\theta)) \cap fn(Q) = \emptyset$$

$$Com_0 : \frac{P \xrightarrow{\bar{x}z} P', Q \xrightarrow{x(y)} Q'}{P|Q \xrightarrow{\langle\|_0\bar{x}z,\|_1x(y)\rangle} P'|Q'\{z/y\}} \qquad Open : \frac{P \xrightarrow{\bar{x}y} P'}{(\nu y)P \xrightarrow{\bar{x}\langle y\rangle} P'}, y \neq x$$

$$Com_1 : \frac{Q \xrightarrow{x(y)} Q', P \xrightarrow{\bar{x}z} P'}{Q|P \xrightarrow{\langle\|_0x(y),\|_1\bar{x}z\rangle} Q'\{z/y\}|P'} \qquad Res : \frac{P \xrightarrow{\theta} P'}{(\nu x)P \xrightarrow{\theta} (\nu x)P'}, x \notin n(\ell(\theta))$$

$$Close_0 : \frac{P \xrightarrow{\bar{x}(z)} P', Q \xrightarrow{x(y)} Q'}{P|Q \xrightarrow{\langle\|_0\bar{x}(z),\|_1x(y)\rangle} (\nu y)(P'|Q'\{z/y\})}$$

$$Close_1 : \frac{Q \xrightarrow{x(y)} Q', P \xrightarrow{\bar{x}(z)} P'}{Q|P \xrightarrow{\langle\|_0x(y),\|_1\bar{x}(z)\rangle} (\nu y)(Q'\{z/y\}|P')}$$

$$S = ((P_1 \mid a(x).P_2) + Q) \mid ((R_1 + \bar{a}\,z.R_2) \mid T)$$

whose syntax tree is

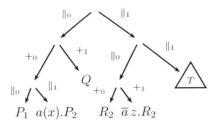

The process $(P_1|a(x).P_2)+Q$ has $\|_0$ as abstract address, while the tree associated to the sub process T is identified by the abstract address $\|_1\|_1$.

Below we introduce the function ∂ for extracting abstract addresses from the proof terms; there is no need to define the function ∂ on pairs because it will be always applied component-wise.

Definition 5. *The function ∂ is inductively defined on proof terms:*

$$\partial(\|_i \vartheta\mu) = \|_i \partial(\vartheta\mu)$$
$$\partial(\mu) = \epsilon$$
$$\partial(+_i\vartheta\mu) = \epsilon$$

For example, consider the transition $S \xrightarrow{\langle\|_0+_0\|_1 a(x),\|_1\|_0+_1\bar{a}\,z\rangle} (P_1 \mid P_2) \mid (R_2 \mid T)$
The proof terms of the communication contain the unique abstract addresses: $\partial(\|_0 +_0 \|_1) = \|_0\|_1$ for the input action and $\partial(\|_1\|_0 +_1) = \|_1\|_0$ for the output action.

5.1   Stochastic Semantics

As it happens for PEPA nets, we associate probabilistic information with actions. Hence, a random variable X_θ, which expresses the time duration of the action described by θ, must be associated to each proof term θ. The values that X_θ can assume are regulated by an exponential function $f_\theta(x) = \lambda e^{-\lambda x}$. Our approach mainly differs from the PEPA one because we do not insert probabilistic parameters in the syntax of the calculus, but we derive them from proof terms. The basic idea is that the operational semantics defines abstract machines and the proofs of transitions (encoded in proof terms) represent the low level routines of the abstract machine needed to implement transitions. We then assign rates to single tags (low level routines) and we give a way of composing them in order to compute rates of the transitions. Thus, for example, an action fired after a choice costs more than the same action occurring deterministically. Therefore, we have two logical phases. First we describe the system functionalities with a specification language. Then we associate quantitative values with the actions of the specification through an interpretation function of the proof terms. Such interpretation function is called *rate* function. Once rates have been associated with transitions, we derive CTMC and perform numerical analysis using the same techniques described in the previous section. Below we give the definition of the rate function that will be used in our case study.

A Rate Function. We assume that the throughput[1] of the communication channels and the size of the messages exchanged are given. We will use two auxiliary functions: *th* and *size*, for associating to each proof term a throughput and a size measure. The function *th* associates a throughput with the triple $(\vartheta_0, \vartheta_1, name)$, where ϑ_0 and ϑ_1 are the abstract addresses of the subprocesses that are communicating. The parameter *name* represents the channel that the partners in a communication use to interact. The function *size* associates a byte size with the couple $(\vartheta, name)$, where *name* is the data sent and ϑ is the abstract

---

[1] The number of bits, characters, or blocks passing through a data communication channel. Throughput may vary greatly from its theoretical maximum. Throughput is expressed in data units per period of time; *e.g.* as blocks per second.

address of the sender process. We use also the function *min* which returns the minimum value between its two arguments.

The definition of the rate function is given for the asynchronous and for the synchronous case:

$$\$(\vartheta\mu) = \frac{size(obj(\mu))}{th(\partial(\vartheta),\epsilon,sbj(\mu))} \times \$_o(\vartheta)$$

$$\$(\vartheta\langle\vartheta_0\mu_0,\vartheta_1\mu_1\rangle) = \frac{size(obj(\mu_i))}{th(\partial(\vartheta\vartheta_0),\partial(\vartheta\vartheta_1),sbj(\mu_i))} \times min(\$_o(\vartheta\vartheta_0),\$_o(\vartheta\vartheta_1))$$

where the value returned by the auxiliary function $\$_o$ represents a *slowing factor* due to the time spent by the run time support. Consider the case when the proof terms record a communication as in $\vartheta\langle\|_0\vartheta_0\mu_0,\|_1\vartheta_1\mu_1\rangle$ (for the other asynchronous case similar, yet simpler, considerations hold). The two partners perform independently some low-level operations locally to their environment. These operations are recorded in ϑ_0 and ϑ_1, inductively built by the application of the rules that fill in the premises of rules *Com* or *Close*. Each of the ϑ_i leads to a delay in the rate of the corresponding μ_i, which we compute through the auxiliary cost function $\$_o$. Then the pairing $\langle\|_0\vartheta_0\mu_0,\|_1\vartheta_1\mu_1\rangle$ occurs and corresponds to the actual communication. Finally, there are those operations, recorded in ϑ, that account for the common context of the two partners. Also, the slow down due to this common context is computed using $\$_o$. Since communication is synchronous and handshaking, we take the minimum of the costs of the operations performed by the participants independently (originated by ϑ_i) to make communications reflect the speed of the slower partner[2].

For example, if a proof term models a service request from a client to a server we could interpret the $+_0$ and $+_1$ tags, contained in the proof term portion of the server ϑ_i, as a time degradation factor due to the waiting time spent in queuing for accessing the server. Also, we can differentiate the slowing factor of an operator taking care of the position where it has been executed by relying on the parallel tags, *i.e.* we can associate with $\|_0\|_1 +_0$ and $\|_0\|_1\|_0 +_0$ different values. For simplicity, here we assume $\$_o(\vartheta) = 1$. A definition of $\$_o$ can be found in [17].

5.2   The π-Calculus Model of a Web Service

We now model the Web service presented in Sect. 2, made of five components: *Client*, *WebService*, *SOAPmsg*, *Discover* and *Database*. In our scenario we consider the Universal Description Discovery Integration (UDDI) registry, modeled by the process *Discover*, which provides to the client the description of the web service. Moreover we assume that the *WebService* process queries a remote database, described as the process *Database*, in order to execute its task.

For the sake of readability, we write x_a for a place-holder that will be replaced with the value a.

---

[2] Recall that the lower the cost, the greater the time needed to complete an action and hence the slower the speed of the transition occurring.

The *Discover* process interacts with the *Client* process by accepting the request ask_Des on the public channel dis. The name ask_Des represents the description of the service that the *Client* needs. The *Discover* sends back to the *Client* the private name des along the channel ask_Des. The name des represents the description of the service that the *Client* asked for.

$$Discover(dis) \overset{def}{=} dis(x\_askDes).(\nu\ des)\overline{x\_askDes}\,des.Discover(dis).$$

The *Client* process interleaves the activity of looking for web-services with various other activities that we express with output actions on the channel *localComp*. When the *Client* needs a web service, it sends the request $askDes$ to the *Discover* on the public channel dis. Then, the *Client* sends the description des, received by the discovery service, to the *SOAPmsg* on the public channel *client*. After that, it executes local operations, $\overline{localComp}$, until it receives the answer *service* from the *SOAPmsg* along the private channel des.

$$Client(localComp, dis, client, y) \overset{def}{=} \overline{localComp}\,y.Client(localComp, dis, client, y)$$
$$+$$
$$((\nu\ askDes)\overline{dis}\,askDes.askDes(x\_des).$$
$$\overline{client}\,x\_des.Client_2(des, localComp, y)$$
$$)$$

$$Client_2(des, localComp, y) \overset{def}{=} \overline{localComp}\,y.Client_2(des, localComp, y)$$
$$+$$
$$des(x\_service).$$
$$Client(localComp, dis, client, y)$$

The *SOAPmsg* process uses the public channel *client* to accept a description of a service, des, from the *Client* seeking for a web service. Then, the *SOAPmsg* is ready to send to the *WebService* the new name *newdes*, representing the client's request, on the public channel *web*. The *SOAPmsg* will receive the answer, *service*, from *WebService* along the private channel *newdes* and then it will send back the answer to the *Client* along the private channel des.

$$SOAPmsg(client, web) \overset{def}{=} client(x\_des).(\nu\ newdes)\overline{web}\,newdes.$$
$$newdes(x\_service)\overline{x\_des}\,x\_service.$$
$$SOAPmsg(client, web)$$

The *WebService* process interacts with the *SOAPmsg* receiving the request on the public channel *web*. Then, it connects with a remote database, using the public channel *data* and the private channel *newdata*, to retrieve the information it needs to complete its task. Finally, it replies the answer *service* to the *SOAPmsg* on the channel *newdes*.

$$WebService(web, data) \overset{def}{=} web(x\_newdes).(\nu\ newdata)\overline{data}\,newdata.$$
$$newdata(x\_service).\overline{x\_newdes}\,x\_service.$$
$$WebService(web, data)$$

The *Database* process simply receives a request from the *WebService* along the public channel name *data* and then gives back the answer using the private channel *newdata*.

248   Linda Brodo et al.

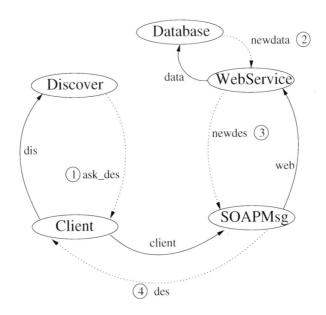

Fig. 4. The changes in the channel topology of the Web services example.

$$Database(data) \overset{def}{=} data(x\_newdata).(\nu\ service)\overline{x\_newdata}\ service.$$
$$Database(data)$$

The complete system is given by composing in parallel the processes defined so far:

$$P(localComp, dis, client, y, web, data) \overset{def}{=}$$
$$(Client(localComp, dis, client, y) \mid Discover(dis)) \mid$$
$$(SOAPmsg(client, web) \mid (WebService(web, data) \mid Database(data)))$$

For the sake of readability from now onwards we shall write the process identifications omitting the parameters. Fig. 4 shows how the processes of the system interact. In particular the arcs between the processes are the communication channels: the ones with dotted lines are auxiliary channels and the circled numbers attached to the channels indicate the temporal order in which they are used.

The transition system generated by applying the enhanced operational semantics is illustrated in Fig. 5. Fig. 6 displays the processes passed through during a computation.

In order to obtain the rates for each proof term, we apply the rate function $ using the measures in Fig. 7. Recall that the function th associates a throughput to a pair of abstract addresses and a channel name; and that the function $size$ associates the byte size of the data communicated to an abstract address and a data name, see Sect. 5.1. Some comments on the quantitative modeling of our example are in order. We do not need to associate a rate to the transitions corresponding to the execution of the asynchronous action $\overline{localComp}\,y$, because the

1	$-\,\|_0\|_0\,+_0 localComp\,y\,\to$	1
1	$-\,\|_0\,\langle\|_0\,+_1 dis\langle askDes\rangle, \|_1\,dis(x\_askDes)\rangle\,\to$	2
2	$-\,\|_0\,\langle\|_0\,askDes(x\_des), \|_1\,askDes\langle des\rangle\rangle\,\to$	3
3	$-\langle\|_0\|_0\,client\langle des\rangle, \|_1\|_0\,client(x\_des)\,\to$	4
4	$-\,\|_1\,\langle\|_0\,web\langle newdes\rangle, \|_1\|_0\,web(x\_newdes)\rangle$	5
4	$-\,\|_0\|_0\,+_0 localComp\,y\,\to$	4
5	$-\,\|_1\|_1\,\langle\|_0\,data\langle newdata\rangle, \|_1\,data(x\_newdata)\rangle\,\to$	6
5	$-\,\|_0\|_0\,+_0 localComp\,y\,\to$	5
6	$-\,\|_1\|_1\,\langle\|_1\,newdata\langle service\rangle, \|_0\,newdata(x\_service)\rangle\,\to$	7
6	$-\,\|_0\|_0\,+_0 localComp\,y\,\to$	6
7	$-\,\|_1\,\langle\|_0\,newdes(x\_service), \|_1\|_0\,newdes\langle service\rangle\rangle\,\to$	8
7	$-\,\|_0\|_0\,+_0 localComp\,y\,\to$	7
8	$-\langle\|_0\|_0\,des(x\_service), \|_1\|_0\,des\langle service\rangle\rangle\,\to$	1

Fig. 5. Transition system of the process P.

self-loops are not represented by the Markov chain model. We assume that the communication connection from the *Client* to the *Discover* has the throughput of $300Kbyte/sec$, and that the communication connection from the *Discover* to the *Client* has a slower throughput of $250Kbyte/sec$ (first and second rows of the tables in Fig. 7). We assume that the communication between the *Client* and the *WebService* is asynchronous, thus we consider that the *Client* requires a shorter time to send the *SOAPmsg* to the *WebService* than the time the *WebService* needs to receive the *SOAPmsg* (third and fourth rows of the tables in Fig. 7). The difference between the sending time and the receiving time could be sensible if the *Client* and the *WebService* are located in two distant geographic regions or else if there are waiting queues for accessing the *WebService*. Recall that the *SOAPmsg* process represents a message which is sent by the *Client* to the *WebService* and then by the *WebService* to the *Client*. The communications between the *WebService* and the *Database* model the time spent by the *WebService* to execute its task (fifth and sixth rows of the tables in Fig. 7). For the last two communications between the *WebService* and the *SOAPmsg* and between the *SOAPmsg* and the *Client* we again suppose that the sending time of the *SOAPmsg* is shorter than the correspond receiving time.

In Fig. 7 we also associate quantitative measures to the private names ask_Des, $newdata$, $newdes$ and des, (when used as data) assuming that they will not vary significantly from one execution of the system to another.

Fig. 8 shows the infinitesimal generator matrix $\mathbf{Q}$ of the CTMC. We solve $\pi\mathbf{Q} = \mathbf{0}$ subject to $\sum \pi = \mathbf{1}$, obtaining the vector
$\pi = (0.014, 0.033, 0.05, 0.063, 0.05, 0.031, 0.255, 0.212)$ as stationary distribution.

Adopting the technique for computing the rewards, described in [4], we can analyze for instance the probability of using the data name des. We consider the following reward array $(0, 1, 0, 0, 0, 0, 0)$ that has value 0 everywhere and value 1 in the position of a state with an outgoing transition whose label contains the

1	$(Client \mid Discover) \mid (SOAPmsg \mid (WebService \mid Database))$
2	$(\ askDes(x\_des).\overline{client}\,x\_des.Client_2(\_des) \mid (\nu\,des)\overline{askDes}\,des.Discover)$ $\mid$ $(SOAPmsg \mid (WebService \mid Database))$
3	$(\ \overline{client}\,des.Client_2(des) \mid Discover) \mid (SOAPmsg \mid (WebService \mid Database))$
4	$(\ Client_2(des) \mid Discover)$ $\mid$ $((\nu\,newdes)\overline{web}\,newdes.newdes(x\_service).\overline{des}\,x\_service.SOAPmsg$ $\mid$ $(WebService \mid Database))$
5	$(\ Client_2(des) \mid Discover)$ $\mid$ $(\overline{newdes}\,x\_service.des(x\_service).SOAPmsg$ $\mid$ $((\nu\,newdata)\overline{data}\,newdata.newdata(x\_service).\overline{newdata}\,sevice.WebService) \mid Database))$
6	$(\ Client_2(des) \mid Discover)$ $\mid$ $(newdes(x\_service).\overline{des}\,x\_service.SOAPmsg$ $\mid$ $((\nu\,newdata)newdata(x\_service).\overline{newdata}\,x\_service.WebService$ $\mid$ $(\nu\,service)\overline{newdata}\langle service \rangle.Database))$
7	$(\ Client_2(des) \mid Discover)$ $\mid$ $(newdes(x\_service).\overline{des}\,x\_service.SOAPmsg \mid ((\nu\,newdata)\overline{newdes}\,service\,WebService) \mid Database))$
8	$(\ Client_2(des) \mid Discover) \mid \overline{des}\,service.SOAPmsg \mid (WebService) \mid Database))$

Fig. 6. Reachable state space of the π-calculus Web service model P.

name des as data (see the transition system in Fig. 5). Thus we obtain that the probability of the system to use the name des as data is 0.033. We also can rely on more specific tags of the proof terms, considering for example the probability that the $SOAPmsg$ and the $WebService$ are interacting. The correspond reward array is $(0,0,0,1,0,1,0)$ that has value 0 everywhere and value 1 in the position of a state with an outgoing transition located at $\|_1\|_0, \|_1\|_1\|_0$. The resulting probability is 0.318.

6   Conclusions

If they were to be viewed purely formally as high-level description languages for specifying continuous-time Markov chains, then PEPA nets and the Stochastic π-calculus would be considered equally expressive. That is to say, for a given CTMC C, it is possible to construct a high-level model in either formalism such that the underlying CTMC derived from the model is isomorphic to C. This is a fundamental agreement in expressive power, but it is a rather weak one, similar to the agreement that all programming languages are Turing complete. In this paper and in related work [3] we have sought to understand the connections between these formalisms more thoroughly.

The modelling paradigms supported by PEPA nets and the Stochastic π-calculus EOS approach have a common root in using interleaving models of

$th : Kbytes/secs.$	
$(\|_0\|_0, \|_0\|_1, dis)$	300.00
$(\|_0\|_0, \|_0\|_1, \mathrm{askDes})$	250.00
$(\|_0\|_0, \|_1\|_0, client)$	250.00
$(\|_0\|_0, \|_1\|_0, web)$	200.00
$(\|_1\|_1\|_0, \|_1\|_1\|_1, data)$	250.00
$(\|_1\|_1\|_0, \|_1\|_1\|_1, \mathrm{newdata})$	200.00
$(\|_1\|_0, \|_1\|_0, \mathrm{newdes})$	250.00
$(\|_0\|_0, \|_1\|_0, \mathrm{des})$	300.00

$size : Kbytes$	
$(\|_0\|_0, \mathrm{askDes})$	10
$(\|_0\|_1, \mathrm{des})$	20
$(\|_0\|_0, \mathrm{des})$	30
$(\|_1\|_0, \mathrm{newdata})$	30
$(\|_1\|_1\|_0, \mathrm{newdata})$	30
$(\|_1\|_1\|_1, \mathrm{service})$	150
$(\|_1\|_1\|_0, \mathrm{service})$	150
$(\|_1\|_0, \mathrm{service})$	150

Fig. 7. The functions th and $size$ applied to the proof terms of the transition system in Fig. 5.

$$1 \xrightarrow{30} 2 \xrightarrow{12.5} 3 \xrightarrow{8.3} 4$$
$$6.66 \uparrow \qquad\qquad\qquad \downarrow 8.33$$
$$8 \xleftarrow{1.33} 7 \xleftarrow{1.66} 6 \xleftarrow{2} 5$$

Fig. 8. The CTMC of the Web services example.

concurrent systems to first describe and then analyse the temporal behaviour of global and mobile code applications. However, there are many opportunities in such an enterprise to exercise creativity in the expression of concepts such as process mobility and performance metrics over models of mobile code systems. The differences between the PEPA nets approach and the EOS approach highlight points where different design choices were made.

Inside the behavioural description of a system the modeller needs to represent sequential execution and causal ordering of events. Over this aspect of the behavioural modelling there is close agreement between PEPA nets and EOS. However, process algebras also need to represent the concurrent composition of sequential behaviours and concepts such as synchronisation, parameterisation, naming and scoping. In stochastically timed process algebras particularly there are many ways to design and justify the synchronisation operator for processes [10, 1] and different design decisions are naturally taken in the PEPA nets and EOS approaches.

Adjacent to this, and perhaps of greater importance, is the use of the process algebra machinery in defining the meaning of terms in the language and legitimising their analysis. The differences between PEPA nets and the EOS approach are most pronounced here. The EOS approach encodes the rules which are used to produce the derivatives of a process as proof terms in their derivations. This information is implicit in a PEPA net one-step derivation although a proof of any derivation could be obtained by revisiting the operational semantics of the language or by using an EOS semantics for PEPA nets [7]. The proof terms play a central role in the performance analysis process for EOS. The evaluation cost function is defined over the proof terms of the language and hence built into the language at the same level as the operational semantics. The cost function and the operational semantics interoperate, with structural congruence rules for operators being disabled by their use in the definition of the evaluation cost function.

In contrast for PEPA nets, performance measures over a model are defined outside the operational semantics for the language, and this separation is highlighted by the use of a separate logical language, PML_ν for the expression of these measures. This separation means that the interpretation of the language constructs is unchanged across models and so tools supporting the language can perform optimisations such as quotienting by PEPA's bisimulation equivalence [8]. This operation is performed by rewriting the terms denoting process derivatives to amalgamate syntactically distinct terms which represent processes which no external observer could distinguish. This has the effect of reducing the state space of the system and therefore reducing the numerical computation effort which is needed to find the steady-state probability distribution for a given assignment of values to the symbolic rates of the model.

Despite these differences in methodology the present paper illustrates that the two modelling approaches can be used effectively in modelling real-world global computing applications and complement each other well in practical use. Both of the modelling methods used here are continuing to develop both in theory and in practical application. When, as in the present paper, we can compare modelling idioms in use we have the opportunity to see how to import analysis methods and techniques from one formalism to the other, to the benefit of both.

Acknowledgements

The authors are supported by the DEGAS (Design Environments for Global ApplicationS) IST-2001-32072 project funded by the FET Proactive Initiative on Global Computing.

References

1. J. T. Bradley and N. Davies. Reliable performance modelling with approximate synchronisations. In *Proceedings of the 7th International Workshop on Process Algebra and Performance Modelling (PAPM'99)*, pages 99–118, Prensas Universitarias de Zaragoza, September 1999.
2. L. Brodo, S. Gilmore, J. Hillston, and C. Priami. A stochastic π-calculus semantics for PEPA nets. In *Proceedings of the workshop on Process Algebras and Stochastically Timed Activities (PASTA)*, pages 1–17, Edinburgh, Scotland, June 2002.
3. L. Brodo, S. Gilmore, J. Hillston, and C. Priami. Mapping coloured stochastic Petri nets to stochastic process algebras. In P. Kemper, editor, *Proceedings of the ICALP Workshop on Stochastic Petri nets*, June 2003. To appear.
4. G. Clark and J. Hillston. Towards automatic derivation of performance measures from PEPA models. In *Proceedings of UKPEW*, 1996.
5. P. Degano and C. Priami. Non-interleaving semantics for mobile processes. *TCS: Theoretical Computer Science*, 216, 1999.

6. P. Degano and C. Priami. Enhanced operational semantics: a tool for describing and analyzing concurrent systems. *ACM Computing Surveys*, 33(2):135–176, 2001.
7. S. Gilmore and J. Hillston. An enhanced operational semantics for PEPA nets. DEGAS project internal document, May 2002.
8. S. Gilmore, J. Hillston, and M. Ribaudo. An efficient algorithm for aggregating PEPA models. *IEEE Transactions on Software Engineering*, 27(5):449–464, May 2001.
9. S. Gilmore, J. Hillston, and M. Ribaudo. PEPA nets: A structured performance modelling formalism. In T. Field, P.G. Harrison, J. Bradley, and U. Harder, editors, *Proceedings of the 12th International Conference on Modelling Tools and Techniques for Computer and Communication System Performance Evaluation*, number 2324 in Lecture Notes in Computer Science, pages 111–130, London, UK, April 2002. Springer-Verlag.
10. J. Hillston. The nature of synchronisation. In U. Herzog and M. Rettelbach, editors, *Proceedings of the Second International Workshop on Process Algebras and Performance Modelling*, pages 51–70, Erlangen, November 1994.
11. J. Hillston. *A Compositional Approach to Performance Modelling*. Cambridge University Press, 1996.
12. J. Hillston and L. Kloul. Formal techniques for performance analysis: blending SAN and PEPA. Submitted for publication, 2002.
13. J. Hillston and L. Kloul. From SAN to PEPA: A technology transfer. In *Proceedings of the workshop on Process Algebras and Stochastically Timed Activities (PASTA)*, pages 56–76, Edinburgh, Scotland, June 2002.
14. K.G. Larsen and A. Skou. Bisimulation through probabilistic testing. *Information and Computation*, 94(1):1–28, September 1991.
15. R. Milner. *Communicating and Mobile Systems: The π Calculus*. Cambridge University Press, Cambridge, England, 1999.
16. R. Milner, J. Parrow, and D. Walker. A calculus of mobile processes. *Information and Computation*, 100(1):1–77, September 1992.
17. C. Nottegar, C. Priami, and P. Degano. Performance evaluation of mobile processes via abstract machines. *IEEE Transactions on Software Engineering*, 27(10):867–889, 2001.
18. C. Priami. Stochastic π-calculus. In S. Gilmore and J. Hillston, editors, *Proceedings of the Third International Workshop on Process Algebras and Performance Modelling*, pages 578–589. Special Issue of *The Computer Journal*, 38(7), December 1995.
19. C. Priami. Language-based performance prediction for distributed and mobile systems. *Information and Computation*, 175(2):119–145, 2002.

Author Index

Lecture Notes in Computer Science

For information about Vols. 1–2820
please contact your bookseller or Springer-Verlag

Vol. 2854: J. Hoffmann, Utilizing Problem Structure in Planning. XIII, 251 pages. 2003. (Subseries LNAI)

Vol. 2855: R. Alur, I. Lee (Eds.), Embedded Software. Proceedings, 2003. X, 373 pages. 2003.

Vol. 2856: M. Smirnov, E. Biersack, C. Blondia, O. Bonaventure, O. Casals, G. Karlsson, George Pavlou, B. Quoitin, J. Roberts, I. Stavrakakis, B. Stiller, P. Trimintzios, P. Van Mieghem (Eds.), Quality of Future Internet Services. IX, 293 pages. 2003.

Vol. 2857: M.A. Nascimento, E.S. de Moura, A.L. Oliveira (Eds.), String Processing and Information Retrieval. Proceedings, 2003. XI, 379 pages. 2003.

Vol. 2858: A. Veidenbaum, K. Joe, H. Amano, H. Aiso (Eds.), High Performance Computing. Proceedings, 2003. XV, 566 pages. 2003.

Vol. 2859: B. Apolloni, M. Marinaro, R. Tagliaferri (Eds.), Neural Nets. Proceedings, 2003. X, 376 pages. 2003.

Vol. 2860: D. Geist, E. Tronci (Eds.), Correct Hardware Design and Verification Methods. Proceedings, 2003. XII, 426 pages. 2003.

Vol. 2861: C. Bliek, C. Jermann, A. Neumaier (Eds.), Global Optimization and Constraint Satisfaction. Proceedings, 2002. XII, 239 pages. 2003.

Vol. 2862: D. Feitelson, L. Rudolph, U. Schwiegelshohn (Eds.), Job Scheduling Strategies for Parallel Processing. Proceedings, 2003. VII, 269 pages. 2003.

Vol. 2863: P. Stevens, J. Whittle, G. Booch (Eds.), «UML» 2003 – The Unified Modeling Language. Proceedings, 2003. XIV, 415 pages. 2003.

Vol. 2864: A.K. Dey, A. Schmidt, J.F. McCarthy (Eds.), UbiComp 2003: Ubiquitous Computing. Proceedings, 2003. XVII, 368 pages. 2003.

Vol. 2865: S. Pierre, M. Barbeau, E. Kranakis (Eds.), Ad-Hoc, Mobile, and Wireless Networks. Proceedings, 2003. X, 293 pages. 2003.

Vol. 2867: M. Brunner, A. Keller (Eds.), Self-Managing Distributed Systems. Proceedings, 2003. XIII, 274 pages. 2003.

Vol. 2868: P. Perner, R. Brause, H.-G. Holzhütter (Eds.), Medical Data Analysis. Proceedings, 2003. VIII, 127 pages. 2003.

Vol. 2869: A. Yazici, C. Şener (Eds.), Computer and Information Sciences – ISCIS 2003. Proceedings, 2003. XIX, 1110 pages. 2003.

Vol. 2870: D. Fensel, K. Sycara, J. Mylopoulos (Eds.), The Semantic Web - ISWC 2003. Proceedings, 2003. XV, 931 pages. 2003.

Vol. 2871: N. Zhong, Z.W. Raś, S. Tsumoto, E. Suzuki (Eds.), Foundations of Intelligent Systems. Proceedings, 2003. XV, 697 pages. 2003. (Subseries LNAI)

Vol. 2873: J. Lawry, J. Shanahan, A. Ralescu (Eds.), Modelling with Words. XIII, 229 pages. 2003. (Subseries LNAI)

Vol. 2874: C. Priami (Ed.), Global Computing. Proceedings, 2003. XIX, 255 pages. 2003.

Vol. 2875: E. Aarts, R. Collier, E. van Loenen, B. de Ruyter (Eds.), Ambient Intelligence. Proceedings, 2003. XI, 432 pages. 2003.

Vol. 2876: M. Schroeder, G. Wagner (Eds.), Rules and Rule Markup Languages for the Semantic Web. Proceedings, 2003. VII, 173 pages. 2003.

Vol. 2877: T. Böhme, G. Heyer, H. Unger (Eds.), Innovative Internet Community Systems. Proceedings, 2003. VIII, 263 pages. 2003.

Vol. 2878: R.E. Ellis, T.M. Peters (Eds.), Medical Image Computing and Computer-Assisted Intervention - MICCAI 2003. Part I. Proceedings, 2003. XXXIII, 819 pages. 2003.

Vol. 2879: R.E. Ellis, T.M. Peters (Eds.), Medical Image Computing and Computer-Assisted Intervention - MICCAI 2003. Part II. Proceedings, 2003. XXXIV, 1003 pages. 2003.

Vol. 2880: H.L. Bodlaender (Ed.), Graph-Theoretic Concepts in Computer Science. Proceedings, 2003. XI, 386 pages. 2003.

Vol. 2881: E. Horlait, T. Magedanz, R.H. Glitho (Eds.), Mobile Agents for Telecommunication Applications. Proceedings, 2003. IX, 297 pages. 2003.

Vol. 2883: J. Schaeffer, M. Müller, Y. Björnsson (Eds.), Computers and Games. Proceedings, 2002. XI, 431 pages. 2003.

Vol. 2884: E. Najm, U. Nestmann, P. Stevens (Eds.), Formal Methods for Open Object-Based Distributed Systems. Proceedings, 2003. X, 293 pages. 2003.

Vol. 2885: J.S. Dong, J. Woodcock (Eds.), Formal Methods and Software Engineering. Proceedings, 2003. XI, 683 pages. 2003.

Vol. 2886: I. Nyström, G. Sanniti di Baja, S. Svensson (Eds.), Discrete Geometry for Computer Imagery. Proceedings, 2003. XII, 556 pages. 2003.

Vol. 2887: T. Johansson (Ed.), Fast Software Encryption. Proceedings, 2003. IX, 397 pages. 2003.

Vol. 2888: R. Meersman, Zahir Tari, D.C. Schmidt et al. (Eds.), On The Move to Meaningful Internet Systems 2003: CoopIS, DOA, and ODBASE. Proceedings, 2003. XXI, 1546 pages. 2003.

Vol. 2889: Robert Meersman, Zahir Tari et al. (Eds.), On The Move to Meaningful Internet Systems 2003: OTM 2003 Workshops. Proceedings, 2003. XXI, 1096 pages. 2003.

Vol. 2891: J. Lee, M. Barley (Eds.), Intelligent Agents and Multi-Agent Systems. Proceedings, 2003. X, 215 pages. 2003. (Subseries LNAI)

Vol. 2893: J.-B. Stefani, I. Demeure, D. Hagimont (Eds.), Distributed Applications and Interoperable Systems. Proceedings, 2003. XIII, 311 pages. 2003.

Vol. 2895: A. Ohori (Ed.), Programming Languages and Systems. Proceedings, 2003. XIII, 427 pages. 2003.

Vol. 2897: O. Balet, G. Subsol, P. Torguet (Eds.), Virtual Storytelling. Proceedings, 2003. XI, 240 pages. 2003.

Vol. 2899: G. Ventre, R. Canonico (Eds.), Interactive Multimedia on Next Generation Networks. Proceedings, 2003. XIV, 420 pages. 2003.

Vol. 2901: F. Bry, N. Henze, J. Maluszyński (Eds.), Principles and Practice of Semantic Web Reasoning. Proceedings, 2003. X, 209 pages. 2003.

Vol. 2902: F. Moura Pires, S. Abreu (Eds.), Progress in Artificial Intelligence. Proceedings, 2003. XV, 504 pages. 2003. (Subseries LNAI).

Vol. 2905: A. Sanfeliu, J. Ruiz-Shulcloper (Eds.), Progress in Pattern Recognition, Speech and Image Analysis. Proceedings, 2003. XVII, 693 pages. 2003.

Printed in the United States
by Baker & Taylor Publisher Services